THE FOUNDATIONS OF THE CONSTITUTION

THE FOUNDATIONS OF THE CONSTITUTION

BY

DAVID HUTCHISON, M.A., Ph.D.

Professor of Government, State College,
Albany, N. Y

INTRODUCTION BY FERDINAND LUNDBERG

UNIVERSITY BOOKS, Inc. *Secaucus, New Jersey*

Published by University Books, Inc.

Manufactured in the United States of America.

Published simultaneously in Canada by
George J. McLeod, Limited, Toronto, Ontario.

The size of this republication has been enlarged to improve
the readability of the text. The original text has been left intact.

INTRODUCTION

1

The publishing history of this superlatively valuable book has been not only undistinguished but, one may say, almost nonexistent. Yet the book itself is priceless in the many arresting ways it throws light on the Constitution. It is, indeed, a treasure trove.

Why? Because it provides at all times a succinct, clear, direct, and often dramatic roadway into the very bones and sinews of the Constitution of the United States. That ultracelebrated instrument, often twisted and tortured beyond recognition by politicians (and often by lawyers and judges, too), becomes more understandable with the aid of this single volume. And this is no small merit against a disturbed background of political distortion and murky academic writings on the subject.

As the Constitution is undeniably important, why not simply read it if one wishes to understand it? Many persons have done just this—a task requiring twenty or so minutes to absorb some four thousand words. Unfortunately, such rapid reading doesn't tell much. One is little wiser than when one started.

The document of 1787 and its amendments read simply, too simply. On the surface it seems crystal clear. But in the hands of lawyers, judges, and often scholars—not to mention politicians—it becomes very complicated, requiring prodigious feats of interpretation. There is, no doubt, a "true" Constitution as distinguished from a casuistic one.

But how to get at the meaning of its various words and phrases? How to arrive at a satisfactory understanding of the document without getting involved in a quagmire of polemical writings?

One way is to go back to the origin of the various lines and phrases and take note of the conditions under which they first saw the light of day. The great service performed by *Foundations of the Constitution* is that it does take one back to the very roots in a way no other book I have ever seen has. It takes us back, as the title suggests, to the very foundation materials. And, as far as I have been able to determine, it does this for the first and only time.

The number of books about the Constitution is virtually endless. Most of them—ponderously analytical, tendentious, argumentative, often bristling with literally thousands of footnotes—repel the healthy mind. Nobody can be as completely right on such intangible matters as the hail of fine-spun footnotes implies. It takes someone with a masochistic taste for medieval-type scholastic lucubrations or German metaphysics to stomach any but a few rare exceptions among them.

But Professor Hutchison's offering—tightly written, factual, compressed, always to the point, and also heavily backed up by source notes—is a continuous splashing fountain of often curious information. It stimulates new interest as one reads along. Cumulatively it begins to generate the excitement of discovery.

In brief, it is not just another dull book on the Constitution. Nor is it another one of those which relates how a group of supernatural figures appeared in 1787 and wrought a miracle in Philadelphia as time stood still and angel choirs sang sweet melodies of peace on earth, good will to men.

What Professor Hutchison sets forth of a purely marginal nature will surprise many readers. For example, he points out that women had the vote under the New Jersey Constitution of 1776 and continued to have it—I won't say "enjoy" it—for thirty-one years. This was long before the nineteenth amendment to the national Constitution and longer still before women's ever-blessed liberation from subordination to the male.

But such minor nuggets apart, the book is made for the true constitutional buff seeking enlightenment amid the shrill cries of contending political hawkers and hucksters—all with visions of government contracts and campaign donations in mind.

2

Despite its obvious merit, the book is practically unknown. If any piece of writing was ever stillborn from the press this one surely was.

Published in 1928 by an obscure publisher who was soon to be out of business, issued in a small edition of possibly no more than two or three thousand copies, written by an obscure professor of government at an obscure little state college (now, however, the nuclear point of the vast University of the State of New York), the book was not reviewed either in the media of general circulation nor in the leading law journals. The only public references to it I could find, apart from a publisher's notice in a trade publication, were in *The American Political Science Review* and *The American Historical Review*. The former gave the book a clearly inadequate six-line notice in its issue of May, 1929, in effect a curt dismissal. Such information was not wanted, thank you very much!

The latter publication (issue of April, 1929) came much nearer to doing the book justice.

"This volume," the reviewer noted, "bears an appropriate title as it contains a more comprehensive and systematic discussion of *The Foundations of the Constitution* than any previous work . . . [Or, one might add today, than any subsequent work, either.] In general, however, as far as the reviewer has been able to test its context and citations, the work maintains a high standard of accuracy."

In only one respect, and that minor, did Herman V. Ames, the reviewer, find fault. It had to do with Hutchison's reliance on Jonathan Elliott's *Debates in the Several State Conventions* for his report of the so-called Pinckney Plan for a constitution rather than on the reconstructed version of the very different original plan as given in Farrand's *Records of the Constitutional Convention*, III, 601-609.

"This volume will serve as a valuable work of reference," the reviewer continued. "As such it is more likely to be used than as a textbook. The vast number of facts noted, together with the condensed and summary treatment employed, does not render it especially attractive to the general reader."

And on this final contention I would say the reviewer of 1929 was completely mistaken.

The book is in fact of vast interest to the mythical general reader, who is supposed to be repelled by anything detailed. Perhaps the general reader of thoroughly demoralized 1929 would not have been interested. But today it is surely different, when the national ambience has been echoing for several years with anguished outcries against crimes committed in the constitutional cathedral during several national administrations.

But why, the plain man naturally asks, all the hullabaloo over what is, seen from the street, merely words written down by a group of long-dead men on a scrap of paper? What is so unusual about these words? Out of what remote circumstances did they first see the light of day? How, and why, did they come to enter into the Constitution of the United States?

Not only the mythical general reader but lawyers, certainly, should find this book of especial interest. I have found that lawyers, with exceptions to one side here and there, are not especially versed in the United States Constitution, even some who profess to be *constitutional lawyers*. Nobody can blame a lawyer for losing a case when the evidence is heavily weighted against him. But lawyers often lose cases *on the law*, sometimes all the way up to the Supreme Court. Had they known the law, one might suppose they might have correctly advised their clients and avoided futile appeals. Daniel Webster, regarded as a great consitutional expert in his day, seriously argued that military conscription was unconstitutional. Although he won cases on appeal, he also lost very many.

And if I am not believed about lawyerly lack of constitutional knowledge, let lawyers stand for a quizzing on the basis of the Hutchison book. And being a constitutional lawyer, oddly, does not insure that one knows the Constitution in all its ins and outs. What is called constitutional law comprises a relatively few cases wherein the Supreme Court has denied, at least for the time being, that the government has the power to do something. It doesn't, in brief, take much in the way of knowledge to be a constitutional lawyer. The general public, however, is apt to suppose that a constitutional lawyer must be a veritable superlawyer.

Most of the time, if I may venture the opinion, most lawyers just don't know too much about the ins and outs of the Constitution.

This book alone will go far to plug a gaping hole in many a lawyer's fund of background knowledge. It could fill in a big knowledge gap, as I suspect it has for a number of constitutional scholars who have shown great aptitude for citing ancient documents but without mentioning Hutchison as a demon cataloguer.

3

The plan of the book is as simple and clear as the writing.

It begins with the very beginning of the document of 1787 and proceeds word by word, phrase by phrase, line by line to the very end with the nineteenth amendment. It then traces to its origin every expression—word by word, phrase by phrase, line by line, through (1) the early state constitutions or other then-contemporary documentary expressions, (2) the Articles of Confederation, (3) colonial charters one after the other, (4) original usages in the distant common law of England, in early English statutes, charters, royal decrees, public documents and judicial *obiter dicta* and the like, and (5) in some cases—such as impeachment—to procedures far earlier than the Norman invasion of 1066 to customs in the Teutonic forests of Europe or even material in the canon law of the Church. And it briefly sketches in the historical context in many of the immediately preceding instances.

One of the advantages this book provides is to give the serious reader a jumping-off place. Reading the Constitution straight off is much like jumping into very deep, seemingly placid, and extremely cold water without knowing how to swim. And approaching it through textbook guides is much like jumping into a large electric fan; one's brain is soon scrambled. The big mistake is attempting to take it all in in one gulp rather than piece by piece, bite by bite, as Hutchison lays it out.

Most of the material in the Constitution, in fact, is very ancient. Much of it was originally wrought, literally, out of blood. The path of the Constitution, both here and in England, is strewn with hundreds of thousands of corpses. The main novelty about the document in 1787 was only in its particular synthesis, its selective codification of very old elements. Had a single writer put it all together, he might well have been accused of plagiarism. The finished structure, it is true, was a new building; but the building under the new coat of paint was constructed for the most part of old timbers and stones, with here and there a new rafter, joist, or even obscure crypt set in place.

I first ran across a reference to this unusual book in one of the bibliographies of the late Professor Edward S. Corwin, the distinguished constitutional scholar of Princeton University. Upon perusing a yellowing copy, I concluded that it was veritably a constitutional gold mine, perhaps known to a few cloistered scholars here and there but quite unknown to the public and to publicists; yet of vast interest to that same public particularly in the aftermath of the Watergate saturnalia of crimes in the highest places.

A book of this nature, in any event, should not be the private preserve of a few scholarly specialists with access to restricted library collections. And despite passing quick references in constitutional guidebooks to ancient sources, such as the unfailingly mentioned Magna Carta, most of the contents of this book are entirely arcane as far as the reading public is concerned and some of it quite astonishing. Not many persons are aware, for example, that some of the language of the Constitution can be traced back to papal bulls, the *non obstante* clause especially. And that most of its stateliest language, indeed, had been legally formalized long before 1787, even before the Pilgrims landed.

4

One group of men that would have been fascinated by this book, positively hypnotized by it, are the framers of the Constitution themselves. While some of them no doubt knew the origins of some of the terms they used, in the case of most terms, they probably did not. All this language and variety of concepts had come to them as something of a heritage in a cumulative flood of legal and governmental documents, one often copied in whole or part from an earlier document. As most of the members of the constitutional convention were lawyers, some educated in England, they had familiarity at least with the most recent documents and political writings. A few among them were heavily read in history and legal affairs.

But in many cases leading men among the founders, and even those who fancied themselves to be brilliant constitutional experts and lawyers such as John Adams, did not realize how derivative their most cherished ideas were, how lacking in originality various supposedly novel elements of the emerging system were.

As Hutchison notes (page 20), Adams, never present at the convention but nevertheless through his voluminous published writings one of its invisible mentors, in the nineteenth century wrote "for anything I recollect this system of checks and balances was an American invention of our own and peculiar to us." Yet James Otis in 1764, Blackstone in his *Commentaries* (1765-69), and Montesquieu in his *Spirit of the Laws* (1748) pointed out checks and balances throughout the British Constitution after 1688. They were also prominent in the colonial and state systems of America. Adams was simply wrong, as were some others of the contemporary leaders in advancing claims for extraordinary constitutional originalities.

As for separation of powers, often supposed to be an original wrinkle, it is nowhere mentioned or even implied in the Constitution although the *doctrine* of separation of powers came from Montesquieu's misreading of the British Constitution. The mistake was not in fact incorporated in the United States Constitution although politicians never tire of claiming it is there. Rather than being "separated," the three branches of government are partially interlocked, no matter what one may hear to the contrary in the street or at political rallies.

5

Just why this book, despite its wealth of precise material, has been ignored and, indeed, unjustly buried and lost, is hard to say. Speculatively, one may attribute some of the neglect to academic snobbishness. Had the book been written by a pundit at a major university and published by Harvard University Press, one may be sure it would have attracted the instant attention it deserved, especially from lawyers and constitutional buffs. And politicians. The latter, armed with this book, might be better aware that they are in a game that can turn highly dangerous, as Richard M. Nixon discovered tardily.

Another reason the book was ignored is that it trod unintentionally on ideological vested interests in various constitutional myths.

For one thing, the myth of great originality on the part of the constitutional convention of 1787 goes right down the drain for the reader of this book. The reader of Hutchison readily sees that except for a few original touches here and there—not all of them exhilarating by any means, such as the underwriting of slavery and giving the slave states representation in Congress for three-fifths of each slave!—the convention turned in what was basically a scissors-and-paste job, an editorial compilation of old English materials.

So, if the convention is due for high praise, as one gathers from the always undiscriminating constitutional cultists, it is for its selections rather than its creativity or even technical expertise. As Prof. John Roche has styled it, the convention was little more than a reform caucus. Its reforms, moreover, related mostly to what had been hastily slapped together under naïve revolutionary auspices by the American states since 1776. The reforms, indeed, were neither historically sweeping nor deep, and aimed mainly at achieving something resembling the American *status quo ante* the Declaration of Independence. Indeed, the inception of the Constitution represented something of a Restoration. The document was, in fact, taken by many of its supporters as a Restoration Constitution, with the central government replacing the British government and many of its members comporting themselves like British grandees.

Individuals at the convention, too, shrink to more ordinary proportions in the light of this book, which shows that they did not develop the main constitutional ideas in their own minds.

All this was apparently enough to earn the disinterest of those who screen devious political operations by inflating and hymning the status of the framers, the convention, and the document. The convention was by no means a gathering of masterminds excogitating constitutional wizardry right and left, although it was fortunate in having a bare handful of keen mentalities present (who, incidentally, were often overruled, and on quite original suggestions, by the entrenched politicos, as the convention record clearly shows).

6

Scholars know, and glancingly acknowledge, that the Constitution has ancient roots. But a difference between accepting (and forgetting) this fleeting secondhand assurance and reading Hutchison's book is that one can now see and feel it vividly oneself, can feel oneself transported back to 1300, 1100, even earlier as one reads familiar words and phrases—due process of law, this constitution, do ordain and establish, speaker, general welfare, ex post facto, bill of attainder, advise and consent, law of the land, necessary and proper, etc., etc.

Yet, although this book shows the remote sources, down to the very language, of most of the Constitution, an historical instance of old wine in a new bottle, it affords no clue at all to how the Constitution has been used and misused by the politicians through the decades since 1788—an altogether different story and one requiring further reading in other quarters. Nor does it show the official *meaning* of each turn of phrase. For the latter, up to 1964, one can turn to the 1,693-paged *The Constitution of the United States of America: Analysis and Interpretation*, published by the U. S. Government Printing Office and designated Senate Document #39, 88th Congress, first session.

A quick and somewhat simplified explanation for the frequent tortured interpretations of the Constitution is that much of all this is beyond the comprehension of most of the citizenry. Phrases such as "substantive due process" and "executive privilege" sound as though they must have a vast and important meaning, and it takes involved books to show that they are so much sound and fury, signifying nothing constitutional. One neither finds them in the Constitution nor any implication of them.

Few in the general populace, in any event, are aware that it took far more than the winning of the War of Independence against England to attain the Constitution, that most of the content of the Constitution long antedates that war.

Yet, even though scholars have long acknowledged the antiquity of the constitutional materials, the constitutional cultists have not been dampened. And, indeed, nothing will ever daunt them. Deprived of originality for the instrument, the stature of the convention itself questioned by intellectual sharpshooters, they have quickly responded by contending that only time-tried and time-tested timbers were taken into the constitutional structure, things that had worked well in the past.

Apart from the fact that many ancient formulas in the Constitution had been in force only off and on, now and then—such as due process and freedom from lawful torture—and that human slavery was as time-honored as anything else and yet repugnant, the contention of the cultists is about as sound as anything they advance to support their general claim that the Constitution is a political masterpiece of the ages, written by master craftsmen for a master race. This it palpably never was.

7

There were, of course, novel features set into the Constitution other than provision for slavery (abolished tardily by the thirteenth, fourteenth, and fifteenth amendments). For such, naturally, Hutchison is unable to trace ancient antecedents.

Perhaps the most absolutely original constructive provision of the document of 1787, arising spontaneously from the convention as little else did, consisted of the provision barring religious tests for the holding of office. (Article VI, paragraph 3). Proposed by Charles Pinckney, it passed without opposition. Here indeed was a sharp departure from European, English, colonial, and even post-revolutionary state practice. There was laid down here an absolute and valuable precedent, one which has served to keep emotionally charged religious prejudices muted if not entirely absent from the American political scene.

The first amendment built on the same idea in forbidding the passage of any law respecting a religious establishment—a precept often since violated by Congress, presidents, and the Supreme Court as boldly as each can be shown to have transgressed other flat constitutional injunctions.

No doubt it is precisely this manipulable aspect of the Constitution that endears it especially to politicians, leading such pretty typical characters as deposed Vice-President Spiro Agnew to eulogize it after his conviction for one of many crimes and his escape from a jail sentence. The instrument contains no automatic self-rectifying provisions, and naturally depends wholly on somebody's intelligent vigilance. *Quis custodiet ipsos custodes?*

What is called "the contract clause," forbidding the impairment of contracts by the states (Article I, Section 10, paragraph 1), is also without deep roots, as Professor Hutchinson concedes. Its presence is usually explained, vaguely, by the fact that James Wilson, its sponsor, was educated in Scotland and therefore trained in Roman law. Yet no specific Roman source for the notion is ever cited.

Actually, as Hutchison makes clear, the law was inspired by conditions of the 1780s and was aimed at the states whose legislatures had freely trammeled contracts, back and forth, so as to favor successive unruly political groups that had won control in the turbulent yearly elections. The object of the groups was to incur contractual obligations, such as for the purchase of land, and then through political control to obtain the license either to defer payments or to pay in something of lesser value, such as new paper money. The clause was aimed, in short, at a certain class of political swindlers who are represented by some historians as honest debtors being ground to dust by wicked creditors. But it was many major debtors of the time who were the villains of the piece, having planned all along to gyp the creditors by manipulating the government through easily obtained control.

As to separation of powers, it is in its rightful place an original notion and also one not to be found in the Constitution nor in subsequent holdings of American courts. It is simply politicians' nonsense, in circulation even prior to 1787. Hutchison leaves this clear, pointing out that the notion originated with Montesquieu in a misunderstanding by this French scholar of the British Constitution. Blackstone relied on Montesquieu's attestation. The nonpresence of any absolute separation of powers in the Constitution was flatly set forth by Chief Justice Taft in *Ex Parte Grossman* 267 U.S. 87 (1925) and, as shown by Hutchison, was similarly viewed as absent by Madison and other leaders of 1787. What the doctrine amounts to in the United States Constitution, Madison said, is merely that no division of the government can exercise the "whole" power of another division. The divisions, however, intermesh in many specific ways under the doctrine of balance. They are far from insulated from each other.

Nor is there anything to be found supporting the notion of "executive privilege." Like many others, it is an invented external notion foisted on the Constitution by dubiously operating politicians. (On this see the incisive study by Raoul Berger, *Executive Privilege: A Constitutional Myth*, Harvard University Press, 1974.) In passing, one should notice that the invention of transiently convenient constitutional notions has been assiduously resorted to from the very inception of the Constitution, notably at the outset by none others than Jefferson and Madison. The Supreme Court finally took to playing this game, and kept it up for a long time—in fact, until pulled up short by the New Dealers of the 1930s.

Some readers will be inclined to feel, in echo of school teachings, that the Electoral College as a means of choosing the president was surely an original contribution, indeed American, but it was first seen in the Constitution of Maryland, where it was used as a means of choosing senators. Yet at the constitutional convention, as Hutchison notes, there were cited similar ways in which both popes and doges of Venice were chosen. The presently accepted method of electing a president, by popular vote for state electors, was in fact flatly rejected by vote of the framers in 1787. And they were against electing a president by direct popular vote, which is what the present electoral system amounts to. The framers were dead set against all crowd commotions, and even against electioneering! They were, too, opposed to political parties. Politicians today do not cite them at all on this point, admittedly a delicate one.

Judicial review, however, is operatively a wholly American procedure although it was first claimed but not instituted as a judicial prerogative in England by Lord Coke (1552-1634). The Americans lifted the idea from Coke's *obiter dicta*, and were applying it in the states before the Constitution was written. Constitutionally it is unquestionably an original feature of the American Constitution although nowhere explicitly mentioned in the document of 1787. To most of the framers, it was a procedure that went without saying although a few were opposed to it.

8

Of the initial ten amendments, which came not from the framers but from opponents and critics of the Constitution, the first eight trace back deeply into bloody English history, as Hutchison shows. And the last one is both entirely original and of doubtful purport—constitutional ambiguity that occasioned much argument and finally wholesale bloodshed in civil war. As to the other amendments up to the nineteenth, most had long-standing antecedent roots, even the nineteenth granting the suffrage to women. For when the nineteenth amendment was passed, women already had the vote in the following states: Wyoming, Colorado, Utah, Idaho, Washington, California, Arizona, Kansas, Oregon, Montana, Nevada, New York, Michigan, Oklahoma, South Dakota, and Alaska Territory. Women already could vote in presidential elections in twelve other states.

The often denounced eighteenth, or prohibition amendment, contrary to the common understanding, also had many long-standing American precedents. As Hutchison points out, as of 1917 thirty-three states had instituted either legislative or constitutional prohibition. Bootlegging itself was an established enterprise long before national prohibition took effect and the prohibition amendment did not go as strongly against the American grain as commonly represented. It was as American as apple pie, no doubt deriving from the Puritan strain transplanted to New England.

In general, this book is an eye-opener for most readers even though accomplished historians may find little to surprise them in it. And its chief informative impact lies in its detailed mosaic of precisely and copiously documented historical sources. Using it as a prolegomena, one can read with infinitely greater understanding Max Farrand's four-volume *Records of the Federal Convention of 1787*, which consists mainly of Madison's highly detailed on-thespot report. For one is, after reading Hutchison, fully aware that the convention members were being cued a long distance of the way by an invisible historical script, were not pulling ideas out of the air or generating them by a group dialectical process.

Naturally, there were minor new things in the Constitution of which one need not take note in an introduction when the book itself is there to read. The staggered age requirements for holding offices—twenty-five years for the House, thirty years for the Senate, and thirty-five years for the president—were certainly novel although some of the best opinion at the convention held out for twenty-one across the board. Most of the members, however, felt that age improved judgment even though it was pointed out to them that some of the most brilliantly successful British political leaders had been in their early twenties—Bolingbroke as prime minister-in-effect and the younger Pitt as prime minister in fact. *Per contra*, many nations have been ruined by mature men. The staggering of elections for the Senate and the fixing of set terms of different lengths all around were also American novelties.

Nevertheless, the historical script followed by the convention, as shown in the long struggle over English law, is brought into naked and vivid view by Hutchison—always to the point. It is above all plain to readers of the convention record who become familiar with this book why many ingenious proposals were voted down. There was simply no extended precedent for them. For most of the way, the convention adhered to precedent, at least as it understood it.

And whatever else this book may be, it is a true teaching gem, in many ways something like a compiled Dead Sea Scrolls of the Constitution. It certainly comes far closer than other books to putting the reader on the earthy ground floor of the constitutional operation—closer than does Farrand's indispensable *Records* and certainly far closer than does *The Federalist*. For this book shows, in a concentrated fashion, the wells from which the constitutional stuff was drawn, often the very vats in which it was distilled, and shows it in a large number of cases as a direct transfer.

Unquestionably, the stylistic finish of the Constitution owes much to the final writer, Gouverneur Morris, a highly erudite and well-read fellow. But Morris could not have written as he did and won the approval of the convention if he had not used terminology that rang a bell with all the signers. When they heard the final script over which they had argued, squabbled, and voted, they were pretty much like trained musicians listening to a transcription of what they recognized as authentic Bach. Despite strong private doubts about parts, all around they knew they were listening to something that might well be an encapsulation of the authentic law of the land.

Nor was the task yet finished.

For the document had yet to run the gauntlet of the state ratification conventions, where it encountered much intelligent opposition and a blizzard of criticism that eventuated in the first ten amendments. These were the residue of 128 amendments proposed by no fewer than seven state conventions.

But practically everything in the main document as well as the amendments came from the sources laid out in this book by Hutchison. Without those sources, left to their own experience, both framers and amenders would have had a comparatively meager store of autonomous ideas to draw upon. The convention was simply not a collection of originators.

Ferdinand Lundberg

FOREWORD

THIS book does not interpret the Constitution. It traces the origins or the historical background, Federal, State, Colonial, and English. The arrangement is that of the Constitution of the United States. Hence, the reader may find what is said on any subject by turning to the section or clause under consideration. The use of the Constitution in reading will make the subject clearer to the reader. The book presents the evidence for entirely new views on many subjects in early American history and this is the author's only apology for its publication. The authoritative references or footnotes will be found at the end of each chapter.

ALBANY, NEW YORK,   THE AUTHOR.
  January 2, 1928.

CONTENTS

THE FOUNDATIONS OF THE CONSTITUTION

FOUNDATIONS
OF THE CONSTITUTION

CHAPTER I

THE CONSTITUTION A GROWTH, ORIGIN OF THE WRITTEN CONSTITUTION AND THE PREAMBLE

The Constitution a Growth. The Constitution of the United States was a growth. It was not a creation of 1787 out of nothing or ex nihilo. The theological and philosophical doctrine ex nihilo nihil fit may be true or false as applied to the creation of the physical universe, but it is certainly true as applied to the Constitution of the United States. "The American Constitution is a growth and the wisdom of the framers of the existing union was shown chiefly in this: that in perfecting the general government they disturbed as little as possible the existing institutions which were the growth of ages, and which were as much a part of their race inheritance as were their own physical and mental peculiarities and tendencies." [1] There is, therefore, little in the Constitution that is new. It contains matter centuries older than Magna Carta, and its provisions establish "organic living institutions transplanted from English soil" [2] to America. The Revolutionary War was not fought by the Americans to destroy existing institutions, but to secure British rights and liberties guaranteed them by the English Constitution. They constantly claimed all the rights and privileges of British subjects, such as the right of trial by jury in the vicinage, the right to the common law, the right to have no taxes imposed on them without their own consent given either personally or by their representatives, and the right to protection against unreasonable searches and seizures. They fought to retain, not to destroy, the old Constitution. They charged George III and Parliament with innovation and violation of their constitutional rights; and claimed all the rights, liberties, and immunities of Englishmen under the English Constitution. [3] George III by his "repeated injuries and usurpations" was denying them the protection guaranteed by the British Constitution and attempting to subject them to "a jurisdiction foreign to our Constitution, and unacknowledged by our laws." [4]   Hence, when the Revolution was over, they simply "changed the form but not the substance of their government" and "retained for the purposes of government all the powers of the British Parliament." [5]   As the growth of centuries, there is a sense, therefore, in which it may be said that the Constitution was not framed at Philadelphia by the Convention of 1787, but was a cumulative Constitution in the making of which Alfred the Great, Ethelred II, the Barons at Runnymede, Simon de Montfort, Henry II, Edward I, Edward III, Edward VI, Elizabeth, James I, Sir Edward Coke, Vattel, John Locke, John Wilkes, Montesquieu, Blackstone, the English Parliament, the English judges, and others all had a share.   They created the material out of which the American statesmen erected the constitutional structure in 1787.   The Constitution of the United States was not an invention of the Convention of 1787, nor borrowed from, nor a conscious imitation of the English Constitution.   The Americans of 1776 were British.   They lived in British possessions, acknowledged allegiance to the British crown, regarded the British Constitution as their own, and claimed rights and protection under it in the same way as other British citizens.   In framing their Constitution, they simply used their own law and constitution.   These belonged to them just as much as to the people of Great Britain and in using them, they neither imitated nor borrowed, but simply used what had always been their own.

2. *The Origin of the Written Constitution.*—A constitution is simply the body of rules in accordance with which the powers of government are distributed and exercised.[6]   In a written constitution, the rules are reduced to a formally enacted written form.   An unwritten constitution is one composed of customs or conventions, decisions of the courts and statutes, as in case of the British Constitution.   How did the United States come to have written constitutions?   There are several converging lines of influence, the result of which is the written constitution.

First among these is the *influence of the colonial charters.*

The colonial charters were modelled after the trading charters.   The charter of the East India Company, December 31,

1600, contains an outline of what is found in all the colonial charters and governments, and which passed into the state and national Constitutions. It was a written constitution for the East India Company. The third charter of Virginia, 1612, by which legislative, executive, and judicial powers are conveyed and distributed, is merely a copy of Queen Elizabeth's Charter to the East India Company. It was a written constitution providing for the government of the colony of Virginia, and is in fact a rough draft or outline of what later developed into the state constitutions, and the Constitution of the United States.[7] The colonial charters constituted the written fundamental law for the government of the Colonies and the new state constitutions were but expansions and amendments of the charters. Connecticut, for example, declared in 1786 they had "a free and excellent constitution" from their ancestors, and that the ancient form of civil government contained in Charles Second's charter should remain as before.[8] While the other states framed constitutions, Connecticut and Rhode Island retained their charters as constitutions till 1818 and 1842. The Americans were always accustomed to government by written constitutions—the charters. The New Jersey Constitution of 1776 calls itself a charter, and speaks of the rights guaranteed therein as "charter rights."[9] It is regarded as the new charter.

A second influence was that of the *church covenants*. Professor A. C. McLaughlin, speaking of the source of written constitutions, says: "Another line is to be traced to the separatist foundation of church government, the principle of religious individualism, and the organization of polity, in agreement and covenant."[10] Charles Borgeaud holds that the origin of written constitutions may be traced to certain English and American documents: namely, the Agreement of the People 1647, the Instrument of Government 1653, the Fundamental Orders of Connecticut 1639, and the Plantation Covenants."[11] Dr. Lobingier thinks we should still have had written constitutions without the church covenant, but they would not have been popular constitutions.[12] The Plantation Covenants were church covenants adapted to political purposes. The origin of the church covenant is not clear. It may have been taken from the Bible and guild statutes,[13] or borrowed from the Anabaptists,[14] or received from Geneva by the English Puritans. In founding a church, the people covenanted or agreed to live in obedience to the laws and government of God, and to hold together as one ecclesiastical body. In 1602 the people of Gainsborough, from which came the Mayflower company, entered into a covenant.[15] In England, the covenants were used for political purposes by the associations or compacts formed for the purpose of supporting Parliament in its struggle against the crown.[16] They were then carried across the Atlantic to America, and used for both political and ecclesiastical purposes. The Mayflower compact was simply the application of the church covenant to political uses. The political and ecclesiastical doctrine of the early New England leaders was that both church and state were organized by means of covenants. In 1639, the clergy declared, "Every state is united by some covenant among themselves." [17] Governor Winthrop said that governmental power "must be limited by constitutions, or political covenants similar to those existing between God and man." [18] Thomas Hooker lays down a similar doctrine in his *Survey of the Summe of Church Discipline*.[19] We may, therefore, expect the application of this doctrine to both state and church by the New England leaders. Consequently, we find that Thomas Hooker applied, or helped to apply, these very principles of the church covenant to the civil government of Connecticut in 1639 in the Fundamental Orders. The freemen of the colony of New Haven adopted a political covenant for the establishment of civil government before they adopted a church covenant, and for the sake of distinction called it "The Plantation Covenant." [20] The Fundamental Articles of New Haven, 1639, explain the situation. "This covenant was called a plantation covenant to distinguish itt from a church covenant wch could nott att thatt time be made, a church nott being then gathered, butt was deferred till a church might be gathered according to God." [21] This is a clear recognition of the adoption of the church covenant for purposes of civil polity. The Fundamental Orders of Connecticut is a written constitution modelled after the church covenant.[22] The Fundamental Agreement of the New Haven Colony was also a church covenant in form.[23] The Guilford Colony adopted such a covenant while still at sea, 1639.[24] The Scotch Covenants also appear on this side of the Atlantic among people of Scotch or Scotch-Irish birth or descent, in the Carolinas and Pennsylvania. The Watauga Compact drawn up by James Robertson, 1774, a Scotch-Irish Presbyterian of Virginian birth, was such a covenant, and the first written constitution adopted west of the mountains.[25] Traces of the British covenants are plainly discernible in John Locke's written constitution for the province of Carolina— the Fundamental Constitutions 1669. Locke was of Puritan origin and had received his training in the Calvinistic school of political thinking.[26] In 1774, the Committee of Correspondence of New Hampshire prepared a covenant, and sent it to all towns in the colony—the New Hampshire Covenant.[27] The church covenant did develop into written constitutions, but what actual contribution was made to the idea of a written constitution is difficult to say.

Third, *the influence of English precedent.* The English people, in the course of long years of struggle against the crown, had acquired a political habit of great value to the nation, namely, the habit of drawing up constitutional documents for the purpose of placing limitations on the king or government, and safeguarding the liberties of the people for the future. This was done at every great crisis in the nation's history, as Magna Carta 1215, the Provisions of Oxford 1258, the Petition of Right, 1628, the Habeas Corpus Act 1679, the Bill of Rights 1689, the Act of Settlement 1701, and many others. The great precedent, however, was the revolutionary convention, or convention parliament of 1689. James Otis said of this: "The present establishment founded on the law of God and nature, was begun by the Convention with a professed and real view, in all parts of the British Empire to put the liberties of the people out of the reach of arbitrary power in all times to come." [28] The convention accomplished this by drawing up a written fundamental law—the Bill of Rights. By means of a written instrument, a check had always been placed on the exercise of arbitrary governmental power, so the Americans, following the ancestral habit, undertake to do the same thing, namely, get rid of the evils complained of and limit the government by formulating a fundamental written law defining the powers and assigning the limits of the government, and declaring what rights were reserved to the people. This was done by revolutionary conventions modelled after the English Convention.[29]   We find the South Carolina Convention declaring itself the legislature of South Carolina just as the English convention declared itself the legislature of England. The fact that the Americans took their Bills of Rights, partly at least, from the English Bill of Rights in their constitution making shows clearly what they had in mind.   The idea of a revolutionary convention and the idea of a written constitutional document limiting the powers of government were inseparable in 1776.

The political philosophy of the Americans, and *the idea of a fundamental law* have been regarded as other influences which helped to create the written constitution.   As to political philosophy, Samuel Adams frequently declared that government must have "a standing rule to live by." [30]   He was also very fond of quoting Vattel's famous declaration that the constitution of the state ought to be fixed.[31]   James Otis said: "The supreme legislature cannot justly assume a power of ruling by extempore, arbitrary decrees, but is bound to dispense justice by known settled rules." "They govern by stated laws." "These are . . . the great barriers of a free state." [32]   Both Adams and Otis are quoting from John Locke's Civil Government.   It was a favorite doctrine of Locke that "the freedom of men under government is to have a standing rule to live by." [33]   According to him the legislature was bound to rule by "promulgated standing laws," "by declared laws," "by declared and received laws," "by established and promulgated laws." [34] The constitution of Massachusetts makes use of Locke's phrase, "standing laws." [35]   Adams and Otis have in mind written laws, or a written constitution, or they would not be standing laws, and the constitution would not be fixed any more than the laws of the Twelve Tables or the laws of Draco were fixed before their reduction to written form.   Locke, whom they are following, brings this out clearly by stating that the law of nature is unwritten, thereby implying that the other is written. Locke's own written constitution also illustrates his meaning. In their quarrel with Great Britain, the Americans had insisted that the constitution was fixed, standing, declared, and when the time came to make constitutions of their own, they made them so.   The influence of political philosophy in this connection is also seen in the statements of John Adams.   Of the

Massachusetts constitution, largely his work, he said: "It is Locke, Sidney and Rousseau, and DeMably reduced to practice in the first instance." [36] Again, he says his researches in Harrington, Sidney, Hobbes, Nedham, and Locke "produced . . . the constitution of Massachusetts, and at length . . . writings . . . some of which undoubtedly contributed to produce the constitution of New York, the Constitution of the United States, and the last constitution of Pennsylvania and Georgia." [37]

The idea of a fundamental law, a law so fundamental that it limited even the King's power, runs far back into English history. The common law and the coronation oath limited the power of the Anglo-Saxon Kings. Henry First's Charter 1100 A.D. and the first and second charters of Stephen 1135, and 1136 A.D. placed definite, written limitations on the royal power. Then Magna Carta 1215 imposed a written limitation on the crown. It laid down the fundamental law binding even on the King.[36] So fundamental was this law, that Coke and Bacon declare laws repugnant to Magna Carta void.[37] The phrase "fundamental laws" soon comes into general use. Bracton and Thornton recognized the existence of a fundamental law.[38] This is too large a subject to trace here, but out of this conception came the written constitution in England. The Republicans of the Puritan Revolution began to fear that the results of the revolution were to be lost, unless some means could be found of placing a check on Parliamentary sovereignty, for Parliament was becoming absolute. That absolutism must be curbed. The means of doing this were found in the old idea of a fundamental law. Magna Carta was "the ancient and fundamental law" [39] which had checked this absolutism of the King and limited royal power when it formerly became dangerous. Therefore, the idea suggested itself that they make a new, written fundamental law which should embody their ideas of what government ought to be, and which should be binding upon and unalterable by Parliament. The result was the written constitution in English history. "In every government," said Cromwell, "there must be a somewhat Fundamental, somewhat like Magna Carta, which should be standing, be unalterable." A law which no legislature could unlaw again, otherwise it would be a mere rope of sand." [40] So, such a funda-

mental law was drawn up by John Lilburne—the Agreement of
the People, 1647. It was beyond the power of Parliament to
revoke it. It defined "the powers of that body, and expressly"
declared "the rights which the nation reserved to itself, and
which no authority might touch with impunity." [41] Though it
never became operative, this was the first written constitution
in history made for a nation—the first written constitution to
limit the power of a national legislature. This was followed
in 1653 by the Instrument of Government, the first written,
national constitution which actually became operative. American writings of the pre-revolutionary period show that Americans were quite familiar with the idea of a fundamental law.[42]
Therefore, in 1776 and following years, the Americans undertake to formulate written fundamental laws defining the powers
and limits of government and declaring what rights were reserved to the people "which no authority might touch with
impunity" and which no legislature could "unlaw again." In
doing this, "the Americans were, however, but following the
example of their British forefathers," says President Goodnow
of Johns Hopkins, "who after having destroyed the monarchy
and set up the short-lived commonwealth of Oliver Cromwell,
drew up in 1654 a written constitution—the Instrument of Government—said to be the earliest written constitution of modern
Europe." [43]

Another thing which ought to be remembered is the fact
that *the first state constitutions were legislative acts,* and,
as such, could not be anything else but written law. The
earliest state constitution, that of New Hampshire, 1776, was
framed and adopted by the Provincial Congress, a body which
performed the functions and exercised the authority and powers
of an ordinary legislature. Consequently, it was drawn up in
the form of a parliamentary resolution.[44] The first constitution of Virginia, 1776, was also framed by a legislative body
which was not, in any sense, a constitutional convention. Jefferson regarded this constitution as a mere bill or legislative
act which could be repealed by the legislature like any other
legislative enactment.[45] The first constitution of South Carolina, 1776, was also framed and adopted by a legislative body
and, therefore, naturally assumed the form of an ordinary
legislative act.[46] The second constitution of South Carolina

was framed and passed as a legislative act, March 19, 1778. It contains an enacting clause and calls itself an act.[47] It required the governor's signature to make it the law of the land. The executive, John Rutledge, refused to sign it, on the ground that the legislature had exceeded its power by transferring the election of the second branch from the general assembly to the people. He resigned and Alexander Middleton was chosen president. He also refused his assent, and Rawlins Lowndes was elected president and gave the assent which transformed the constitution into the law of the state.[48] The people of South Carolina regarded the constitutions of 1776 and 1778 as legislative acts, and this view was adopted in 1823 by the highest state court—the constitutional court of South Carolina—in the case of Athanatius Thomas vs. Chesley Daniel.[49] "Of the eleven new constitutions," says Professor Hart, "ten were put into force by the congress or convention which drew them—but those conventions were also the legislatures of the time." [50] These conventions were following their predecessor, the English convention or Convention Parliament of 1688-89. The first state constitutions, especially the Bill of Rights and constitution of Virginia, served as models for the other states.

3. *The Preamble.* "We the people of the United States." This refers to the general body of electors, or the people in their sovereign, political capacity. This doctrine of the sovereignty of the people was an established doctrine of the British Constitution long before 1787. It had been asserted by the English Parliament as early as 1366 in Edward Third's reign. It is also found in the Declaration of the Army, and the Agreement of the People 1647; in the acts abolishing the Kingship and declaring England a commonwealth, 1649, and it was declared by the Parliament which erected the High Court of Justice for the trial of Charles First.[51] Popular sovereignty was established in England by the Revolution of 1688, and this inspired John Locke, whose Civil Government taught the American colonists. The Continental Congress in an address to the inhabitants of the United Colonies, February 13, 1776, correctly stated the doctrine to be a maxim of the English Constitution.[52] Again, *political philosophy* taught the doctrine and had made a deep impression on the Revolutionary statesmen. James Otis follows John Locke in declaring the

supreme power to be "originally and ultimately in the people."
He quotes over a page from the Treatise on Civil Government
and says the sentiments of the colonists regarding their rights
were drawn chiefly from Locke.[53]   Samuel Adams also quotes
freely from the Civil Government on the same subject.[54]   The
Massachusetts Proclamation of January 19, 1776, declared the
consent of the people was the foundation of government; that
every exercise of sovereignty against or without that consent
is injustice, usurpation and tyranny; and the supreme sovereign power resides in the people.[55]   The Council ordered this
to be read at every annual town meeting, in all the courts, and
from every pulpit in Massachusetts.   The Preamble of the constitution of Massachusetts, 1780, contains the same phraseology as the preamble of the Federal Constitution.[56]   The Virginia Convention also adopted Locke's doctrine as clause two
of the Bill of Rights,[57] and the Declaration of Independence
soon promulgated the same teaching.   The state constitutions
do the same thing as the New Hampshire constitution, 1784,
which says: "All government of right originates from the
people, is founded in consent, and instituted for the general
good." [58]   The Continental Congress in the Address to the Inhabitants of Quebec, October 26, 1774, attributes the same
doctrine to Montesquieu.[59]   However, by 1787 Americans seem
to be chiefly conscious of Locke as the author.   James Wilson,
for example, said in the Pennsylvania convention that the leading principle in American Constitutions, namely, that supreme
power resides in the people, was Locke's doctrine.   "The great
and penetrating mind of Locke," he said, "seems to be the only
one that pointed towards even the theory of this great truth." [60]

   The State Constitutions also contained statements on the
subject.   When the Declaration of Independence was issued in
1776, all the powers of the British Crown and Parliament
passed to the people of the several states,[61] and the doctrine
of popular sovereignty was immediately given a leading place
in the new state constitutions.   Virginia adopted the principle
as early as June 12, 1776,[62] while in Rhode Island and Connecticut it appeared as early as 1636 and 1638, due to the
influence there of the church covenants and town compacts
which embodied the *doctrine of common consent*.   In 1647, the
Rhode Island Assembly declared their form of government was

"Democratical, that is to say, a government held by the free and voluntary consent of all or the greater part of the inhabitants." The same doctrine is found in the constitution for the civil government of New Haven, 1639. The people of all the states is meant, not the people of one state." [63]

"*Of the United States.*" The New England Articles of Confederation, 1643, use the term "United Colonies." [64] The Continental Congress used this name for the first time in Gen. Washington's commission. [65] It was also inserted in the Address to the Inhabitants of Great Britain in the Declaration of Causes and Necessity of Taking up Arms, [67] and in Franklin's draft of a constitution, July 25, 1775. [68] When the resolution recommending South Carolina to establish a government was under discussion in Congress in 1775. John Adams labored hard to have the words, "colony" and "colonies" stricken out, and the words "state" and "states" substituted: He was unsuccessful because "the child was not yet weaned." [69] Then, Jefferson used "United States" July 4, 1776, in the Declaration of Independence. [70] The terms "states" and "United States" came into use with the Declaration. Dickinson's Draft of July 12, 1776, makes use of the name "United States." [71] Then, on September 9, 1776, the official change was made by Congress passing the following resolution: "Resolved, That in all continental commissions, and other instruments where heretofore, the words 'United Colonies' have been used, the stile be altered for the future to the United States." [72] The Articles of Confederation adopted by Congress November 15, 1777, fixed the name in the written constitution by declaring: "The stile of this confederacy shall be 'The United States of America.' " [73] The Convention of 1787 took the name from the Articles August 6. [74] The committee on style then changed it to read: "We, the people of the United States," in order that it might apply to nine states if the constitution should be ratified by nine instead of thirteen as had been required by the Articles. Montesquieu speaks of states in a Confederate Republic as "United States." It is just possible that this may have influenced the American statesmen in their adoption of the name.

"*In order to form a more perfect union.*" The union under the Articles of Confederation had consisted in the states enter-

ing "into a firm league of friendship with each other." [75]
American experience had found this so imperfect in practice
that it almost wrecked the union and proved utterly unsuited
to the exigencies of government. It gave Congress no power
to regulate commerce, secure a revenue, execute the laws of the
union, enforce treaties, or to protect the states against the
turbulence of insurrection as evidenced, for example, by Shays's
rebellion in Massachusetts. The British had failed to solve the
problem of imperial organization. Their attempt brought on
the Revolution. The Americans had also failed to solve the
problem after the Revolution. The convention of 1787 was
called to undertake a second attempt by making "such alterations and further provisions" as might be necessary "to render
the federal constitution adequate to the exigencies of union." [76]
That is, to form a more perfect union than under the Articles—
a union which would remedy the defects of the Articles of Confederation and solve the pressing problems of American government.

"To establish justice." Under the Articles, there was no
national system of courts to which the people could resort
for justice. There was no supreme court of appellate jurisdiction to which appeals could be taken to correct the errors
of state courts relating either to national affairs or to the
citizens of other states. Motives of policy and justice rendered it extremely desirable that this situation be remedied.
The United States had also become amenable to the law of
nations and responsible for foreign relations, but under the
Articles the union had no power to compel states to obey the
law of nations or fulfil treaty obligations. As a matter of
fact, treaties were violated by the states and the United States
was helpless, as in the case of the treaty of 1783. It was worse
than useless to refer such questions to the courts of delinquent
states. It was necessary, therefore, that the United States
should be given power to cause justice to be done to each
state "and the citizens of each, but also to cause justice to
be done by each, and the citizens of each, and that not by
violence and force, but in a stable, sedate and regular course
of judicial procedure." "What is the precise sense and lati-
tude in which the words 'to establish justice'—are to be understood?" The answer is found in Article III, section 2 of the

Constitution where it is declared that the judicial power of the United States shall extend to ten classes of cases.[77] The Constitution establishes justice by creating Federal courts and giving them jurisdiction over such cases.

"*To insure domestic tranquillity.*" American statesmen had had two bitter experiences in this connection. The first in 1783, when a band of eighty mutinous soldiers from Lancaster, Pennsylvania, uttering offensive words against the members of congress and pointing their muskets at the windows of the hall in which the delegates were in session, insulted and threatened the representatives of the nation. Congress found itself without any means of self-protection. An appeal for protection was made to the Governor of Pennsylvania, but he expressed "doubts concerning the disposition of the militia to act unless some actual outrage were offered to persons or property." It was also uncertain "whether a repetition of the insult to congress would be a sufficient provocation" for the use of the state militia. The mutineers, whose avowed purpose was to obtain a settlement of their accounts from congress, threatened to kidnap members of Congress to guarantee indemnity for their offence. Unable to secure any definite promise or assurance of protection from the state authorities, the President summoned congress to meet at Trenton, New Jersey, instead of Philadelphia. The United States was so weak that a mutiny of eighty soldiers forced Congress to flee and seek asylum in another state.[78] Again, when Shays's rebellion occurred in Massachusetts, Madison admitted that under the Articles of Confederation Congress had no authority to interfere in the internal controversies of a state. True, Congress began to enlist troops, but for what purpose? Was it to aid Massachusetts in quelling insurrection and securing "the tranquillity of the union?" Congress, being helpless, did not dare say that, but began the enlistment of troops ostensibly to be used against the Indians, though the real object of the military preparations was to quell the disturbances in Massachusetts.[79] This affair startled the nation, showed the states their insecurity and taught the need of such a change as would confer on the government of the United States constitutional power to protect the states and the union by enabling it to suppress domestic insurrection and guarantee to each state a republican form of government.

Domestic tranquillity also "requires that the contentions of
states should be peaceably terminated by a common judiciary,"
and to prevent "danger of irritation and criminations arising
from apprehensions and suspicions of partiality" that controversies between states and citizens of other states should
be settled by a national court.[80]   This has been done by the
Constitution.

"*To provide for the common defence.*"   This was taken
from the Articles of Confederation.[81]   It goes back to the New
England Articles of Confederation, 1643, which uses the phrase
"for offence and defence." [82]   In the preamble to the Albany
Plan, 1754, Dr. Franklin used the phrase "for their mutual
defence," [83] while in his Draft, 1775, "common defence" appears.[84]   At first, he wrote the words found in the New England
Articles.[85]   The Dickinson Draft used the words of Franklin's
Draft,[86] and as the Dickinson Draft, when slightly amended and
adopted by Congress, became the Articles of Confederation, it
is clear that Dr. Franklin was really the author of the phrase.
The words "common defence and safety" were frequently used
by the states during the Revolutionary period.[87]   One important
purpose of the Articles was to provide for defence, but the
Constitution by giving Congress power to tax and raise armies
furnished more adequate means of protection.

"*To promote the general welfare.*"   The immediate source
for this was the Articles of Confederation in Article three of
which the words "their mutual and general welfare" appear.
Madison said the terms were not new but "well known to the
people of America" and "found in the old Articles of Confederation." [90]   Similar phraseology is found in English and
colonial documents, as "for the common profit" in Confirmatio
Cartarun, 1297; "for the weal and common good" in the Commission for negotiating a Union with Scotland, 1604; [91] "the
present good and welfare" in the New Jersey Commissions and
Agreement; [92] the Third Charter of Virginia, 1611, "the general
weal," "for the general good," "for the good and welfare,"
"the weal public and general good"; [93] the Ordinance of Virginia, 1621, "the public weal"; the Fundamental Orders of
Connecticut, 1638, "the good of the public"; [95] and the New
England Articles of Confederation make use of the phrase "for
their own mutual safety and welfare."   The Articles of Con-

federation, of course, took the phrase from the Dickinson Draft, 1776, while the Dickinson Draft took it from Dr. Franklin's Draft of July 21, 1775. This is not a grant of power to Congress to do anything that will promote the general welfare. No new or additional powers are delegated to Congress by the preamble.[96]

"To secure the blessings of liberty to ourselves and our posterity." One of the objects of the union under the Articles of Confederation was "the security of their liberties." [96] This was found in Article two of the Dickinson Draft which took it from Article two of Franklin's Draft, 1775.[97] Randolph's propositions of May 30, 1787 in the Federal Convention refer the phrase to the Articles of Confederation.[98]

"Do ordain and establish this constitution." This language is legislative in character. The English King in Council legislated by ordinance in the early history of England, and in doing so used the phraseology of the preamble—"ordain and establish"—in many such laws.[99] In earlier documents, "ordain" sometimes stands alone but not so in the later as in the Statute of Provisors, 1351, and Ordinance of the Staple, 1353. An ordinance was primarily an executive act. A statute was a legislative act. The former was temporary, the latter permanent. Ordinances, when confirmed by Parliament, were statutes "to endure forever." [100] That is, they became permanent enactments. In the fourteenth century, statutes and ordinances are scarcely distinguishable. In 1406, an act to regulate the succession passed by the lords and commons in Parliament was "ordained and established." In the same year, an act regulating the manner of electing knights of the shire to Parliament was "ordained and established" "by the assent of the lords spiritual and temporal, and of all the commonality of the realm in this present parliament." Another act of 1413 providing that residence within the shire be required as a qualification for members of parliament, was also "ordained and established." [101] In the fifteenth century, legislation by ordinance disappeared, but reappeared in the sixteenth as Proclamations. The words *"to enact"* appear in 1295. Later, acts, as the famous act providing that allegiance to a de facto king should not be treason, make use of the words "ordained, established and enacted," or "enact, establish and ordain," or "enacted,

ordained and established," [102] by authority of parliament.
Sometimes "be it ordained and established" and at other times
"be it enacted" is used as the enacting clause in different sections of the same act.[103] Finally, the words "ordained and established" are dropped and "Be it enacted" remains as the
enacting clause.

The Colonial Charters also make use of these words. The
second charter of Virginia, for example, 1609, uses the words
"grant, declare and ordain" and "ordain and establish." [104]
The charter of Connecticut 1662 employs the words, "We doe
hereby establish and ordain," "We have ordained, constituted
and declared." The Governor, Deputy Governor, and Assistants are authorized to make, ordain and establish all manner
of reasonable laws, statutes, and ordinances not contrary to the
laws of England. In the Rhode Island Charter, 1663, we have
"ordeyned, constituted and declared," and "established and ordeyned." [105] The words appear in the preamble of several of
the *state constitutions*. The Pennsylvania constitution of 1776
used "ordain, declare and establish." New York, 1776, uses
"the people of the state doth ordain, determine and declare."
Georgia, 1777, wrote "We, therefore, the representatives of the
people—do ordain and declare, and it is hereby ordained and
declared." Vermont, 1777, uses the Pennsylvania phraseology.
Massachusetts, 1780, used "ordain and establish"; New Hampshire, 1784, follows Massachusetts,[106] which appears to be the
immediate source of the words in the Federal Constitution. The
committee of detail in its report of August 6 used the Pennsylvania phraseology,[107] doubtless due to the fact that Wilson was
a member of that committee. He would naturally use the words
in the constitution of his own state. The committee on style
adopted the phraseology of the Massachusetts constitution.
That instrument was very highly regarded and contributed
quite largely to the Constitution of the United States. King of
Massachusetts, Johnson of Connecticut, and Madison of Virginia were members of this committee.[108] All were familiar with
the wording of the Massachusetts constitution, the latter two
through their state charters. By using these words the state
constitutions announced that the people of the state legislated
by using an extraordinary method, and that the state constitutions were direct legislative enactments of the sovereign will.

By adopting the form used in the state constitutions, the Federal Convention of 1787 intended to proclaim that the people of the United States also legislated by an extraordinary method which made the Constitution the supreme law of the land and not merely a treaty or league of states.

"This constitution." In the Constitutions of Clarendon, 1164, the term is used to denote certain statutes of Henry Second.[108] In England and the colonies during the Provincial period, the word was used "to designate the political system, and also certain rights and privileges which were claimed to be the natural inheritance of Englishmen."[109] The Second Charter of Virginia, 1609, and the Charter of Carolina, 1665, speak of laws and constitutions, while in the Pennsylvania Frame of 1682 the established system of government is called a constitution.[110] Hamilton, in Congress April 1, 1783, and in his recommendation for a convention, 1786, spoke of the Articles of Confederation as "the Federal Constitution," and "the constitution of the federal government." The law of Virginia complying with the recommendation from Annapolis used the same words.[111] By 1787 the name had been adopted by all the state constitutions to indicate that each was the fundamental law of the state. Therefore, after ten years' experience in constitution making, the term had come to be commonly used for the fundamental law of the state or United States.

NOTES TO CHAPTER I

1. Cooley, Const. Hist. as seen in Am. Law, p. 30.
2. Gompers v. U. S. 233 U. S. 604; Bryce, Am. Commonwealth, I, ch. III, p. 28.
3. Declaration of Rights, 1774.
4. Decl. of Independence.
5. Munn v. Ill. McClain, Cases, 947.
6. Cooley, Const. Law, p. 21.
7. Prothero, Stats. 448; MacDonald, Sel. Charters, 1, 2, 17.
8. Stats. of Conn. 1786, p. 1.
9. Poore, Charters and Constitutions, 1311, 1313, 1314.
10. Mich. Law Rev. V, 617.
11. Borgeaud, Pol. Sc. Q., VII, 614.
12. Lobingier, The People's Law.
13. Borgeaud, Rise of Democracy, 87.
14. Lobingier, The People's Law, p. 25, note.
15. Id. p. 54.
16. Id. 55.
17. Osgood, Pol. Ideas of the Puritans, in Pol. Sc. Q., 1891.
18. Id. p. 20.

19. Id. p. 46, 68; Osgood, Pol. Sc. Q., 1891, p. 25.
20. MacDonald, Sel. Charters, p. 68.
21. Id.
22. Poore, Charters and Constitutions, p. 249.
23. MacDonald, Sel. Charters, p. 67.
24. Lobingier, The People's Law, p. 98.
25. Id. 105-121; Roosevelt, Winning of the West, I, 183.
26. MacDonald, Sel. Charters, 149.
27. Walker, N. H's Five Provincial Congresses, pp. 9-10, 73-74, 75.
28. Otis, Rights of the Colonies, 1764, p. 16.
29. Jameson, Constitutional Conventions, 144, 112-144.
30. Works, II, 357.
31. Vattel, Law of Nature and of Nations, Bk. 1, ch. III, p. 10; S. Adams, Writings, 1, 156, 170, 174, 185, 190, 196.
32. Otis, Rights of the Colonies, pp. 36, 37.
33. II, ch. XI, II, IV.
34. II. ch. XI.
35. Poore, 966.
36. McIlwain, High Court of Parliament, p. 65; Adams, Origin of Eng. Parlt., 296.
37. Id. 65.
38. Id. Coke, Rep. 8.
39. McIlwain, High Court of Parlt., 65.
40. Carlyle, Oliver Cromwell's Letters and Speeches, Pt. VIII, Speech III.
41. Borgeaud, Adoption and Amendment of Constitutions, p. 6.
42. Baldwin, Two Centuries of Am. Law, 22; MacDonald, Sel. Charters, 332; S. Adams Writings, I, 65, 134, 147, 156, 174, 180, 185, 190, 196, 197; II, 210; Otis, Rights of the Colonies, 16, 36, 37.
43. Goodnow, Principles of Const. Government, p. 7.
44. N. H. State Papers, Vol. 7, 690-3, 703; N. H. Prov. Papers, Vol. 7, 49, 57, 59, 62, 64.
45. Jefferson, Works (Marsh Ed.), VIII, 353-4; 363-4; Id. (Ford ed.), 89, 29, 30.
46. Ramsey, Hist. S. C. I., 269; II, 135.
47. Poore, Charters & Const'ns 1620-21.
48. Ramsey, Hist. of the Revolution in S. C., I, 132-3.
49. McChord's S. C. Reports, Vol. 2, 259, 260.
50. Hart, Actual Government, 47.
51. Adams and Stephens, Sel. Docs., 130, 398, 399, 400.
52. Journals of Congress under date.
53. Rights of the Colonies, 12, 22, 26, 30; Comp. Civil Gov. II, ch. 4; VIII, ch. XI, 141, 149, 229.
54. Writings, II, 257-8.
55. Force, Am. Archives, Series 4, Vol. 4, 1776, p. 834.
56. Poore, Charters, 959.
57. Journals, Va. Convention, 42.
58. Const. N. H. I, VII, VIII, Comp. Civil Gov. II, Ch. IX, VIII, XI, Sec. 141.
59. Journals, I, 59, or under date.
60. Elliot, Debates, II, 456.
61. McClain, Cases, 947, 1009; 119 N. Y. 232; Munn, v. III, 94 U. S. 113.
62. N. C. Art. I. S. C. Preamble, Md., Art. I, Pa., Arts. III, IV; Ga. Preamble; Vt., 1777, Art. IV; 1786, Art. VI; Mass. Art. VI; N. H. Arts. I, VII, VIII; Va. sec. 2.

63. Lobingier, People's Law, 79, 80; MacDonald, Sel. Charters, 93, 116; Coll Coun. Hist. Soc. III; Twitchell, Hist. Address; 3 Stat. of Conn. I; R. I. Laws, 1647 p. 18; Blue Laws of Conn. 115, 117; Hall, Cases in Const. Law, 939.
64. MacDonald, Sel. Charters, 95.
65. Journals, I, 114, 117.
67. Macdonald, Sel. Charters, 374; Journals, I, 142.
68. Am. Hist. Leaflets, No. 20, p. 1.
69. Adams Works, p. 22.
70. Decl. of Indep.
71. Am. Hist. Leaflets, 20, p. 8.
72. Journals of Cong., Sept. 9, 1776.
73. Arts. of Confed.
74. Elliot, Debates, V, 376-7.
75. Arts. of Confed, III.
76. Elliot, Debates, II, 117; 7 Wall. 700.
77. Chisholm v. Ga. 2 Dall. 419.
78. Elliot, Debates, V, 92-3; Journals of Cong. June 21, 30, 1783.
79. Elliot, V, 94-5.
80. 2 Dall. 419.
81. Art. III.
82. MacDonald, Sel. Charters, 94.
83. MacDonald, Sel. Charters, 254.
84. Art. II.
85. Am. Hist. Leaflets, No. 20, p. 3.
86. Art. VI.
87. R. I. Acts and Resolves, 1779, p. 34, passim.
90. Elliot, IV, 428.
91. Adams and Stephens, Sel. Documents, 86, 328.
92. MacDonald, Sel. Charters, 142.
93. Poore, Charters, 1903-4.
94. MacDonald, Sel. Charters, 36.
95. Id. 64, Arts. 2, 12; Am. Hist. Leaflets, No. 20, p. 3; Jacobson v. Mass., 197 U. S. II.
96. Art. III.
97. Am. Hist. Leaflets, No. 20, p. 3.
98. Elliot, Debates, V, 132.
99. Adams and Stephens, Select Docs. of Eng. Const. Hist., 68, 92, 93, 94, 95, 100, 119, 124, 126, 173, 174, 180, 213, 224, 228, 240, 246.
100. Id. 127.
101. Adams and Stephens, Sel. Docs., 173, 174, 180.
102. Adams and Stephens, Sel. Docs., 216, 217, 227, 231, 245, 288.
103. Id. 232-4.
104. Poore, Charters, 1899, 1901.
105. Poore, Charters, 252, 255, 1597, 1599; MacDonald, Sel. Charters, 13. 14, 118, 130, 207.
106. Poore, Charters, 1540, 1541, 1332, 378, 1858, 1859, 956, 957.
107. Elliot, Debates, V, 377.
108. Id. 330; Adams and Stephens, Sel. Docs. II.
109. A. C. Goodell, Harvard Law Rev., VII, 424.
110. Poore, Charters, 1391, 1392, 1899, 1519, 1520.
111. Elliot, Debates, V, 81, 116, 117.

CHAPTER II

The Separation of Powers, and a Bicameral Legislature

"All *legislative* powers . . . shall be vested in a Congress." "The *executive* power shall be vested in a President." "The *judicial* power . . . shall be vested in one supreme court, and in such inferior courts as the Congress may from time to time ordain and establish."[1] These three clauses taken together contain a statement of the doctrine of the separation of powers. The framers of the Constitution did not understand this doctrine to mean complete and absolute separation of the three departments, but rather, as explained by Davie of North Carolina, "that these three branches must not be entirely blended into one body."[2] Madison pointed out that in none of the state constitutions had the several departments of power been kept absolutely separate and distinct and that Montesquieu did not mean that the "departments ought to have no *partial agency* in, or *no control over*, the acts of each other." He meant that "the whole power of one department" should not be "exercised by the same hands which possess the whole power of another department." This would be destructive of liberty. Even in the British Constitution which Montesquieu regarded as the standard or mirror of political liberty, the departments are not "totally separate and distinct from each other."[3]

This doctrine originated in Montesquieu's Spirit of Laws. This celebrated author believed he found the doctrine in the British Constitution and laid down the maxim that "there can be no liberty where the legislative and executive powers are united in the same person or body of magistrates," or "if the power of judging be not separated from the legislative and executive powers." Blackstone in his Commentaries follows Montesquieu. Locke teaches the same doctrine in his Civil Government, but differs slightly from Montesquieu. The British Constitution was to him (Montesquieu), says Madison, the perfect model, the standard or mirror of political liberty and the source from which the maxim was drawn.[4] The Americans,

20

however, regarded Montesquieu as the real author of the maxim.
James Madison wrote: "The oracle who is always consulted
and cited on this subject is the celebrated Montesquieu."
Hamilton also quotes him as the author of the great political
axiom.   On October 26, 1774, the whole Congress in the Address to the Inhabitants of Quebec accepted the idea of Montesquieu's authorship.   Davie in the North Carolina Convention
said, the great Montesquieu and several other writers have
laid it down as a maxim not to be departed from "that the
legislative, executive and judicial powers should be separate
and distinct." [5]   Justice Howell in his defence of the judges
before the Rhode Island Assembly for the part they had played
in the case of Trevett v. Weeden, 1786, quotes Montesquieu as
the author of the doctrine and adds, "Judge Blackstone hath
adopted the same idea." [6]   In Kamper v. Hawkins, 1793, Judge
Roane of Virginia quotes Montesquieu as responsible for the
doctrine of the separation of powers being incorporated by the
convention into the state constitution.   Although expounding
the British Constitution, Montesquieu "has the merit at least
of displaying and recommending" the doctrine "most effectually
to the attention of mankind." [7]

A *second* source of the doctrine was *American experience*
(1) under the Articles of Confederation;
(2) under the state constitutions.

The Articles of Confederation vested all powers legislative,
executive, and judicial in the legislature of one house.   This
was found by experience to work badly in practice.   Jefferson,
speaking of the defects of the Confederation, says: "The want,
too, of a separation of the legislative, executive, and judiciary
functions worked disadvantageously in practice."   In a letter
to Edward Carrington written from Paris, August 4, 1787,
he says, he hopes that the powers in the hands of Congress
will be separated and adds: "the want of it has been the source
of more evil than we have experienced from any other cause." [8]
Hamilton, in his resolutions for a General Convention, June
30, 1783, declared the Confederation defective, "In confound-
ing legislative and executive powers in a single body—contrary
to the most approved and well-founded maxims of free government, which require that the legislative, executive, and judicial
authorities should be deposited in distinct and separate

hands." [9] Americans, by experience, had learned that this defect needed to be corrected as much as lack of power to tax or regulate commerce. Hence, the Convention of 1787 undertook to remedy this political weakness by constitutional provision. Madison's plan, outlined in his letter to Randolph, April 8, 1787, proposed the adoption of the doctrine as a working principle of the constitution. Then, Randolph's Resolutions of May 29, 1787, proposed it to the convention.[10] At first, the committee of detail intended to make an express statement on the subject as the state constitutions did, but omitted such a provision, probably because other statements rendered it unnecessary.

Lastly, all the state constitutions had incorporated the doctrine. When Rutledge asked John Adams in Congress what he considered a proper form of government for a state, his reply was that he hoped they would "preserve the English Constitution in its spirit and substance as far as the circumstances" of the colonies "required or would admit," and that "*the three branches of the legislature* would be preserved, an executive independent of the senate or council and the house, and above all things the independence of the judges." "But governors and councils we have always had, as well as representatives. A legislature in three branches ought to be preserved and independent judges." [11] This recognizes the existence of the separation of powers in the English, colonial, and state governments. All the state constitutions had acted upon Montesquieu's world-famous maxim for the purpose of securing the safety of the life, liberty, and property of the citizens, and American experience insisted that the same political axiom be made a working principle of the Constitution of the United States to guarantee the liberty and safety of the citizens as against the national government. The basis for the doctrine was the English common law principle "that an act done by any official person or law-making body beyond his or its legal competence is simply void." [13]

As supplemental to the principle of the separation of powers, is *the system of checks and balances.* This simply means that each department of the government acts as a check and balance against abuse of power by the other departments. The President, for example, by his veto power, acts as a check and balance against abuse of power by the legislature; the courts by their power to declare laws void check legislative power; the legislature, by its power to impeach, acts as a check against abuse of power by the executive and judiciary; the right of the senate to ratify appointments and treaties is a check on the President, while the executive by his power to pardon, reprieve, or commute acts as a check upon abuse of power by the courts; the senate may veto acts of the House and the people by their power in periodical elections may check abuses in the departments.

One source of this doctrine was the *British Constitution.* John Adams in a letter to John Taylor wrote: "for anything I recollect this system of checks and balances was an American invention of our own and peculiar to us." Judge Cooley, commenting on this, says: "The invention, nevertheless, was suggested by the British Constitution, in which a system almost equally elaborate was in force." [14] On the question of English origin, James Otis, 1764, said: "See here the grandeur of the British Constitution! See the wisdom of our ancestors! The supreme legislative, and the supreme executive, are a perpetual check and balance to each other. If the supreme executive errs, it is informed by the supreme legislative in Parliament. If the supreme legislative errs, it is informed by the supreme executive in the courts of law." [15] Montesquieu, expounding the doctrine, says that man invested with power is apt to abuse his authority. To prevent this, it is necessary that "power should be a check to power." After describing the working of the three departments and showing how they mutually check and balance one another in the Constitution of England, he wrote: "The legislative body being composed of two parts, they check one another by the mutual privilege of rejecting. They are both restrained by the executive power as the executive is by the legislative." [16] Blackstone in his Commentaries also gives a splendid exposition of the system of checks and balances in the English government.[17]

Further, this system was to be found *in the colonial and state governments.* Checks and balances existed in the colonial governments as witnessed, for example, by the impeachment of Deputy-Governor Carey of North Carolina in 1711; Chief Justice Trot and Chief Justice Allen of South Carolina, 1717 and 1727; and Chief Justice Oliver of Massachusetts in 1774.[18] All the state constitutions embodied the principle so that the framers of the Federal Constitution were familiar with the axiom in practice in both the state and colonial systems. Each had its legislature, executive, and judiciary which in greater or less degree, were balanced against and checked by the others. This was especially true of the states.[19] The statesmen of the Revolutionary period believed in the truth of these doctrines just as they believed in the truth of the law of gravitation. They held there could be no liberty where the separation of powers did not exist. The truth of Montesquieu's doctrine is no longer believed in by political scientists, namely, that there can be no liberty without it. It is regarded as a little too absurd to say there is no liberty in Great Britain because the doctrine is violated by the cabinet system, and there is liberty in Mexico, where the doctrine is obeyed. The late Goldwin Smith characterized Montesquieu's idea as a dream, and Professor Stephen Leacock regards it as undoubtedly false when stated as a universal principle.[20]

A *bicameral legislature*, the Senate and House of Representatives, is created.[21] The legislature of two houses originated in England, where it was bicameral from about 1332 A.D. The first distinct record of the houses sitting in separate session is found about that date, and the separation was complete by about 1339 A.D.[22] Originally all sat in one house, but the knights of the shire who sat with the barons, gradually drew away from them, and united with the burgesses, while the clergy by degrees ceased to attend Parliament. The knights were drawn towards the burgesses by common local, social, and commercial interests. After the clergy ceased to attend Parliament, they were represented in the commons by the members they helped to elect by their votes. The final result was a legislature of two houses—one composed of prelates, earls, and barons, and the other of the commons of the land, or lords and commons.[23] English precedent, therefore, urged the adoption of bicameral legislatures in America. It was the only legislature with which the Americans were acquainted, and it was a race inheritance.

A *second source was colonial experience.* The first representative legislature in America, that of Virginia, 1619, adopted the idea of two houses—upper and lower. It was organized by John Pory, a Master of Arts of Cambridge University and a former member of Parliament in England, and was composed of Englishmen, so that, as a matter of course, it followed the English model. What else would Englishmen do? The two houses sat and deliberated together and were not definitely separated until 1680.[24] The first legislature was followed as a model by the other colonies.

In Massachusetts, the legislature was at first unicameral, but the bicameral system was introduced in 1644.[25] In Maryland, the bicameral system was established in 1650 by an act providing as follows: "Be it enacted . . . That prnt Assembly during the continuance thereof be held by way of Upper and Lower house to sitt in two distinct rooms a part."[26] A legislature of two houses was established in New Hampshire from the first, March, 1680;[27] in Connecticut, 1698, though the Fundamental Orders, 1639, introduced the beginnings;[28] in Rhode Island, 1696;[29] New York was always bicameral; in North Carolina, 1691 or earlier; in South Carolina from the first, 1674; in Georgia, 1754, though the Constitution of 1777, followed Pennsylvania in adopting a unicameral legislature.[30]

A *third* source was *the state constitutions.* All the state constitutions, except those of Pennsylvania and Georgia, had established legislatures of two houses.[31] In adopting two houses, the convention simply provided for the creation of a national legislature modelled after that of the states.

A *fourth* reason, for the adoption of a bicameral legislature, was *the fact that American experience under the unicameral Articles of Confederation had been unfortunate.* They had followed Franklin's Draft and the Continental Congress. In February, 1783, Pelatiah Webster had proposed a scheme for a congress of two houses. Madison suggested such a legislature to Edmund Randolph, April 8, 1787.[32] The convention adopted this suggestion: (1) To restrain the power of the legislature by providing that each house act as a check on the other. Without this, James Wilson declared there could be neither liberty nor stability. Edmund Randolph declared a senate had been created for the purpose of curbing the turbulence and follies of democracy.[33]

(2) To remove the danger of giving Congress additional

powers. Davie said this could not be done in case of a single body without danger, so the legislature was divided in order that one branch might act as a check on the other.[34]

(3) To remove the danger of entrusting important powers to Congress by the states. This ought not to be done in case of a single body, Charles Pinckney said, and therefore, the convention divided the legislature, and gave the executive a limited revisionary power over their proceedings.[35]

(4) James Bryce suggests that there was a practical reason for the adoption of a legislature of two houses, namely, that it enabled the convention to settle the dispute between the large and small states. The latter were satisfied by being given equal representation in the Senate, while the former were satisfied with proportional representation in the House of Representatives.[36] "As a way out of a practical difficulty," says Professor Hart, "the nation returned to the English and Colonial bicameral system." [37]

Origin of the Names "Senate" and "House of Representatives." These were taken from the state constitutions. Several state constitutions contained provisions similar to Art. I, Sec. 1 of the Constitution of the United States. The New Hampshire constitution of 1784 declared: "The supreme legislative power within this state shall be vested in the senate and house of representatives." Massachusetts used both names in the constitution of 1780. New York used "senate" in the constitution of 1777. North Carolina did the same in her constitution of 1776. Pennsylvania called her lower house "House of Representatives," while South Carolina used both names in the constitution of 1778.[38]

The section, as reported by the committee of detail on August 6, appears to have been taken from the Massachusetts and New York constitutions. It read: "The legislative power shall be vested in a congress to consist of two separate and distinct bodies of men, a house of Representatives and a Senate, each of which shall in all cases have a negative on the other." The phrase, "Two separate and distinct bodies of men" was the language of the New York constitution of 1777. The remainder is the exact language of the Massachusetts constitution of 1780. In Massachusetts the name, House of Representatives, was in use long before the days of the Revolution or the framing of state constitutions. It was first used in the Explanatory Charter of Massachusetts Bay granted by George I in 1726. The name, thus originating in England, was carried forward into the constitution of Massachusetts. In DeLolme's Constitution of England 1777, the members of the House of Commons are called 'representatives' and 'representatives of the people.' "The people act only through their representatives" he wrote. The framers of the Massachusetts constitution of 1780 copied even the language of DeLolme.[39]

The Origin of the Name "Congress." The Massachusetts Assembly issued a circular letter to the other colonies on June 8, 1765, inviting them to send delegates to a congress to be held in New York, the first Tuesday of October, to consider the Stamp Act duties, and to petition King and Parliament for relief. This body assembled as the *first congress* of the American Colonies.

Benjamin Franklin suggested the first continental congress in 1774. He wrote a letter from London, England, July 7, 1773, to Thomas Cushing, Speaker of the Massachusetts Assembly, suggesting a general *congress* of all the colonies to assert and declare their rights.[40]

NOTES TO CHAPTER II

1. Const. U. S., Art. 1, sec. I, II, sec. I, cl. i, III sec. I.
2. Elliot, Debates, IV, 121-2; II, 479, 504-5; Federalist, Nos. 46, 47.
3. Federalist, No. 47.
4. Montesquieu, Sp. of Laws, Bk. XI, ch. VI; Blackstone, Com. I, 308; Locke, Civil Gov., Bk. II, ch. 12; Federalist, 47; McClain, Cases, 84, 86.
5. Federalist, Nos. 47, 78; Journals of Cong., I, 59; Dickinson, Writings II, 12; Elliot, Debates, IV, 121.
6. Varnum's Pamphlet, Trevett v. Weeden, 40.
7. Virginia Cases, 142-3; McClain, Cases, 86.
8. Jefferson, Works (Ford ed.), V, 117, 319.
9. Elliott, V, 117; Am. Hist. Leaflets, No. 28, p. 15; Hamilton, Works, I, 289.
10. Elliot, Debates, V, 107, 120-121, 127. See also letter of Mar. 19, and Apr. 16, p. 121.
11. Adams, Works, III, 17, 18, 20.
13. Bryce, Am. Commonwealth, I, chap. III, 30.
14. Adams, Works, VI, 467-8; Cooley, Const. Law, VII, 148.
15. Otis, Rights of the Colonies, etc., 47.
16. Sp. of Laws, Bk. XI, ch. VI.
17. Commentaries, I, ch. II, 145, 147, 155.
18. Chalmers, Introd. to the Hist. of the Revolt of the Colonies, Bk. VII, ch. XI.
19. Federalist, 47, p. 304 seq. (Lodge ed.).

20. Goldwin Smith, The Bystander, Toronto, May, 1880, p. 64, quoted by Leacock, Elements of Pol. Science, p. 151; Roger Foster, Commentaries on the Constitution, p. 302.

21. Art. I, sec. I.

22. Medley, Eng. Const. Hist., 140; Taswell-Langmead, Eng. Const. Hist., chap. VIII, p. 211.

23. Adams and Stephens, Sel. Docs., 104, 106, 135, 136, 140, 142, 160, 165; Taswell-Langmead, ch. VIII; Medley, 139; Feilden, 96, 135; Stubbs, passim, charters, 483.

24. Col. Records of Va., p. 1, seq; Bruce, Institutional Hist. of Va., 590-1.

25. J. H. Univ. Studies in Hist. and Pol. Sc., XIII, 213-216.

26. Id. 249.

27. Id. 219.

28. Col. Records of Conn., 267.

29. J. H. Univ. Studies in Hist. and Pol. Sc., XIII, p. 230.

30. Id 240; Id. 252-3; Id 253; Id 254.

31. Const. N. Y. 1777, Art. II, p. 1332, Poore Charters; Const. Mass. Art. I; 960, Poore; N. H. 1784, p. 1284, Poore; Thorpe or Poore, Charters and Consts., passim.

32. Am. Hist. Leaflets, No. 28, p. 9; Elliot, Debates, V, 108.

33. Elliot, Debates, V, 197, 138.

34. Id IV, 21.

35. Elliot, IV, 256.

36. Am. Commonwealth, I, 186.

37. Actual Government, 217.

38. Thorpe, Constits. and Charters, Vol. 8, p. 2458; Id. 1803; Id. vol. 5, 3084; Thorpe, Vol. 6, 3248.

39. Elliot, Debates, V, 377; Poore, Charters, 1332, 960, 955, 966; DeLolme, The Const. of Eng., chaps. VI, VII, VIII, 213, 222, 224, 243, 244; Coffin v. Coffin, 4 Mass. 11.

40. Bradford, Mass. State Papers, p. 36; Journal of the House 1765, p. 109; Franklin, Writings, VI, 77 (Smyth).

CHAPTER III

THE HOUSE OF REPRESENTATIVES

1. The representative principle in government is of English origin. The earliest use, apart from church councils, was for financial and judicial purposes in the local communities. The reeve, priest, and four men were sent as representatives to the hundred moot, and twelve lawful men were sent to represent the hundred in the shire moot. The boroughs sent the reeve and four men. The shire moots assessed and collected the sums granted by the commune concilium through knights elected for the purpose. In 1085 A.D., William the Norman summoned representatives from the hundreds and townships to secure information for the Domesday book.[1] The priest, reeve, and six men from each vill were summoned. Henry Second applied the principle to financial and judicial purposes. Then, under Richard First, the knights were elected "and not merely nominated." Magna Carta provided that the assizes should be held four times a year in each county by two justices and four knights elected by the county.[2] This completes two steps in the development of the representative idea:

(1) Representation.

(2) Election. The third step was

(3) Concentration, which soon began to take shape. The representatives from several or all of the counties were summoned to meet at one central place for consultation. The earliest instances of concentration have been accepted as those of August and November, 1213, when King John summoned representatives from the whole of England to meet at St. Albans and Oxford.[3] Professor A. B. White argues that the first known instance of concentration was in 1227, when one hundred and forty knights met at Westminster for a political purpose.[4] From this time, the several steps are clear to 1295—the Model Parliament.

In the first representative Assembly in America—in Virginia in 1619—were "two Burgesses out of every town, Hun-

29

dred or other particular plantation, to be respectively chosen by the inhabitants." [5]   The representative idea was naturally adopted by all the colonies—a race inheritance.

2. *Biennial Elections.* All the states but one had adopted annual elections from the ancient usage of England as a guarantee of security and a safeguard against tyranny.[6]   Annual, biennial, and triennial elections were proposed in the convention.[7]   Edmund Randolph moved June 21 that elections be biennial. Colonel Mason supported him and this was adopted nem. con.[8]   The convention adopted biennial elections from the practice of South Carolina.[9]   Both Randolph and Mason mentioned this in their speeches.[10]   It was evidently a continuation in the South Carolina constitution of the provision found in the Fundamental Constitutions of Carolina framed by John Locke in 1669, which provided for biennial elections.[11]   This traces the provision in the Federal Constitution back to John Locke as the author.

What caused the Convention of 1787 to adopt biennial elections?   (1) Charles Pinckney said that being short, they would render members dependent enough on their constituents, would guarantee security against tyranny, and would be less burdensome and less expensive than annual elections.[12]

(2) The provision for biennial elections was a compromise. Caleb Strong said in the Massachusetts Convention that the majority in the Federal Convention had favored triennial elections, but the Southern states, less populous than the Eastern, urged that frequency of elections would be very expensive, and this produced the compromise arrangement of the constitution, though it was agreeable to the practice of South Carolina.[13]

(3) The abuse of the English practice. The statutes of 1330 and 1362 provided for annual Parliaments. Earlier statutes had provided for calling Parliaments once, twice, or three times a year. In spite of laws, Parliaments were not summoned by the Kings. The Long Parliament passed the Triennial Act to end this in 1641, which provided for Parliament meeting in spite of the King. This was repealed in 1664, and in 1694 a second Triennial Act was passed. In 1715, the Septennial Act was passed, increasing the life of Parliament to seven years.[14]   That is, Parliament continued itself in exist-

ence or its members in office for four years for which they had
never been elected by the people. "An attention to these dangerous practices," says the Federalist, "has produced a very
natural alarm in the votaries of free government, of which
frequency of elections is the corner-stone; and has led them to
seek for some security to liberty against the danger to which
it is exposed." This security was found in "biennial elections
unalterably fixed" by the written constitution,[15] which circum-
scribes the powers of Congress.

3. *The Qualifications of Electors.* The difficulty confront-
ing the Convention here lay in the fact that every state had
adopted different qualifications for its electors.[16] Each state
was a law unto itself. The framers of the constitution, therefore, saw that the adoption of a uniform qualification for federal voting was impossible, as it would embarrass and inconvenience all the states, no matter what qualifications might be
adopted. Should the convention, for example, adopt the qualifications required by Vermont or Massachusetts it would an-
noy and embarrass all the other states. Should an entirely
new qualification be adopted, it would perplex and trouble all,
and cause irritation by excluding some from voting for members of Congress, who would be able to vote for members of
the state legislatures, or vice versa.[17] The convention, therefore, wisely adopted the qualifications fixed by the states in
their constitutions and laws for the election "of the most numerous branch of the State Legislature." This left the existing qualifications of each state in force within its bounds,
avoided all interference by the Federal Government, and secured to the states the right to prescribe the qualifications for
their own and federal voters.[18]

Qualifications of Representatives.[19] 1. An age qualification of twenty-five years. Why twenty-five years? Some of
the states required twenty-one years.[20] The convention believed
that a man was mentally and politically immature at twenty-
one. Colonel Mason, who moved in convention that twenty-
five years be the age qualification required, was the spokesman
for this view. He declared that at twenty-one his own political opinions were too crude and erroneous to merit an influence
on public measures. It was absurd that a man should not even
be permitted to make a bargain for himself to-day, and be

authorized to-morrow to manage the affairs of a great nation.
It was said that Congress had been a good school for young
men, but he preferred that they bear the expense of their own
education. Mason was from Virginia, and the constitution of
that state required members of the senate to be "upwards of
twenty-five years of age." [21]   The Delaware Constitution of
1776 required an age qualification for the upper branch of
the legislature.[22]   The Virginia Constitution doubtless suggested this age qualification to Colonel Mason.

Wilson opposed Mason's proposition on the ground "that
it tended to dampen the efforts of genius and laudable ambition.
There was no more reason for incapacitating youth than age
where the requisite qualifications were found," and he cited Mr.
Pitt and Lord Bolingbroke as examples of men who rendered
signal services to the state before reaching the age of twenty-
five. He "was against abridging the rights of electors in any
shape." This was strong common sense argument, but Colonel
Mason's motion, by a vote of seven to three states, was
adopted.[23]

2. *A Citizenship Requirement of Seven Years.* Why seven
years? The report of the committee of detail of August 6,
provided for a citizenship requirement of three years.[24]   On
August 8th, Colonel Mason said that while he favored opening
wide the door for emigrants yet he "did not choose to let
foreigners and adventurers make laws for us and govern us."
A rich foreign nation like Great Britain might send over tools
who could secure election to the national legislature by bribery
for insidious purposes. If Americans are not a simple folk,
they will at the present moment be strongly impressed with
Colonel Mason's wisdom. He moved the substitution of seven
years for three, which was seconded by Gouverneur Morris, and
agreed to by all the states except Connecticut.[25]

3. *A Residence Requirement.* The provision, as formulated
by the committee of detail, required that a representative be
"a resident of the state." [26]   On August 8, Sherman moved to
strike out 'resident' and insert 'inhabitant' on the ground that
it would be less liable to misconstruction. Madison seconded
this, saying that 'inhabitant' was not so vague in common acceptation, would not exclude persons absent on public or private business, and that great disputes had arisen in Virginia

over the meaning of the word 'residence.' On June 19, Madison had also pointed out that Chief Justice McKean of Pennsylvania had represented Delaware in the Congress of Confederation from 1774 to 1783, and that on February 2, 1782, Chief Justice McKean and Samuel Wharton, citizens of Pennsylvania, and Philemon Dickinson, a citizen of New Jersey, had been elected to Congress to represent the State of Delaware. This was to avoid paying the delegates, but whatever the motive, the effect was "the vote of one state was doubled and the influence of another increased by it." [27]

Gouverneur Morris instanced bitter disputes in New York over the meaning of these words and was opposed to both. Mercer told of violent disputes in Maryland over the meaning of the word 'residence.' The convention inserted 'inhabitant' for 'resident' on the ground that it would be less liable to be misunderstood or misconstrued. The same term was used in the constitutions of Massachusetts, New Hampshire, and New Jersey. An attempt to insert a requirement for a definite period of residence—one, three, or seven years—was voted down.[28] In England, the requirement of habitancy was repealed by statute 14 Geo. III, c. 58.[29] To avoid disputes, misconstruction, misunderstanding, and misrepresentation, the word 'inhabitant' was, therefore, inserted in the constitution instead of resident as a qualification for President. "Residence implies permanency, or at least an intention to remain. Habitancy may be temporary. A man's residence is often a legal conclusion from statements showing his intention. Habitancy is a physical fact which may be proved by eye-witnesses." [30]

Appointment of Representatives and Direct Taxes. The convention could not agree on the question of counting slaves in the basis of representation.[31] Therefore, Gouverneur Morris moved without any intention of making it part of the Constitution "that taxation shall be in proportion to representation." [32] His motive was to lessen the desire of the South for a large representation by increasing the burden of taxation proportionately, and to lessen the opposition against the South for the same reason. He "meant it as a bridge to assist us over a certain gulf," [33] he said. Customs duties and other indirect taxes could not be levied on this principle. Mason declared it might embarrass Congress, and drive it to requisitions. Morris then inserted the word 'direct,' thereby making the rule apply to direct taxation only. It was then adopted nem. con.[34]

1. *Origin of the Term 'Direct' Taxes.* (1) *European economic writers.* Philip Dunbar argues that the distinction between direct and indirect taxes was suggested to Gouverneur Morris by the French Economists, and especially by Turgot. He makes a clear-cut distinction between direct and indirect taxes. "And of all Americans, Gouverneur Morris and James Wilson were most likely to give him attention," because the former was familiar with French literature and politics, while the latter had acted as Advocate General of France from 1779 to 1783. Turgot's work on taxation was published in 1764, and was in circulation in the United States. Dupont de Nemours published in Paris and Philadelphia in 1782, his Memoires sur la Vie et les Ouvrages de M. Turgot. Who proposed the use of the term in convention? Gouverneur Morris, while James Wilson approved it.[35] Adam Smith's Wealth of Nations had been published in 1776. He uses the term "direct tax," and "direct taxes," and speaks of things being "taxed directly" and "taxed indirectly."[36] An examination and comparison of what Gouverneur Morris says with what Adam Smith writes on the subject might lead one to conclude that the Wealth of Nations had influenced Morris. It is inconceivable that James Wilson, born and educated in Scotland, could have been ignorant of what his great countryman had to say upon the subject. Albert Gallatin said: "The remarkable coincidence of the clause of the constitution with this passage (quoted by Gallatin from the Wealth of Nations) in using 'capitation' as a general expression, *including the different species* of direct taxes, an acceptation of the word peculiar, it is believed, to Dr. Smith, leaves little doubt that the framers of the one had the other in mind at the time."[37] In Hylton v. U. S., Justice Patterson "quoted copiously from Adam Smith in support of his conclusions."[38] It is clear that the Wealth of Nations had a strong influence on the men who framed the Constitution. Patterson was a member of the convention.

(2) *American state experience.* The states were accustomed to levying direct taxes. The people were so familiar with the phrase in 1787 that it was "a household phrase."[39] The discussions in the conventions show familiarity with the term, and

that the people understood that their taxes were largely direct taxes. John Marshall said in the Virginia convention: "The objects of direct taxes are well understood: they are but few. What are they? Lands, slaves, stock of all kinds, and a few other articles of domestic property." [40] The power given to Congress to levy direct taxes was a system well understood and in actual operation in the states. Dawes of Massachusetts said there was a prejudice against it, caused by "the manner in which it has been abused by the errors of the old confederation." [41] From 1785 to 1789 an annual direct tax of over two million dollars was raised in Pennsylvania.[42] *Direct taxes* were also constantly raised by the colonial legislatures. The legislative records of the colonies contain act after act passed for this purpose. The acts of New York, Rhode Island, Connecticut, or Massachusetts in this connection are so numerous, it would be a waste of time to quote them. The same is true of other colonies.

2. *The Rule of Apportionment.*[43] There were two steps in the development of this clause:

(1) In the Congress of 1783.

(2) In the Convention of 1787.

There was a prevalent idea that representation and taxation ought to be based on population. It is found in the New England Confederation 1643, Franklin's Albany Plan 1754, Franklin's Draft 1775, and other documents. In the Continental Congress, the lack of any accurate census prevented the adoption of such a plan.[44] On March 6, 1783, the Committee on Revenue made a report to Congress, one part of which proposed to abolish article eight of the Articles of Confederation which made land the basis of taxation, and to substitute an article providing that the common treasury be supplied by the several states "in proportion to the number of inhabitants of every age, sex, and condition, except Indians not paying taxes in each state, which number shall be triennially taken, and transmitted to the United States in Congress assembled in such mode as they shall direct, and appoint, provided always that in such enumeration no persons shall be included, who are bound to servitude for life, according to the laws of the state to which they belong, other than such as may be between the ages of — years." [45] It is obvious that we have here the first outline of the clause in the constitution. Article eleven of the Dickinson Draft supplied part of the language, and the principle.[46] It based taxation on population, and the Southern states would have numbers rather than land as the basis, but it was found impossible to compromise between North and South. The South wanted half their slaves included. The Eastern States refused this,[47] so land was adopted in the Articles of Confederation as the basis instead of numbers.[48] The clause was recommitted to fill the blank and fix the proportion in absolute numbers. The Committee reported March 28, 1783, recommending that two blacks be rated as one freeman. Messrs. Wolcott, Higginson, Holten, and Osgood proposed that they be rated as four to three; Carroll four to one; Rutledge would agree to two to one but thought three to one would be more just. A vote was taken on the question of voting slaves three to one, and it stood five to five with Rhode Island divided. All the Southern states voted 'no.' It was agreed to postpone the question for further reflection and deliberation,[49] but as the general opinion of Congress was that no compromise would be agreed to, and the necessity of adopting "some simple and practicable rule of apportionment" was urgent, Madison said, that "in order to give proof of the sincerity of his professions of liberality, he would propose that the slaves be rated as five to three." Rutledge seconded the motion, and Wilson said he would sacrifice his opinion in the compromise. New Hampshire, New Jersey, and Pennsylvania voted with the Southern states for Madison's proposition.[50] Hamilton, on April the first, moved to reconsider the question on the ground of his absence. "The rate of three-fifths was agreed to without opposition." [51] The great need, and despair of a more favorable compromise were the motives at work. On April 18th, the revenue plan was passed by Congress as amended, "all the states present concurring except Rhode Island which was in the negative, and New York which was divided—Mr. Floyd, ay, and Mr. Hamilton, no." [52] Madison was, therefore, the author of the three-fifths compromise in the Congress of 1783.

2. *In the Convention of 1787*. The men who discussed the subject in 1783 were in the Convention of 1787, namely, Ellsworth, Fitzsimmons, Gilman, Gorham, Hamilton, Lee, Mercer, Madison, Rutledge, Wilson, Williamson, and Carroll. On June

11, 1787, Wilson proposed in the Federal Convention that the three-fifths ratio be adopted as "being the rule in the act of congress agreed to by eleven states for apportioning quotas of revenue on the states." [53] The rule of apportionment of the Revenue Amendment of 1783 was offered by Wilson, because it had been accepted by eleven of the thirteen states "as unexceptionable before." King gave the same reason: "It was adopted, because it was the language of all America." [54] Professor Van Tyne, in reviewing Volume III of Channing's History of the United States calls attention to the fact that the "federal ratio is not an artificial number," but "was *reasoned*— based upon the fact that it was generally agreed that a slave did about three-fifths as much work as a free white laborer." [55] The debate in congress, March 27, 1783, reveals this.[56] Gorham said the argument offered then convinced him that three-fifths was pretty near the just proportion as a rule of taxation. General Pinckney said the rule they employed was "the productive labor of the inhabitants." It was an attempt to fix the ratio between free labor and slave labor.[57] In the Federal Convention, July 11, General Pinckney and Pierce Butler of South Carolina demanded that all the slaves be counted. Williamson suggested the three-fifths ratio as a compromise. Davie declared emphatically that North Carolina would never confederate unless the slaves were rated at least as three-fifths. If the Eastern states meant to exclude them, the business was ended. Randolph supported Davie, and, under threat of secession, the Eastern states consented to the compromise which was adopted.[58] The purpose was to secure Southern support and adhesion to the new Constitution. Alexander Hamilton, speaking on the three-fifths clause in the New York Convention, June 20, 1788, declared it was the "result of a spirit of accommodation" without which "no union could possibly have been formed." [59] The problem of the convention at this point was union or secession, and it was more expedient to compromise and save the union, than to refuse and have the union disrupted.

3. *The Census.* There were several precedents for the taking of a census, such as the triennial census of the males between sixteen and sixty of Franklin's Draft;[60] the triennial census of Dickinson's Draft; the New York Constitution of

1777 provided for taking a census every seven years. Proposals were made in convention for a census every ten, fifteen, or twenty years. A ten year period was adopted, the census to be taken "in the manner and according to the ratio recommended by congress in their resolution of the 18th of April 1783." [61] Congress had taken a rough census in April 1783, and on the basis of that census had divided $1,500,000, to be raised annually among the states.[62] The idea of a ten year period may have been taken from the constitution of Massachusetts, which required an assessment or valuation of property to be taken every ten years for purposes of taxation. Apportionment of representatives and taxation on the basis of a census was not therefore new in 1787.[63]

Vacancies in Representation.[64] No uniform rule existed for the issuing of writs of election among the states. Precedents existed for issuing writs by the House (upper or lower), the Speaker, or the Executive. This provision gave uniformity throughout the United States. Randolph's committee draft shows that the original intention of the convention was to give the Speaker power to issue the writs.[65] Certain statutes of South Carolina provided for the issuance of writs by the Governor and Council. The Governor of Connecticut issued writs for the election of new deputies in case of the death or absence of a member. By the law of Delaware, the Governor, on application of the Speaker, issued the election writs.[66]

The Pennsylvania Frame of Government, 1692, provided for the issuing of writs by the executive or governor to the sheriff of the county within ten days after a vacancy by death or otherwise.[67] The Duke of York's Charter of Liberties, 1683, provided that writs were to be issued by the governor to "Townes, Cittyes, Shires, Countyes, or Divisions" for the election of new members in case of the death or removal of representatives. The New Jersey Concession and Agreement of 1665 conferred power on the governor and council "to issue writs for elections to fill vacancies in the Assembly." The practice of issuing writs of election originated in England. The King issued his writ to the sheriff of the county directing him to cause knights, citizens, and burgesses to be elected to Parliament.[68] When vacancies occurred during the session, the speaker, by order of the House, sent his warrant to the clerk of the crown in chancery, who then issued the writ to the sheriff. If in time of recess for over twenty days, the speaker could issue the writ without order of the House in case of a vacancy caused by death, or elevation to the peerage.[69] This practice was carried to the colonies.

The immediate precedent, however, appears to have been found in the Ordinance of 1787 passed by Congress July 13th, while the Convention was in session. This required the governor to issue a writ to the county or township to elect another in his stead, in case of the death of a representative or his removal from office.[70]

The House.[71] (1) To "*choose their speaker.*" The speaker is of English origin. From 1377, when Thomas Hungerford was chosen speaker, the English Parliament has had an unbroken line of speakers who have presided over the deliberations of Parliament and acted as the medium of communication between the crown and the house. Down to 1679, the King virtually chose the speaker, but since that date, the speaker has been chosen by the House of Commons.[72]

Then, the first legislative assembly held in America, 1619, in Virginia, following English precedent, elected John Pory, a former member of the English Parliament, as speaker. Once introduced, the speaker became the presiding officer in all colonial legislatures. The Fundamental Constitutions of Carolina, 1669, provided for a speaker. The Pennsylvania Frame of Government 1696, the Charter of Privileges 1701, the Explanatory Charter of Massachusetts 1725, and the Albany Plan of Union 1754, all provided for a speaker to be elected by the Assembly or Grand Council. In Massachusetts, he was to be elected by the representatives and approved by the governor. Virginia had had her speaker for over a century and a half.[73]

The state constitutions then provided for the election of a speaker by the lower house of the legislature. The constitution of Maryland, 1776, and all the other state constitutions provided for the election of a speaker by the lower house. The exact phraseology of the clause appears in the constitution of New York 1777, Massachusetts 1780, and New Hampshire 1784. The committee of detail reported the provision in convention.[73]

(2) *"And other officers."* The charters and state constitutions provided for this. The first Virginia legislature, 1619, exercised the power, and provision was made for this by the Pennsylvania charter of Privileges 1701. The state constitutions all provided for the exercise of this power.[74] The convention simply adopted what had long been familiar to the people in their colonial and state governments.

(3) *"And shall have the sole power of impeachment."* The sources of this are to be found among the ancient Germans who sometimes tried capital cases relating to the public welfare in their assemblies.[75] (a) *Impeachment trials, however, originated in England,* where the practice grew up of trying offenders before the House of Lords as a high court of justice and a jury, the commons acting as accusers and prosecutors at the bar of the Lords.[76] It was a relic of barbarous times when powerful offenders could not be reached by other means. The first impeachment case occurred in England in 1376, when Lords Latimer and Neville and four commoners, Bury, Ellys, Lyons, and Peachey were impeached for maladministration in office, convicted, and "sentenced to imprisonment, fine, and banishment." [77] The case of Lord Melville 1804, was the last impeachment trial in England. Such trials are now regarded as among the antiquities of the constitution. Parliament could impeach only when regularly called by the executive. It could not meet of its own initiative for the purpose.[78] The House of Commons had "the sole power of impeachment."

(b) *In the American colonies.* When English local parliaments or legislatures were established in the colonies, English parliamentary practice followed the institution, and impeachment became a part of the colonial system. The Pennsylvania Frame of Government 1682, the Pennsylvania and Delaware Frame 1683, the Pennsylvania Frame, 1696, and the Charter of Privileges 1701, all provided for impeachment trials.[79] Where the charters were silent, the Colonial Assemblies claimed and exercised the right of impeaching judges, and other colonial officials before their councils as an upper house. In 1689 Governor Sothell of North Carolina, in 1706 William Rouse and five others in Massachusetts, in 1711 Deputy Governor Carey of North Carolina, in 1717 Chief Justice Trot of South Carolina, and in 1727 Chief Justice Allen of the same state were

impeached.[80]   Later, Chief Justice Peter Oliver of Massachusetts 1774, and Francis Hopkinson, state judge of admiralty
of Pennsylvania, 1780, were also impeached.[81]

(3) *In the state constitutions.*   The state constitutions
adopted the English practice, and made provision for impeaching state officials for misconduct in office or after the term of
office had expired.[82]   In the ten state constitutions referred to
below, the lower house had "the sole power of impeachment."
The practice is as old as 1376 anyway.   The whole history of
impeachments in England, the colonies, and the states follows
this rule of the Federal Constitution—the lower branch im-
peaches.

NOTES TO CHAPTER III

1. Art. 1, sec. 1, cl. 1; Taswell-Langmead, Const. Hist. of Eng., 131;
Stubs, Sel. Charters, 72, 86, 155, 299.
2. Adams and Stephens, p. 2; Id. 14, 18, 20; Id. 29; Medley, 131,
Adams etc., p. 45.
3. Adams and Stephens, p. 40.
4. Am. Hist. Rev., July, 1914—Some Early Instances of Concentration of Reps. in Eng.
5. Col. Records of Va., p. 81.
6. Elliot, V, 224; Id. III, 246; V, 184.
7. Elliot, V, 183.
8. Id. 224, 225, 226.
9. Poore, 1622.
10. Elliot, V, 224, 225; Federalist, No. 52.
11. Poore, 1405; The S. C. Act of 1694 provided assemblies continue
two years, and the Act of 1721, three years; Trott's Laws of S. C., pp.
36, 379.
12. Elliot, IV.
13. Elliot, II, 6, 7.
14. Adams and Stephens, No. 34, No. 51, No. 57, Hen. VII, Hen.
VIII, Jas. I, Chas. I; Adams and Stephens, No. 139; Id. No. 247.
15. Federalist, No. 52; Id.
16. Vt. Poore, 1861; Mass. Id. 964; N. H. Id. 1285; N. Y. Id. 1334;
N. J. Id. 1311; Pa. Id. 1542; Md., S. C. and Ga., Id. 871, 1411, 1623, 379, etc.
17. Elliot, V, 385, 389.
18. Const. U. S., Art. 1, sec. 2, cl. 1.
19. Id. Art. 1, sec, 2, cl. 2.
20. Poore, Charters, 379, 821.
21. Elliot, Debates, V, 228; Poore, Charters, 1910.
22. Id. 274.
23. Elliot, V, 228, 229; Eng. required 21 yrs.; Blackstone, Com. I, 175.
24. Elliot, V, 377.
25. Elliot, V, 389.
26. Id. 377; Poore, 1543, 1623; Wilson and Rutledge.
27. Elliot, Debates, V, 389, 210, 596.
28. Elliot, Debates, V, 389-90; Poore, 963, 1286, 1311.

29. Blackstone, Com. I, 175.
30. Foster, Commentaries, sec. 62, Willoughby on the Const., I, 525.
31. Art. 1, sec. 1, cl. 3.
32. Elliot, Debates, V, 302.
33. Elliot, V, 363.
34. Id. 302.
35. Q. J. Economics, Vol. 3, 437, seq—Quesnay, Mercier de la Riviere Dupont de Nemours, Id. 438; 157 U. S. 467; Q. J. Econ., Vol. 3, 439; Id. 157 U. S. 467; Q. J. Econ., Vol. 3, 439; Elliot, V, 302.
36. Wealth of Nations, Bk. V. ch. II, pt. ii, app. to Arts. I and II, Article IV.
37. Gallatin, Writings, III (Adams ed.) 74-5; quoted by C. J. Field in Pollock v. Farmer's Loan and Trust Co., 157 U. S. 455, 569-70.
38. Id. 429.
39. 157 U. S. 456-7; Pa. Stats. at L, XI, 65, 81, 470; Henning, Stats. XII, 93, 112, 418; X, 166; Am. State Papers, Finance, I, 414-441; 157 U. S. 467.
40. Elliot, III, 229.
41. Id. II, 441.
42. Id. III, 97, IV, 146, II, 93, I, 369; 157 U. S. 459; R. I. Acts and Resolves (1769), p. 15 (1778), p. 19, 30, Laws of Conn. 1715, pp. 184, 190, 198.
43. Art. 1, sec. 2, cl. 3.
44. Elliot, V, 181.
45. Elliot, Debates, V, 62-64.
46. Art. II, Am. Hist. Leaflets, No. 20, p. 10.
47. Elliot, V, 79.
48. See testimony of Wilson and Clark, Elliot, V, 79.
49. Id.
50. Elliot, V, 79.
51. Elliot, V, 81.
52. Id. 87.
53. Elliot, V, 181.
54. Elliot, II, 452; d. 36.
55. Am. Hist. Rev., Apr., 1913, p. 605.
56. Elliot, V, 78, 79.
57. Elliot, V, 296; See also debate in Fed. Convention July 11 to July 13, Id. IV, 283, 157 U. S. 467, Elliot V, 31.
58. Elliot, Debates, V, 296, 302, 303, 306.
59. Childs, Debates and Proceedings (1788), p. 26; Hening, Statutes, XI, 402.
60. Am. Hist. Leaflets, No. 20, p. 5.
61. Am. Hist. Leaflets, No. 20, p. 10; Thorpe, Vol. 5, 2629, 2631; Id. 3252; Elliot, V, 301, 305.
62. Id. 82.
63. Poore, 961; Pennsylvania also provided for a septennial census, and reapportionment; Poore, 1544; Farrand, Records, III, 260; Laws of N. Y., Vol. 1, 428; see also Acts and Res. of R. I., 1774, pp. 20-1, 54, 71; Id. 1776, p. 95.
64. Art. 1, sec. 2, cl. 4.
65. Meigs, Growth of the Const., p. 316, seq. (III, 17).
66. Public Laws of S. C. (Grimke), p. 113; Stats. of S. C., II, 687; Blue Laws of Conn., p. 16; Laws of Del., I, 152.
67. Macdonald, Sel. Charters, 220.

68. Colonial Laws of N. Y., Vol. 1, 113; Macdonald, Sel. Charters, 145; Adams and Stephens, pp. 40, 55, 83, 84.

69. Blackstone, Commentaries, I, 203.

70. Poore, 430 (sec. 10).

71. Art. 1, sec. 2, cl. 5.

72. Col. Records of Va., pp. 10-11; Macdonald Sel. Charters, 156; Comp. Blackstone, Com. I, 211; Col. Rec. of Va., pp. 10-11.

73. Thorpe, Vol. 3, 1692; Id. Vol. 7, 3816; Vol. 5, 2595; 3084, 3085; Vol. 1, 563; Vol. 6, 3756; Vol. 2, 779; Vol. 3, 1899; Poore, 1334, 1287, 964; Elliot, V, 377.

74. Col. Records of Va., 10-11; Macdonald, Sel. Charters, 226; Poore, 823, 964, 1287, 1334; Thorpe, 7, 3816; 4, 2462, 2790, 2595; 5, 3085; 1, 563; 2, 1779; 3, 1897, 1899.

75. Tacitus, Germania, 12; Anson, Law and Custom of Const., 362.

76. May, Parliamentary Practice, 663.

77. Adams and Stephens, No. 82; May, Parliamentary Practice, 51 seq.

78. Dicey, Law of the Constitution, 368; see Sulzer Trial, and rejected constitution of New York, 1915; Blackstone, IV, 259, 261.

79. Poore, 1523, 1528, 1535, 1538.

80. Roger Foster, Commentaries on the Constitution—Appendix.

81. Roger Foster, Commentaries—Appendix.

82. Poore, 276, 964, 1287, 1337, 1312, 1413, 1543, 1624, 1870, 1912.

CHAPTER IV

THE SENATE

1. *Senators Are to be Chosen by the State Legislatures.*[1] Four plans for the election of senators came before the convention: (1) Election by the House of Representatives from nominations made by the state legislatures—the Virginia plan.[2] (2) Election by the President from a number of nominations made by the state legislatures—Read's plan.[3] (3) Popular election of senators—Wilson's plan.[4] (4) Election by the state legislatures—plan of Spaight and Sherman.[5] The clause for the election of senators remained blank till June 7, when Dickinson proposed that the second branch be chosen by the state legislatures.[6] The motion was adopted by the vote of ten states, and agreed to again on June 25 by a vote of nine to two states.[7]

The reasons given in 1787 for the adoption of this method were: (1) The legislatures would know the mind of the states better than the people. (2) The state legislatures would be most likely to select men distinguished for their rank and wealth and this would result in the upper house "bearing as strong a likeness to the British House of Lords as possible."[8] (3) "The commercial and moneyed interest would be more secure in the hands of the state legislatures than of the people at large."[9]

The unanimity of the vote is accounted for by the fact that though the large states favored proportional representation, nevertheless, the delegates from the large states voted with the small states for the purpose of securing the importance of the state governments.[10] In adopting this method of election, the convention simply retained the arrangement for the election of delegates to the Continental Congress and Congress of Confederation. This had been done by the colonial or state legislatures.[11] The state constitutions provided for the election of delegates by the legislatures of the states.[12] The Albany

44

Plan of Union, 1754, provided that the members of the Grand Council should be chosen by the colonial assemblies.[13] The Dickinson Draft and Articles of Confederation provided that the delegates to congress were to be "appointed in such manner as the Legislature of each colony shall direct." The Articles substituted "state" for "colony." [14] The convention, therefore, simply applied to the senate the practice in use for some years in electing delegates to the American unicameral congress.

2. *"Two senators from each state,"* or *Equal Representation in the Senate.* On June 11, Sherman moved in the Convention of 1787 that suffrage in the first branch be in proportion to numbers, and that there be equal representation in the second branch, [15] each state to have one vote. This was rejected and proportional representation in both branches favored.[16] Doctor Johnson of Connecticut pointed out that since the states were in some respects to retain their political capacity, and in others were to be districts of individuals, the two ideas ought to be combined [17] "that in one branch the people ought to be represented, in the other, the states." [18] On July 2, a motion offered by Ellsworth, proposing that each state have one vote in the second branch, was lost by an equal division with Georgia divided.[19] The small states feared they would be destroyed in some mysterious way by the machinations of the large state delegates. They were afraid of the loss of their sovereignty, or that they would be "swallowed up." This was the most perilous hour in the history of the Convention. Would the small states remain or would they bolt the Convention? Madison declared the real antagonism was not between the large and small states but between North and South caused by climate and slavery, and the situation had become distressing and seriously alarming.[20] "We were on the verge of dissolution, scarce held together by the strength of a hair," wrote Luther Martin of Maryland.[21] It was during the debate on this subject that Doctor Franklin said: "In this situation of this assembly, groping as it were in the dark, to find political truth and scarce able to distinguish it when presented to us, how has it happened, sir, that we have not hitherto once thought of humbly applying to the Father of lights to illuminate our understandings? . . . I have lived, sir, a long time, and, the

longer I live, the more convincing proofs I see of this truth—
that God governs in the affairs of men. And if a sparrow
cannot fall to the ground without his notice, is it possible
that an empire can rise without his aid? We have been as-
sured, sir, in the sacred writings, that 'except the Lord build
the house, they labor in vain that build it.' I firmly believe
this—I therefore beg to move that, henceforth, prayers im-
ploring the assistance of Heaven, and its blessings on our deliberations, be held in this assembly every morning before we
proceed to business." Williamson said the cause of the omission was they had no funds.[22] "We are now at a full stop,"
said Sherman, and he supposed nobody meant they should break
up without doing something.[23] Gerry said they faced either
compromise or secession. He had rather agree to it than have
no accommodation.[24] Williamson of North Carolina declared:
"If we do not concede on both sides, our business must soon be
at an end." [25] "If no accommodation takes place," said Strong
of Massachusetts, "the union itself must soon be dissolved." [26]
Luther Martin of Maryland declared emphatically, he would
never confederate if it could not be done on just principles.[27]
The Convention evidently had come to a dead halt. Where?
At the foot of an insurmountable precipice, or could it be scaled
by the ladder of compromise? The Convention knew full well,
the choice was either dissolution or compromise. Therefore,
General Pinckney moved on July 2 that a committee consisting
of one member from each state should be appointed to devise
and report a compromise.[28] In spite of the opposition of Wilson and Madison the question was carried, and the committee
appointed by ballot.[29] The committee was clearly a compromise committee for not one of the strong, national leaders was
given a place on it. It reported through Gerry on July 5:
(1) That there should be proportional representation in the
first branch; that all money bills shall originate there, and shall
not be altered or amended by the second branch. (2) That
in the second branch each state shall have an equal vote [30]—
the Connecticut Compromise. Dr. Franklin offered the motion
in committee on which the report was based.[31] The report
was adopted by a vote of six to three July 7.[32] The large
state delegates held a caucus next day to decide whether they
were to accept the result, or frame a constitution of their own.

Fortunately, they could not agree to agree on a disagreement and the danger passed.[33] The vote of July 7 stood as follows:

AY	NO	DIVIDED
Connecticut	Pennsylvania	Massachusetts
New York	Virginia	Georgia = 2
New Jersey	South Carolina = 3	
Delaware		
Maryland		
North Carolina = 6 [34]		

The effect of this note was to make the Constitution partly federal, partly national. North Carolina was the only Southern state to vote for the federal principle contained in the compromise. In 1787 Virginia and South Carolina voted against the federal idea, yet it was not North Carolina but South Carolina which seceded in 1861.

Massachusetts was divided—Gerry and Strong against King and Gorham—because the two former believed they must compromise or see the union dissolved.[35] On a vote on July 16 on the whole report as amended, Georgia voted "No" with the large states.[36] The cause of this, according to Bedford, was that though a small state, she hoped soon to become a large state, the population was increasing so rapidly.[37] The defection of North Carolina to the ranks of the small states, and the division of Massachusetts enabled the small states to carry the compromise.[38] North Carolina voted with the small states to save the union. "The lesser states," said Davie in the North Carolina Convention, "would never have concurred unless the check had been given them, as a security for their political existence against the power and encroachments of the great states."[39] Of the four delegates from North Carolina two at least favored the compromise, Williamson to save the union, and Davie for the same reason, though he favored it on general principles.[40]

The principle of an equal vote was found in Article V, Articles of Confederation, which provided that "each state shall have one vote."[41] This was taken from Article 17 of the Dickinson Draft,[42] which again, was simply the adoption by Dickinson and his committee of the rule operative in Congress since 1765. When the Stamp Act Congress met in New York on October 7 it was: "Resolved, That the committee of each colony shall have one voice only, in determining any questions that shall arise in congress." [43]   On the assembling of the first continental congress at Philadelphia, September 5, 1774, it was resolved: "That in determining questions in this Congress, each colony or province shall have one vote." The reason for this was that congress had no census at hand and could not ascertain "the importance of each colony," therefore, the principle of equal representation was adopted,[44] not, however, without vigorous opposition.   Wilson said, "it was submitted to originally by Congress under a conviction of its impropriety, inequality and injustice," "owing to the urgent circumstances of the time." [45]   Gouverneur Morris adds to this by saying: "On the declaration of independence, a government was to be formed.   The small states aware of the necessity of preventing anarchy, and taking advantage of the moment, extorted from the large ones an equality of votes." [46]   On the questions of suffrage and slavery, there was the same division into large and small states in the continental congress that showed itself later in the Federal Convention.[47]   It is believed by some that the Americans were influenced in their adoption of equal suffrage by the fact that the Dutch, Germanic, and Belgic Confederacies voted by states.   This was well known and discussed by American statesmen.[48]   Doctor Rush condemned the method, as the cause of the decay of Dutch liberties, and Wilson declared the Germanic Confederacy a burlesque on government.[49] He always stood for proportional representation, and against equal suffrage.   Dr. Friedenwald thinks, however, that this was the real origin of giving each state one vote.[50]

"*Two senators.*"   On July 23, Gorham suggested that two senators be chosen from each state, as a small number would be more convenient for the despatch of business.   Gouverneur Morris had moved that three be elected but the Convention agreed to two nem. con.[51]   The reasons were (1) To prevent the senate from becoming too large.   (2) To prevent unnecessary expense.   It was expected that many new states would be added, hence, there would be an increase in the number of senators.[52]

The number *two* was probably suggested by the Articles of Confederation, which provided that no state should be represented in Congress by less than two members.[53] As a result of this rule, the states frequently sent but two members and became more or less accustomed to sending but two delegates to congress. For example, in congress on November 4, 1782, seven states were represented by two delegates. It was a rule on which the states had been already acting for sometime.[54]

3. *"for six years."* The committee of the whole provided that senators should hold office for seven years. On June 25, Gorham suggested a four year term, one fourth to be elected every year. Williamson then suggested six years on the ground that it would be more convenient for rotation. Read proposed they hold office *"during good behavior."* General Pinckney also proposed four years. The vote on the question stood five to five with Maryland divided.[55] On June 26th, Gorham proposed that Williamson's suggestion "to fill the blank with six years, one third of the members to go out every second year," be adopted. Read proposed nine years, one third to go out triennially. Six years, one third to go out biennially was adopted by a vote of seven to four states.[56] No delegate, according to the Articles of Confederation could serve in congress for more than three years out of a term of six years. The Dickinson Draft contained the same provision.[57] This, as well as greater convenience for purposes of rotation may have suggested the six year term to Williamson.

4. *"Each senator shall have one vote."* On July 23, Gouverneur Morris moved, seconded by King, that the members in the second branch vote per capita. Luther Martin opposed this, because it departed from the idea of the states being represented in the second branch, but it was adopted.[58] The committee of detail on August 6 reported the provision in the following form: "Each member shall have one vote."[59] The words were again agreed to as part of the section on August 9.[60] "Senator" was substituted for "member" by the committee on style and arrangement. The Fundamental Constitutions of Carolina, 1669, contain a similar clause: "And have every member one vote."[61] The phraseology is simply that of the Articles of Confederation with the substitution of "senator" for the word "state."[62] From this point of view the language runs back through the Dickinson Draft, and the resolutions of Congress of 1765, 1774, and 1777.[63] "The Senate is really a

continuation of the old Congress of Confederation in which there was an equal vote of states, with the great improvement that the two members vote separately." [64]

1. *Rotation in the Senate.*[65]   On April 8, 1787, Madison wrote to Randolph that the second branch should go "out in rotation." [66]   Gorham moved on June 26 that one third of the senators go out every second year.   The committee of detail worked this clause into shape, and the lot was to be used to divide the senators into three classes.[67]   This had been changed by the committee on style, and again inserted, and on September 14 Madison moved that the words "by lot" be stricken out, that some rule might prevail which would prevent both senators from the same state from going out at the same time.[68]   This rotative principle was taken from the constitution of New York, according to Madison.   Wilson declared it was proposed "avowedly on the plan of the New York Senate." [69]   The New York constitution of 1777 divided the senators into four classes by lot.   Virginia also divided her senators into four classes by means of the lot, though the plan was not the same as that of New York.[70]   This principle of rotation appears in Franklin's Draft of July 21, 1775 in connection with the executive council, one third of which was to go out every year.[71]   It was doubtless suggested to Franklin by the Pennsylvania Frame of 1682 which is identical with Franklin's proposition of 1775.[72]   The Pennsylvania and Delaware Frame, 1683, also contains the same principle in a somewhat altered form.[73]   Both were drawn by William Penn.   Delaware retained this rotative principle in her constitution of 1776 for the upper branch of the legislature in which the members were to be divided into three classes to go out by rotation.[74]   The motive of the convention, according to Charles Pinckney, was that the rotative principle removed all danger of aristocratic influence in the senate, while, on the other hand, election for six years gave it "all the advantages of an aristocracy—wisdom, experience, and a consistency of measures." [75]   The rotative principle would supply opportunity to destroy any nascent aristocratic influence, while the six year term would always leave a sufficient number of experi-

enced senators to conduct the business of state wisely and intelligently.

2. *Vacancies in the Senate.* In the colonies, the Governor made temporary appointments to the council in case of a vacancy.[76] This provision is from that practice.

QUALIFICATIONS OF SENATORS

1. *An Age Requirement of Thirty Years.* (Art. I, Sec. 3, cl. 3.) The convention decided first, by a vote of seven states to four, and again unanimously, that the age qualification should be thirty years for the senate.[77] Two state constitutions, New Hampshire, and South Carolina required this age qualification for senators.[78]

2. *A Citizenship Qualification of Nine Years.* Gouverneur Morris proposed fourteen years. Butler opposed the admission of foreigners without long residence because they would naturally be attached to other countries, and possess ideas of government so different as to be dangerous to the United States. Madison and Doctor Franklin opposed fourteen years on the ground that it would insert a principle of illiberality in the Constitution, discourage the most desirable people from emigrating to the United States, and destroy the friendship of European nations.[79] Wilson said he would be placed in the strange position of being incapacitated for office under the constitution he had helped to frame. |Randolph reminded the Convention of the language of the patriots, the liberal principles of the American state constitutions, and declared that fourteen years would cause all foreigners who had settled in the United States under these invitations to become hostile. He proposed nine years instead. This was agreed to by six states to four.[80]

3. *A Residence Qualification.* (See Art. I, Sec. 3, cl. 2). The New Hampshire Constitution provided that senators must be inhabitants of the district they represented.[81] Massachusetts required a senator to be five years an inhabitant of the state. South Carolina required five years' residence and New Hampshire seven.[82]

THE VICE-PRESIDENT [83]

1. *To be President of the Senate.* This originated in the committee on postponed and unfinished portions, which reported

on September 4 through Brearly. It provided, "The Vice-President shall be ex officio president of the senate." Gerry declared it improper to place the Vice-President at the head of the senate owing to the close and intimate connection between him and the President.[84] Colonel Mason urged that it was an encroachment on the rights of the senate, and a mixing of legislative and executive functions.[85] Williamson, a member of the committee, said such an officer was not wanted, but "was introduced merely for the sake of a valuable mode of election which required two to be chosen at the same time."[86] That is, the adoption of the electoral college caused a Vice-President to be chosen because the new method of electing the President required the electors to vote for two persons. Once introduced, the Vice-President must be given some place and some function in the system. There was no place and no work for him unless they made him President of the senate. So Sherman, another member of the committee, says: "If the Vice-President were not to be President of the senate, he would be without employment."[87]

This was taken from the constitution of New York, 1777, which made the Lieutenant-Governor President of the senate.[88] The Pennsylvania Frame of Government provided that the Deputy Governor should sometimes preside over the provincial council or upper house. The Pennsylvania and Delaware Frames contained a similar provision.[89] In South Carolina the Vice-President was President of the Privy Council.[90] In Massachusetts, the Lieutenant-Governor was President of the council in the absence of the Governor.[91]

There is also an analogy between the English Upper House and the Senate. The presiding officer might also be "appointed" by the King's commission, but if none be so appointed, the House of Lords might then elect.[92] In the same way, the senate may elect a President pro tempore in the absence of the Vice-President, or in case he acts as President. That is, in Lords and Senate, the presiding officer is in general provided, but if none be provided, then the presiding officer is chosen by the House. The members of the convention knew their Blackstone well enough to understand that.

2. To "have no vote unless they be equally divided." (1) The purpose—to prevent a deadlock in the government should

there be an equal division in the senate on any question. Maclaine said in the North Carolina convention the provision was "calculated to prevent the operation of the government from being impeded."[93] Davie said, where there was an equal division it was necessary to have some person decide the question impartially, and the vice-president as "the officer and representative of the union" was "the most proper person to decide in cases of this kind," as he was the representative of all the states. "These I believe to be the principles upon which the convention formed this officer." He makes the significant remark that commercial jealousy between the Eastern and Southern states had a principal share in this business.[94] The Vice-President was to be an impartial judge in case the Eastern and Southern states came into conflict in the senate, and an equal division took place. (2) The provision originated in a principle common to all deliberative bodies—the application of a common and universally recognized parliamentary principle. Caldwell objected in the North Carolina convention that the provision gave legislative power to the Vice-president. Maclaine replied that "a provision of this kind was to be found in all deliberative bodies."[94] (3) The whole provision is taken from the constitution of New York 1777, which provided that the Lieutenant-Governor should be President of the senate and have a casting voice in their deliberations, but should not vote on any other occasion.[95] In the deliberative bodies of the colonies, the presiding officer had a casting vote.[96] The speaker of the English Parliament also had a casting vote in case of equal division in the House.[97]

ORGANIZATION OF THE SENATE.[98]

1. *The Senate is to "choose their other officers."* See Art. I, sec. 2, cl. 4.

2. *To Choose "a President pro tempore" in Two Cases,* (1) when he shall exercise the office of President, (2) when he shall exercise the office of Vice-President. The Constitution of New York, 1777, contributed this provision. It provided that the senate might choose a president in the absence of the Lieutenant-Governor, or when he exercised the office of governor. The senate of Massachusetts also had power to choose its own President.[99]

IMPEACHMENTS [100]

1. *The Senate Is to Have "sole power to try all impeachments."* This simply affirms or restates the old English,[101] colonial, and state practice which runs back to the impeachment of Lords Latimer and Neville, and Richard Lyons in A.D. 1376—the first impeachment trial in England. "The model from which the idea of the institution has been borrowed pointed out that course to the convention," says the Federalist. "In Great Britain, it is the province of the House of Commons to prefer the impeachment; and of the House of Lords to decide upon it. Several of the state constitutions have followed the example." [102] The constitution of Massachusetts provided that the senate should try all impeachments.[103] The New Hampshire, Delaware, Pennsylvania, and South Carolina constitutions also provided that the upper house try impeachments.[104]

2. *The Members of the Court Are to Take an Oath.*[105] Massachusetts, South Carolina, and New Hampshire constitutions contained a similar provision.[106] The provision was proposed by Gouverneur Morris.[107]

3. *The Chief Justice Is to Preside at the Trial of the President.* This was suggested by the committee of eleven to the Federal Convention, September 4, 1787.[108] Madison and others desired to give the trial of impeachments to the Supreme Court. This was opposed because (1) it was feared the court might thereby be warped or corrupted; (2) it was believed it would be an improper tribunal to try the President since the judges would be appointed by him; [109] (3) the Supreme Court was to try the President after the impeachment was over.[110] The Vice-President, it was believed, might be connected with the President in the same crime, and would, therefore, be an improper person to sit in judgment on the President, and also, since the Vice-President succeeded to the presidential office, he might endeavor to influence the senate against the executive for the purpose of securing the presidential office himself. The Chief Justice was chosen to preside for these reasons.[111] In England, the Lord High Steward presided at the trial of a peer.

4. *The Concurrence of Two-thirds Required to Convict.* This provision was found in the constitution of New York.[112] The constitution of South Carolina and the rejected constitu-

tion of Massachusetts, 1778, contained the same provision.[113]

Judgment in Cases of Impeachment. (Art. I, Sec. 3, cl. 7.) This clause was also taken from the constitution of New York, 1777, almost word for word.[115] The only changes were the substitution of the word "office" for "place," "United States" for "state," and "according to law" for "according to the laws of the land." The reason for this last change was that "law of the land" meant the law of each separate state, and would, therefore, have conveyed a false idea in 1787.[116] The constitutions of Massachusetts, 1780, and New Hampshire, 1784, repeat the language of the New York constitution of 1777.[117]

1. *The Times, Places, and Manner of Holding Elections Prescribed by the State Legislatures.* (Art. I, Sec. 4, cl. 1.) This clause originated in the committee of detail.[118] Randolph's draft, used in that committee, reads, "the place shall be fixed by the legislatures from time to time, or on their default by the national legislature." [119]

This makes clear the motive which influenced the Convention. The state might "default" and the provision is intended to meet that emergency. As a matter of fact, the states had defaulted, therefore, the clause finds its origin in American experience under the Articles of Confederation. In order that there may be no future defaulting Congress is given power to "make or alter such regulations." [120] The states might fail or refuse to send delegates to Congress, Madison said.[121] Davie declared the purpose of the clause was to give Congress power to control the combinations of large states formed with the design of destroying the union, and to prevent states from refusing to send representatives to Congress. Rhode Island is cited as an example of the kind. A faction was in possession of the state government which had frequently deprived the people of the benefit of representation in the union, and embarrassed Congress by their absence. "The same evil may again result from the same cause, and Congress ought, therefore, to possess constitutional power to give the people an opportunity of electing representatives, if the states refuse or neglect to do it." With this power, Congress can give the people representation in spite of any faction in any state. It gives Congress the constitutional means of self-preservation.[122]

2. *"Except as to the place of choosing senators."* This
was added on September 14 for the purpose of exempting the
state capitals from the power of Congress.[123]   In the North
Carolina convention, J. Taylor asked why it was that "the
states had control over the place of electing senators, but not
over that of choosing the representatives." Spraight, a member of the Federal Convention, answered that "the reason of
that reservation was to prevent Congress from altering the
places for holding the legislative assemblies in the different
states." [124]   Congress shall have no control over the *places*
where legislatures shall choose senators.

MEETINGS OF CONGRESS

1. *Annual Meetings.* Some of the *charters*, as those of
Rhode Island and Connecticut, required two meetings of the
legislature yearly, but annual meetings were provided for, and
this became the more general practice.   The Pennsylvania
Frame of 1696, and the Charter of Massachusetts 1691, required yearly meetings.[125]

The *state constitutions* provided for annual legislative meetings.   The Virginia constitution of 1776 required that "they
shall meet once or oftener every year," [126] the Maryland Constitution provided: "The General Assembly shall meet annually
on the first Monday of November."   The constitutions of New
Jersey 1776, Pennsylvania 1776, Massachusetts 1780, and New
Hampshire 1784, all provided for annual meetings of the legislature.[127]

The English Constitution was another source for the provision.   As early as A.D. 1311 the New Ordinance required
annual meetings of the English Parliament.   The Bill of Rights
provided "that for redress of grievances, and for the amending,
strengthening, and preserving of the laws Parliament ought to
be held frequently." [128]   This had an influence on the origin of
the provision in the Constitution of the United States by operating through the state constitutions.   Though quoted by some
without naming any special date for the meeting of the legislative body, yet, in practice, it was interpreted to mean annual
meetings at least.   The Maryland constitution incorporates the
provision and interprets it in that way.   The constitutions of
North Carolina, Massachusetts, and New Hampshire interpret

the provision to mean annual meetings.[129] This was apparently the continuation of the practice with which Massachusetts had been familiar for nearly one hundred years. The charter of 1691 and the explanatory charter of 1726 provided for annual legislatures.[130]

2. *"On the first Monday in December."* The time for the meeting of Congress was fixed by the committee of detail. Why was December chosen? Gouverneur Morris [131] moved to substitute May for December. Three members of the committee of detail replied to Morris giving their reasons for fixing the meetings in December.

(1) Wilson—Winter was the most convenient season for business.

(2) Ellsworth—As nearly all members of Congress would be more or less connected with agriculture, the summer would interfere too much with private business.

(3) Randolph—He had examined the state constitutions and found that the times of the state elections would suit December better than May, and, as the national representatives would doubtless be elected then, he thought it advisable "to render our innovations as little incommodious as possible." [132]

This provision originated in the charters and constitutions. Gorham said in the New England states the annual time of meeting had long been fixed by their charters and constitutions.

(1) *The charters.* These fixed the exact days of the week and month on which the assemblies were to meet, just as the Constitution of the United States does. The Pennsylvania charters give the exact date instead of the day of the week. In fixing the meeting of Congress for a certain day in a certain month, by means of a constitutional provision, the Convention of 1787 was simply following long established custom.[133]

(2) *The state constitutions.* The Pennsylvania constitution required the General Assembly to meet on the fourth Monday of October. The constitutions of South Carolina, New Jersey, Vermont 1777 and 1786, Massachusetts 1780, and New Hampshire, 1784, all contained a similar provision.[134] The South Carolina constitution of 1776, required the assembly to meet "on the first Monday in December," as does the Constitution of the United States.[135] John Rutledge, a member of the committee of detail from South Carolina, may have suggested

this in committee. The Articles of Confederation fixed the meeting of Congress for the first Monday in November.[136] The Constitution of the United States simply follows American experience—colonial, state, and national.

3. *"Unless they shall by law appoint a different day."* Randolph was the author of this clause. He was opposed to fixing the day irrevocably by means of a constitutional provision, but some precise time must be fixed, he said, until the legislature could meet and make provision by law. Therefore, he moved to add these words which Madison seconded, and the clause was approved by a vote of eight states to two in the Convention.[137]

NOTES TO CHAPTER IV

1. Art. 1, 3 cl. i.
2. Elliot, V, 127.
3. Id. 167.
4. Id. 138.
5. Id. 137, 138.
6. Id. 166; Farrand, Records, III, 554.
7. Elliot, V., 170, 240.
8. Elliot, V, 166.
9. Id. 169.
10. Id. 170, 240, 241.
11. Journals of Cont. Cong. 11, 25, 54, 55, 261, 454 (Nov. 30, 1776).
12. Thorpe, Consts. IV, 2467; V, 2635, 2793, 3085; VI, 3246, 3253, 3759; VII, 3817.
13. Macdonald, Sel. Charters, 255.
14. Am. Hist. Leaflets, No. 20, pp. 11, 18.
15. Elliot, V, 178.
16. Id. 182.
17. See Dickinson's claim to be the author, Farrand, Records, III, 554.
18. Elliot, V, 255.
19. Id. I, 507.
20. Id. I, 507.
21. Elliot, I, 358.
22. Elliot, V, 253-4.
23. Id. 270.
24. Id. 278, 285.
25. Id. 273.
26. Id. 313.
27. Id. 267.
28. Elliot, Debates, V, 270, 272.
29. Id. 273.
30. Elliot, Debates, V, 263-4.
31. Elliot, V, 286, 316.
32. Id. 286.
33. Id. 286, 319.
34. Id. 286.
35. Elliot, V, 278, 312, 313.

36. Id. 316.
37. Id. 268, 292, 309.
38. Elliot, V, 273.
39. Id. IV, 21.
40. Id. 273, 266, 281, 267.
41. Am. Hist. Leaflets, No. 20, p. 18; Journals, III, 333.
42. Id. p. 11.
43. Elliot, Debates, IV, 341.
44. Journals of Cong., I, II; Elliot, I, 42.
45. Elliot, V, 181, 177.
46. Elliot, V, 286-7.
47. Id. I, 71-2, 74-5, 77, 78; Id. V, 287.
48. Elliot, I, 77; Id. V, 314.
49. Elliot, I, 77.
50. Am. Hist. Assoc. Rep., 1896, I, 223 seq.
51. Elliot, V, 356, 357.
52. Elliot, V, 256, 357.
53. Art. V.
54. Elliot, V. 1.
55. Elliot, Debates, V, 1, 241.
56. Elliot, V, 242, 245.
57. Am. Hist. Leaflets, No. 20, 18, 14.
58. Elliot, V, 356, 357.
59. Id. 377.
60. Id. 357.
61. Poore, 1404.
62. Art. V.
63. Art. 17, Elliot, IV, 341; Journals of Cong. I, ii; III, 333.
64. Prof. A. B. Hart, Actual Government, 218.
65. Art. 1, sec. 3, cl. 2.
66. Elliot, V, 108.
67. Elliot, V, 377.
68. Id. 541.
69. Id. I, 393.
70. Poore, 1334, 1914.
71. Am. Hist. Leaflets, No. 20 (Art. IX), p. 5.
72. Macdonald, Sel. Charters, 193.
73. Id. 200.
74. Thorpe, Vol. 1, 562.
75. Elliot, IV, 329.
76. Bruce, Inst. Hist. of Va., 320.
77. Elliot, V, 186, 241.
78. Poore, Charters, 1286, 1622.
79. Elliot, .V, 398.
80. Elliot, V, 399, 401.
81. Poore, Charters, 1286.
82. Thorpe, Charters and Constitutions, III, 1897; VI, 3250; IV, 2460.
83. Art. 1, sec. 3, cl. 4.
84. Elliot, Debates, V, 507, 522.
85. Elliot, V, 527.
86. Id. 522.
87. Elliot, V, 522.
88. Poore, 1336.
89. Macdonald, Sel. Charters, 194, 202.
90. Poore, 1617; see also N. J. Poore, 1312.
91. Id. 967.

92. Blackstone, Commentaries, I, 211, 181.
93. Elliot, IV, 26.
94. Elliot, IV, 26.
95. Poore, 1336.
96. Macdonald, Sel. Charters, 65; see also Connecticut Acts, 1784, p. 29, and Statutes of Conn., 1786, p. 29.
97. May, Parliamentary Law, 343.
98. Art. 1, sec. 3, cl. 5.
99. Poore, Charters and Constitutions, 1336, 963.
100. Art. 1, sec. 3, cl. 6.
101. Adams and Stephens, Sel. Documents, 132; Taswell-Languead, Const. Hist. of Eng., 224.
102. Federalist, No. 64 (Dawson Ed.), 465.
103. Poore, 963.
104. Id. 1286, 1545, 277, 1625; for colonial impeachments, see Roger Foster, Constitution, the appendix.
105. Poore, 1337.
106. Id. 963, 1624, 1286.
107. Elliot, V, 529.
108. Elliot, V, 507.
109. Id. 528, 529.
110. Elliot, V, 508.
111. Elliot, IV, 44; for further study, see Elliot, V, 128, 205, 302, 380, 508, 522, 507, 528, 529, 540, 541, 580.
112. Poore, 1337.
113. Id. 1625.
115. Poore, 1337.
116. Brinton Cox, Judicial Power and Unconstitutional Legislation, p. VIII.
117. Thorpe, chapters Vol. 3, 1895, Vol. 4, 2461.
118. Elliot, V, 377.
119. Meigs, Growth of the Const., 11, 7, 8.
120. Elliot, V, 402.
121. Id.
122. Elliot, V, 60, 66; IV, 60.
123. Elliot, V, 542.
124. Elliot, IV, 70.
125. Macdonald, Sel. Charters, 35; Poore, Charters, 949; Macdonald, 218.
126. Poore, 1910.
127. Poore, 823, 1311, 1543, 960, 1284.
128. Adams and Stephens, p. 93; Id. p. 465.
129. Poore, Charters, 818, 823, 1410, 1412, 959, 960.
130. Id. 949, 955.
131. Elliot, Debates, V, 377.
132. Elliot, V, 384.
133. Elliot, V, 383; Mass. 1629, Poore, 937; Conn. 1639, Id. 249; New Eng. Confed. 1643; MacD. Sel. Charters, p. 98; New Haven 1643; Id. 103; Conn. 1662, Poore, 253; R. I., Id. 1598; Fund. Consts. of Carolina, 1669; Poore, 1405; Pa. Frame, 1682, MacD. Sel. Charters, 196, 218, 202; Pa. and Del. Frame, 16, 93; Poore, 949; Mass. 1691, Pa. 1696, Poore, 1543, 1622, 1311, 1861, 1870, 960, 1284, 1618.
134. Poore, 1405; Macdonald, Sel. Charters, 196, 218, 202; Poore, 949, 1543, 1622, 1311, 1861, 1870, 960, 1284, 1618.
135. Poore, 1618.
136. Id. 8.
137. Elliot, Debates, V, 382.

CHAPTER V

THE POWERS, DUTIES, RESTRICTIONS, AND PRIVILEGES OF EACH
HOUSE

THE LAW-MAKING BODY

1. *Each House to Be the Judge of Elections, Returns and
Qualifications of Its Own Members.*[1] This clause was drafted
by the committee of detail and adopted on August 10 without
debate or change.[2] The origins of this are found:

(1) *In the English Constitution.* The right of the House
of Commons to determine contested elections was first distinctly
asserted in England in 1586 in the case of the Norfolk election.[3]
The right was not, however, definitely acknowledged and settled
beyond dispute till the famous Goodwin's case in the reign of
James I, 1604. After a sharp struggle, the King yielded, and
acknowledged the House of Commons "was a court of record
and judge of returns." [4] The right of the Commons was never
again questioned and was given further legal sanction and
confirmation by the Courts in the cases of Bernardiston v.
Soame, 1674, Onslow, 1680, and Prideaux v. Morris, 1702,
while it received legislative recognition by an act of the English
Parliament in 1696.[5] The right of the House of Commons
to decide on the qualifications of its own members was first
asserted and established in the case of Doctor Alex Nowell,
1553, who was declared disqualified because a member of con-
vocation.[6] In 1559, the House decided that John Smyth, Burgess elect for Camelford, who had been declared an outlaw,
was "a member of this House." [7] In 1576, the House of Commons decided in Lord Russel's Case that "he shall continue a
member of this House." [8] The *Commons* have exercised the
right ever since that time.

(2) *In the charters.* The Fundamental Orders of Connecticut, 1638-9, the Pennsylvania Frame of Government, 1682
and 1696, and the Pennsylvania Charter of Privileges, 1701,
all contain a provision on the subject. The latter provides

61

that the Assembly "shall be Judges of the Qualifications and Elections of their own Members." [9] The first legislative assembly in America, 1619, began its proceedings by examining the qualifications of members, and excluded some on grounds of disqualification. In Virginia in 1653, Robert Bracewell, a minister, was suspended and declared ineligible to a seat in the House of Burgesses.[10] Therefore, this function had been exer· cised by the legislatures from earliest times in America.

(3) *In the state constitutions.* The committee of detail apparently took this from the constitution of Massachusetts, where the exact phraseology of the Federal Constitution is found. New Hampshire follows Massachusetts,[11] and the state constitutions nearly all contained a similar provision. This was true of Delaware, New Jersey, New York, Pennsylvania, Vermont, Maryland, and North Carolina.[12] Connecticut retained her Colonial Charter of 1662 as the constitution of the state after the Revolution, but the deputies had been authorized by statute to determine contested elections.[13] Precedents for the provision in the Constitution of the United States were, therefore, both ancient and numerous.

2. *A Majority Shall Constitute a Quorum.* This came from the committee of detail.[14] In Virginia, the constitution required a majority of the Senate to be present in order to do business.[15] The New York constitution provided "that a majority of the said members shall, from time to time, constitute a house, to proceed upon business." [16] Maryland, New Jersey, Massachusetts and New Hampshire required a majority for a quorum.[17] Gorham, in the Federal Convention, said a majority "was the quorum almost everywhere fixed in the United States." [18] The Convention follows American experience in providing, as Ellsworth said, that no law or burden could be imposed by a few men.[19] Magna Carta provided (Ch. 61) that a majority of the twenty-five barons should constitute a quorum. The majority principle first appears in Anglo-Saxon law in the reign of Henry the First.[20] The Provisions of Oxford, A.D. 1258 contain a clear, definite statement of the principle: "And if they cannot all be present, that which the majority shall do shall be firm and established." [21]

3. *"A smaller number may adjourn from day to day."* The committee of detail reported this provision on August 6.[22] The

principle was found in the constitutions of North and South Carolina. It also appears in substance in article nine of the Articles of Confederation. The phraseology was apparently taken from the constitution of South Carolina. John Rutledge, chairman of the committee of detail, was from South Carolina, and was doubtless responsible for the use of the phraseology of his own state constitution.[23] An act of the Rhode Island legislature, 1752, authorized so many of the deputies as may be present to adjourn from day to day.[24] For the English rules, see Blackstone, I, 186, and Jefferson's Manual, section L.

4. "*To compel attendance of absent members.*" This provision was proposed by Randolph and seconded by Madison on August 10 in the Federal Convention of 1787. The purpose was to prevent secessions on the part of the members of Congress in order to hinder the assembling of a quorum with the intention of paralyzing business, or obstructing the passage of certain measures. Ellsworth suggested that secessions might be guarded against by giving each an authority to require the attendance of absent members.[25] American experience under the Articles of Confederation dictated the provision. The members of Congress from the states had failed to attend, which resulted in great inconvenience, delay, annoyance, and rendered Congress powerless for half the year to transact important business. Even before Confederation, on November 16, 1775, Congress found it necessary to check non-attendance by passing the following resolution: "Resolved, That for the future, no member absent himself from Congress without leave of Congress." [26] Speaking of the difficulties of 1781-2, John Rutledge said in the South Carolina convention: "In those times, business of vast importance stood still, because nine states could not be kept together." Davie cited Rhode Island as a conspicuous sinner in this regard.[27] So troublesome was this neglect, or refusal of members to attend Congress, that the Report on Trade and Revenue of August 14, 1786, recommended the state legislatures to adopt an amendment giving Congress power to compel the attendance of members on pain of disqualification for membership in Congress, or for any office of trust or profit under the states, or the United States.[28] The Convention of 1787 felt it necessary to curb this evil.

The constitution of New Hampshire gave the House of Representatives power to compel attendance. The Fundamental Orders of Connecticut, 1639, gave the deputies power to "fyne any . . . for not coming in due tyme."[29] In 1659-60, the Virginia legislature passed an act to compel attendance of members of the House of Burgesses. The law imposed a fine of three hundred pounds of tobacco for every twenty-four hours' absence, unless an acceptable excuse could be given. The reason for the law was to prevent delay in the election of a Speaker, or election of an unacceptable one. In 1691, the House of Burgesses instructed the Speaker to issue a warrant for the arrest of James Bray, who had neglected to attend. He was detained by the sheriff, till he apologized to the House.[30] This principle originated in England. As early as 1382, Knights neglecting to attend Parliament were fined, and in Henry Eighth's reign members leaving without permission of Parliament were also fined.[31] This is the same practice which later prevailed in the colonies and states. The members of the Hundred Court were likewise compelled to attend under penalty of a fine in early England.[32] A law of 1662 in Rhode Island provided for enforcing attendance by fine and seizure of goods to pay it, if not paid. Members leaving the House after business had begun were to forfeit the whole of their wages. Another act provided for imposing a fine for non-attendance the first day of the session.[33]

1. *Each House is to Determine the Rules of its Proceedings.* (Art. I, Sec. 5, cl. 2.) The committee of detail originated and reported this clause as it appears in the Constitution. Charles Pinckney proposed a similar provision.[34]

(1) *The real source was the state constitutions.* The committee of detail took this from the constitution of Massachusetts. New Hampshire followed Massachusetts. The constitutions of Delaware, 1776, Maryland, 1776, Virginia, 1776, and Georgia, 1777, contained practically the same provision.[35]

(2) *Colonial procedure.* The Virginia Assembly of 1619 proceeded to settle the rules of its proceedings in English fashion, and the whole system of English Parliamentary procedure became colonial procedure.[36]

(3) *The English Constitution.* In the reign of Richard II, the judges of England declared the right belonged to the Parliament.[37] It was important that Parliament exercise this power

in England, otherwise money would have been granted, and Parliament dissolved by the King before redress of grievances. By demanding redress of grievances first, the Commons were able to control the crown and limit the prerogative.

2. To "*punish its members.*" This originated in the committee of detail. The immediate source was:

(1) *The state constitutions.* The provision was evidently taken from the constitution of Massachusetts, which gave each house this power. The same identical provision was found in the constitution of New Hampshire 1784, while the Maryland constitution of 1776 gave similar power.[38]

(2) *Colonial charters and practices.* The Fundamental Orders of Connecticut gave the General Court power "to fyne any that shall be disorderly at their meetings." On many occasions, the Virginia House of Burgesses fined members for offences.[39]

(3) *The Constitution of England.* It arose in England as part of "the right to the exclusive cognizance of matters arising within the house."[40] In 1548, John Storie was imprisoned in the Tower apparently for using disrespectful language towards the Speaker and Protector Somerset. Other instances of punishment by imprisoning members are Thomas Copley, 1558, Peter Wentworth, 1576 and 1587, Cope, 1587, and Palmer, 1641. Both Commons and Lords frequently exercised the right in England. It was carried to America, and has become a part of the American system.

3. "*Expel a member.*" This also originated in the committee of detail. Madison declared on August 10, that the right of expulsion was too important to be exercised by a bare majority or quorum, and in factional emergencies might be dangerously abused. In view of this, he moved that the words "with the concurrence of two thirds" be added. Gouverneur Morris opposed this on the ground that it would enable a few men to keep a member in Congress who ought to be expelled. Madison's proposal was agreed to by ten States to one with Pennsylvania divided.[41] The origin was to be found:

(1) *In the state constitutions.* The power to expel a member was found in the constitutions of Vermont, 1777, and 1786, Delaware, 1776, Maryland, 1776, and Pennsylvania, 1776.[42]

(2) *The right of expulsion was of English origin.* The first case of expulsion in England was that of Thomas Long expelled for bribing the borough of Westbury to elect him to Parliament in 1571. In 1581, Arthur Hall was expelled for publishing a book slandering the Speaker, Sir Robert Bell, Dr. Parry 1585, Sir John Trevor, Speaker, for taking bribes 1694, Robert Walpole for corruption and embezzlement, 1712, and Sir Richard Steele for writing a pamphlet, "The Crisis," reflecting on the Tory ministry of Queen Anne, were expelled by the Commons.[43]   The right of the House to expel a member was unquestioned, and the case of Wilkes, expelled for seditious libel, 1769, decided that expulsion did not disqualify for service in Parliament again if reelected.[44]   For this reason, some of the state constitutions provided that the house should have the right to expel a member, "but not a second time for the same offence, if re-elected." [45]   From England, the right of expulsion came through the colonial governments and first state constitutions to the Constitution of the United States.

1. *Each House to Keep a Journal.*[46]   (Art. I, Sec. 5, cl. 3.) This clause originated in the committee of detail on August 6.[47] Gerry, however, was the author of the clause, "except such parts thereof as in their judgment require secrecy," which he proposed on August 10.[48]   The provision was taken from article nine of the Articles of Confederation.[49]   Even the clause proposed by Gerry was taken from article nine. In the discussion in Convention, Wilson said, "this is a clause in the existing Confederation."   Any delegate on request might have the yeas and nays entered on the Journal according to article nine.   Randolph believed this clause should have been adopted also, and seconded Gouverneur Morris's motion to that effect.   On August 10,[50] Gorham declared that in Massachusetts it led to great abuses, the frivolous stuffing of the journals with yeas and nays and the misleading of the people.   Gorham's strong opposition caused disagreement on the question of allowing a single member to call for the yeas and nays—that is, the provision of the Articles of Confederation—and caused the adoption of the provision, "at the desire of one-fifth of those present" instead.[51]   The Dickinson Draft uses the same language as the Articles of Confederation.[52]   The New Hampshire constitution of 1784 provided for entering the

yeas and nays on motion of an individual.[53] The state legislatures kept their journals, and the colonial assemblies had kept a record of their proceedings from the first legislative meeting in 1619 in Virginia.[54] The English House of Commons had kept its journal since 1547, and the House of Lords since 1509. Before that, the proceedings of Parliament were recorded in the Rolls of Parliament, A.D. 1278-1503.[55]

Adjournment.[56] The power of adjournment belongs solely to each house, as in the English Parliament.[57] This provision was reported by the committee of detail on August 6, which took it from the constitution of South Carolina, 1778. Other state constitutions gave power to adjourn,[58] but South Carolina was the only one that gave power to do so for three days.[59] The Randolph draft gave power to adjourn for "one week." The words "one Week" are stricken out, and "3 days" inserted instead in the handwriting of John Rutledge of South Carolina.[60] Since these words are in Rutledge's handwriting in the Randolph draft used in the committee of detail, we conclude Rutledge was responsible for this insertion in the report of the committee, and, therefore, for its being in the Constitution of the United States. Some of the charters also contained a provision giving the legislature power to adjourn, as the Concessions and Agreements of West New Jersey, 1677, and the Pennsylvania Frame of 1696.[61]

The words "during the session of Congress" were added on August 11 on motion of Gouverneur Morris to meet the objection of King that the provision authorized the two houses to adjourn to a new place.[62]

COMPENSATION AND PRIVILEGES OF CONGRESSMEN.[63]

1. *Senators and Representatives to be Paid for Their Services.* The question in the Convention of 1787 was, whether members of Congress should be paid by the state or the nation. After a long discussion, it was decided they should be paid by the nation. They were paid by the states under the Articles of Confederation.[64] The reasons urged against state payment were:

(1) It would make the members of Congress improperly dependent on the state legislatures. This was urged by many.

"Those who pay," said Hamilton, "are the masters of those who are paid."[65]   (2) It would create inequality because different states would make different provision.[66]   (3) The states might be so parsimonious that the best equipped men would refuse to serve.[67]   (4) As the legislature was national, it would be unfair to throw an unequal burden on the distant states.[68] (5) The nation ought to pay because the service was national.[69]

The practice of paying legislators was firmly established in the United States in 1787.   The Articles of Confederation required the states to pay their members or delegates to Congress.[70]   The constitution of Pennsylvania, 1776, provided for payment of the wages of representatives out of the state treasury.[71]   The South Carolina constitution of 1778 provided that public officers should receive adequate yearly salaries "fixed by law."   The American colonies were accustomed to paying their legislators from very early times.   As early as 1636, at least, the Virginia Assembly provided for the payment of its members by the county which they represented.[73]   The records of Virginia do not show whether the members were paid or not from 1619 to 1636.   At first, payment simply covered travelling expenses to and from Jamestown and the cost of living there during the meeting of the House of Burgesses.[74]   A salary or fixed sum appears to have been paid to the burgesses in 1660-1661 for the first time.   An act provided for the payment of one hundred and fifty pounds of tobacco per day to each burgess, and in addition, travelling expenses to and from Jamestown.[75]   Once introduced, the practice of paying members in the colonies remained, while in England it declined.   The Pennsylvania Frame of Government, 1696, provided for paying members of assembly 4s. per day, and travelling expenses at the rate of 2d. per mile both ways.   The Speaker received 5s. per day.[76]   Doctor Franklin's Albany Plan provided for paying the forty-eight members of the Grand Council ten shillings per diem and travelling expenses.[77]   The Concessions and Agreements of West New Jersey, 1676, allowed the member of assembly one shilling per day.[78]   All this was an inheritance from England.   There, knights and burgesses were entitled to payment of expenses at least, as in early Virginia.   In Edward the Third's time, knights were paid 4s. per day and citizens or burgesses 2s. by their constituents.[79]   In Edward the Se-

cond's time the members received the same amount. Payment
was regulated by Act of Parliament in 1388 and 1544. Writs
for payment of members can be traced to the end of the reign
of Henry the Eighth. Thomas King was the last man to receive pay for attending Parliament in 1681. He sued his constituents for wages and Lord Chancellor Nottingham gave
judgment in his favor.[80] King was member for Harwich. The
practice of paying members was established in the American
colonies before it died out in England, and this passed into the
Constitution of the United States.

2. *The Privileges of Freedom from Arrest and Freedom of
Speech.* The committee of detail originated this practically
as it stands.[81] The sources are:

(1) *The Articles of Confederation.* Comparison of the report of the committee of detail with the Articles of Confederation shows that with a few slight changes the committee's report was taken bodily from Article V.[82] The privileges of members had been asserted in the good old-fashioned English way
in Congress as early as June 14, 1777, in the case of Gunning
Bedford.[83]

(2) *The state constitutions.* Some of the state constitutions provided for these privileges. Freedom from arrest was
provided for by the constitutions of Maryland, 1776, Massachusetts, 1780, and New Hampshire, 1784, and freedom of
speech by the same state constitutions.[84] Part of the phraseology is identical with that of the Federal Constitution. In
Rhode Island and Connecticut which had no state constitutions,
the laws provided for these privileges.[85]

(3) *Colonial laws and charters.* As early as 1623, the
legislature of Virginia passed an act giving the burgesses the
privilege of *freedom from arrest* for at least seven days before
the meeting of assembly, and for at least a week after adjournment. Any creditor attempting to interfere with a member
thereby forfeited the debt. Even a sheriff who served a warrant in such a case rendered himself liable to punishment.[86]
The idea was that a burgess owed duty first to the state, and
prevention of service was an injury to the state. Another law
of 1643 extended the privilege from the day after election to
ten days after the dissolution of the assembly.[87] In 1676, Nathaniel Bacon was arrested on his way to the assembly by Cap-

tain Gardiner, who was fined about $1500 for violating the privilege in Bacon's case.[88]   The privilege became general, once it was introduced, and assemblies were extremely jealous of its violation. The Fundamental Orders of Connecticut, 1639, provided for the privilege of *freedom of speech in the General Court*.[89] The Pennsylvania Charter of Privileges granted the assembly "all the privileges of an assembly according to the rights of the freeborn subjects of England." [90]

(4) *The English Constitution.* The real historical origin of these privileges lies far back in English history, or, perhaps, even back of that in old Gothic law which says: "Extenditur haec pax et securitas ad quattuordecim dies convocato regni senatu." [91]   The privilege of a member to freedom from arrest goes back in England to a law of Ethelred, A.D. 600, which imposed a fine on anyone violating the privilege.[92]   It is also found in the laws of Edward the Confessor,[93] and a law of Canute declared: "Every man is entitled to grith to the gemot and from the gemot, except he be a notorious thief." [94]   The privilege was recognized in the case of the Bishop of St. David's in the reign of Edward I, and in the case of the Prior of Malton in Edward the Second's reign.[96]   In Atwyll's Case, 1477, the Commons declared that the privilege had existed "whereof time that mannys minde is not the contrairie." [97]   In the case of Sir Thomas Shirley, 1603, the first legislative recognition of the privilege was given.[98]

This clause of the Federal Constitution grants the privilege "in all cases, except treason, felony, or breach of the peace." The privilege was never regarded as applicable to such cases. In Thorpe's case, 1453, the judges so decided,[99] hence, the Constitution of the United States excludes the privilege in these cases.[100]   (See also Stats. of Conn. 1786, p. 28, 1784, p. 28). Freedom of speech existed in Edward Third's reign.[101]   The privilege was violated and given definite legal recognition in Haxey's case, 1397. The King, Lords, and Commons acknowledged it as a legally existing right,[102] and it was confirmed in the cases of Young and Strode.[103]   The Speaker first claimed the privilege in 1541, and it was finally fixed as law in the Bill of Rights, 1689, which declared that "the freedom of speech and debates or proceedings in Parliament ought not to be impeached or questioned in any court or place out of Parliament." [104]   The framers of the Articles of Confederation took this provision of the Bill of Rights and changing it slightly, embodied it as Article V. The constitution of Maryland, 1776, and Massachusetts, 1780, also contain the provision.[105]   The principle passes from the Bill of Rights to the Constitution of the United States in this way.[106]

1. *No Senator or Representative to Hold Any Civil Office.*[107]   The sources of this are found:

(1) *In the Articles of Confederation.*   Article V provided that no delegate to Congress could hold any office under the United States for which he shall receive any compensation.[108] The Dickinson Draft contained the same provision.[109]   On November 15, 1779, Gerry and Sherman offered a resolution in Congress dealing with the same subject and using part of the language found in the Articles of Confederation. It was rejected twice.[110]

(2) *The state constitutions and laws.*   Some state governments disqualified members of the legislature for office and some did not do so.[111]   The Maryland constitution of 1776 contained several provisions on the subject. One clause disqualified officeholders from sitting in Congress.[112]   Another disqualified Senators, Assemblymen and members of the Council from holding office "during the time for which" they "shall be elected." [113]   This clause, found at different stages in the development of the section in the Constitution, would indicate that the members of the Convention had the Maryland Constitution in mind. The constitutions of South Carolina, 1776, and 1778, provided that acceptance of office vacated the seats of members.[114]   The constitutions of North Carolina and Georgia, 1776 and 1777, permitted the holding of one lucrative office.[115]   The constitution of Pennsylvania prohibited members of the house of representatives from holding office,[116] while the constitution of New Hampshire, following the Articles of Confederation, provided that no congressman could hold any office or place of profit under the United States.[117]   A law of Rhode Island prohibited justices from holding any office of trust or profit. In 1780, Paul Mumford and Peter Phillips resigned as members of the upper house, and were then chosen as judges of the Superior Court of Judicature of Rhode Island.[118]   State experience, therefore, provided many precedents for the principle.

(3) *The charters.* The charter of Georgia, 1732, contains practically the same provision as the Constitution of the United States.[118] The Concessions of West New Jersey, 1676, provided that no person could hold two offices at once.[119]

(4) *The English Constitution.* A comparison of the Articles of Confederation, the Dickinson Draft, the constitutions of Maryland, North and South Carolina, Georgia, New Hampshire, and the Charter of Georgia, 1732, with the Act of Settlement, 1701, and the Place Act of 1707, shows that the English Acts are the original source from which the principle is derived. The language is identical. Identity of principle and phraseology cannot be the result of accident. Part of the identical phraseology of the English Place Act appears in the Constitution of the United States.[120] The principles found in the above acts are those of the Federal Constitution. (1) No member to be appointed to a new office, or an office with increased emoluments during the term for which he was elected. (2) No officeholder to be a member of the House of Commons.[121]

In 1742, the Place Bill further disqualified a large number of the members of the Commons.[122] The purpose of these acts was to prevent Parliament from being controlled by the Executive through the officeholders and use of corruption. This principle of legislative disqualification goes back to the commissioners of Stamps and Excise, 1694 and 1699, though a disqualifying act of 1693 was rejected by the Lords.

The purpose of the Convention in adopting this clause was the same as that of the English Parliament. The declarations of Ellsworth and Wilson show that the prevention of corruption was uppermost in the minds of the framers of the Constitution.[123] The Federalist quotes the clause as evidence that "the Constitution has provided some important guards against the danger of executive influence upon the legislative body."

James Bryce says the purpose was to prevent the President not merely from winning over members of Congress by alluring promises of office, but also to prevent the President's ministers from corrupting or unduly influencing the representatives, as George III and his ministers corrupted the English Parliament. He quotes No. 40 of the Federalist in support of his view and says the Fathers were determined to avert this form of corruption, hence, the provision in the Constitution.[124]

REVENUE BILLS TO ORIGINATE IN THE LOWER HOUSE [125]

To compensate the large states for the sacrifice they had made in giving the small states equal representation in the Senate, the exclusive right of originating money bills was given the lower house. This would enable the large states to control money bills, as they would have a majority of members in that body.[126] It was part of a compromise between the large and small states. The sources lie:

(1) *In the state constitutions.* Wilson said in Convention that this provision had been transcribed from the British into several American constitutions,[127] and Madison remarked that both Great Britain and the states possessed the regulation.[128] In Maryland, the House of Delegates originated all money bills.[129] In Delaware, though money bills originated in the lower house, they might "be altered, amended, or rejected by the legislative council." [130] In New Jersey, South Carolina, and Virginia the upper house could not amend.[131] The constitutions of Massachusetts and New Hampshire, 1780 and 1784, contained the provision in the Federal Constitution.[132] The Convention took this clause from the constitution of Massachusetts. The only difference is, the Massachusetts constitution says: "All money bills," instead of "all bills for raising revenue." Strong of Massachusetts was responsible for part of the phraseology.[133] The reason why they gave the Senate power to amend is given by James Madison: "When you send a bill to the Senate without the power of making any alteration, you force them to reject the bill. The power of proposing alterations removes this inconvenience." [134]

(2) *The English Constitution.* As early as 1395, money granted was given "by the Commons with the advice and assent of the Lords." [135] The principle was given definite recognition for the first time in 1407 by the king, that all money bills should originate in the lower house.[136] The Lords acknowledged the sole right of the Commons to originate money bills in 1640 in the Short Parliament.[137] The Commons denied the right of the Lords to amend money bills in two resolutions, 1671, and 1678.[138] Sir Matthew Hale mentions that the Lords could amend a money bill by changing the time. A supply bill, or grant of tunnage and poundage for one year, might be

changed by the Lords to two years.[139]   The Commons recognized the right of the Lords to reject a money bill in 1671 and 1689, "to pass all or reject all without dimunition or alteration." [140]   Some of the state constitutions, as New Jersey, Virginia, and South Carolina, followed the British model closely in providing that the bill might be rejected, but not altered.   "These clauses in the Constitutions of the States," said Rutledge of South Carolina, "had been put there through a blind adherence to the British model." [141]   Delaware, Massachusetts, and New Hampshire gave the upper house what the English House of Lords did not have, namely, power to alter or amend money bills.   The convention follows these constitutions for the reasons given above by Madison.[142]

1. *The President's Veto Power.*[143]   Madison, in planning for the new Constitution, had the veto of the King in Council in mind, and says so.[144]   Consequently, we are not surprised to find that the Virginia Plan proposed that the Executive and a convenient number of the national judiciary should act as a council of revision.[145]   This was to be the American King in Council.   Gerry and King objected to the judges acting as a council of revision on the ground that they ought to be able to expound the law when it came "before them free from the bias of having participated in its formation," and that their exposition of the laws which involved the power of deciding on their constitutionality would give them a sufficient check against encroachments on their own department.   Gerry moved and King seconded a resolution proposing to give the executive a negative on any legislative act, unless "afterwards passed by ———— parts of each branch of the national legislature."   The blank was finally filled with "two thirds" and agreed to by the Convention.[146]

Clause three was proposed by Randolph after Madison had failed to secure the words "or resolve" added after the word "bill" with an exception as to votes of adjournment.[147]   Madison's reason for the change was if the President's veto were "confined to bills, it would be evaded by acts under the form and name of resolutions, votes, etc." [148]   Clause three was intended to prevent such evasion of the veto, the purpose of which was: (1) To enable the Executive to defend his rights. (2) To prevent popular, factious, or legislative injustice and encroachments. State experience had proven their checks insufficient.[149] The source was to be found:

(1) *In the state constitutions.* The immediate source was the New York state constitution of 1777. The provision here is almost identical in principle and wording even to the two thirds and ten days requirements.[150] The constitution of Massachusetts, 1780, also contained a provision similar in principle and phraseology to that of New York.[151] About the only difference is that the Governor is required to return the bill within five days instead of ten days as in New York. The Massachusetts provision was suggested by the constitution of New York, while the framers of the Constitution of the United States had both in mind. "Similar powers," said James Wilson, "are known in more than one of the States. The Governors of Massachusetts and New York have a power similar to this, and it has been exercised frequently to good effect." [152] In his draft, he wrote after the clause, "(Massachusetts Constitution of 1780, Ch. I, sec. I, Art. II)." [153] Hamilton regards the constitution of Massachusetts as the source of the suspensive veto of the President.[154]

(2) *In American experience.* (a) Under the Articles of Confederation. Article thirteen of the Articles required the consent of every state legislature to any amendment. So, Rhode Island was able to veto the five per cent amendment of 1781, and New York the Revenue Amendment of 1783, while five states could veto any important act of Congress.[155] Congress begged and prayed the states to give it enough power to enable it to live, but one state by its veto could destroy the union. This bitter experience taught American statesmen to provide that in the future no such veto should stand in the way of needful legislation.

(b) Of the veto of the King in Council and colonial governors. With the exception of the charter colonies of Rhode Island and Connecticut, and the Proprietary colony of Maryland, the King retained power to veto any act of the colonial legislatures, even though the Governor of the colony might approve the law.[156] One colonial grievance was: "He has refused his assent to laws the most wholesome and necessary for the public good. He has forbidden his Governors to pass laws of immediate and pressing importance." [157] In addition, "loud complaints" against the Governors for vetoing acts of the colonial legislatures had been made in all the colonies except Rhode Island and Connecticut where the Governor was elected for one year. This bit of experience was not forgotten by the framers of the state constitutions, hence, only one state constitution gave the Governor veto power—a suspensive veto—the constitution of Massachusetts, 1780. In New York, a suspensive veto was exercised by a council of revision.[157] Doctor Franklin declared that the Governor's negative was constantly used to extort money, and that in Pennsylvania no good law could be passed without making a bargain with the Governor, and it became the regular practice to send orders on the treasury in favor of the Governor along with the bill to be signed, so that he might receive the favor before signing the bill.[158] The result was the suspensive veto in the Constitution of the United States.

(3) *In the colonial charters.* The Ordinance of Virginia, 1621, reserved to the Governor a negative voice.[159] The charter of Massachusetts' Bay, 1691, and the Explanatory Charter of Massachusetts, 1725, contained a similar provision.[160]

(4) *The English Constitution.* The Charter of Pennsylvania, 1681, the Charter of Massachusetts Bay, 1691, and the Charter of Georgia, 1732, provided for sending laws to the King in Council to be approved or disapproved.[161] Madison proposed such a veto "as the King of Great Britain heretofore had," [162] hence the council of revision of the Randolph draft and State of New York. In England, the King originally possessed the right to assent or withhold assent to bills passed by Parliament. Acts of Parliament were drawn up in the form of petitions for laws to which the King assented or dissented, granted or refused to grant the petitions. Elizabeth vetoed forty-eight of the ninety-one bills passed by Parliament in one session.[163] William III made frequent use of his veto.[164] Queen Anne was the last English sovereign to veto a bill—the Scotch Militia Bill, 1707.[165] Due largely to the rise of ministerial responsibility, the veto power became obsolete. In the conflict between Charles the First and his Parliament, he refused his assent to the Militia Bill, and Parliament practically passed it over his veto by transforming it into a Parliamentary ordinance to be enforced without the consent of the Crown.[166]   A. C.

Mason thinks that it may have been this the Massachusetts convention had in mind when the Governor was given a suspensive veto.[167]

2. *The Concurrence of Both Houses Necessary to Legislation.* (1) This principle was of English origin. It goes back for its establishment and recognition to 1318 at least. From that year, the form of legislation runs: "by the assent of the prelates, earls and barons, and the commonality of the realm." [168] So that "no bill is an act of Parliament . . . until both the houses severally have agreed unto it." [169]

(2) Bicameral legislatures were established in the colonies in which the concurrence of both branches was necessary to the enactment of laws. Colonial charters, as Pennsylvania, 1683 and 1701, and the Charter of Massachusetts Bay, 1691, provided for this.[170]

(3) The state constitutions provided for the same thing.

The first state constitution, New Hampshire, 1776, declared: "No act shall be valid unless agreed to and passed by both branches of the legislature." [171] Other state constitutions provided for the same thing.[172] Connecticut, not having a state constitution, passed an act in 1784, which provided: "Any act may be originated by either branch, but not be valid without the concurrence of both." [173] This was simply declaratory of the well-known parliamentary rule.

NOTES TO CHAPTER V

1. Art. I, Sec. 5, ch. 1.
2. Elliot, V. 378, 406.
3. Medley, Eng. Const. Hist. 277. Prothero, Stats. 130.
4. Id. 325-331; Adams and Stephens, Sel. Docs. 324.
5. Medley, 620; Taswell-Langmead, Eng. Const. Hist. 271.
6. Howell St. Tr. 1119; 2 Ventris 37; 2 Salkeld 502; 7 W. III C. 7; Medley, 276.
7. Prothero, Stats. 131.
8. Prothero, Stats. 131.
9. Macdonald, Sel. Charters, 64, 224; Poore, Charters, 1524, 1538.
10. Col. Records of Va. 9-14, 18, Hening, Statutes, I, 378.
11. Poore, Charters, 962, 964, 1285.
12. Id. 273, 1312, 1334, 1543, 1861, 822, 823, 1412.
13. Laws of Conn. 1715. p. 27.
14. Elliot, Debates, V, 378.
15. Poore, Charters, 1910.
16. Poore, Charters, 1334.
17. Poore, Charters, 822, 823, 1311, 963, 964, 1287.
18. Elliot, Debates, V, 430.
19. Id. 406.
20. C. 5, S. 6, McKechnie, Magna Carta, 478.

21. Adams and Stephens, Select Documents of Eng. Const. Hist. 59, 62.
22. Elliot, V, 376.
23. Poore, 1412, 1618, 1622. Fisher, Evolution of the Const. 102.
24. Laws of R. I. 1752. p. 54, Laws of 1730, p. 118, Blackstone, I, 186.
25. Elliot, V, 406.
26. Moore, Am. Eloquence, I, 369. Journals of Congress, I, 233.
27. Elliot, IV, 268, Id. 60, 66.
28. Am. Hist. Leaflets, No. 28, p. 30-31.
29. Poore, 1287. Poore, Charters, 251.
30. Hening, Statutes, I, 532. Bruce, Inst. Hist. of Va. V. I, 464.
31. Feilden, Const. Hist. of Eng. 136.
32. Feilden, Const. Hist. of Eng. p. 70.
33. Laws of R. I. 1717, p. 12. Id. 1776. Id. 1769, 63.
34. Elliot, V. 378; Moore, Am. Eloquence, II, 369.
35. Poore, 963, 1286, 274, 823, 1910, 379.
36. Col. Records of Va. 1-14.
37. Feilden, Constitutional Hist. of Eng. 113.
38. Elliot, V, 378. Poore, 964; 1287, 822.
39. Poore, 251; Bruce, Inst. Hist. of Va. 465-66.
40. Medley, Const. Hist. of Eng. 278.
41. Taswell-Langmead, 386, 380, 477-80; Medley, 278; Prothero, 120, 123-4.
42. Elliot, V, 378, 407; Meigs, Growth of the Const. 316 (III, 12. seq.); Poore, 1861, 1870, 274, 822, 1543.
43. Feilden, Eng. Const. Hist. 117; Medley, 183; Taswell-Langmead 387; Prothero, 136, 592; Medley, 276. See DeLolme Const. of Eng. (1777), pp. 326-7 for three important cases.
44. May, Parliamentary Practice, 55.
45. Poore, Charters and Constitutions, 274, 1543.
46. Art. I, Sec. 5, Cl. 3.
47. Elliot, V, 407.
48. Elliot, V, 408-9.
49. Am. Hist. Leaflets, no. 20, p. 24.
50. Art. IX; Elliot, V, 407.
51. Elliot, V, 407-409.
52. Art. 18.
53. Poore, 1287.
54. Colonial Records of Va.
55. May, Parliamentary Practice, 202.
56. Art. I, Sec. 5, Cl. 4.
57. Id. 46. Blackstone, Com. I, 183; Jefferson Manual I.
58. As. N. Y., Mass.
59. Poore, 1335, 963, 964, 1622.
60. Meigs, Growth of the Constitution, p. 316 (III, 19); Poore, 1335, 1622.
61. MacDonald, Sel. Charters, 181, Id. 222.
62. Elliot, V, 409, 410.
63. Art. I, Sec. 6, Cl. 1.
64. Am. Hist. Leaflet, No. 20, p. 18.
65. Elliot, V, 184, 228, 246, 247, 425-427, 277.
66. Id, 425.
67. Id.
68. Id. 425.
69. Elliot, V, 226.
70. Art. V. Art. 16. Dickinson draft.
71. Poore, 1544.

73. Bruce, Inst. Hist. of Va. II, 435.
74. Id. 435-437.
75. Id. 439. See Laws of R. I. 1719, pp. 1, 2; 1776, 23, 29.
76. Poore, 1534.
77. Macdonald, Sel. Charters, 256.
78. Id. 181.
79. May, Parliamentary Practice, 22.
80. Taswell-Langmead, Eng. Const. Hist. 220, Medley, Eng. Const. Hist. 207.
81. Elliot, V, 378, Meigs, Growth of the Constitution, 316 (III. 14), (IV. 8).
82. Am. Hist. Leaflets, No. 20, p. 18, Elliot, V, 378.
83. Journals of Congress, III, 195.
84. Poore, 822, Id. 964, Id. 1287, Poore, 181, 959, 1283.
85. Laws of R. I. 1719, p. 18. Act of 1666; Acts and Laws of Conn. 1784, p. 28. Statutes of Conn. 1786, p. 28.
86. Hening's Statues, Vol. I, p. 125.
87. Hening's Statutes, V. I, 203, 444, 550.
88. Bruce, Inst. Hist. of Va. V. II, 447.
89. Poore, 251.
90. Poore, 1538.
91. May, Parl. Practice, Ch. V. Taswell-Langmead, Eng. Const. Hist. 261-266; Medley, Eng. Const. Hist. 265-8. Quoted by Blackstone, Commentaries, I, 164, from Sternh, de jure Goth. I: 3, c. 8.
92. May, Parl. Procedure, 103.
93. Id. 103. In fact, all suitors in the shire and hundred courts were protected by the law. Feilden, 68.
94. Stubbs, Sel. Charters, 74; Taswell-Langmead, Eng. Const. Hist. 261.
96. May, Parl. Practice, 104, Taswell-Langmead, 261.
97. May, Parl. Practice, 104.
98. Id. 106-107; Taswell-Langmead, 264-265.
99. Medley, Eng. Const. Hist. 267; Taswell-Langmead, 262.
100. U. S. Const. Art. I, sec. 6, cl. 1.
101. May 96, Taswell-Langmead, 256.
102. Adams and Stephens, p. 224.
103. May, Parl. Practice, 97; Taswell-Langmead, 258; Adams and Stephens 224.
104. Adams and Stephens, 465.
105. Poore, 818, 959. See resolution of Cong. Nov. 12, 1777, adding these privileges to Arts. of Confed., Journals of Cong. II, 324.
106. Of course, this does not mean that the privileges were not well known as working principles of American legislative bodies, Colonial, State and national. As such, they were American as much as British.
107. Art. I. sec. 6, cl. 2.
108. Am. Hist. Leaflets, no. 20. p. 18.
109. Id. 14.
110. Journals of Cong. V. 412, 430-2.
111. Elliot, V. 505.
112. Poore, 824.
113. Poore, 825.
114. Id. 1618, 1624.
115. Id. 1414, 380.
116. Poore, 1543.
117. Id. 1291.
118. Acts and Resolves of R. I. 1780. p. 4. Id. 372.
119. Macdonald, Sel. Charters, 182.

120. Comp. Art. I. Sec. VI. Cl. 2, with sections 24 and 25 of the Place Act.
121. Adams and Stephens, 479, 484, 483.
122. Taswell-Langmead, Eng. Const. Hist. 550.
123. Elliot, V, 373, Id. II, 484, Id. V. 506.
124. Bryce, Am. Commonwealth, V, I, Ch. IX, p. 86.
125. Art. I, sec. 7, cl. 1.
126. Elliot, V, 418.
127. Id. 282.
128. Elliot, V, 274.
129. Poore, 822.
130. Poore, 274.
131. Poore, 1312, 1617, 1624, 1910.
132. Id. 1280, 1287, 964.
133. Elliot, V, 427, 510, 529.
134. Id. III, 376.
135. Medley, Eng. Const. Hist. 237.
136. Adams and Stephens, 175, 176.
137. Feilden, Eng. Const. Hist. 114; Gardiner, Hist. V. IX. 56, 216.
138. Medley, 284.
139. Blackstone, com. I. 190.
140. Taswell-Langmead, 461.
141. Elliot, V, 419.
142. Id. III, 376. See Stats. of Del. I. 34.
143. Art. I, sec. 8, cl. 3.
144. Elliot, V, 121, 108, 128.
145. Id. V, 128.
146. Elliot, V, 151, 154, 155.
147. Id. 431, 535.
148. Id. 431.
149. Id. 538.
150. Poore, 1332.
151. Id. 960.
152. Elliot, II, 472.
153. Am. Hist. Assoc. Rep. 1902, I. 155.
154. Federalist, no. 68, p. 479.
155. Am. Hist. Leaflets, no. 28, pp. 12, 24, 25.
156. A. C. Mason, Veto Power, 17; Woodburn, Am. Republic, 147; Macdonald, Sel. Charters, 187, 211, 243; Decl. of Indep.
157. A. C. Mason, Veto Power, 18, 19.
158. Elliot, v, 154.
159. Bruce, Inst. Hist. of Va. II, 320; Macdonald, Sel. Charters, 36.
160. Poore, 952, 955.
161. Poore, 952, 1512, 372.
162. Elliot, V, 108; IV. 623.
163. Hansard, Series V, 1180, 1182.
164. Medley, Eng. Const. Hist. 319.
165. Id.
166. Gardiner, Documents, no. 50.
167. A. C. Mason, Veto Power, 16.
168. Medley 236, Taswell-Langmead, 217, 221.
169. Prothero, Statutes, 178.
170. Poore, 1528, 1538, 951.
171. Poore, 1280.
172. Poore, 1412, 1617, 1624, 1910, 1862, 960, N. C., S. C., Va., Vt., Mass.
173. Conn. Acts and Laws, 1784, p. 27.

CHAPTER VI

THE ORIGIN OF THE DIVISION OF POWERS IN THE AMERICAN FEDERAL SYSTEM

This originated in the division of powers which existed in practice in the Old Colonial System. The colonists held that their relation to the government of Great Britain was merely a federal relation. John Adams, Lee, and Wythe argued in the Continental Congress on June 8, 1776, that the connection of the Colonies with Great Britain "had been federal only." [1] Madison argued in the Federal Convention, June 29, 1787, that "the States ought to be placed under control of the general government—at least as much so as they formerly were under the King and British Parliament." [2] According to the later American theory of the British Constitution, the Empire was a confederacy "united by a common executive sovereign, but not united by any common legislative sovereign." Massachusetts, New York, Pennsylvania, Virginia, and the other colonies had each its own parliament which had as much power within its territorial limits as the Parliament of Great Britain or Ireland had within the territorial limits of Great Britain or Ireland. The Parliament of New York or Virginia had as much right to pass laws for Great Britain as the Parliament of Great Britain had to enact laws for Virginia or New York. According to the Petition of Right, no taxes can be levied but by common consent in Parliament. The people of America not having any representatives in Parliament to make a part of that common consent, could never, therefore, be taxed by the British Parliament. "They have Parliaments of their own with the right of granting their own money by their own representatives." [3]

Franklin, Jefferson, and Madison state the American theory clearly. Franklin writes: "America is not a part of the dominion of England, but of the King's dominions. England is a dominion itself and has no dominions. . . . Their only bond of union is the King. The British legislature are undoubtedly

81

the only proper judges of what concerns the welfare of that state; the Irish legislature are the proper judges of what concerns the Irish State; and the American legislatures of what concerns the American States respectively." [4]   Jefferson says of the act suspending the legislature of New York, "One free and independent legislature hereby takes upon itself to suspend the powers of another free and independent as itself." [5]   Madison, in his Report on the Virginia and Kentucky Resolutions, says: "The fundamental principle of the revolution was, that the Colonies were coordinate members, with each other, and with Great Britain of an empire united by a common executive sovereign, but not united by any common legislative sovereign. The legislative power was maintained to be as complete in each American Parliament, as in the British Parliament. And the royal prerogative was in force in each colony, by virtue of its acknowledging the King for its executive magistrate, as it was in Great Britain by virtue of a like acknowledgment there. A denial of these principles by Great Britain, and the assertion of them by America, produced the revolution." The British Parliament passed the Declaratory Act in 1766 which asserted that Parliament had power to make laws "to bind the colonies . . . in all cases whatsoever." That is, the act made the British theory of the Empire the supreme law of the Empire, and it was the attempt of George III to enforce that law that "produced the revolution." The British attempt to organize their empire, or solve the problem of imperial organization, had failed.

After the revolution, the Americans had the same old problem on their hands—the problem of imperial organization, and at first they naturally attempted to solve it by applying the American theory of the empire to the problem. Hence, they wrote their theory into the first Constitution of the United States—the Articles of Confederation. Under this, the states retained their "sovereignty, freedom, and independence," and there was no real provision made for "any common legislative sovereign." The Americans failed in their first attempt to solve the imperial problem. The Articles would not work, and this forced American statesmen to frame the Constitution of the United States in 1787. This great instrument provided for "a common legislative sovereign" for certain definite, enumerated objects while the states remained sovereign as to all the powers reserved. This solution was a compromise between the American and British theories and combined the best elements of both. The Supreme Court of the United States has stated this frequently, holding that for purposes of government the states have retained all the powers of the British Crown and Parliament, and may do anything the British Parliament may do unless prohibited from doing it by (1) the Constitution of the United States or (2) by the constitution of the state.[6]

In practice, however, the British Parliament regulated trade with foreign nations and between the different parts of the empire. This was natural, as that part of the empire was the oldest and largest and bore the principal share of the public burdens. The exercise of this regulating power was tacitly acquiesced in by the other parts of the Empire until Great Britain claimed the power to make laws to bind the colonies in all cases whatsoever. Franklin also declared the power to regulate general commerce could nowhere so properly be placed as in the British Parliament.[7] According to the British theory, the colonies were merely settlements for trade purposes under the absolute jurisdiction of Parliament. The question as to whether the American or British theory of the Constitution was correct is of no practical importance now and need not here concern us. It is, however, of vast importance that England, either unconscious of the fact or wilfully refusing to recognize the fact, had built up a composite empire in which in practice there was in operation a very real division of powers between the central or imperial government and the colonial governments. This same division was carried forward through the Albany Plan, Continental Congress, Franklin Draft, Dickinson Draft, and Articles of Confederation into the Constitution of the United States. "Even in the division of authority between the States and national government," says Professor A. C. McLaughlin, "we see a readjustment of the old practical relationship between the Colonies and the mother country."[8] "As they formerly were under the King and British Parliament," the imperial government controlled peace and war, foreign affairs, and all subjects falling within the provinces of international law, such as treaties and admiralty jurisdiction.

Parliament legislated for the whole Empire in matters of general concern. "His majesty's high Court of Parliament is the supreme legislative power over the whole empire," says Samuel Adams over and over again.[9] Imperial defence was in the hands of the general government—the control of the general army and navy and power on the high seas.[10] Indian affairs were partly controlled by the central government, and partly by the Colonies.[11] The post-office was controlled by the central government,[12] which also regulated general commerce,[13] coinage,[14] and whatever of taxation there was through the Post-Office Act and some others.[15] As to the judiciary, the colonial judges were appointed during the pleasure of the crown though dependent on the colonial legislatures for their salaries. Local courts modelled after the English courts retained control of local justice, civil and criminal.[16] The central government had also created for all America a vice-admiralty court acting without juries,[17] while the King in Council formed a supreme court for the Empire to which appeals were carried from the colonies. There was also an imperial citizenship for all the colonies, and a system of common law.[18] The colonies exercised extensive powers of local government, taxing themselves internally, and controlling their own local or internal police, militia, justice, commerce, education, religion, and legislation. We find, therefore, a definitely recognized division of powers established by custom in practical operation between the imperial or central government, and the local or colonial governments, similar to the division of powers under the Articles of Confederation, and the Constitution of the United States. This is shown by the following diagram:

DIVISION OF POWERS UNDER THE OLD COLONIAL SYSTEM

POWERS OF THE IMPERIAL GOVERNMENT	POWERS OF THE COLONIAL GOVERNMENTS
1. Peace and war	1. Local taxation
2. Sending and receiving ambassadors	2. Local justice
3. Treaties and alliances	3. Local militia
4. General commerce	4. Local commerce
5. Coinage	5. Local education
6. Post-office	6. Local religion

POWERS OF THE IMPERIAL GOVERNMENT	POWERS OF THE COLONIAL GOVERNMENT
7. General or imperial army	7. Local police
8. Navy, naval defence and power on high seas	8. Local legislation
9. Indian affairs (in part after middle of 18th century)	9. Elected local officers
10. Legislated on matters of general or Imperial concern	10. Indian affairs (partly)
11. Granted land in royal Colonies	1. The securing of men and money for defence of the empire
12. Was an imperial citizenship	2. Indian affairs and
13. Was a system of common law	3. The founding of new Colonies were unsettled. These were the things that gave trouble in the system.*
14. A Supreme Imperial Court, The King in Council	
15. Naturalization for the Empire	

The British Empire, therefore, consisted of a composite state in which in practice there was a very real division of powers between the central and local governments. If the British government could have legalized the system, given it a fixed, permanent form, and provided for representation of the colonies in Parliament, it would, doubtless, as James Otis said, have firmly united "all parts of the British empire in the greatest peace and prosperity," and have rendered "it unvulnerable and perpetual." [19]   The American Revolution would have been unnecessary because it would have remedied the very defects that brought on the Revolution. The first Assembly of Virginia exercised all the above powers of local government.[20]

The Albany Plan of Union, 1754, was intended to remedy the defects of the Old Colonial System by giving the central government additional powers by systematizing and legalizing the scheme of colonial government, in order that the British Empire might be able to use the whole strength of the Empire in defence of the Empire. This was especially necessary in view of the fact that England foresaw clearly that the Empire was

* See also Professor A. C. McLaughlin Lectures, and the Supreme Court and the Constitution; Beer, Br. Col. Policy, Passim; Munro. Government, p. 57.

about to engage in a struggle with France. The additional powers given the central government were:

(1) *Power to regulate Indian affairs.* It had been found impossible to get the colonies to cooperate properly on this subject, hence, experience dictated the necessity of giving the central government control.

(2) *Power to establish new settlements and make laws for their regulation till formed by the crown into self-governing colonies.*

(3) *Power to make laws, levy taxes, duties, and imposts, enlist men, build forts, and equip a fleet for defence of the colonies.*[21] This was an attempt to remedy the defects of the old colonial system. It was not adopted because the colonies "all thought there was too much prerogative in it, and in England it was judged to have too much of the democratic," said Doctor Franklin. He also declared that, if adopted, the American Revolution would never have occurred. The reason is, it would have been unnecessary because the Plan solved the problem of organizing the empire. It remedied the very defects in the imperial organization that brought on the Revolution, by solving the acute problem of getting men and money for defence of the Empire. The fundamental principle of the division of powers in the Albany Plan was that the colonies retained all power not granted. This passed into the Constitution of the United States and became fundamental in that instrument.

When the Revolution came, Congress took the place of the King and began to take over and exercise all the powers formerly exercised by the British government under the Old Colonial System, leaving the colonies, as before, to exercise the same powers of local government. Congress assumed:

(1) *Control of the Post-Office.* On May 29, 1775, Congress appointed a committee to consider and report on the best means of establishing a postal system. It reported July 25, and Congress then organized a postal system, and appointed Benjamin Franklin Postmaster-General for the United Colonies at a salary of one thousand dollars per year.[22]

(2) *Congress began "to raise and support armies," and assumed control of all military affairs and defence of the United Colonies.* On June 14, 1775, Congress began to raise an army by resolving that six companies of riflemen should be raised

in Pennsylvania, two in Maryland, and two in Virginia to join the army near Boston. The pay of officers and men was fixed, and the army known as the American Continental Army.[23] Congress also drafted and adopted "rules for the government and regulation" of the army.[24] The British military code, the Military Act and the British Articles of War of 1686 were adopted with some modifications, because American troops were already familiar with these.[25] Congress assumed charge of the defence of America, and began to speak of the American army. On June 15, 1775, George Washington was unanimously elected Commander-in-chief by ballot. One Adjutant-General, one Quarter-Master General and other officers were also chosen.[26] On July 18, 1775, Congress recommended to the United Colonies, that all able bodied men between the ages of sixteen and fifty in each colony be formed into regular companies of militia; [27] and on the 21, passed a resolution authorizing General Washington to increase the army in Massachusetts, not to exceed twenty-two thousand men.[28] On June 12, 1776, Congress organized a war office. A Board of War and Ordinance of five members was appointed and their duties prescribed,[29] and on October 17, 1777, Congress created a new Board of War to consist of three members with extensive duties. They were not to be members of Congress.[30] Congress was consciously assuming powers hitherto exercised by the Imperial Government which also had its Articles of War, Board of War and Ordinance Board.[31]

(3) *Congress assumed control of the navy, naval defence, and power on the high seas.* Congress began by fitting out four armed vessels for the defence of the United Colonies, adopted rules for the regulation of the navy, and fixed the pay of officers and men.[32] A naval committee consisting of seven members of Congress was appointed to take charge of the navy, and the seizure of all British vessels carrying stores to the enemy, or used in war against the Colonies was ordered by Congress.[33] Laws were made for the regulation of admiralty courts in prize cases.[34] Letters of marque and reprisal were issued April 3, 1776, signed by the President of Congress.[35] On the same date, Congress issued instructions to the "commanders of private ships or vessels of war, which have commissions or letters of marque and reprisal authorizing them to make cap-

tures of British vessels and cargoes." The inhabitants were authorized to fit out privateers to prey on British commerce, and a Board of Admiralty of five members was established "to superintend the naval affairs of these United States." On December 8, 1779, Congress transferred all matters, referred before to the Marine Committee, to the Board of Admiralty.[36] In 1708, an admiralty Board had been substituted for the office of Lord High Admiral in England.[37] In doing all this, Congress is consciously taking over and doing the things formerly done by the British government for the whole empire under the Old Colonial System.

(4) *Congress emitted bills of credit, borrowed money on the credit of the United States and established a national treasury.* Congress, on June 22, 1775, resolved to issue two millions of dollars in bills of credit in the form of continental currency for the defence of America, and pledged the twelve confederated colonies for their redemption.[38] On July 25, 1775, Congress resolved to emit another million dollars in bills of thirty dollars each, and on November 29, resolved to emit bills to the value of three million dollars, and borrowed five million dollars at four per cent, pledging the faith of the United States for principal and interest, and on December 2, 1777, Congress resolved to direct their commissioners at the Court of France and Spain to endeavor to secure a loan of two millions sterling on the faith of the thirteen United States.[39] Two treasurers were appointed on July 29, 1775, to reside at Philadelphia. The quotas of contribution were divided and assigned to the several colonies. Congress continued to make requisitions on the colonies, as Great Britain did under the Old Colonial System. On February 17, 1776, Congress appointed a standing committee of five to superintend the treasury, and on April 1, 1776, a treasury office of accounts was established, and placed under the control of a committee of five. An Auditor-General was also appointed. Later, a committee appointed for the purpose recommended that a Comptroller, Treasurer, and an Auditor be appointed to conduct affairs of the treasury.[40]

(5) *Congress assumed control of Indian affairs.*[41] Congress created three departments of Indian affairs—a northern, a middle, and a southern department—and on July 11, 1775, appointed commissioners to superintend Indian affairs. Laws

were made for the regulation of Indian trade, and steps taken
to prevent the Indians from being charged exorbitant prices.*
    (6) *Congress assumed control of the external trade of the
colonies.*   On July 11, 1775, Congress appointed Jay, Franklin, Gadsden, Deane, and Lee a committee to devise ways and
means to protect the trade of the colonies.   On October 26,
Congress recommended the provincial assemblies to trade with
the West Indies,[42] and on November 1, resolved that no produce should be exported before March 1, without its permission;
that no rice be exported to the British dominions; and that no
livestock be exported anywhere.   On December 29, 1776, Congress gave Virginia and North Carolina permission to export
produce to any part of the world, except Great Britain, Ireland, Alderney, Guernsey, Jersey, Sark, Man, and the British
West Indies; and on April 6, 1776, passed resolutions for the
regulation of trade in the United Colonies, which threw their
ports open to all the world except Great Britain.   Then on
October 28, 1778, the Committee of Commerce was directed and
empowered by Congress to assume control of the commerce of
the United States;[43] and on December 14, 1778, Congress appointed a new committee of commerce of five members to "conduct the commercial affairs of the United States."[44]   Congress
uses the language of the Navigation Acts, and by adopting
regulations is consciously taking over control of commerce and
assuming the powers formerly exercised by the British government in the regulation of trade for all the colonies.
    (7) *Congress assumed control of foreign affairs.*   As early
as November 29, 1775, Congress had appointed a committee
of five "for the sole purpose of corresponding with our friends
in Great Britain, Ireland and other parts of the world," said
committee to lay their correspondence before Congress, when
directed to do so.[45]   On April 17, 1777, Congress changed the
name "committee of secret correspondence" to "the committee
of foreign affairs."   Thomas Paine was made secretary, and
two additional members were added on May 26, 1777.   Then,
Congress took over the treaty-making power from the crown,
and on February 6, 1778, Franklin, Arthur Lee, and Silas
Deane, as commissioners representing the United States, concluded a treaty with France, or rather one of amity and commerce and another of alliance, which was ratified and declared

binding on all the states of the Union, May 4, 1778.[46]   We
have here a division of powers between Congress, or the central
or revolutionary government of the colonies or states, practically the same as under the Old Colonial System.   Franklin's
Draft reduced the unwritten system under which Congress was
working to the form of a written constitution, July 21, 1775.
The division of powers here was almost identical with that of
the Old Colonial System.   Dickinson's Draft of July 12, 1776,
follows Franklin's Draft, although the latter was in some respects superior to the former.   The division in the Articles
of Confederation was that of the Dickinson Draft, while the
Constitution of the United States adopted the division of powers
contained in the Articles,[47] and added a few powers which
American experience under the Articles had shown to be necessary to provide for the exigencies of government and the preservation of the union.[48]   Certain powers, as the power to tax
and regulate commerce, were withheld from the central government by the Articles.   The states retained these.   Why
should the colonies quarrel and fight with Great Britain over
the power to tax, and then surrender it to a government, which
might be as tyrannical as George III?   That seemed to the
colonies to give up everything for which they had been fight-
ing.   Therefore, it required the bitter experience of Confederation to enlighten and persuade them that it was absolutely necessary to surrender this power to *their* central government, if
the Union was to continue to exist.

When Congress established a post-office, Indian departments, asumed control of the general army and navy, etc., the
colonies had not yet committed themselves to independence, and
Congress had not then decided on the necessity of creating a
new, independent, national government.   The colonists still
looked forward to reconciliation with the mother country, when
the powers they had assumed temporarily would return to the
central government of the Empire.[49]   But when independence
came, the powers Congress had taken over from the government
of Great Britain, temporarily for the conduct of the war, remained in the hands of Congress, and became a permanent part
of the American federal system.   The attempt of the British
to organize the Empire had failed because it brought on the
Revolution.   After the civil war was over, and the Americans

POWERS OF THE CENTRAL GOVERNMENT

EVOLUTION OR STEPS IN THE GROWTH OF THE DIVISION OF POWERS IN THE AMERICAN FEDERAL SYSTEM

Old Colonial System	Albany Plan	Continental Congress	Franklin Draft	Dickinson's Draft	Articles of Confederation	Constitution of United States
Peace and war, etc., as on page 84.	Same as Old Colonial System except that control of 1. Indian affairs. 2. Western lands. 3. Power to tax, raise armies and maintain a navy are given to the central authority.	Takes the place of the British Government, and takes over and exercises practically all the powers of the Albany Plan. It constitutes a revolutionary central government for all the colonies.	Practically the same as in Albany Plan. The expense of wars and general expenses are to be paid out of a common treasury. Each Colony is to levy taxes to pay its allotment in proportion to the number of males in the colony between sixteen and sixty.	Powers are practically the same as in Franklin's Draft and the Old Colonial System, but 1. The power to tax. 2. To regulate general commerce are retained by the States.	Same as in Dickinson's Draft.	Practically the same as in Articles of Confederation except that several additional powers are given Congress which experience had shown to be necessary, and among these were: 1. Power to tax. 2. Power to regulate general commerce.

had won their independence, the same old problem—the problem of imperial organization [50]—remained in American hands unsolved. Their first attempt—the Articles of Confederation —also failed, because "they constituted a government which should have the power which they had contended belonged to the British government, and no more." [51] Such a government could not long exist. The division of powers, withholding both the power to tax and regulate trade, was too imperfect. The second attempt of the Americans to solve the problem succeeded—the Constitution of the United States. The development from the Old Colonial System to the Federal Constitution is traced in the diagram on page 91. It is unnecessary to insert the powers of the colonial or state governments, as, in general, they remain the same throughout the period. There are, of course, some additions at the Revolution, such as the transfer from the crown to the people, in their right of sovereignty of title to all lands within the state. [52]

NOTES TO CHAPTER VI

1. Elliot, I, 57, 58; Jefferson, Writings, I, 10. Am. Eloquence, I. 365.
2. Elliot, I, 462.
3. Franklin, Works IV. 441.
4. Id.
5. Summary View, Am. Hist. Leaflets, no. 11, p. 10, 14, 19. The recent British Imperial Conference practically adopted the American theory as the theory of the existing empire. Pol. Sc. Rev. May 1927, p. 377.
6. Elliot, Debates, IV. 562; 2 Dallas, 419, 4 wh. 316; 94 U. S. 113; 3 Dall. 54; McClain cases, 947.
7. Works, III, 21, 238; Const. of Md. 1776, preamble. Poore, Charters, 817 Const. Ga. 1777. Id. 377; Const. S. C. 1776. Id. 1615.
8. Confederation and Constitution, 275.
9. S. Adams, Works II. 185, 197. See also Cooley, Const. Law, Chap. I. Jas. Otis, Rights of the Colonies, 33. Franklin, Works IV. 709 seq.
10. Beer, British Colonial Policy, 7, 10, 11, 200, Mass. Circ. Letter.
11. Beer, Br. Col. Policy, 10, 253, 254.
12. For history of the Colonial post-office, see Am. Hist. Rev. Jan. 1916. The Colonial Post-Office by William Smith.
13. Farrand, Records III, 522.
14. Beer, British Colonial Policy, 307.
15. Id. 31-36, 162-3, 284-5, Am. Hist. Rev. The Col. Post-Office, Smith, Jan. 1916.
16. Beer, BR. Col. Policy, 188.
17. Id. 289. Col. Statutes. passim.
18. Poore, 255, 374, 930, 940, 950, 1380, 1385, 1602, 1891.
19. Otis, Rights of the Colonies. 65.
20. Brown, First Republic in America, 320.
21. Macdonald, Sel. Charters, 254. Franklin, Wks. III, 35-65.

22. Journals of Congress I, 102; Elliot, Debates, I, 46, 49.   Dr. Franklin had been Deputy Postmaster-General under the old Colonial system before the Revolution.
23. Journals of Con. I, 110, 111.
24. Id. 111, 120, II, 343.
25. Brig.-Gen. Geo. B. Davis, A Treatise on the Milit. Law of the U. S. 3, 4.
26. Journals of Cong. I, 118, 119, 150, 117, 111-112, 112-113.
27. Id. 158.
28. Id. 162.
29. Id. II, 198, 199.
30. Journals of Cong. III, 351.
31. Medley, Eng. Const. Hist. 483, 484.
32. Journals of Cong. I, 203, 211-212, 244, 249.
33. Id.
34. Journals of Cong. I, 203, 204, 255, 256, 260, 211, 277, 242.
35. Journals of Cong. II, 102.
36. Id. 102, 114.   Id. V. 447.
37. Medley, Eng. Const. Hist. 490.
38. Journals of Cong. I. 117, 118.
39. Journals of Cong. I, 165, 254.   Id. II, 374.   Id. III, 431.
40. Journals of Cong. I, 173, 174.   Id. II. 64, 109, 115, 119.   Journals of Congress (Ford. Ed), XI, 780.
41. Hart, Actual Government, 359.
* The British government in 1756 had organized two departments, a Northern and a Southern, and had appointed as agents, Sir William Johnson for the Northern Indians, and Edmund Atkin for the Southern.   Beer, British Colonial Policy, p. 254.
42. Journals of Congress, I, 151; Id. II, 44, 147; Id. I, 152, 209.
43. Journals of Congress I, 212-213, 288; Id. II, 117-118; Id. IV, 622.
44. Journals of Cong. IV, 712.
45. Journals of Cong. I, 254, II, 159, III, 66, 113, 164.
46. Id. IV. 256, XI, 418, XII, 256, 257.   C. H. Butler, The Treaty-Making Power of the United States, 260-261.
47. Franklin gave regulation of "general Commerce" to Congress, Dickinson to the States.
48. Federalist, 39; Elliot, II, 482; Am. Hist. Leaflets, no. 20.
49. Poore, 1279, 1314, 1329, 1617, 1620.   Franklin's Draft Arts. V. and XIII; Const. of N. Y. 1777, Preamble.
50. A. C. McLaughlin, Confed. and Constitution, Chap. III.
51. Edward Channing, Student's Hist. of U. S. 239.
52. Const. N. Y. I. 10.

CHAPTER VII

☊The Powers of Congress

1. *Congress is "to lay and collect taxes, duties, imposts, and excises."* (Art. I, Sec. 8, cl. 1.) Charles Pinckney's draft seems to have provided for this.[1] The report of the committee of detail submitted August 6, by Rutledge, provided that Congress should exercise the above powers.[2] The sources are to be found:

(1) *In American experience under the Articles of Confederation.* Under the Articles, Congress had no power to raise revenue to pay the debt, interest on the debt, civil service, foreign representatives, or even the army.[3] To such straits was Congress reduced that early in January, 1783, Robert Morris, Superintendent of Finance, informed Congress that "further drafts were indispensable to prevent a stop in the public service," and he actually proposed to draw on such "contingent funds" as a loan John Adams was instructed to secure, and "the friendship of France." He declared "that the last account of our money affairs in Europe showed that . . . there were three and a half millions of livres short of the bills actually drawn."[4] Dyer opposed the proposition as dishonorable, but consented on being told it was either that, or the public credit would be stabbed abroad and the public service would be wrecked at home, and the very existence of the nation endangered.[5] James Wilson of Pennsylvania defended the giving of this power to Congress on the ground that without it, they must again compel their friends in Europe to advance the money to the United States to enable the country to pay them the interest on their own loans. "This," he said, "was actually the case in Holland last year."[6] This shameful condition which compelled the United States to borrow money from their creditors to enable the government to pay them the interest on their own loans, was entirely due to the fact that Congress had no power of taxation, direct or indirect. The only means

94

at the disposal of Congress was to use the old colonial method to supply the treasury of the United States, namely, make requisitions on the states, but experience had proved that the states "shamefully neglected to pay their quotas," and that "no dependence could be placed on such requisitions." [7] On February 3, 1786, a committee reported to Congress that experience had evinced that requisitions had failed, that it would be impolitic, if not impossible, to borrow more, and that the emission of paper bills of credit would be altogether ineffectual and inadmissible and that unless some other more efficient and productive fund can be found "we shall suffer the highest national difficulties." [8] So requisitions failed as a source of revenue. Bankruptcy and disunion threatened the United States, and as a result several attempts were made to amend the Articles of Confederation, to place in the hands of Congress the means of securing a permanent revenue. These failed, due to the selfishness of Rhode Island and New York,[9] who refused their assent. Money could not be borrowed under such circumstances. In the spring of 1783, the Count of Vergennes wrote to the President of Congress and "sundry members urging the necessity of establishing permanent revenues for paying our debts and supporting a national character," and said no one could be found who would risk lending money to the United States under the circumstances.[10] Neither could more paper money be issued, as it was worthless. Jefferson says "one thousand dollars was worth about one dollar." [11] So, bitter and humiliating experience taught Americans that power to tax for the purpose of securing a steady, permanent revenue must be given to Congress, or the Union would be dissolved. American experience dictated the provision. Further, experience had taught the necessity of giving Congress this power for the purpose of regulating trade, encouraging commerce, and manufactures, and securing reciprocal commercial advantages from other nations.[12]

(2) *State, colonial, and English precedents.* The Constitution of Massachusetts gave the legislature power to levy taxes, duties, and excises.[13] New York and Pennsylvania had also levied excise duties. The terms were in common use in the statutes of Pennsylvania. "Imposts" is used in the Act of 1700, and "excises" appears in the Statutes of 1712.[14] The com-

mittee of detail simply gave Congress a power already exercised by the state governments.

In the colonies, the Albany Plan of Union, 1754, proposed to give the general government power to levy taxes, duties, and imposts.[15] In 1646, the General Court of the Colony of New Plymouth passed a law imposing an excise on wines and tobacco.[16] Massachusetts levied excise duties on many articles, both before and after the Revolution under the Articles of Confederation.[17] In New York, formerly a Dutch colony, we should naturally expect to find excises. In June, 1629, the West India Company granted the colonists of the Patroons in New Netherland, freedom from customs, taxes, excise, and imposts for ten years.[18] The Director and Council of New Netherland, June 21, 1644, passed an ordinance levying an excise on beer, wine, brandy, and beavers for the purpose of raising money to pay the soldiers. On August 4, 1644, a similar ordinance was passed. Additional excises were imposed from time to time till 1656, when an excise was levied on slaughtered cattle, hogs, goats, and sheep, for the purpose of preventing the Indians from stealing, slaughtering, and selling the stock of the colonists.[19] A curious instance of the use of the excise is found on November 21, 1661, when the Director General of New Netherland passed an ordinance levying an excise on beer, wine, and brandy for one year at Esopus for the purpose of raising money to help to pay for the building of the minister's house at Wiltwyck. "From every tun of strong Beer" was to be levied "four guilders. From a hogshead of French Wine, sixteen guilders. From an anker of Spanish Wine . . . Brandy or distilled liquors . . . six guilders." [20] Therefore, when New Netherland passed into the hands of the English in 1664, excises already held a prominent place in the revenue system of the Province; and excises were also levied after the territory passed under English control. On May 15, 1699, an excise act was passed by the New York Assembly, imposing excise duties on liquors, the first of many such acts in New York.[21] The trading classes, who controlled the middle colonies, favored excises as the best method of taxation. Pennsylvania passed an act in 1700 levying an excise on ale, cider, beer, and wine. This was followed by many similar acts.[22] Taxation was a sovereign right, and the phraseology of the clause was common in the states where excises existed in 1787. In fact, all the terms—taxes, duties, imposts and excises—are to be found in the freedoms and exemptions granted by the West India Company in 1629, to the Colonists of New Netherland,[23] and in the Statutes of Pennsylvania.[24]

In England, an excise was first proposed by Pym in March, 1643, but rejected because of its unpopularity. The need of money was so urgent, however, as to overcome all objections, and Parliament passed an excise ordinance, July 21, 1643.[25] The English borrowed the idea from Holland, and levied the excise on ale, cider, beer, starch, and other articles.[26] In 1660, the English Parliament passed the Act Abolishing Relics of Feudalism, and Fixing an Excise, which levied an excise on ale, beer, cider, mead, aquæ vitæ, chocolate, tea, coffee, and other articles and turned the revenue over to the King in return for his surrender of the right of purveyance and feudal dues.[27] Justice Chase in Hylton v. U. S., 1796, said: "The term duty is the most comprehensive next to the general term tax; and practically in Great Britain (whence we take our general idea of taxes, duties, imposts, excises, customs, etc.) embraces taxes on stamps . . ."[28] Excises, borrowed from Holland by the English, became part of the English system, and were almost immediately transferred to the American Colonies.

2. *Taxes Are to Be Levied by Congress, the Representative Body of the Nation.* The political theory of the Revolution was that no taxes could "be imposed on them but with their own consent, given personally, or by their representatives."[29] In the Massachusetts Circular Letter, this is laid down as "an essential unalterable right in nature," and a fundamental law of the British Constitution "that what a man has honestly acquired is absolutely his own, which he may freely give, but cannot be taken from him without his consent."[30] This is the language of Locke's Civil Government.[31] The principle was embodied in the state constitutions of Massachusetts, 1780, Virginia, Maryland, Pennsylvania, and North Carolina, 1776, Vermont, 1777 and 1786, and New Hampshire, 1784.[32] The Constitution of the United States follows the political theory of John Locke, the Revolution, and the state constitutions.

The colonial governments controlled taxation, and the principle goes back to Magna Carta or even beyond that. All taxation required the consent of the Witan, as Danegeld first levied in A.D. 991. Magna Carta provided that no aid or scutage should be imposed, but by the common consent of the kingdom.[33]   Sir Edward Coke shows that duties were first granted to Edward I by the English Parliament in 1275.[34] An impost of three pence on the pound was granted him in the thirty-first year of his reign on the imports and exports of all foreign merchants.[35]   In 1295, Edward summoned representatives of the whole nation to meet in Parliament, because he recognized that taxation could be imposed only with the approval of those taxed. He quoted Justinian: "Quod omnes similiter tangit ab omnes approbetur," which expressed the theory of the English Constitution then as now.[36]   The Confirmatio Cartarum, 1297, expressly recognized the principle. This confirmed and fixed the right of taxation by Parliament alone as a principle of the English Constitution, and made all unparliamentary taxation illegal.   In spite of this, English Kings, as James I and Charles I, continued to levy illegal taxation.   The Petition of Right, 1628, prohibited that; and the Bill of Rights, 1689, declared all levying of money without Parliament illegal.[37]   This principle was transferred to the colonies and state constitutions, and is one of the great fundamental principles of the English Constitution.

3. *Congress Is Empowered to Levy Taxes "to pay the debts and provide for the common defence and general welfare of the United States."*   This states the purpose of the power to tax. It is power to *levy taxes* for the general welfare that is given to Congress, not power to do anything for the general welfare.

This clause was suggested by Sherman in Convention "for the object of the old debt."[38]   The Convention disagreed to it, but the committee of eleven recommended the same thing in their report of September 4th, which was agreed to nem. con.[39] The clause was suggested to Sherman and the committee by Article VIII of the Articles of Confederation.[40]   Sherman and Ellsworth in a letter to Governor Huntington, September 26, 1787, say: "The objects for which Congress may apply moneys are the same mentioned in the eighth article of the Confederation, viz., for the common defence and general welfare, and for the payment of debts incurred for those purposes."[41]   Madison, in a letter to Andrew Stevenson, November 17, 1830, says the phraseology was copied or borrowed from the eighth Article of the Articles of Confederation, and is "used in one instrument as in the other." [42] Article VIII goes back to Dickinson's Draft,[43] while this in its turn, is indebted to Articles II and VI of Franklin's Draft.[44]

4. *"All duties, imposts and excises shall be uniform."* McHenry and General Pinckney offered the proposition, which became the clause in the Constitution. It was referred to a committee of eleven which reported August 28, and was agreed to August 31, nem. con.[44] The committee on style omitted the clause, and Gouverneur Morris recalled it by offering a motion on September 14. Doctor Witherspoon on February 3, 1781, had moved in Congress that duties and imposts be uniform throughout the United States. The resolution was rejected.[45] *American experience* was responsible for that proposal and for this clause in the Constitution. No uniform system of duties, imposts, and excises existed in the states under Confederation. Every state was a law unto itself, with the result that in some states the duty on an article would be very low, while the duty on the same article in another state would be outrageously high. The table on page 100 shows by comparison this conflicting system of duties on tea, coffee, and sugar.

The depressing effect of this conflicting and exasperating system of duties on trade is quite obvious. There was also a complicated and conflicting system of ad valorem duties ranging from one per cent in Pennsylvania,[46] to twenty-five per cent in Rhode Island.[47] The specific duties on many other articles were as conflicting as in case of tea, coffee, and sugar. The vexations, heartburnings, and difficulties of trade under so many different, discriminating, and conflicting systems of duties were extremely many. In addition, discriminating tonnage duties also existed. The laws of Virginia classed all vessels from other states as vessels from "foreign ports," and levied a duty of one shilling and three pence per ton on all vessels from other states of the Union entering the ports of Virginia. Virginia passed an act in 1783 repealing an act imposing tonnage on Virginia vessels, and granting exemption from such duties to vessels of sixty tons burthen from Maryland. In 1786, Vir-

TEA

State	Duty	Date
New York........	4d. per lb.........	Act of 1784 [1]
Virginia..........	6d. per lb.........	Act of 1786 [2]
Virginia..........	2s. per lb.........	Act of 1787 [3]
Virginia..........	1s. per lb. (Bohea)	Act of 1787
Pennsylvania......	1d. per lb. (Bohea)	Act of 1780 [4]
Pennsylvania......	6d. per lb.........	Act of 1780
Pennsylvania......	1s. per lb.........	Act of 1782 [5]
Pennsylvania......	2d. per lb. (Bohea)	Act of 1782
Pennsylvania......	2d. per lb.........	Act of 1785 [6]
Pennsylvania......	6d. per lb. (Hyson)	Act of 1785
Rhode Island......	3d. per lb. (Bohea)	.... [7]
Rhode Island......	1s. per lb.........	....

COFFEE

State	Duty
New York........	1d. per lb. [8]
Virginia..........	1d. per lb. [9]
Pennsylvania......	1s. per 100 lbs. in 1780 [10]
Pennsylvania......	2s. per 100 lbs. in 1782
Rhode Island.....	1d. per lb. [11]

LOAF SUGAR

State	Duty
New York........	3d. per lb. [12]
Virginia..........	4s. 2d. per hundred [13]
Pennsylvania......	1s. 6d. per hundred, Act 1780 [14]
Pennsylvania......	3s. per hundred, by Act of 1782
Pennsylvania......	2d. per lb., by Act of 1783
Rhode Island......	2d. per lb. in 1783 [15]
Rhode Island......	3d. per lb. in 1785

[1] Laws of N. Y., Vol. 1, p. 599.
[2] Hening, Statutes, 12, p. 289.
[3] Id. 414.
[4] Statutes at Large of Pa., 10, 253.
[5] Id., Vol. 11, p. 9.
[6] Id., Vol. 12, p. 100.
[7] R. I. Colonial Records, Vol. 9, p. 666.
[8] Laws of N. Y., Vol. 1, p. 599.
[9] Hening, Statutes, Vol. 10, p. 511; Vol. 11, p. 122.
[10] Statutes at Large, Vol. 10, p. 253.
[11] R. I. Col. Records, Vol. 9, p. 666.
[12] Laws of N. Y., Vol. 1, p. 599.
[13] Hening, Statutes at Large; or Pa., Vol. 10, p. 253; Vol. 11, p. 9–68.
[14] Statues at Large, Vol. 10, p. 253.
[15] R. I. Col. Records, Vol. 9, p. 666; Vol. 10, p. 115.

ginia imposed a tax of one shilling on every seaman entering a harbor of the state.[48] The American people had had enough of this. For the United States to possess the power of levying such duties would be discriminating, oppressive, and destructive of trade, therefore, to remedy existing evils and safeguard the future, duties shall be uniform throughout the United States.

Congress Is Authorized "to borrow money on the credit of the United States." (Art. I, Sec. 8, cl. 2.) This clause originated in the committee of detail which reported the provision on August 6. It also contained the words, "and emit bills," after "money." To prohibit Congress from issuing paper money, and to win the moneyed class to the support of the Constitution, this clause was stricken out, and the clause for borrowing money agreed to nem. con. The committee on style then readded the words "on the credit of the United States." [49] The sources are:

(1) *The Articles of Confederation.* The articles gave Congress power "to borrow money . . . on the credit of the United States," if nine states consented. The Dickinson Draft gave Congress the same power in the same words. The Continental Congress borrowed money on the credit of the United Colonies.[50]

(2) *England after the Revolution of 1688.* English Kings borrowed money from Italian and Jewish bankers. Edward III repudiated his debt in 1345. Charles II did the same in 1672, although he had promised interest at six per cent which was paid till repudiation. Owing to expensive wars, the debt increased so rapidly after 1688 that it was not deemed advisable to levy taxes sufficient to pay the annual expenses for fear the people might revolt. The expedient was then adopted of borrowing money for the state, and then levying taxes enough to pay the interest on the debt, which was then converted into property capable of being transferred as shares from one person to another. This policy laid the foundation of the national debt. The system originated in 1344, in Florence. The Florentine government finding itself unable to pay £60,000, formed the principal into "an aggregate sum" called "a mount or bank," "the shares whereof were transferable like our stocks with interest at five per cent." [51]

1. *"To regulate commerce."* (Art. I, Sec. 8, cl. 3.)

The clause originated in the committee of detail. If, as his speeches seem to show, Charles Pinckney's draft contained the provision found in his plan, the committee of detail appears to have used this provision with the change of a single word.[52] Madison on August 18, submitted a proposition, "To regulate affairs with the Indians," to be referred to the committee of detail.[53] The committee reported August 22, but no action was taken, and the committee on postponed and unfinished portions recommended the addition of the words, "and with the Indian tribes," which was agreed to nem. con.[54] The sources are to be found:

(1) *In American experience under the Articles of Confederation.* The Federal Convention was called to remedy defects in those Articles, and experience had proven that lack of power to regulate commerce was one of the greatest weaknesses. Article IX practically prohibited Congress from making any commercial treaty that would interfere with the power of the states to regulate trade as they pleased.[55] Great Britain, correctly enough, did not believe the United States could make any treaty of commerce that would bind all the states, and, therefore, determined to deal with the United States as a collection of rival, hostile trading states. In July, 1783, American shipping was shut out of the West Indies by an order-in-council, so that in April, 1784, Congress said: "Great Britain" has "adopted regulations destructive of our commerce with her West India Islands." [56] An Act of Parliament of 1784 prohibited Americans from trading with Newfoundland.[57] Other nations prohibited American vessels from entering their ports and imposed heavy duties on American products. American trade was paralyzed, and Congress was absolutely powerless to protect American commerce, to command reciprocal trade advantages, or to withhold them for the purpose of securing advantages in return, to impose retaliatory duties, or to prohibit foreign vessels from entering American ports. "Our whole commerce is going to ruin," said Dawes in the Massachusetts convention. "Congress has not had the power to make even a trade law, which shall confine the importation of foreign goods to the ships of the producing or consuming country." [59] "For want of this power in our national head," said Samuel Adams, "our friends are grieved, and our enemies insult us. Our am-

bassador at the Court of London is considered as a mere cipher, instead of as the representative of the United States." [60]   Any commercial treaty made by the United States might be reduced to a nullity by the perverse action of a single state.[61]   The carrying trade, commerce, agriculture, and manufactures of the United States declined, so that bitter experience taught the American people "that a power to remedy this defect should be given to Congress, and the remedy applied as soon as possible." [62]

(2) *Another defect was the lack of uniformity in the commercial regulations of the United States.*   The states could not act together, were hostile, and no uniformity existed in duties, imposts, and excises.   Laws for the regulation of trade were frequently flatly contradictory.   Some states taxed the goods of other states and greatly irritated their neighbors.   Connecticut taxed the imports of Massachusetts.   Rhode Island taxed her neighbors.   New York, New Jersey, Pennsylvania, and Maryland passed navigation laws which treated the citizens of the other states of the Union as aliens.[63]   The laws of Maryland, in violation of the Articles of Confederation,[64] granted exclusive privileges to her own vessels, yet all Congress could do was to recommend the contrary.   Virginia did the same thing.[65]   New York, Pennsylvania, Virginia, and South Carolina "taxed and irritated the adjoining States trading through them." [66]   A New York law of 1785 imposed on all wares and merchandise brought into the state from Rhode Island, Connecticut, New Jersey, and Pennsylvania, the same duties as were imposed on goods imported in British ships, or ships owned by British subjects, unless they could prove to the satisfaction of the collector that the goods had not been taken into their state by a British ship.   Goods brought into New York in British, or British-owned ships paid double duty.[67]   Charles Pinckney declared that the navigation laws and other commercial regulations passed to remedy the existing evils, only made them worse by interfering with each other, and in almost every case with treaties existing under the Union.[68]   Partial and iniquitous laws, Davie said, had ruined the commerce of North Carolina and many other states.[69]   On June 25, 1778, Congress declared "that the sole and exclusive power of regulating the trade of the United States with foreign nations ought to be

clearly vested in the Congress." [70]   The Commerce Amendment
of April 30, 1784, proposing to give Congress power to pass
navigation laws was rejected by the states.[71]   Monroe's proposal on Commerce giving Congress power to regulate trade,
was discussed in Congress, July 13-14, 1785, but no action
taken.[72]   The commercial interests and prosperity of the United
States were being utterly destroyed.   Therefore, the Convention remedied the defect by giving Congress the above power.[73]
Madison says the clause grew out of the abuse of power by the
importing states in taxing the non-importing, "and was intended
as a negative and preventive provision against injustice among
the States themselves." [74]

(3) *Other pre-convention sources.*   The principle was to
be found in many documents of the period, suggested in some
cases by the defects in the Articles of Confederation.   It is
found in Madison's outline of a constitution in his letter to
Jefferson, March 19, 1787, to Washington, April 16, and to
Randolph, April 8, and in Monroe's proposal on commerce,
March 28, 1785; the Report on Trade and Revenue, August
14, 1786, in Pelatiah Webster's Scheme, 1783, and in the New
Jersey resolution of 1778.   The Franklin Draft made provision for the regulation of general commerce by Congress,[75]
while the Continental Congress had actually exercised control
over trade, taking over power from the central government of
the Empire under the Old Colonial System.   This was the real
origin.

2. *"And with the Indian tribes."*   The Articles of Confederation gave Congress power to regulate "the trade," and
manage "all affairs with the Indians not members of any of
the States, provided that the legislative right of any State
within its own limits be not infringed or violated."   This was
an expansion of the Article in Dickinson's Draft.   Franklin's
Draft also gave regulation of Indian affairs to Congress.   The
Continental Congress assumed control of Indian affairs early
in its history.[76]   The Albany Plan, 1754, gave regulation of
Indian affairs and Indian trade to the President and Grand
Council.[77]   Under the Old Colonial System, Indian affairs had
been controlled partly by the colonial governments, and partly
by the Imperial government.   This was found to work badly
in practice, because when an Indian uprising threatened one

colony, the colonies remote from the scene of danger cared little about the matter, and felt no need of giving aid or cooperating with their sister colonies in the danger zone. It was found impossible to get the colonies to cooperate properly, hence, this experience led Doctor Franklin to give control of Indian affairs to the central government in his Albany Plan. "The real basis of the whole Indian system is the precedent of government control in Colonial and Revolutionary times." [78]

1. *"To establish an uniform rule of naturalization."* (Art. I, Sec. 8, cl. 4.) The Pinckney, and Patterson, or New Jersey Plans contained a provision for a uniform rule of naturalization.[79] The clause was reported by the committee of detail August 6, and adopted on August 16th.[80] This provision originated in American experience of the many conflicting laws of naturalization in operation among the states. Under Confederation, Congress lacked power to regulate naturalization throughout the union. The want of uniformity was severely felt, and caused the members of the Federal Convention to adopt a provision giving Congress power to adopt a uniform rule.[81] In New York, for example, an alien might be naturalized by means of a legislative act for the purpose, taking an oath of allegiance to the state, and renouncing allegiance to any foreign prince or state "in all matters ecclesiastical as well as civil." [82] In Pennsylvania, a man could become a citizen by taking the oath of allegiance to the state, and renouncing allegiance to George III, his heirs and successors.[83] In Virginia, an alien could become a citizen by going before a court of record, and declaring on oath his intention to reside in the state, and taking an oath of fidelity to the commonwealth. But this Act of 1783, disabled such citizens from being elected or appointed to office legislative, executive, or judicial, until they had acquired an actual residence in the state of two years after taking the oaths, "or until they have evinced a permanent attachment to the State by having intermarried with a citizen of this commonwealth, or a citizen of any other of the United States, or purchased lands to the value of one hundred pounds therein." [84] An act of 1786 disabled naturalized citizens for five years.[85] That is, the laws of one state naturalized an alien, while by the laws of another state, he was incapacitated, and incapable of holding office, while at the same time he was entitled to all

the privileges and immunities of citizens in every other state.[86] As soon as admitted to citizenship in Pennsylvania or New York, the alien became entitled to citizenship rights in all the states, but at the same time, he was denied those rights by the laws of Virginia and other states.[87]   Each state retained "the very improper power" "of naturalizing aliens in every other State.   In one State, residence for a short time confers all the rights of citizenship; in another, qualifications of greater importance are required.   An alien, therefore, legally incapacitated for certain rights in the latter, may, by previous residence only in the former, elude his incapacity; and thus the law of one State be preposterously rendered paramount to the law of another, within the jurisdiction of the other." [87]   In some states, the residence qualification which enabled an alien to hold any office, would not in other states even entitle him to vote at elections.[88]   This jumble of contradictory laws on the subject of naturalization soon led to embarrassment and complaints, when citizenship began to be transferred from state to state.[89]   It was open to any citizen interdicted by the laws of one state, to secure citizenship in another state, and then assert his rights of citizenship in the state which proscribed him.[90]   This was also a dangerous situation, which might at any time embroil the United States in a foreign war.   Davie of North Carolina cited a case in the state convention, where a vessel and cargo belonging to some Holland merchants, was stolen by a man who then sought refuge in Rhode Island.   The minister of the United Netherlands demanded his surrender as a citizen of Holland.   In the meantime, the thief had taken the oath of allegiance to Rhode Island, and had become, thereby, a citizen of that state.   The demand was refused, and Rhode Island protected the pirate in his villainy in spite of Holland's desire to punish him for his crime.[91]   This lack of uniformity was severely felt, and a uniform law ought to be recommended to the states, Madison declared on August 27, 1782.[92]   The charters provided for a common, imperial citizenship, and English or Imperial citizens were created by the central government of the Empire, by letters patent or Act of Parliament.[93]   A foreigner serving two years in the English navy, all foreign Protestants, serving for two years as soldiers in the colonies or whale fisheries, and Jews and Protestants re-

siding for seven years in the colonies, could on taking the oaths
of allegiance and abjuration, or making an affirmation, be naturalized.[94]   The colonies admitted to colonial citizenship by
act of the legislature.[95]   After the Revolution, the states continued to naturalize aliens, and naturalization by the central
government disappeared though the earlier common citizenship rendered "intercitizenship in the Federation inevitable." [96]
The failure of this method of naturalization under Confederation forced American statesmen to give the regulation of naturalization to the central government as under the Old Colonial
System.

2. *A Uniform Bankruptcy Law.*   On August 16, while
Article 16 of the report of the committee of detail was under
discussion, Charles Pinckney moved to submit a proposition
with Article 16, proposing "to establish uniform laws upon the
subject of bankruptcies," which was done.   The committee reported September 1, recommending the addition of the clause,
and this was agreed to on September 3rd.[97]   The clause originated in American experience.   Under Confederation, the want
of a uniform bankruptcy law was, says Madison, severely felt
by the people of the several states, and the establishment of
such a law would prevent many frauds "where the parties or
their property may lie or be removed into different states." [98]
The states had their own bankruptcy laws, as South Carolina,
Pennsylvania, and New York, 1784.[99]   Pennsylvania also passed
a number of special acts for the relief of insolvent debtors
named in the acts, and a stringent law was enacted in 1785.
The state constitution also provided that "the person of a
debtor, where there is not a strong presumption of fraud, shall
not be continued in prison, after delivering up, bona fide, all
his estate, real and personal, for the use of his creditors, in
such manner as shall be hereafter regulated by law." [100]   This
principle of the bankruptcy law of the times was as old as the
bankruptcy law of Julius Caesar.   To protect their citizens,
Virginia and North Carolina found it necessary to pass laws
to prevent debtors from leaving the state for the purpose of
defrauding their creditors.[101]   Therefore, experience of the
difficulties, and of the absolute inability of the states to prevent
fraud under the existing state laws, led the Convention to give
regulation of bankruptcy laws to Congress.   In 1787, bank-

ruptcy and insolvency had different meanings in English law, the former being applied to the case of a trader who had committed fraud upon his creditors. They might then institute proceedings against him to have him declared a bankrupt and his property taken and distributed to pay his debts. In such a case, the trader or merchant might be discharged from further liability or be imprisoned as they thought best. Insolvency was used to describe a debtor, who was not a merchant or trader, who, to secure a discharge from liability for his debt, might surrender his property to his creditors in payment of his debt. This distinction never obtained in the colonies or United States.[102] The uniformity provided for is a geographical uniformity. That is, laws equally applicable to all the states. This was what American experience dictated as necessary to solve their problem. The foundation of American bankruptcy law was the law of Henry VIII, 1542, followed by the laws of 1570, 1706, and 1755. The laws of New York, 1755, and Rhode Island, 1756, were copied almost verbatim from the law of 1755.[103]

1. *The Currency.* (Art. I, Sec. 8, cl. 5.) Pinckney's Plan appears to have contained this provision.[104] On August 6, the committee of detail reported three propositions.

"To coin money.
"To regulate the value of foreign coin.
"To fix the standard of weights and measures." [105]

The Convention agreed to these on August 16. The committee on style wove the three propositions into one sentence and inserted "thereof." This provision finds its source in the Articles of Confederation, which gave the exclusive right to Congress to coin money and regulate the value thereof.[106] The power to regulate the value of foreign coin was not given. Charles Pinckney also had the Articles of Confederation in mind.[107] The Dickinson Draft gave Congress the same power, while the Franklin Draft gave Congress the power of regulating "general Currency." [108] Alexander Hamilton had pointed out in his Resolutions for a General Convention that the Articles of Confederation were defective "in granting the United States the sole power of regulating the alloy and value of coin struck by their own authority, or by that of the respective states, without the power of regulating the foreign coin in circulation." The Federalist points out that this would destroy the proposed uniformity in the value of the coin which would be subjected to the different regulations of the several states. It might circulate at par in one state, and be of little or no value in another state.[109] The giving of this power to Congress, therefore, remedied a defect, which American experience had taught existed in the Articles of Confederation.

2. *"Fix the standard of weights and measures."* This was found in the Articles of Confederation. The Dickinson Draft gave Congress the same power.[110] To secure uniformity in weights and measures, the King fixed the standard in early England. By the law of King Edgar, the standard was kept at Winchester. By the law of 1197, Parliament ordained there should be a standard of weights and measures throughout the Kingdom, and that the custody of these should be given to certain persons in every city and borough. Later, the standards were kept in the exchequer and weights and measures were regulated by Parliament. In Connecticut, state, county, and town standards existed. The county standards were tested by the state standards and those of the town by the county standards.[111]

"To provide for the punishment of counterfeiting." (Art. I, Sec. 8, cl. 6.) The clause originated in the committee of detail.[112] It grew out of American experience. The question of dealing with counterfeiters became a serious one during the later period of the Continental Congress, and the half dozen years under the Articles of Confederation. So numerous and audacious were the counterfeiters, that they actually endangered the financial security of the government,[113] and the success of the Revolution. Samuel Adams, writing to John Winthrop, February 6, 1779, said that the depreciation of the paper currency was due to two causes: (1) to the flood of it which had been issued; (2) to the fact that a great quantity, especially of the emission of May 20, 1777, and April 11, 1778, had been counterfeited.[114] In fact, so many were the counterfeits issued of the bills of credit emitted on the above dates, and so distressing were the results in enhancing prices, defraud-

ing individuals, and injuring the credit of the paper currency of the United States, that on June 2, 1779, Congress felt it necessary to recall and destroy both these issues by June first of that year.[115] On January 14, Congress ordered that for the purpose of preventing the new issue from being counterfeited, "new stamps with additional checks be provided," and that the signatures of the signers be sent to the assemblies, counties, towns, and districts for the protection of the inhabitants.[116] Washington felt constrained to write Congress on the subject of counterfeiting bills of credit, December 7, 1779; and on June 19, 1780, Congress offered a reward of $2,000 to any person securing the conviction of any counterfeiter of bills of credit, or of anyone knowingly passing or receiving such bills.[117]

Early in 1776, South Carolina found it necessary to pass stringent laws against counterfeiting the current coin and bills of credit issued by the Continental Congress. On April 9, 1776, the Legislature felt it necessary to pass an act making it a felony to counterfeit, raze, or alter any notes, orders, certificates, or bills of credit issued by South Carolina, or the Continental Congress. This Act was signed by John Rutledge.[118] The delegates in Congress from New Jersey laid before it a number of counterfeit Continental bills of credit, and on May 30, 1776, a committee of six was appointed to consider the whole question, and report to Congress.[119] The committee reported on June 7, recommending that the Convention of the Province of New Jersey direct the counterfeiters to make satisfaction to the injured parties who had received the bills, imprison the offenders, and "That it be recommended to the Legislatures of the United Colonies to pass acts of legislation for making the Continental bills of credit a lawful tender in all payments, and for the most effectual preventing the counterfeiting thereof." [120] The report was "ordered to lie on the table for consideration," and on June 24, 1776, Congress resolved: "That it be recommended to the several legislatures of the United Colonies to pass laws for punishing in such manner as they shall think fit, persons who shall counterfeit, or aid or abet in counterfeiting, the Continental bills of credit, or who shall pass any such bill in payment, knowing it to be counterfeit." [121] That is, Congress, helpless to cope with the situation, appeals to the colonies for aid. Later, the Articles of Confederation gave it no power to punish counterfeiters, hence Congress in its helplessness looked to the state governments for protection. Other appeals were made on October 7, 1776, and January 1, 1779.[122]

Among the many state laws passed as the result of these appeals, was one by Virginia, 1779, making it a felony to counterfeit, alter, or erase any bill of credit, or treasury note, or loan office certificate of the United States of America.[123] New York passed three statutes, March 8, 1779, November 20, 1781, and April 25, 1785, making it a felony to counterfeit any bill of credit, money, or certificates of the United States, of New York State, or the coin of any foreign country.[124] South Carolina on March 12, 1783, passed an act making it a felony to counterfeit foreign coin,[125] while Connecticut in 1786 placed a law on the statute books inflicting twenty stripes, and a fine of £500 on any person counterfeiting bills of credit or notes of the United States.[126]

Out of all this experience, and a great deal more of the same kind, came the idea that it was necessary to insert a provision in the Constitution of the United States which would give the American government power to protect itself and the people of the country against counterfeiters of its coin or securities. Many of the members of the Federal Convention had been members of Congress, and had been present when the counterfeit troubles were discussed. Among these were Madison, Wilson, Dickinson, Few, Gerry, Sherman, and Ellsworth. The two latter were members of the Congress of 1780, which offered a reward of $2,000 for the conviction of counterfeiters.[127] Sherman had been a member of the committee of six appointed on May 30, 1776, to investigate and report on the subject.[128] The committee of detail which reported the provision to the convention was composed of Ellsworth, Gorham, Randolph, Rutledge, and Wilson. They had discussed the subject in Congress, and voted on the recommendations appealing to the states for aid.

John Rutledge, as Governor, had signed the first act of South Carolina against counterfeiters, and in the convention had written on Randolph's committee draft, "And of declaring the crime and punishment of counterfeiting." [129] The draft did not contain anything dealing with the subject, and it is probable that it was Rutledge who suggested the clause to the committee of detail, as it is found in his handwriting on the margin. All were familiar with the counterfeiting difficulties of Congress, and this American experience—unfortunate experience—dictated the provision in the Constitution of the United States.

"To establish post-offices and post-roads." (Art. I, Sec. 8, cl. 7.) Pinckney's Plan gave Congress power "to establish post-offices." [130] The report of the committee of detail, August 6, contained an identical provision. On August 16, Gerry moved that the words "and post-roads" be added. This was seconded by Mercer and the Convention agreed.[132] The sources were:

(1) *The Articles of Confederation.* These gave Congress power to establish post-offices, and Charles Pinckney had this in mind when he offered his provision in Convention. Dickinson's Draft gave Congress the same power,[133] while Franklin's Draft extended the power of Congress "to the establishment of posts." [134]

(2) *The states had exercised the power.* "The States before the union was formed could establish post-offices and post-roads," said the Supreme Court of the United States in the Rapier case. The power was surrendered to Congress.[135]

(3) *The colonies, under authority of the British Parliament, had exercised this power.* In 1685, the King on Governor Dongan's advice instructed him to proceed to the establishment of a post-office. The Council of New York then passed an ordinance for the purpose.[136] In 1692, on the request of Andrew Hamilton, an Edinburgh merchant appointed to manage the colonial post-office, the legislature of New York passed a law establishing a general letter office in New York, fixing the rates, and authorizing Hamilton to appoint a post-master of the general office.[137] Other colonies had exercised the same power.[138]

(4) *The British government had established the post-office in Britain and the colonies.* James the First established the post-office in England for carrying letters to and from foreign ports for the convenience of English traders. Charles I organized it for carrying letters in England and Scotland, 1635.[139] The real establishment of the postal system in the colonies was under William III. The Post-Office Act of 1710 was so com-

prehensive as to embrace for the first time the postal arrange-
ments of Great Britain, Ireland, the West Indies, and the
American colonies, and placed the whole system throughout
the Empire under the control of the British Postmaster General.[140] The Continental Congress took over control of the
post-office from the central government of the Empire, and
this became a national power under the Articles of Confederation and passed from there into the Constitution of the United
States.

Copyrights and Patents. (Art. I, Sec. 8, cl. 8.) On
August 18, 1787, Madison offered certain propositions on the
subject to the Convention to be referred to the committee of
detail. Pinckney also offered several on the same subject.[141]
No report was made by the committee of detail, and the propositions went to the committee on postponed and unfinished portions which reported the following proposition on September
5th: "To promote the progress of science and the useful arts,
by securing for limited times, to authors and inventors the
exclusive right to their respective writings and discoveries,"
which was agreed to nem. con.[142] The phraseology of Madison
and Pinckney appears here. The committee on style reported
on September 12, with the change of but a single word—the
omission of the article "the" before the word "useful." [143] The
sources were:

(1) *The state laws and constitutions.* On May 2, 1783,
on the report of a committee consisting of Williamson, Izard,
and Madison, Congress recommended that the several states
take action to secure to authors and publishers the copyright
of their works for a period of fourteen years, with an additional
fourteen years at the end of the first, by enacting such laws as
the states might think proper for the purpose.[144] Congress
possessed no power in 1783 to enact a uniform copyright law
for the United States. It did all it possibly could—made a
recommendation to the states. The result was a flood of state
copyright laws, some for twenty-one years, and some for fourteen years. Vermont failed to act on the recommendation.[145]
The South Carolina act granted inventors the exclusive privilege of making and selling their inventions for fourteen years.
In general, the acts followed the recommendations of Congress.

Again, some of the state constitutions provided for encouragement to arts, science, and literature.[146]   In Pennsylvania, other precedents are found in the Charters. The Frames of Government of 1682, and 1696, contained the following provision: "The Governor and Provincial Council shall . . . encourage and reward the authors of useful sciences and laudable inventions in the said province." [147]   By the Constitution, the power exercised by the states is surrendered to the United States in order to "make effectual provision" for authors and inventors.[148]   This could not be done by the states separately.

(2) *English copyright and patent law.* The first copyright issued to an author in England was to John Palsgrave, 1530, for a French grammar. This was really a printer's license or printing privilege for seven years, which was the form taken by copyright down to the middle of the sixteenth century.[149]   But the foundation of all English and American copyright law was the statute of Anne's reign, 1710.[150]   This gave authors of books already printed the sole right of printing for twenty-one years. Some of the states adopted this. Authors of books not printed were given the sole right of printing for fourteen years. After this term of fourteen years expired, the author, if living, was given the sole right of publishing for another term of fourteen years. That is, Congress requested the states in 1783 to adopt this law as theirs, which several of them did, as South Carolina, New York, and Connecticut. The Congressional Copyright Law of March 31, 1790, also followed the English Act of 1710.[151]

As to patents, the Statute of Monopolies, 1624, secured to inventors the sole right to their inventions for fourteen years.[152] All patent law is based on this statute.[153]   The South Carolina act, passed on the recommendation of Congress simply embodied the principle of the Monopoly act of 1624. This provision gives Congress power to do what the states and British government had been accustomed to do in the past.

"To constitute inferior tribunals." (Art. I, Sec. 8, cl. 9.) The Virginia Plan provided for "inferior tribunals" to hear and determine cases in the first instance. The Pinckney Plan provided for giving Congress power to erect inferior tribunals.[154]   On June 4, the Convention added to the Virginia Plan the words: "to consist of one supreme tribunal, and of one or more inferior tribunals." Next day, Rutledge moved that

the words "inferior tribunals" be stricken out on the ground that such tribunals would encroach on the jurisdiction of the state courts, and this was done.[155]

The report of the committee of the whole, June 13, contained the clause "that the national legislature be empowered to appoint inferior tribunals," moved by Madison and Wilson to give Congress "discretionary power." [156] Hamilton's plan contained a similar provision.[157] On July 18, Butler and Martin opposed the resolution on the ground that such courts would interfere with the jurisdiction of the state courts and were unnecessary, as these could do the work. Randolph replied that state courts could not be trusted to administer the national laws as the interests of state and nation would clash, and the state courts would favor the states against the United States.[157] Gorham pointed out that federal courts for the trial of piracies already existed in the states and no complaints had been urged against them by the states or state courts. The Convention adopted the resolution, and the committee of detail reported it on August 6.[158] The sources are:

(1) *The Continental Congress and Articles of Confederation.* Courts in America are the creations of legislative bodies. The Continental Congress had erected federal courts, December 4, 1776, January 15, 1780, and April 5, 1781.[159] The Articles of Confederation gave Congress power to establish courts for the trial of piracies and felonies committed on the high seas and for determining finally appeals in cases of capture,[160] and Congress had exercised the power.[161] The Dickinson Draft gave the same power and the Report on Trade and Revenue proposed to give Congress power to establish a federal court for the trial of United States officers guilty of crimes and misbehaviours in office, to which appeals could be taken from the state courts.[162]

(2) *The state constitutions and legislatures.* Some state constitutions expressly gave the legislature this power.[163] The state legislatures had erected courts. The Connecticut statute of 1786 used the phraseology of the Madison and Wilson resolution.

(3) *The colonial charters and legislatures.* The Charters of Connecticut, 1662, Rhode Island, 1663, and the Pennsylvania Frames of 1682, and 1683, gave similar powers.[164] The Charter

of Massachusetts Bay, 1691, granted the power to the Assembly in the same language, as is found in the constitution of 1780.[165] The Charter of Georgia, 1732, conveyed the same power.[166] The colonial legislatures instituted judicatories under their charters.

(4) *The English Constitution.* Under the ancient English Constitution, all courts of justice were derived from the power of the King. In law, the courts were the King's courts, and he was always present to administer justice. The judges were the King's judges to whom he had delegated his judicial power. Whether the courts were created by Act of Parliament, or by letters-patent, in theory they were erected by the King's consent.[167] In the charters, the King delegated this power to erect courts to the Governor and Company. The Charter of Connecticut, for example, gave the Governor and Company power to erect judicatories for the trial of all causes in dispute within the colony.[168] The Charter of Rhode Island, 1663, contained an identical provision.[169] This power was exercised by the colonial legislatures, and when the Revolution came, the power was transferred to the sovereign people to be exercised by them through their representatives in their state or national legislatures.

Piracies and Felonies on the High Seas. (Art. I, Sec. 8, cl. 10.) This clause originated in the committee of detail which reported on August 6.[170] The word "punish" was inserted before piracies on motion of Gouverneur Morris. Madison and Randolph moved to insert "define and" before punish.[171] Wilson objected that "felonies" were sufficiently defined by the common law and Dickinson agreed, but Madison replied that felony at common law was vague and defective. If the state laws prevailed on this subject, the citizens of different states would be subject to different penalties for the same offence committed at sea, and "there would be neither uniformity nor stability in the law. The proper remedy for all these difficulties was to vest the power proposed by the term 'define' in the national legislature," so the motion was adopted.[172] The word "punish" stood before offences, therefore, on September 14, Gouverneur Morris moved that it be stricken out in order that "offences against the law of nations" would be definable as well as punishable by Congress by virtue of the preceding clause.

Wilson opposed the alteration, because "to pretend to define the law of nations, which depended on the authority of all the civilized nations of the world would have a look of arrogance" which would make the United States ridiculous. Gouverneur Morris insisted that the law of nations was often too vague and deficient to be a rule, and the word was stricken out.[173] The sources of this provision are to be found in the Articles of Confederation and American experience under those articles. They gave Congress power to appoint courts "for the trial of piracies and felonies committed on the high seas." The Dickinson Draft gave Congress the same power.[174] The Continental Congress had taken over power on the high seas formerly exercised by the Imperial government under the Old Colonial System. The Constitution, however, is an improvement intended to remedy defects in the Articles of Confederation on two points.

(1) *The term "felony" had various and uncertain meanings.* In the English common and statute law, the term "felony" was one of loose and various meanings, while under Confederation the term did not have the same meaning in any two states of the union, and every time the states revised their criminal law, the word was given a new meaning. In fact, South Carolina was dissatisfied with the clause in the Articles of Confederation from the very beginning, and in 1778 the legislature instructed their delegates in Congress to ask that the clause be amended. Therefore, on June 25, the delegates proposed that the clause giving Congress power to appoint courts for the trial of piracies and felonies committed on the high seas be stricken out, and another substituted, giving Congress power to declare "what acts committed on the high seas shall be deemed piracies and felonies." That is, South Carolina asked that Congress be given power to define piracies and felonies. The request was rejected.[174] So severely was this defect felt by both states and Congress, that in 1786 an attempt was made to remedy it by amending the Articles of Confederation. A Grand Committee recommended the adoption of seven new articles, one of which gave Congress the sole power of declaring "what offences shall be deemed piracy or felonies on the high seas and to annex suitable punishments."[175] Congress did not take action on the report. But the Convention of 1787, many of whose members had been in Congress in 1778, and 1786, adopted

the South Carolina proposition and remedied the defect by giving Congress power to say what "felony" was—to define it—so that it would be the same thing throughout the United States. This gave certainty and uniformity.[176]

(2) *Offences against the law of nations were neither definable nor punishable by Congress under Confederation.* Control of foreign affairs was vested in the Federal Government without empowering it to pass laws in support of, or to define offences against or to try, and punish offences against the law of nations, "for the want of which authority the faith of the United States may be broken, their reputation sullied, and their peace interrupted by the negligence or misconception of any particular State." The United States might be embarrassed and embroiled with foreign nations by citizens, and the Federal Government had absolutely no power to prevent it by enforcing obedience or punishing infractions of the law. To prevent this, and enable the United States to say what the law was when vague or deficient, Congress was given power to define and punish offences against the law of nations.[177] It remedied a defect in the Articles of Confederation. The English Parliament had by statute defined what acts committed on the high seas should constitute piracy.[178]

"To declare war . . . water." (Art. I, Sec. 8, cl. 11.) The committee of detail reported a provision, August 6, empowering Congress:

(1) *"To make rules concerning captures on land and water."* [179] On August 17, the first clause was agreed to nem. con. and Madison and Gerry moved to strike out the word "make" and insert "declare" instead, "leaving to the executive the power to repel sudden attacks." Sherman said the Executive should be able to repel, not to commence war, so "make" was better than *declare*, which narrowed the power too much. The Convention agreed to insert "declare." [180] On August 18, Pinckney offered a proposition to be referred to the committee of detail, which read: "To grant letters of marque and reprisal." Gerry offered a similar motion.[181] No report was made on these propositions, and they went to the committee on postponed and unfinished portions which reported September 5, through Brearly recommending that the words "and grant letters of marque and reprisal" be added to the proposition "To declare war." [182]

The source of this clause was Article nine of the Articles of Confederation which gave Congress these powers. The Dickinson Draft conferred the same powers, and Franklin's Draft gave power to determine on war and peace.[183] The Continental Congress had exercised all these powers, taking them over from the Imperial government which had exercised the same powers under the Old Colonial System. Blackstone says, the prerogative of granting letters of marque and reprisal is "nearly related to" and plainly derived from the power of making war.[184] As early as 1328, the English Parliament began to exercise control over questions of peace and war,[185] though the Witan had done so long before, and the New Ordinance of 1311 provided that the King "should not undertake against anyone deed of war, without the common assent of his baronage, and that in Parliament." [186] This required a legislative declaration of war. The Lord High Admiral issued letters of marque and reprisal under the Act. 29, Geo. II, c. 34, 11, and 17, Geo. II, c. 34, 11. The United States annexed the power to grant letters of marque and reprisal to the power to declare war. Such a letter is simply a commission or license given to a private vessel by the government authorizing reprisals on the ships of the enemy.

"*To raise and support armies, etc.*" (Art. I, Sec. 8, cl. 12.) Pinckney's plan gave Congress power "To raise armies," which was intended to give "an unqualified power of raising troops, either in peace or in war, in any manner the union may direct." [187] The committee of detail reported the same provision, and on August 18, Gorham moved to add the word "raise," which was done, and the clause adopted as amended.[188] Gerry pointed out that no check against the danger of standing armies in time of peace had been provided. The people would offer strong opposition to the Constitution in case of such an omission. He could never consent to give Congress power to keep an indefinite number of troops, and he proposed "that there should not be kept up in time of peace more than ———— thousand troops." He intended to fill the blank with two or three thousand. Martin and Gerry offered such a resolution, but it was rejected on the ground that the appropriation of money for a limited time as in England was safeguard enough. Mason had already moved that the appropriation of revenue be limited "as the best guard in the case." On

August 10, Pinckney moved that "no grants of money shall be made by the legislature for supporting land forces for more than one year at a time." [189] The committee on postponed and unfinished portions, to which it went, reported September 5, through Brearly recommending that there be added to the clause, "to raise and support armies," the provision, "but no appropriation of money to that use shall be for a longer term than two years," which was agreed to nem. con.[190] The sources were:

(1) *American experience.* Under the Articles of Confederation, the United States could not raise a single regiment, or build a single ship, "before a declaration of war, or an actual commencement of hostilities." All Congress could do was to agree on the number of land forces to be raised, and then requisition each state for its quota; and it had no authority to do even this unless nine states assented.[191] The colonists had complained bitterly of the King keeping standing armies in time of peace without consent of their legislatures.[192] Hence, when the Americans framed the Articles of Confederation, they took care to deprive Congress of all such power by making the government of the United States dependent on the states. In practice, it was found that the Union could not defend its rights or protect its property. The states obeyed or disobeyed as they chose. This unfortunate experience led the Convention to discard "the fallacious scheme of quotas and requisitions, as equally impracticable and unjust." [193]

(2) *The Continental Congress.* The Congress took over military power and control of the general army from the central government of the empire, and appointed the officers. The Albany Plan gave the President and Grand Council power to "raise and pay soldiers." [194] These were precedents.

(3) *The English Constitution.* That part of the clause regarding the appropriation of money was taken from the English Constitution. The Bill of Rights, 1689, provided that no standing army could be raised, or kept in time of peace without the consent of Parliament. The Mutiny Act was, therefore, passed first in 1689, and annually thereafter, giving the necessary permission to keep a specified number of troops, and appropriating the required money to support such an army.[195] It was necessary for Parliament to meet annually to pass this act, or else the army had no legal status, no means of discipline,

and no money to support it. This gave Parliament absolute control over the army, and the framers of the Constitution adopted this principle of a legislative appropriation of money for a limited time for the support of the army. Another part of the act, specifying a certain number of troops, was rejected though proposed by Gerry and Luther Martin. The principle of the Mutiny Act checks any abuse of power by the President or commander-in-chief. Colonel Mason said, "he considered the caution observed in Great Britain on this point, as the palladium of public liberty." The Federal Convention adopted the idea as being in Madison's words, "the best possible precaution against danger from standing armies." [196] Charles Pinckney had proposed that the appropriation be made for one year at a time, as in England, but the committee on postponed and unfinished portions recommended two years. Why two years instead of one year? One of the objections urged in the Pennsylvania Convention against the Constitution was: "Appropriations may be made for two years, though in the British Parliament they are made but for one." [197] In the Federal Convention, Gerry also objected to an appropriation for two years instead of one year, saying he could not conceive a reason for the change. Sherman, who was a member of the committee, explained "that the appropriations were permitted only, not required for two years," and that the reason for making the appropriation for two years instead of one (as in the British Constitution) was that since the legislature was to be elected biennially, it would be inconvenient to limit appropriations to one year, as no session of Congress might be held within the specified time inside of which renewal was required.[198]

"To provide and maintain a navy." (Art. I, Sec. 8, cl. 13.)

(1) This clause originated in the committee of detail, whose report gave Congress power "to build and equip fleets." On August 18, the Convention agreed unanimously without discussion to substitute "to provide and maintain a navy" on the ground that it was a more convenient definition of the power.[199]

(2) *The Articles of Confederation were the immediate source.* They gave Congress power "to build and equip a navy." The Dickinson Draft proposed to give Congress power "to raise naval forces." [200]

The Continental Congress began very early to take over from the imperial government the control of the navy, and provide and maintain a fleet. On October 13, 1775, "Congress ordered two armed vessels to be fitted out," and on October 30 two more vessels were ordered to be fitted for sea. On November 10, 1775, Congress resolved to raise two battalions of marines, and on December 13, 1775, Congress sanctioned a report for the fitting out of a navy of thirteen ships, five of thirty-two guns. That is, Congress was taking over power from the government of the Empire under the Old Colonial System, and this power, reduced to written form, and embodied in the Articles of Confederation, passed into the Constitution of the United States. The Albany Plan, 1754, as a precedent, gave the President and Grand Council power "to equip vessels of force." [201]

"*To make rules and regulations for the land and naval forces.*" (Art. I, Sec. 8, cl. 14.) The Convention took this from the Articles of Confederation on August 18. The Dickinson Draft contained the clause, while Franklin's Draft gave Congress "the regulation of our common forces." The Continental Congress had exercised this power as early as June 14, 1775, when it appointed a committee to prepare rules and regulations for the government of the army, and on June 30 adopted Articles of war, or sixty-nine rules which were replaced by those of September 30, 1776. On November 28, 1775, Congress adopted rules for the regulation of the navy of the United Colonies. The Albany Plan gave the same powers to the President and Grand Council.[202] The power given in this clause was taken over from the central government of the Empire by the Continental Congress, and embodied in the written Constitution of the United States—the Articles of Confederation of 1781—and transferred by the Convention of 1787 to the Constitution of the United States.

The ultimate source of the clause was the English Constitution. In early times in England, military law existed only in time of war, and articles of war were issued by the Crown, or by the commander-in-chief under authority of the crown. Charles the Second's Articles of 1672 constituted the basis of all later British military law. In the later history of Britain, Articles of War were issued by statutory authority. The

British Government had enacted articles in 1774, 1686, and the Mutiny Act in 1689. The members of Congress and American soldiers were familiar with the British Mutiny Act and Articles of War, and this naturally caused Congress to turn to these as a model. The result was the adoption for the regulation of the American army on June 30, 1775, of the Mutiny Act, Articles of War, and the British Military code of 1774, with some changes and omissions. A comparison of the American articles of 1776, with the British Military code of 1774, shows that they were practically identical.[203] At the outbreak of the Revolution, the British military code was the American code. The Continental Congress assumed the power of the British government to make rules for the regulation of the army, and the exercise of this power was legalized by the written Constitution—the Articles of Confederation—and from there it passed into the Constitution of the United States.

"*To provide for the calling forth the militia.*" This also originated in the committee of detail. The provision is found in Rutledge's handwriting. Charles Pinckney, another South Carolinian, seems to have inserted a similar provision in his draft, and it is probable that Rutledge or the committee got it from Pinckney.[204]

American experience originated the clause. Under the Articles of Confederation, Congress had no power to direct the militia, or call it forth to suppress insurrection, execute the laws of the union, or repel invasion. They were dependent on the states to carry out their recommendations. Shays's rebellion in Massachusetts made the utter helplessness of Congress clear to the whole country. Congress began to raise troops to aid Massachusetts, but did not dare to make the purpose known. Congress pretended the troops were to be used against the Indians. They had no power to interfere in the internal controversies of a state.[205] This danger was never absent from the minds of American statesmen after Shays's rebellion. "The insurrection in Massachusetts," said Madison, "admonished all the States of the danger to which they were exposed," and he objected to the Patterson Plan because it did not remedy "the defect of the Confederation on this point." [206]

"Ask the citizens of Massachusetts if the Confederation protected them during the insurrection of Shays," said General

Pinckney in the legislature of South Carolina. "When Massachusetts was distressed by the late insurrection Congress could not relieve her," said Randolph in the Virginia convention.[206] In the North Carolina convention, Davie urged the need of adopting a Constitution which would remedy the defects of the Articles of Confederation, especially the defect which prevented Congress from defending a state. "If the rebellion in Massachusetts had been planned and executed with any kind of ability," he said, "that state must have been ruined, for Congress was not in a situation to render them any assistance." [207] This alarming experience convinced the American people of the absolute necessity of providing against such danger in future, by giving Congress power to call forth the militia to execute the laws of the union, suppress insurrection, and repel invasion.

"*To provide for organizing, arming, and disciplining the militia,*" etc. (Art. I, Sec. 8, cl. 16.) This clause was formulated for a threefold purpose.

(1) *To secure uniformity in the regulation of the militia throughout the United States.* The great dissimilarity in the militia of different states had produced disastrous results during the Revolution.[208]

(2) *To give Congress power to defend the nation.* Butler and Madison urged that as Congress was responsible for national defence, regulation of the militia belonged of right to them.[209]

(3) *To secure a properly disciplined, efficient militia force for the defence of the nation.* Madison said the primary object was "to secure an effectual discipline of the militia." The states would neglect this as they had their requisitions, and the more they were consolidated into one nation, the more they would rely on the central government for defence, and the less on their local militia, and, therefore, the less prepared the state militia would be. The discipline of the militia was "a national concern, which ought to be provided for in the national constitution." [210] The regulation and discipline of the militia under the Articles of Confederation had been left to the states, with the result that there was neither uniformity nor a well-disciplined militia.

Charles Pinckney's draft, apparently, contained the provision.[211] The committee of detail failed to report on the subject on August 6, doubtless, because the members did not agree

on the question.[212]   On August 18, Mason offered a resolution
giving Congress power over the regulation and discipline of
the militia, but withdrew it in favor of another providing for a
select militia.   General Pinckney revived Colonel Mason's original motion.   These were referred to a grand committee of one
from each state appointed on August 18.   Governor Livingston reported from this committee on August 21, the clause in
the Constitution, except that the words "make laws" stood in
place of "provide" and "the United States" in place of "Congress."   Gerry said it made the states mere drill-sergeants,
but all attempts to amend were voted down.[209]

   *Congress Is Given Exclusive Jurisdiction Over the District
of Columbia and Ceded Districts.*   (Art. I, Sec. 8, cl. 17.)
Pinckney's Plan evidently contained some provision for fixing
the seat of government.[210]   On July 26, Colonel Mason declared
there were two objections against fixing the seat of the national government at the same place as the seat of the state
government.   (1) It would result in disputes concerning jurisdiction between the two governments.   (2) It would give, or
tend to give, the national deliberations a provincial tone.

   He moved that the committee of detail be instructed to receive a clause preventing the seat of the national government
from being fixed at the same place as a state government for
a longer time than it took to erect the public buildings.   He
withdrew it for the time being because afraid it might excite
hostile passions against the Constitution.   Gouverneur Morris said he feared the provision might cause a feeling of enmity between Philadelphia and New York which expected to
become the seat of the national government.[211]   On August
18, Madison referred a series of propositions to the committee
of detail, one of which gave Congress power to exercise exclusively, legislative authority at the seat of the general government over a district not exceeding ———— square miles, the
consent of the legislature of the state or states to be obtained.
Charles Pinckney submitted a similar proposition.   No report
was made by the committee, and the propositions went to the
committee on postponed and unfinished portions which reported
through Brearly, September 5, recommending a provision practically as it stands in the Constitution.   It was clearly based
on Madison's proposition of August 18.   The first part was

agreed to nem. con.[212]   The second part beginning, "And to exercise like authority etc." was objected to by Gerry, who said such power might be used to enslave a state by buying up its territory, and the strongholds proposed might be used to awe the state into undue obedience to the general government. To obviate this objection, King moved to insert the words "by the consent of the legislature of the State," after the word "purchased." "This would certainly make the power safe," he said. Gouverneur Morris seconded this, and the whole clause, as amended, was adopted.[213]

   Why Did the Convention of 1787 Give Congress This Power? (1) To prevent clashing of jurisdiction between the state and federal government. (2) Because of the insurrection of 1783 in Pennsylvania. Grayson, in the Virginia Convention, said: "What originated the idea of exclusive legislation was, some insurrection in Pennsylvania, whereby Congress was insulted— on account of which, it is supposed, they left the State." Strong, a member of the Federal Convention, told the Massachusetts Convention that the purpose in erecting a federal town was to enable Congress to protect itself against insult.[214]   In June, 1783, eighty soldiers mutinied, surrounded the state-house at Philadelphia, where Congress was in session, uttered insulting language and threatened to fire through the windows. Outrages were committed on persons and property; they threatened to loot the bank, and demanded justice from Congress or settlement of their accounts. The state government either could not, or would not protect Congress, or suppress the mutiny. Rumors of intended violence and kidnapping of members of Congress being rife, Elias Boudinot, the President, summoned Congress to meet at Trenton, New Jersey.[215]   To enable Congress to protect itself against insult, humiliation, or danger, without dependence on state governments, exclusive jurisdiction over the seat of the central government was given by the Convention.

   The first part of the clause giving Congress power to legislate for the district "in all cases whatsoever," whether intentional or unintentional, is the language of the hated Declaratory Act of 1766.

   Implied Powers. (Art. I, Sec. 8, cl. 18.)   This clause originated in the committee of detail, whose report contained the clause as it stands in the Constitution.[216]   Alexander Hamilton asked and answered the question: "Why was this provision inserted in the Constitution?" "But suspicion may ask, why then was it introduced? The answer is, that it could only have been done for greater caution, and to guard against all cavilling refinements in those who might hereafter feel a disposition to curtail and evade the legitimate authorities of the Union." [217] Wilson, a member of the committee of detail, said it was intended to give Congress "the power of carrying into effect the laws which they shall make under the powers vested in them by this Constitution." It simply declares that the means for executing the powers of Congress are "included in the grant." [218]

(1) Madison, in his Report on Coercion of March 16, 1781, said that the thirteenth article of the Confederation gave Congress *"a general and implied power"* "to enforce and carry into effect all the articles of the said Confederation against any of the States which refuse or neglect to abide by such their determinations, or shall otherwise violate any of the Articles; but no determinate and particular provision is made for that purpose." [219] American experience was thoroughly familiar with the doctrine under the Continental Congress, where all powers had been implied.

(2) *Implied powers are granted in some of the Charters.* The Charter for the Province of Pennsylvania, 1681, grants power to the Proprietor "to doe all and every other thing and things which unto *the compleate Establishment of Justice,* unto Courts and Tribunalls, formes of Judicature and Manner of Proceedings doe belong altho in these presents express mention be not made thereof." The Charters of Carolina, 1663, and 1665, contain almost an identical statement. [220]

(3) *The doctrine of implied powers was not unknown to English legal theory.* Sir John French, Chief Justice of the Common Pleas, argued for implied powers in Hampden's Case, 1637. The fundamental laws, he argued, had given the King sole power to levy money for the defence of the Kingdom, and that the law which had given this power to the King to do these things hath also given him the means to put these things in execution. "No axiom is more clearly established in law or in reason," said Madison, "than that where the end is required, the means are authorized." [221]

NOTES TO CHAPTER VII

1. Moore, Am. Eloquence, I. 366, 367.
2. Elliot, V, 378.
3. Elliot, V, 21.
4. Id.
5. Elliot, V, 22.
6. Id. II, 466.
7. Id. II, 56.
8. Journals of Congress, Feb. 3, 1786.
9. Elliot, V, 11, 13, 40, 63-67, Am. Hist. Leaflets No. 28, pp. 12, 20.
10. Elliot, V, 76.
11. Jefferson, Writings (Ford ed.), IV, 154, See same statement by Mason, Elliot, III, 472, 473.
12. Elliot, II, 57-9, 83.
13. Poore, 961.
14. See Index. Statutes at Large of Pa. 1700-1787. Id. I, 252. Id. III, 26.
15. Macdonald, Sel. Charters, 256.
16. Plymouth Colony Laws, 85.
17. Elliot, V, 40. Dewey, Financial Hist. of U. S. 12.
18. Laws and Ordinances of New Netherland, p. 7.
19. Laws and Ordinances of New Netherland, p. 38, 39, 40, 41, 208.
20. Laws and Ordinances of New Netherland, p. 418, 419.
21. Dewey, Financial Hist. 13, 14. Colonial Laws of New York, I, 419, seq. 1059.
22. Statutes at Large of Penn. II (1700-1712), p. 107. See Index, Statutes at Large, 1700-1787.
23. Laws and Ordinances of New Netherland, p. 7. See XVIII.
24. Statues at Large, V, 10, p. 252.
25. Pol. Hist. of Eng. VII, Montague (Ed. by Poole).
26. Blackstone, Com. I, 288, 319, 322, and note. See also his earlier date for excises.
27. Adams and Stephens, Sel. Documents, 422.
28. 3 Dall. 175.
29. Resolutions of the Stamp Act Congress, Macdonald, Sel. Charters, 314.
30. Macdonald, Sel. Charters, 314.
31. Locke, Civil Govt. II, Ch. XI. 142, 140.
32. Poore, Charters, 958, 1909, 818, 1541, 1410, 1860, 1868, 1281.
33. Medley, Eng. Const. Hist. 120; Taswell-Langmead, Const. Hist. of Eng. 27-28; Adams and Stephens, 29.
34. Inst. 2, 58, 59; Adams and Stephens, 69.
35. Coke, Inst. 4, 29; Blackstone, Com. I, 314.
36. Cod. V, LVI, 5. Taswell-Langmead, Eng. Const. Hist. 199, 200.
37. Adams and Stephens, 339, 464.
38. Elliot, V, 476.
39. Id. 477, 476, 503, 506, 507.
40. Articles of Confederation, Art. VIII.
41. Elliot, I, 492. IV, 612, 42.
42. Farrand, Records, III, 485, 486, 487, 491, 494, 495.
43. Am. Hist. Leaflets, no. 20, p. 9, 3, 4.
44. Elliot, V, 479, 483, 484, 503; nem. con. i.e. unanimously.
45. Id. 543; Meigs, Growth of the Constitution, 351; Elliot, I, 92.

46. Statutes at Large, Vol. 10, p. 253.

47. Id. Laws of N. Y. Vol. 2, p. 790. Hening, Statutes at Large of Va. Vol. 10, p. 511; V. 11, p. 375; V. 12, p. 290. R. I. Col. Records, Vol 10, p. 115.

48. Hening, Statutes at Large of Va. Vol. 11, pp. 70, 121, 289. Id. Vol. 12, p. 305. The resolution of August 28, included the word "tonnage" which was stricken out. Elliot, V, 484, 503.

49. Elliot, V, 378, 434, 435. Meigs, Growth of the Constitution, p. 351 (app.).

50. Art. IX; Am. Hist. Leaflets, No. 20.

51. Blackstone, Com. I, 370-371. Medley, Eng. Const. Hist. 542. Taswell-Langmead, Eng. Const. Hist. 494, 495.

52. Elliot, V, 378. Meigs, Growth of the Constitution 316 (V). Moore, Am. Eloquence, I, 366, 367. Elliot, V, 130.

53. Id. 439.

54. Id. 507.

55. Art. IX. Arts. of Confed.

56. Am. Hist. Leaflets, No. 28. p. 20.

57. 25. Geo. III. cap. 1.

59. Elliot, II, 58.

60. Elliot, II, 124, 129.

61. Federalist, no. 22.

62. Elliot, II, 83, 106, 124.

63. Elliot, II, 59. Id. V, 119, 118. Black, Const. Law, p. 214-5.

64. Art. IV.

65. Elliot, V, 19, IV, 20. Hening, Stat. 11. p. 70.

66. Elliot, V, 119.

67. Laws of New York, Vol. 2, p. 65.

68. Elliot, IV, 254.

69. Id. 20.

70. Journals of Cong. (Ford. ed.), Vol. XI, p. 648.

71. Elliot, V, 66. Am. Hist. Leaflets, no. 28.

72. Washington Writings (Sparks), Vol. IX, 503.

73. Art. I, sec. VIII, Cl. 3, Const. U. S.

74. Farrand, III, 478.

75. Madison, Writings (Cong. ed.), Vol. I (See under dates.) Elliot, V, 107; Washington, Writings (Sparks), V, IX, 503. Am. Hist. Leaflets, no. 28, pp. 26, 8. Journals of Cong. V, 11, 648. Am. Hist. Leaflets, no. 20, p. 12. For. Eng. origin, see Cong. Rec. Vol. 52, 63 Cong. 3 sess. p. 528.

76. Am. Hist. Leaflets, no. 20, p. 22, 12. Id. p. 6. Elliot, I, 52.

77. Macdonald, Sel. Charters, 256.

78. Hart, Actual Government, 359.

79. Moore, Am. Eloquence, I, 368. Elliot, V, 192.

80. Elliot, V, 378, I, 245. Meigs, Growth of the Constitution, p. 316. (V. 11. seq.) 351.

81. Elliot, V, 120.

82. Laws of N. Y. Vol. 1, 460, 703; Vol. 2, 146, 182, 592.

83. Statutes at Large, V, IX, 111, 304, 306; Vol. XII, 179, 180. Poore, 1547.

84. Hening, Stats. at Large. Vol. 11, p. 323, 129.

85. Id. Vol. 12, 261, 262.

86. Art. IV. Arts. of Confed.; Moore, Am. Eloquence, Vol. I, p. 368.

87. Federalist, no. 41. (Dawson ed.).

88. Moore, Am. Eloquence, I, 368; Poore, 1872.

89. Am. Hist. Assoc. Rept. 1901, I, p. 305.

90. Federalist, no. 41.

91. Elliot, IV, 19.

92. Id. V, 120; Am. Hist. Assoc. Rep. 1901, I, 305; Fed. no. 41. Poore, 255, 375, 940, 1732, 1901. passim.

93. Am. Hist. Assoc. Rep. I, 304. Taswell-Langmead, Eng. Const. Hist. 534. Medley, Const. Hist. of Eng. 450. Blackstone, Com. I, 426, 427, 273, 374.

94. Blackstone, Com. I, 273, 374.

95. Colonial Laws of N. Y. Vol. I, 123, 124, 858, 999, 1034.

96. Am. Hist. Assoc. Rep. 1901. I, 304.

97. Elliot, V, 488, 503, 504.

98. Elliot, V, 120. Federalist, no. 42, p. 266 (Lodge ed.).

99. Laws of N. Y. I, 650; Stats. at Large, IV, 86, 172; V, 79.

100. Stats. at Large. X, 421. XI, 1, 52, 158, 180, 186-7, 195-6, 330, 334. XII, 70, 80; Poore, Charters, 1546. N. C. Const. Poore, 1414.

101. Hening, Stats. Vol. 9, 186; Poore, 1414.

102. Sturgis v. Crowninshield, 4 wh. 122; Story, Com. VI.

103. 4 Wh. 130; 4 Ann. 17; 13 Eliz.; 34 Hen. VIII, 4; 1 Geo. 3, 17; Stats. at. Large, IV, 86; V, 79; Id. Pa. IV, 172; IX, 6; Laws of N. Y. i, 650; Laws of U. S. 2, 19.

104. Elliot, V, 130. Moore, Am. Eloquence, I, 367.

105. Elliot, V, 378, Elliot, V, 434. Meigs, Growth of the Const. 351.

106. Art. IX.

107. Moore, Am. Eloquence, I, 369.

108. American Hist. Leaflets. no. 20, p. 12, 4.

* The States and Colonies had exercised this power—the regulation of the value of the coinage. R. I. in 1763, passed an act regulating the value of foreign coin.
See Laws of R. I. 1767, pp. 166-167. Acts. & Res. 1782, p. 23. Acts. & Laws of Conn. 1784, p. 160. Blackstone, Com. I, 277.

109. Hamilton, Works (Lodge), I, 288-295. Am. Hist. Leaflets, no. 20, p. 19. Fed. No. 41 (Dawson ed.), 42 (Ford ed.).

110. Am. Hist. Leaflets, no. 20, p. 13, Art. IX.

111. Blackstone, Com. I, 275-6. Laws of Conn. 1715, 253; 1784, 262; 1786, 261.

112. Elliot, V, 378, 436, 437.

113. Am. Hist. Leaflets, no. 20, p. 13.

114. S. Adams, Writings (Cushing), IV, 121.

115. Journals of Congress, Vol. 13 (Ford), pp. 21-22.

116. Journals of Cong. XIII, p. 64 (Ford ed.).

117. Id. XV, p. 1368; Id. XVII, 530.

118. The Public Laws of S. C. (J. F. Grimke), 1694-1790, p. 283.

119. Journals of Cong. IV (Ford. ed.), p. 321.

120. Journals of Cong. V (Ford. ed.), p. 426.

121. Id. p. 476.

122. Journals of Cong. V (Ford. Ed.), 849-50; XIII, 11.

123. Hening, Stats. at Large. Vol. 10, p. 94.

124. Laws of N. Y. Vol. 1, 120, 368, 412, 464.

125. Public Laws of S. C. 1640-1790, p. 314.

126. Statutes of Conn. 1786.

127. Journals of Cong. XVII, 526, 527.

128. Journals, V (Ford), 417; IV, 87; V, 417.

129. Meigs, Growth of the Constitution, p. 316 (V, 14), seq.

130. Moore, Am. Eloquence, I, 367; Elliot, V, 130.
131. Id. 378.
132. Id. 434.
133. Art. IX; Moore Am. Eloquence, I, 367; Am. Hist. Leaflets, no. 20, p. 12.
134. Am. Hist. Leaflets, no. 20, p. 4.
135. 143 U. S. 110; McClain Cases, p. 479.
136. Am. Hist. Rev. Vol. XXI, no. 2, Jan. 1916, pp. 259, 260.
137. Laws of the Colony of N. Y. I, 294, 295. For other laws see I, 347, 410, 581.
138. For Va. see Hening, I, 112; Pa. Stats. at Large. II, 58. Conn. Laws of Conn. 1715, p. 98.
139. Blackstone, Com. I, 322.
140. Statutes at Large, V, 12, 9, Anne c. 8; (or p. 112). 12 Car. II, 365.
141. Elliot, V, 440.
142. Elliot, V, 440.
143. Meigs, Growth of the Constitution, p. 351.
144. Journals of Cong. under date, May 2, 1783.
145. R. I., Mass., N. H. and Va. for *twenty-one years*. R. I. Col. Records, Vol. 9, 736. Perpetual Laws of the Commonwealth of Mass. Vol. 1, p. 94. Laws of N. H. 1783, p. 294. Hening, Stats. at Large, Vol. 12, p. 30.
For *fourteen years*, Conn. Public Statute Laws of the State of Conn. Bk. I, p. 474. Statutes and Laws, 1786, p. 133. Statutes at Large of Pa. Vol. XI, p. 272. Laws of S. C. 1694-1790 (J. F. Grimke). Stats. at Large IV, 618. Laws of N. Y. Vol. 2, p. 298. Laws of N. C. Vol 5. Digest of the Laws of the State of Ga. (Marbury and Crawford), p. 342.
146. Among these N. C. Poore, 1414; Mass. Poore, 970; N. H. 1521; Pa. Poore, 1547.
147. Poore, 1535, 1538.
148. Federalist, No. 42 (Dawson ed.).
149. Bowker, Copyright, Its History and Law, p. 20.
150. 8 Anne, c. 19.
151. U. S. Stats. at Large, Vol. 1, p. 124.
152. 21, Jac. I, c. 3.
153. Blackstone, Com. I, 407.
154. Elliot, V, 128, 130; Moore, Am. Eloquence, I, 367.
155. Elliot, V, 155; I, 160 (Res. 9, cl. 1); Elliot, V, 159.
156. Elliot, V, 159, 160.
157. Id. V, 331.
158. Elliot, V, 331, 378.
159. Journals of Congress under dates.
160. Article IX.
161. Journals of Congress, August 28, 1782, and December 24, 1784.
162. Am. Hist. Leaflets, no. 20, pp. 16, 29.
163. Mass. (1780), 960; Poore, N. H. 1284; Vt. 1861, 1870. Moore, Am. Eloquence, I, 367. As Va. Journal House of Delegates, 1776, pp· 47, 71. R. I. Acts and Res. 1780, p. 9, 13. Conn. 1784, Acts and Laws, p. 29; Statutes of Conn. 1786, p. 27.
164. Poore, 255, 1598, 1521, 1529.
165. Id. 951.
166. Poore, 375; As Va. 1623 seq. Hening, Statutes, I, 125, 132, 163, 168, 169, 185, 273, 462, 448, 466. R. I. Laws of R. I. 1745-52, p. 27. Conn. Laws of 1715, p. 23, 1750, p. 105.

167. Blackstone, Com. III, 24.
168. Poore, Charters, 255.
169. Id. 1598.
170. Elliot, V, 378.
171. Id. 437.
172. Elliot, V, 437.
173. Elliot, V, 543; McClain, Cases, 502.
174. Art. IX, Am. Hist. Leaflets, no. 20, p. 11. In 1779, the State of R. I. had passed an act giving the Superior Court of Judicature jurisdiction in cases of "piracy and felony committed on the high sea." R. I. Acts and Res. 1779, p. 16.
174. Elliot, I, 91.
175. Am. Hist. Leaflets, no. 28, p. 29.
* Among these were Madison, Wilson, Charles Pinckney, Ellsworth, Sherman and Few. See Journals of Congress.
176. Federalist, no. 41 (Dawson); Elliot, V, 437.
177. Hamilton, Works (Lodge), I, 295; Elliot, V, 543. In 1782, the State of Connecticut passed an act giving the Superior Court and County Courts jurisdiction to try offences against the law of nations. Acts and Laws of Conn. p. 602.
178. See Blackstone, Com. IV, 71-2.
179. Elliot, V, 378, 379.
180. Id. 439.
181. Elliot, V, 440.
182. Id. 440, 441; Id. 510, I, 285.
183. Art. IX, Am. Hist. Leaflets, no. 20, pp. 20, 11. Letters of marque and reprisal were issued by the Governor of Rhode Island in 1776. See Acts. and Res. of R. I. Dec. 1776, p. 5.
184. Blackstone, Com. I, 297.
185. Taswell-Langmead, Const. Hist. of Eng. 210 (note), 225-227.
186. Id. 215, Adams and Stephens, Sel. Docs. p. 93.
187. Elliot, V, 130; Moore, Am. Eloquence, I, 366.
188. Elliot, V, 379, 442.
189. Elliot, V, 442, 443, 440, 445.
190. Elliot, V, 510, 511.
191. Am. Hist. Leaflets, no. 20, p. 17; Art. IX.
192. Decl. of Independence.
193. Shays's rebellion is an example. Federalist (Dawson ed.), no. 23.
194. Elliot, I, 47; Journals of Cong. I; Macdonald, Sel. Charters, p. 256.
195. Blackstone, Com. I, 415, 416; Medley, Eng. Const. Hist. p. 479. Adams and Stephens, Sel. Documents, p. 457. Skottowe, Hist. of Parliament, 133.
196. Elliot, V, 443, 441; Federalist, No. 40 (Dawson ed.).
197. Elliot, V, 510; Elliot, II, 465.
198. Elliot, V, 503, 511.
199. Elliot, V, 379, 443.
200. Art. IX; Am. Hist. Leaflets, no. 20, p. 12.
201. Elliot, I, 50; Journals of Cong. I, 203, 211, 212; Elliot, I, 51; Ibid. 52; Macdonald Sel. Charters, p. 256.
202. Elliot, V, 443; Art. IX, Articles of Confed.; Elliot I, 47-8, 51, 248. Am. Hist. Leaflets, 20, p. 12, 4; Journals, I, 90, 435-482, 244. Macdonald, Sel. Charters, 256.
203. Davis, A Treatise on the Military Law of the U. S. App. B, and C, pp. 581-618, and Chap. XIX, p. 342; Military Laws of the U. S. 962-63; Willoughby, Const. II, 1192.

204. Elliot, V, 379; Meigs, Growth of the Constitution, 316 seq. (V. 12);
Elliot, V, 130; Moore, Am. Eloquence, I, 368.
205. Elliot, V, 94, 95.
206. Elliot, V, 209. Elliot, IV, 282. Id. III, 82.
207. Elliot, IV, 20. Federalist, No. 21.
208. Elliot, V, 443; Federalist, No. 25.
209. Elliot, V, 444, 466.
210. Am. Eloquence, I, 369.
211. Moore Am. Eloquence, I, 367, 368.
    Elliot, V, 374, 410.
212. Comp. Elliot, V, 443, with 466.
    Elliot, V, 410, 440, 510-11, 516.
213. Elliot, V, 511.
214. Elliot, III, 431, 433-4; Id. II, 99.
215. Elliot, V, 93, 94, 92; III, 433. The state executive refused to act.
216. Elliot, V, 379, 447.
217. Federalist, No. 33.
218. Elliot, II, 449; Cooley, Const. Law Ch. IV, sec. 15.
219. Am. Hist. Leaflets, no. 28, p. 3.
220. Poore, 1511, 1384, 1392.
221. Howell, St. Tr. II, 1224. Federalist, No. 43 (Dawson).

CHAPTER VIII

LIMITATIONS ON THE POWER OF CONGRESS

The Slave Trade. (Art. I, Sec. 9, cl. 1.) The first part of the clause originated in the committee of detail.[1] On August 8, King urged that a time limit be placed on the importation of slaves, as "he never could agree to let them be imported without limitation, and then be represented in the national legislature."[2] Therefore, on August 21, Luther Martin proposed that the importation of slaves be limited by taxing them. Without this, he said, the clause would encourage the slave traffic to increase representation of the southern states, since five slaves were to be counted as three freemen. "It was inconsistent with the principles of the revolution, and dishonorable to the American character, to have such a feature in the constitution."[3] Wilson pointed out that all importations were taxed except slaves which was "in fact a bounty on that article."[4] After a bitter debate, General Pinckney moved the commitment of the clause to a committee for the purpose of reporting a compromise provision levying on slaves an equal tax with other imports which was right and would remove the objection.[5] The committee of eleven—one from each state—to which it was referred,[6] reported August 24 through Governor Livingston of New Jersey, the clause in the constitution except that it proposed 1800 instead of 1808, and instead of levying ten dollars on each person a tax or duty was to be imposed "at a rate not exceeding the average of the duties laid on imports."[7] The report embodied the ideas of King, Luther Martin, and General Pinckney, namely: (1) A time limit. (2) Limitation by taxation. (3) Taxation of slaves to be the same as that on other imports.

On August 25, General Pinckney moved to strike out "the year 1800" and insert "eighteen hundred and eight."[8] Madison said twenty years would produce all the mischief that can be apprehended from liberty to import slaves. "So long a term will be more dishonorable to the American character than

134

to say nothing about it in the constitution." It passed in the affirmative. Baldwin moved to strike out the words "average of the duties laid on imports," and to insert "common impost on articles not enumerated" instead, which was done. But Sherman objected that this acknowledged men to be property by taxing them as such under the character of slaves, and Madison declared it wrong to admit in the Constitution the idea that there could be property in men. It was, therefore, agreed to amend the second part to read: "but a tax or duty, may be imposed on such importation not exceeding ten dollars for each person." [9] This tax or duty of ten dollars was regarded as "equivalent to the five per cent on imported articles," [10] said Edward Rutledge. Boudinot said in Congress in 1790 that all parties in the Convention understood the tax of ten dollars to be the equivalent of "five per cent ad valorem." [11] Both Gerry and Madison were present and offered no correction or contradiction, so we may assume the correctness of Boudinot's statement. It was General Pinckney's suggestion that slaves be made liable to an equal tax with other imports.[12]

A precedent for imposing a duty on the importation of slaves was found in state and colonial laws. North Carolina in 1787 imposed a duty of £5 on slaves imported from Africa, £10 on each slave from elsewhere, and £50 on each slave imported from a state licensing manumission.[13] The laws of Virginia, Pennsylvania, and South Carolina imposed a duty on negroes imported into those states. In 1705, Massachusetts passed an act imposing a duty of £4 on every negro imported.[14] On the first cargo of slaves brought into New York, an ordinance imposed a duty of 10 per cent ad valorem.[15]

Why Was This Clause Inserted in the Constitution? The majority in the Convention opposed the principle. It was inserted as a compromise with North and South Carolina, and Georgia. In fact, Gouverneur Morris wanted the importation of slaves to be extended by name to these three states only, to show that it was a compromise with them, but withdrew his motion for fear of giving offence.[16] These states refused to be "parties to the union," if their right to import slaves was prohibited. "If the Convention thinks, that North Carolina, South Carolina, and Georgia will ever agree to the plan, unless their right to import slaves be untouched, the expectation is vain.

The people of those states will never be such fools as to give up so important an interest," said Rutledge of South Carolina. "South Carolina can never receive the plan if it prohibits the slave trade," said Charles Pinckney. Williamson, though against slavery both in opinion and practice, "thought the Southern states could not be members of the union if the clause should be rejected." He "thought it more in favor of humanity from a view of all the circumstances to let in South Carolina and Georgia on these terms, than to exclude them from the union." General Pinckney said he "should consider a rejection of the clause as an exclusion of South Carolina from the union." [17] Baldwin declared emphatically that Georgia was decided on the point. This was a local matter and Georgia would not agree to any attempt to abridge one of her favorite prerogatives. Sherman said it was better to permit the Southern states to import slaves "than to part with them if they made that a sine qua non." Luther Martin also testifies that the Southern states refused to enter the union if they were prohibited from importing slaves. Iredell says South Carolina and Georgia wished to replenish their supply of negroes, many of which they had lost during the war, and this was what caused them to oppose any prohibition on the power to import slaves.[18] In the North Carolina convention, McDowell asked why the clause had been adopted. Spaight, a member of the Federal Convention, explained that a contest had occurred in the Federal Convention between the Southern and Northern states. The latter wished to exclude the importation of slaves absolutely. The former would not consent as they needed hands to cultivate their lands. Therefore, South Carolina and Georgia insisted on the clause. In twenty years, they would be fully supplied, and the trade would then be abolished. Madison declared this was a compromise with the Southern states. Wilson said, it was all that could be obtained.[20] The Convention of 1787 faced either union or disunion. Three states declared emphatically that they would not be parties to the union if their right to import slaves was prohibited. Of the two evils, probably disunion was the worse, therefore, compromise was believed to be expedient, hence, the adoption of this clause.

Why did the Convention use the terms "migration" and "importation"?

The first referred to free persons coming into the country. The second referred to slaves. Free persons could not be spoken of as being imported, or as importations, Iredell said in the North Carolina Convention. The tax was to be paid on persons imported, not on persons migrating.[21] Wilson declared that the convention selected their language with great care, and when a tax or duty is mentioned the term migration is dropped, so that congress has power to impose the tax only on those imported, that is, on slaves.[22] Why are slaves not mentioned in the clause? Luther Martin said the convention anxiously sought to avoid any expressions that might be odious to the ears of Americans, therefore, slaves are not mentioned.[23]

The Suspension of the Privilege of the Writ of Habeas Corpus. Charles Pinckney had proposed a provision dealing with the suspension of the privilege of the writ of habeas corpus, but Gouverneur Morris moved the clause as it stands.[24] The sources are:

(1) *The constitution of Massachusetts.* The Convention gives the government of the United States a power previously exercised by the states. Pinckney took his propositions of August 20, and 28, from the constitution of Massachusetts. He used the same phraseology and time limit.[25] Gouverneur Morris used the same provision in part. The New Hampshire Constitution contained the Massachusetts provision.[26]

(2) *The colonial charters.* In the colonies, the right to the writ of habeas corpus seems to have rested on the common law, except in South Carolina where the English Habeas Corpus Act of 1679 had been practically reenacted.[27] A declaration of martial law suspended the operation of the common law, and, therefore, suspended the privilege of the writ of habeas corpus. In some cases, it must have been suspended under the provisions of the charters. The charter of New England, 1620, and the Grant of Maine, 1664, gave the governors power to exercise and declare martial law.[28] The charter of Massachusetts Bay, 1691, gave the governor power to use "the Law Martiall in time of actual warr Invasion or Rebellion."[29] The charter of Georgia, 1732, gave the same power in the same words.[30] The words "invasion or rebellion" appear in the Constitution of the United States.

(3) *The English Constitution.* The habeas corpus existed

at the common law from very early times in England, and any freeman could, if imprisoned, demand from the Court of King's Bench a writ of habeas corpus by which the court inquired into the cause of detention, and discharged, or bailed, or remanded the prisoner.[31]   The writ is believed to be older than Magna Carta.   In 1592, "the Resolution in Anderson," a dictum of the Bench, swept away the historical accidents of the writ, and definitely established the habeas corpus as a remedy which existed of right for all prisoners.[32]   The great security of civil liberty, however, was the Habeas Corpus Act of 1679, intended to remedy all defects in the existing law.   In England in times of great danger, as in rebellion or invasion, the act had been suspended.   There is never such a thing as a general suspension of the writ in all cases, but it is suspended in the case of certain persons charged with certain specified crimes.[33]   The Act was suspended in England during the rebellion of 1715, during the Jacobite conspiracy of 1722, and the invasion of England in 1745 by Charles Edward, the Pretender.[34]   That is, the Act had been suspended in times of invasion or rebellion. This is the origin of the words "rebellion or invasion" in the Constitution.   Chief Justice Pearson of North Carolina in "In re Cain" 1864, gives a clear account of the matter.   He says it was a vexed question in England whether Parliament could suspend the privilege of the writ of habeas corpus except in the two cases of rebellion or invasion.   The precedents for the suspension of the writ in other cases were questioned.   Lord North in 1777 introduced a bill for the purpose of suspending the writ in cases of treason and sedition committed in the colonies.   There was no rebellion or invasion in Great Britain, and violent opposition arose, "and it was denounced as unconstitutional and dangerous to liberty."   So violently was the bill opposed that Lord North was compelled to yield, and submit to amendment by inserting a proviso as follows: "Nothing in this Act shall be construed to extend to persons resident in Great Britain."   When the Constitution of the United States was framed, the members of the Convention determined to settle this vexed question for America, and to do so, expressly limited the power of Congress to suspend the privilege of the writ to times of rebellion or invasion.   The Constitution, in express terms, limits the occasions to these two; so that there may in future be no question or cavil as to treason or sedition, as there had been in England.[35] Similarly, Justice Manly in "In re P. Rafter," said: "This is a negative pregnant and implies a power in Congress to suspend the writ, as the Parliament of England was wont to do, subject to the limitation that the power shall be exercised only in cases of rebellion and invasion when the public safety may require it." [36]

Congress first suspended the privilege of the writ in 1863. The power to suspend the privilege of the writ is placed among the powers of Congress, and is, therefore, a legislative and not an executive power.[37] The Convention, in doing this, followed the English practice as laid down by Blackstone. "But the happiness of our constitution is, that it is not left to the executive power to determine when the danger of the state is so great as to render this measure expedient, for it is the Parliament only, or legislative power, that whenever it sees proper, can authorize the crown, by suspending the habeas corpus act for a short and limited time, to imprison suspected persons without giving any reason for so doing." [38]

No Bill of Attainder or Ex Post Facto Law. (Art. I, Sec. 9, cl. 3.) Gerry and McHenry moved the insertion of this clause on August 22,[39] on the ground that Congress was more to be feared than the state legislatures. It was opposed by Gouverneur Morris, Ellsworth, and Wilson as unnecessary, because ex post facto laws were void anyway, and, therefore, its insertion would proclaim American ignorance to the world. The clause was divided, and the first part relating to bills of attainder agreed to nem. con.[40] The second part was adopted seven to three with North Carolina divided. The term ex post facto was understood to relate to criminal cases only, as in Blackstone.[41] Many of the members associated violation of contracts with the clause. The ruinous stay and tender laws and paper money of Massachusetts, Rhode Island, North Carolina, and other states violated contracts, so Gerry attempted to secure the extension of the prohibition to civil cases, but it was unanimously rejected.[42] The sources were:

(1) *American experience.* Experience, Carroll said, overruled all other calculations on this subject. The state legislatures had passed such laws.[43] Many cases had occurred in American history. The acts of the states confiscating the

property of the loyalists during the Revolution were bills of attainder.[44] Virginia and New York roused bitter resentment by passing such bills. Jefferson drew up a bill of attainder after a conference with Patrick Henry, which was passed by the Virginia legislature for the purpose of putting Josiah Phillips to death for committing depredations and murders in Norfolk and Princess Anne. The Assembly was accused of murder, and Governor Randolph denounced the act in the Virginia convention, June 16, 1788, as a shocking example of the violation of the Constitution.[45] "He was attainted very speedily and precipitately, without any proof better than vague reports, without being confronted with his accusers and witnesses, without the privilege of calling for evidence in his behalf, he was sentenced to death, and was afterward actually executed." John Marshall also denounced it, and said: "Can we pretend to the enjoyment of political freedom or security, when we are told that a man has been, by an act of Assembly, struck out of existence without a jury trial, without examination, without being confronted with accusers and witnesses, without the benefits of the law of the land?" [46]

The New York Assembly on October 22, 1779, passed a bill of attainder to attaint fifty-eight persons. The act banished all the persons named in the bill, amongst them being three women, and enacted that, if at any time thereafter, they should be found in the state, they should be adjudged guilty of felony, and should suffer death without benefit of clergy.[47] The persons named were condemned in their absence and without trial. The constitution of 1777 expressly gave the New York legislature power to pass bills of attainder attainting of crimes committed before the end of the Revolutionary War.[48] Georgia passed a bill of attainder on May 4, 1782, banishing a man named Cooper, and confiscating all his property and debts to the state.[49] In 1706, Massachusetts proceeded against six men by bill of attainder, and convicted and fined them. A separate act was passed fining each from £60 to £1100. Next year, Queen Anne in council repealed the acts on the ground that jurisdiction over the cases lay in the courts and not in the assembly.[50] The supreme court of the state had affirmed the right of Georgia to pass a bill of attainder, as the constitution did not interdict it. "Such acts of attainder and confiscation were not novelties in America, any more than in England." [51] If England and the states had passed bills of attainder, why might Congress not do the same thing? Therefore, the cautious thing to do is to insert a provision to protect the citizen against punishment by legislative acts having a retrospective operation, warned American experience.

(2) *The state constitutions.* The Federalist points out that the Convention of 1787 could find precedents for this in the state constitutions. [52] The fundamental law of Maryland 177 ,, North Carolina 1776, Massachusetts 1780, and New Hampshire 1784, expressly prohibited the passage of such laws. The constitution of New York, 1777, provided "that no acts of attainder shall be passed by the legislature" for crimes other than those committed before the end of the war. [53]

(3) *The English Constitution.* Bills of attainder originated in England. Such a bill was first used in 1321, to banish the Despencers. This was "the earliest notable instance of its employment." [54] The Lancastrians and Yorkists used acts of attainder to destroy each other. The Tudors also used them. Such an act was used in England for the last time in 1696 in the case of Sir John Fenwick. [55] This was a violation of the subject's personal liberty, a common law right guaranteed by Magna Carta. The framers of the Constitution knowing full well the abuses of attainder in England, determined to provide against such a thing in the United States, so that "bills of attainder and other acts of party violence," might not ruin individuals here "as they have frequently done in England." [56]

Ex post facto laws were not unknown in England. The Treason Act of Edward III gave Parliament power to create ex post facto treasons. [57] Thomas Haxey was condemned to death 1397 by an ex post law. Sir Edward Coke performed a service for England by laying it down in "The Case of Proclamations" that the King could not create an "ex post facto law" by proclamation. The terms "ex post facto" and "retrospective laws" are both found in Blackstone's Commentaries. [58] The state constitutions, doubtless, were framed with this in mind. Blackstone defines and condemns ex post facto laws. Chief Justice Chase in 1798, in the case of Calder v. Bull said, that the prohibition was introduced from the knowledge that the Parliament of Great Britain claimed and exercised a power to pass such laws under the denomination of bills of attainder, or bills of pains and penalties. "To prevent such and similar acts of violence and injustice, I believe the federal and state legislatures were prohibited from passing any bill of attainder or ex post facto law." [59]

Direct Taxes. (Art. I, Sec. 9, cl. 4.) On August 6, the committee of detail reported what was practically the above clause: "No capitation tax shall be laid, unless in proportion to the census hereinbefore directed to be taken." [60] On September 14, Read moved to insert after "capitation" the words "or other direct tax," on the ground that this would take away all pretext for saddling the states with a readjustment of past requisitions of Congress. This was adopted. Colonel Mason moved the insertion of the words "or enumeration" as explanatory of the word "census" which was done. [61]

The purpose, Justice Patterson said, was to favor the Southern states. "They possessed a large number of slaves; they had extensive tracts of territory, thinly settled and not very productive. A majority of the states had but few slaves, and several of them a limited territory, well settled, and in a high state of cultivation. The Southern states, if no provision had been introduced in the Constitution, would have been wholly at the mercy of the other states," because Congress could then have taxed the slaves at discretion or arbitrarily, and the land in every part of the union, whether poor or rich and highly productive at the same rate "so much a head in the first instance, and so much an acre in the second." [62] To guard the South against this, the clause was placed in the Constitution. [63] In the Federal Convention, there arose the difficult question as to whether the slaves should be treated as property or persons. The South did not want the slaves to be counted in the population for purposes of taxation. The North had no desire to inflict injustice on the South, but at the same time was determined that the South should not have the slaves counted for the purposes of representation, and omitted in the count for purposes of taxation, which would be an injustice to the North. Rather than lose in representation, the South preferred to assume the additional burden of taxation. So a compromise was arranged by which the rule for representation was adopted for purposes of taxation. [64] Abraham Baldwin, a member of the

Federal Convention from Georgia, declared in the House of Representatives, February 13, 1790, "this was intended to prevent Congress from laying any special tax upon negro slaves, as they might in this way, so burthen the possessors of them as to induce a general emancipation." [65]   Hugh Williamson, a member of the Federal Convention from North Carolina, referring to the clause, in the House of Representatives, February 3, 1792, said: "Another article had defended us (the South) from unequal direct taxes." [66]

Exports Not to Be Taxed. (Art. I, Sec. 9, cl. 5.)   The Pinckney draft contained a provision against taxing exports, or what purported to be the draft whether so or not.   General Pinckney on July 12 urged the insertion of a clause restraining Congress from taxing exports.   The committee of detail reported the provision on August 6. [67]   It originated:

(1) *In Southern economic fear and opposition.*   The staple products of the South, tobacco, rice, and indigo, furnished one third of the exports of the country.   South Carolina alone had in one year exported products valued at £600,000. [68]   In the Convention, therefore, the South, led by South Carolina, bitterly opposed giving Congress power to tax exports, because it would discriminate against her products, and lay on them an additional burden.   The South feared a combination of the Eastern and Middle states against her for trade purposes. [69]   On July 12, General Pinckney expressed alarm at Gouverneur Morris' mention of taxing exports, and said that South Carolina would not be represented in proportion to her £600,000 of exports and ought not to be taxed for that. [70]   It was then, he urged that Congress be prohibited from taxing exports by a constitutional provision.   On July 23, he warned the convention that if the committee of detail failed to insert some constitutional guarantee to the Southern states against taxing exports, in their report of a constitution, he should be bound to vote against it in duty to his state. [71]   On August 16 and 21, Mason urged the necessity of the provision as a security for the Southern products. [72]   Williamson of North Carolina declared emphatically that should Congress be given power to tax exports, it would destroy the last hope of the adoption of the Constitution. [73]   With the South emphatic in its protest, and determined to oppose giving Congress such power, even to

the point of rejecting the Constitution, there was nothing to do but insert the limitation on the power of Congress. In the House of Representatives, on November 5, 1792, Williamson said the purpose of the provision was to "defend the great staples of the southern states—tobacco, rice, and indigo—from the operation of unequal regulations of commerce or unequal direct taxes." [74]   Another purpose was evidently to allay Southern fear that negroes exported from one state to another might be taxed. [75]

(2) *In American state experience.*   Several states taxed the exports of their neighbors who had no ports of their own.   Pennsylvania taxed the exports of New Jersey, Maryland, and Delaware, and expected to "export for New York." [76]   Virginia and South Carolina exported for North Carolina; while Rhode Island exported the produce of Connecticut and Massachusetts. [77]   As a result, it was said that New Jersey was like a cask tapped at both ends, as New York also taxed her exports, and North Carolina was like a patient bleeding at both arms. [78] On August 21, Langdon protested against leaving the exporting states free to tax the exports of New Hampshire and other non-exporting states.   "The exporting states," said Madison, "wished to retain the power of laying duties on exports," while "the states whose produce is exported by other states opposed the laying of heavy duties on their commodities." [79]   The purpose of the non-exporting states was, therefore, to put an end to an intolerable and depressing trade situation in which they were taxed for the privilege of exporting their produce through other states.   The delegates from those states felt that the only way to meet such a situation was to deprive both the central and state governments of the power to tax exports.

No Preference to Be Given to the Ports of One State over Those of Another.   Maryland was responsible for this clause being inserted in the Constitution. [80]   The Maryland delegates, Carroll and Luther Martin, expressed apprehension on August 25 lest Congress under the power of regulating trade "might favor the ports of particular states by requiring vessels destined to or from other states to enter and clear thereat, as vessels belonging or bound to Baltimore to enter and clear at Norfolk," and they offered a proposition prohibiting Congress from exercising such power. [81]   This, with another proposal by

McHenry and General Pinckney, was referred to a committee of one from each state which reported through Sherman on August 28.[82] On August 31, Carroll and Jenifer urged the Convention to agree to the clause, as it was a tender point with Maryland, and it was adopted.[83]

The reason for its adoption was that it was believed Congress might compel all vessels sailing into, or out of Chesapeake Bay for Baltimore or other Maryland port, to enter and clear at Norfolk, or some other port in Virginia. The Maryland delegates thought this would be extremely injurious to the commerce of their state, and were determined to secure some safeguard against any such commercial discrimination.[84] Under the Articles of Confederation, some states had levied discriminating duties on the shipping of other states, as New York, Massachusetts, and Pennsylvania.[85] Rhode Island, New Jersey, Connecticut and Pennsylvania were discriminated against by New York.[86] The United States government had no power to prevent this. Maryland suggested and secured a constitutional clause prohibiting such discriminations in future.

Money Must Be Appropriated by Law. (Art. I, Sec. 9, cl. 7.) This clause was suggested by the committee appointed July 2 to devise and bring in a compromise on representation.[87] The committee of detail reported it on August 6 in slightly altered form, while the committee on postponed and unfinished portions of the Constitution gave it final form in its report of September 5.[88] The second part of the clause was suggested by Colonel Mason who moved on September 14, a provision requiring "that an account of the public expenditures should be annually published." [89] Gouverneur Morris declared it impossible, and King impracticable to include every minute shilling; and Madison moved to strike out "annually" and insert "from time to time," instead, on the ground that it would require frequent publications, and yet leave enough to the discretion of Congress. If too much were required, nothing would be done as under the Articles of Confederation which required half-yearly accounts. It was found impossible to comply punctually, with the result that the practice of giving accounts had ceased. The substitution was agreed to, and the amended resolution added to the clause after the word "law." [90] The origins of the clause are to be found:

(1) *In the Articles of Confederation.* Congress had the power "to appropriate and apply 'all moneys' raised for the service of the United States," and was required to publish and transmit accounts to the states every half-year.

Pelatiah Webster's scheme 1783, also provided that no money be paid for any purpose without an express appropriation made by law.[91]

(2) *The state constitutions and state practice.* After the Declaration of Independence, the states passed annual appropriation bills.[92] They also provided for rendering accounts of receipts and expenditures of all public monies as Virginia, 1776.[94] The other states did the same thing. The constitution of Massachusetts, 1780, provided for payment only in consequence of appropriations made by law.[95] New Hampshire adopted the provision as part of her constitution in 1784.[96] All the state governments made appropriations and rendered accounts of such monies.

(3) *The colonial practice.* All the colonial legislatures appropriated money to particular uses. The Virginia Assembly did so as early as 1629 at least.[97] Pennsylvania, New York, and other states did the same.[98] The colonial legislatures, as Rhode Island, Connecticut, and New York, also provided for examining and publishing statements of the accounts.[99] The Albany Plan 1754, provided for appropriating money.[100] This was the established colonial practice.

(4) *The English Constitution.* The practice originated in England and was carried to the colonies. After Parliament secured control over taxation, it was found necessary to go a step further, and actually see that the money it voted was really applied to the purposes for which it was granted. An attempt was made in the reign of Henry III to take from the King his right to expend the public money.[101] In 1340 money was appropriated to be "spent upon the maintenance of the safeguard of our said realm of England, and of our wars in Scotland, France, and Germany, and in no places elsewhere." [102] In 1348 Parliament appropriated a grant "solely for the war of our lord the King." [103] The money raised north of the Trent was appropriated for war with Scotland. In 1346 the same thing was done. In 1353 a subsidy on wool was granted for purposes of war. This is regarded as the first unequivocal in-

stance of the appropriation of supplies, as this covered the whole of England.[104]   In 1413, Henry V was given a grant of a subsidy and tonnage and poundage "for the safeguard of the sea." [105]   And another in 1415 "for the defence of the realm." [106]   The practice fell into disuse under the Tudors, was revived in 1624 under James I,[107] and firmly established in the reign of Charles II, 1665.   The King asked Parliament for a large sum to carry on the war against Holland.   Sir George Downing, a Teller in the Exchequer, seized the opportunity to introduce into the subsidy bill a proviso that the money (£1,250,000) should be used solely for the war, and that no money should be issued out of the Exchequer except on a warrant stating that the money had been spent for the war.[108] Charles the Second's Appropriation Act firmly established the principle.   A provision had been inserted in the annual supply bill, since the time of William III providing severe penalties for the expenditure of money for any other purpose than that for which it had been appropriated.

How Could Parliament Be Certain That the Money Voted Had Been Used for the Purpose for which It Had Been Granted? This involved the auditing of the accounts.   So in 1340, Parliament appointed a committee to examine the accounts of the collectors of the last subsidy.   In 1341, Parliament requested that a commission be appointed to audit the accounts, which was also done.   In 1376, and 1377, auditors were demanded, and two treasurers were appointed "to render faithful account." [109]   In 1378, Parliament demanded an account.   The King, Richard II, replied that it had never been known that the King must render an account, but for the satisfaction of the Commons, he ordered the receipts and expenditures to be set forth in writing by Walworth, the treasurer.[110]   In 1379, the King presented the accounts for audit on his own initiative.[111]   In 1406, Henry IV made an attempt to regain control, declaring emphatically that "Kings do not render accounts," but in 1407, he laid the accounts before Parliament.[112]   The practice was not finally established till 1667 when Charles II was compelled by the Commons to assent to the passage of a bill appointing a committee with extensive powers to audit the accounts.   The colonies and states audited their accounts as the mother country did.[113]   Committees were appointed to audit them as in England.[114]

No Titles of Nobility to be Granted. (Art. I, Sec. 9, cl. 8.)
This clause originated in the committee of detail. Their re-
port·provided that "the United States shall not grant any
title of nobility." The Convention agreed to this nem. con. on
August 23.[115] Charles Pinckney immediately urged the necessity of adding a clause to preserve the foreign ministers and
other officers of the United States from the danger of external
or foreign influence, and for this purpose offered the clause in
the Constitution.[116] The sources of the provision were:

(1) *The Articles of Confederation.* "The prohibition with
respect to titles of nobility is copied from the Articles of Confederation," says the Federalist.[117] Pinckney's proposition was
taken from Article VI. He added the words "without the consent of the legislature." The committee on style changed
"legislature" to "congress" in their report of September 12.[118]
With the exception of this addition, the clause is also found in
Dickinson's Draft, and Randolph's Report on Powers of Congress, August 22, 1781, proposed to institute an oath to be
taken by officers of the United States "against presents, emoluments, office or title of any kind from a King, prince or foreign state." [119] So that there appears in this report part of
the phraseology of the clause in the Constitution. In Dickin-.
son's Draft and the Articles of Confederation, the prohibition
is absolute while in the Constitution it is conditional, "without
the consent of Congress." This was not satisfactory to several
of the states. Massachusetts asked for an amendment providing that "Congress shall at no time consent" to any such
thing. New Hampshire, following Massachusetts, asked for
the same amendment. New York and Rhode Island asked "that
the words 'without the consent of Congress' be expunged." [120]

(2) *The state constitutions.* Article forty of the Maryland Declaration of Rights 1776, provides "that no title of
nobility be granted" by the state, and article thirty-two reads:
"Nor ought any person, in public trust receive any present
from any foreign prince or state . . . without the approbation
of this state." [121] The phrase "without the approbation of this
state" evidently suggested the words "without the consent of
the legislature" in Pinckney's proposition, which became "without the consent of Congress" in the Constitution. The constitution of North Carolina, 1776, also prohibited the state from

conferring or granting hereditary emoluments, privileges, or honors,[122] while the Georgia constitution of 1777, deprived any person holding a title of nobility of the right to vote, or hold office under the state. To enjoy the rights of citizenship, he must surrender his title "in the manner directed by any future legislation." [123] It is just possible that the Dickinson Draft of July 12, 1776, may have suggested the idea to the state constitutions, as the Maryland convention did not meet till August 14, 1776, or complete its work till November 11, 1776. The North Carolina congress did not meet till November 12, 1776.

(3) *American experience.* In the Virginia Convention, Governor Randolph said that an incident which had actually happened caused the convention to place the restriction in the constitution. The King of France had presented the American ambassador with a box or present, therefore, it was thought proper to prohibit American officials from accepting such things from foreign rulers or states. The *purpose* was to prevent corruption and intrigue with foreign governments, to secure the nation against the danger of "foreign influence in the affairs of government," and to prohibit anyone in office from receiving or holding any emoluments from foreign states.[124] Mason also referred to the incident, and it is said that Doctor Franklin was the person to whom they referred.[125]

In the debate in Congress, May 11, 1789, Madison said he opposed titles because they were not reconcilable with the nature of American government, or the genius of the American people. They diminished the true dignity and importance of a republic instead of increasing it.[126] Samuel Adams said that the framers "probably foresaw that such titles, vain and insignificant in themselves," might in time lead to the absurd and unnatural claims in America of exclusive and hereditary privileges.[127] These things have no place in a republic "based upon equality of rights." [128] Several of the state constitutions make a similar statement as to the cause of inserting the provision, namely, the government ought to be instituted for the common benefit, protection, and security of the people, and not for the particular emolument, or advantage of any single man, family, or set of men.[129]

NOTES TO CHAPTER VIII

1. Elliot, V, 379; Meigs, Growth of the Constitution, 316 (V seq.).
2. Elliot, V, 392.
3. Elliot, V, 457.
4. Id. 459.
5. Id. 460.
6. Id. 461.
7. Elliot, V, 471.
8. Id. 477.
9. Elliot, V, 477, 478.
10. Elliot, V, 277.
11. Id. IV, 411.
12. Id. V, 460.
13. Elliot, V, 460.
14. Ancient Laws and Charters of Mass. Bay. app. 748.
15. Ordinance of Aug. 6, 1655.
16. Elliot, V, 477.
17. Elliot, V, 460, 457, 477, 459.
18. Elliot, V, 459, 461; Id. I, 273; Id. IV, 178.
20. Elliot, IV, 100; Farrand, Records, III, 436; Elliot, II, 452.
21. Elliot, IV, p. 102.
22. Elliot, II, 452.
23. Elliot, I, p. 373, Luther Martin's Letter.
24. Moore, Am. Eloquence, I, 369; Elliot V, 445, 484.
25. Poore, 972; Elliot, V, 445, 484.
26. Id. I, 375, Poore, 1292.
27. Am. Hist. Rev., Vol. 8, p. 24 seq. 22, 23, 24.
28. Poore, 784, 925.
29. Id. 953.
30. Id. 377. For the history of habeas corpus in the colonies see American Hist. Review, Vol. 8, Habeas Corpus in the Colonies, A. H. Carpenter.
31. For the various writs in use, see Jenks, Sel. Essays in Anglo Saxon Legal History, II, 534, 538, 541, 543, 544; Blackstone, III, 127-132; McKechnie, Magna Carta, 361-365; Ridges, Const. Law, 410 seq.
32. Jenks, II, 541-544.
33. Medley, Eng. Const. Hist. 446.
34. Id. and May, Const. Hist. 11, ch. XI.
35. 2 Winston, 145, 146 (N. C. Reports).
36. 2 Winston, 154 (N. C. Reports).
37. See Ex parte Merryman, Campbell's Reports, 246; 9 Am. Law Reg. 524; Ex Parte Bollman, 4 Cranch 75.
38. Blackstone, Com. I, 145.
39. Elliot, V, 462.
40. Id. 462, 463.
41. Id. 488, III, 477, 481.
42. Elliot, V, 488, 545.
43. Id. III, 477, 481.
44. Cooley, Const. Law, ch. XV, sec. 1.
45. Hening Statutes, Vol. 9, 463, 464; Elliot, III, 140, 236. For case of Josiah Phillips, see Burk, Hist. of Va., IV, 305-306, Tucker's Blackstone, app. I, 293, Roger Foster, Const. of U. S. attainder, 4 Calls. Rep., 135 Elliot, III, 66-67.
46. Elliot, III, 66-67, 223, 236.

47. Laws of N. Y. Vol. I, p. 173.
48. Sec. 41, Const. of N. Y.; Poore, 1339.
49. 4 Dall, 14, 15.
50. Palfrey, Hist. of New England, 271-281.
51. 4 Dall. 14-20.
52. 4 Dall. 14, seq., Federalist, No. 44.
53. Federalist, No. 44 (Lodge ed.); Poore, 818, 1410, 959, 1282, 1339, see Calder v. Bull, for the statement of supr. ct., 3 Dall. 386.
54. Taswell-Langmead, Eng. Const. Hist. p. 305.
55. Feilden, Const. Hist. of Eng., 156, Hallam, Const. Hist. of Eng., chap. XV.
56. McRee, Life and Correspondence of Iredell, Vol. 2, p. 172.
57. Medley, Eng. Const. Hist., 168.
58. Taswell-Langmead, Eng. Const. Hist., p. 241, 375, Adams and Stephens, p. 336, Blackstone, Com. I, 46, and Note to Hammond Ed. p. 133.
59. 3, Dall. 389.
60. Elliot, V, 379, Meigs, Growth of the Const., V (seq. 316).
61. Elliot, V, 545.
62. 4 Dall. 252.
63. 2 Dall. 177.
64. 157, U. S. 524.
65. Farrand, Records, III, 360.
66. Farrand, Records, III, 366.
67. Elliot, I, 148; V, 130, 302; Elliot, V, 379.
68. Id. 302.
69. Elliot, V, 456.
70. Id. 302.
71. Elliot, V, 357.
72. Id. 432, 456.
73. Id. 454.
74. Farrand, Records, III, 360.
75. Id. 360, 366.
76. Elliot, V, 455, 112, 119, III, 483.
77. Id.
78. Elliot, V, 112.
79. Id. 454; Id. II, 483.
80. Elliot, V, 478, 479, 503.
81. Id. 479.
82. Id. 483, 484, 502.
83. Elliot, V, 502, 503.
84. Luther Martin's Letter, Elliot, I, 375.
85. Hart, Actual Government, 395.
86. Laws of N. Y., 1783-1788, p. 66. See also Laws of 1784, p. 585; Vol. 2, p. 46, 1787, p. 509, p. 11, 65, 511; Act of 1788, p. 90, Stats. at Large of Pa., 1786, p. 234.
87. Gen. Pinckney's Compromise Committee.
88. Elliot, V, 274, I, 194, 206, 222, 224; V, 316, 375, 377, 510.
89. Id. 545.
90. Elliot, V, 546; Art. IX, Arts. of Confed.
91. Art. IX; Elliot, V, 546, Am. Hist. Leaflets, No. 28, p. 10.
92. Laws of N. Y. I, 75, 96, 138, 196, 255, 285, 322, 398, 425, 491, 573, 759, II, 854 for examples; Virginia, Hening, Statutes, Vol. II, p. 12, 247.
93. Pa. Statute at Large, Vol. IX, 360, 443.
94. Hening Stat., Vol. X, 204.
95. Poore, 966.

96. Id. 1289.

97. Hening, Statutes, I, 142, 171, 195, 229, Vol. VI, 467.

98. Statutes at Large, II, 387. See Index "appropriations," of other volumes, as Vol. VI, Laws of the Colony of N. Y. I, 237, 669.

99. Id. 430, Acts and Resolves of R. I., 1770, p. 64, 74, 18, 95.

100. MacDonald, Sel. Charters, 256.

101. Medley, Eng. Const. Hist., 245.

102. 14 Ed. III, 2.

103. Adams and Stephens, Sel. Documents, p. 114.

104. Taswell-Langmead, Eng. Const. Hist. 219.

105. Adams and Stephens, 178.

106. Id. 183.

107. Prothero, Statutes and Constitutional Documents, 278-9, 318.

108. Taswell-Langmead, 494; Medley, 245-6; Cooley's Blackstone, I, 334 note.

109. Adams and Stephens, p. 105, 136.

110. Adams and Stephens, 137.

111. Id. p. 138.

112. Medley, Eng. Const. Hist. 246.

113. Acts and Resolves of R. I. for example 1768-1777, 1770, p. 1864, 95 and 74.

114. Acts and Resolves of R. I. 1770, p. 18, 64, 74, 95.

115. Id. 1777, Elliot, I, 227, V, 379, 467.

116. Id. 467, I, 301.

117. Lodge ed. no. 44, p. 279, Dawson, ed. No. 43.

118. Art. VI, Elliot, I, 301.

119. Am. Hist. Leaflets, No. 20, p. 8, Id. no. 28, p. 5.

120. Elliot, I, 323, Id. 326, Id. 323, 326.

121. Poore, 820, 819.

122. Poore, 1410.

123. Id. 379.

124. Elliot, III, 465, 486.

125. Farrand, Records of the Federal Convention, III, 327.

126. Annals of Cong. I, 521.

127. Works, IV (Cushing Ed.), 357.

128. Cooley, Const. Law, Chap. IV, sec. 16.

129. Const. of Pa., 5, Va., 4, Vt. 6; Mass. I, 6.

CHAPTER IX

LIMITATIONS ON THE POWERS OF THE STATES

No State to Enter into Any Treaty, Alliance or Confederation, etc. These clauses originated in the committee of detail,[1] and were reported on August 6. On August 28, on motion of Wilson and Sherman, the clause prohibiting the states from emitting bills of credit, or making anything but specie a tender in payment of debts, was transferred from Article XIII, to Article XII of the committee's report, and inserted after the words "coin money." [2] The effect of the transfer was to make the prohibition on the states absolute, as according to Article XIII, the states might emit bills of credit with the consent of Congress. The motive was to make the provisions of the clause unconditionally and absolutely binding on the states for the purpose of crushing paper money. Sherman feared paper money partisans would secure election to Congress for the purpose of voting its consent to emitting paper money.[3] On August 28, King moved to add a provision of the North West Ordinance of 1787 prohibiting the states from interfering in private contracts.[4] Rutledge moved that the clause, "nor pass any bill of attainder or ex post facto laws" be substituted for King's motion which was done.[5] This was taken from the prohibition already placed on Congress.[6] Next day, Dickinson told the Convention that on examining Blackstone's Commentaries, he had found that the term 'ex post facto' applied to criminal cases only, and as the states would not be restrained from passing ex post facto laws in civil cases, some further provision would be necessary for that purpose.[7] The committee on style, of which King was a member, did not forget this. The result was a new clause to meet the situation, "nor laws altering or impairing the obligation of contracts." The words "altering or" were stricken out on September 14.[8]

The origins of the several clauses may now be traced.

(1) *"No State shall enter into any treaty, alliance, or*

confederation." [9]   The condition, "with the consent of Congress," was omitted, and the provision made absolute under the Constitution.   The reason for this change was that the states had violated the article by making treaties and alliances without consent of Congress, or giving Congress notice of such compacts.   Some states had made treaties with the Indians.[10] Virginia and Maryland had entered into compacts in violation of the Articles of Confederation.[11]   It was well known to Americans that this was a principle of the Republic of Holland.   Montesquieu stated it forcibly, and pointed out that its omission in the Germanic Constitution left the way open for misfortunes to overtake the Confederacy, "through the imprudence, ambition, or avarice of a single member.[12]   While these facts, doubtless, had their influence on the development of the original proposition, the provision was, however, well known to American statesmen as a law of the Old Colonial System.   No colony could enter into any treaty, alliance, or confederation with foreign powers, and treaties made by the central government of the Empire were binding on the colonies.[13]   The Dickinson Draft of July 12, 1776, also contained the provision.[14] This was merely a reduction to formal written rule of what had been the actual situation in practice under the Old Colonial System.

(2) *"Grant letters of marque and reprisal."*   "These letters are grantable," says Blackstone, "by the law of nations, whenever the subjects of one state are oppressed and injured by those of another; and justice is denied by that state to which the oppressor belongs."   This was the law of that day.[15] The states had issued such letters after the Declaration of Independence was adopted, as, for example, Rhode Island in 1776.[16]   The Articles of Confederation prohibited the states from granting letters of marque and reprisal.[17]   The Dickinson Draft contained a similar provision.[18]   "The prohibition of letters of marque," says Madison, "is another part of the old system." [19]   Under this system, however, the states could issue such letters after a declaration of war by Congress under regulations established by the United States, or in case of attack by pirates.   The purpose of giving the United States sole power to issue them was to secure "the advantage of uniformity in all points which relate to foreign powers"; and "immediate

responsibility to the Nation in all those, for whose conduct the Nation itself is to be responsible." [20]

(3) *"Coin money."* The coining of money is the act of the sovereign power.[21] The right of the states to coin money was retained under Confederation "as a concurrent right with that of Congress," though the United States was given authority to regulate the alloy and value of coin struck by their own authority, or by that of the states.[22] The Dickinson Draft gave the United States in Congress assembled, "the sole and exclusive right and power" of "coining money and regulating the value thereof."[23] The Constitution improved on the Articles of Confederation by taking the right to coin money from the states, as proposed by the Dickinson Draft. The purpose of this was to preserve "the uniformity and purity" of the standard of value,[24] for "a right of coinage in the particular states," says Madison, "could have no other effect than to multiply expensive mints, and diversify the forms and weights of the circulating pieces." [25] No uniform system of coinage existed under Confederation, and this lack of a uniform, stable, fixed standard of value, common to all the states, which could be used as a medium of exchange in all commercial transactions between business man and business man everywhere, was felt severely.[26] The result was a jumble of all kinds of coins, which tended to discourage and destroy business. Therefore, the framers of the Constitution decided to remedy these evils by giving Congress absolute control over the monetary system.

(5) *"Emit bills of credit; make anything but gold and silver coin a tender in payment of debts."* Both the colonies and the states issued large amounts of paper money. Massachusetts was the first to do so, as early as 1690. Rhode Island did so in 1715, and 1719; New York, 1709; Virginia, 1756; Maryland, 1769.[27] Sometimes, the sums emitted were quite large, especially for that day. New York, for example, emitted £120,000 in 1770, and Pennsylvania £200,000 in 1777.[28] So serious did the paper money pest become that in 1751 the British government prohibited the colonies from issuing more, but they still continued to do so. The prohibition did not prohibit.[29] This money was by law made legal tender in all cases (except for his Majesty's quit rents) in most of the colonies and states.[30] The usual, inevitable results fol-

lowed: a depreciation of the paper money, and an impairment of the public credit defrauded many people, by compelling them to receive payment in the depreciated currency, or else lose the amount of the debt.[31] The gold and silver were driven out, which impoverished the country and commerce was depressed and destroyed, as foreign merchants and traders avoided a country where they were cheated, and forced to suffer heavy losses by being paid in worthless paper money.[32]

"The injustice and pernicious tendency of this disgraceful policy," said Mr. Davie in the North Carolina convention, "were viewed with great indignation by the states which adhered to the principles of justice. In Rhode Island, the paper money had depreciated to eight for one, and a hundred per cent with us. The people of Massachusetts and Connecticut had been great sufferers by the dishonesty of Rhode Island, and similar complaints existed against this state."[33] James Wilson spoke in a similar strain in the Pennsylvania convention: "Fatal experience has taught us, dearly taught us, the value of these restraints. What is the consequence even at this moment? It is true, we have no tender law in Pennsylvania; but the moment you are conveyed across the Delaware, you find it haunt your journey, and follow close upon your heels. The paper passes commonly at twenty-five or thirty per cent discount. How insecure is property!"[34] The tender laws of some states also compelled creditors to receive land of appraised value, but frequently barren and useless, in payment for debts contracted to be paid in gold and silver.[35] Other things, as produce and live stock, were also made legal tender. Mr. Davie declared with heat in the convention of North Carolina, that the commerce of North Carolina and many of the states was ruined by partial and iniquitous laws, "which basely warranted and legalized the payment of just debts by paper, which represents nothing, or property of very trivial value."[36] As early as November 19, 1779, Congress entertained a resolution recommending the state legislatures to revise their laws for making paper currency a tender in payment of debts, and "so to frame them that injustice to creditors and debtors may be prevented." Witherspoon moved to add as an amendment, "and that the injustice which has already taken place may be remedied as far as may be practicable," but conditions became worse instead of better.

This was the situation when the Federal Convention met for the purpose of remedying defects in the existing government. One defect to be remedied was that arising from paper money and tender laws of the states. The Convention knew that the states having large amounts of paper money in circulation would never consent to have it destroyed immediately, or ratify any constitution having that effect. So they determined that all they could do was to place some limitation on the growing evil. The Convention, therefore, prohibited any future increase of paper money, and left the way clear for its gradual extinguishment by the states calling in and redeeming their emissions in circulation.[37] "This clause," says Mr. Davie, "became in some measure a preliminary with the gentlemen who represented the other states." "You have," said they, "by your iniquitous laws and paper emissions, shamefully defrauded our citizens. The Confederation prevented our compelling you to do them justice; but before we confederate with you again, you must not only agree to be honest,[38] but put it out of your power to do otherwise." American experience of paper money, therefore, dictated the provision. So bitter had been that experience, that when the committee of detail reported the clause as prohibiting the states from emitting bills of credit without consent of Congress, "the Convention," says Luther Martin, "was so smitten with the paper money dread that they insisted the prohibition should be absolute." [39] Madison testifies that the cause of the insertion of the clause in the Constitution "was the practice of the states in making bills of credit, and in some instances appraised property a 'legal tender.' " [40]

(6) *"Pass any bill of attainder, ex post facto law, or law impairing the obligation of contracts."* Some of the state constitutions prohibited the states from passing bills of attainder or ex post facto laws. This extends the prohibition to all the states absolutely. For origins, see Art. I, Sec. IX, cl. 3. For ex post facto laws, see McClain, Cases in Const. Law. p. 981-2, or Calder v. Bull, 3 Dallas, 386.

The purpose of the clause, which forbids the states to pass any laws impairing the obligation of contracts seems to have been to prevent the states from passing stay and tender laws which prevented or delayed the collection of private debts.[41] The tender laws have already been mentioned. An example of such laws is the South Carolina Act of 1782, postponing suits for debts till ten days after the next meeting of assembly.[42] In 1786, the Massachusetts legislature passed an Act suspending for eight months all laws in force in the commonwealth for the collection of private debts in specie.[43] On January 30, 1787, another act was passed continuing the act of 1786 in force.[44] Chief Justice Marshall said in Sturges v. Crowninshield, this law grew out of the distress following the war of independence. "To relieve this distress, paper money was issued, worthless lands, and other property of no use to the creditor, were made a tender in payment of debts, and the time of payment stipulated in the contract was extended by law. These were the peculiar evils of the day. So much mischief was done, and so much more was apprehended, that general distrust prevailed, and all confidence between man and man destroyed." [45] These measures were subversive of private contracts and public faith,[46] and called out this clause prohibiting the states from enacting any law impairing the obligation of contracts. The intention or purpose of the Convention was not only to prevent a repetition of such evils, but also to establish the great principle that contracts should be forever inviolable against legislative interference.[47] The state governments are not to have even the power to interfere with private contracts, such as that between debtor and creditor. The sources may be summarized as follows:

(1) The history of the times, or American experience.
(2) The North West Ordinance.
(3) Blackstone's Commentaries.
(4) The Civil Law.

"Impairing the obligation of contracts," are words which are not taken from the English common or statute law, or state statutes. "The tradition is that Mr. Justice Wilson, who was a member of the Convention, and a Scottish lawyer, and learned in the civil law, was the author of this phrase." [48]

Patrick Henry and George Mason objected in the Virginia convention that states and individual speculators had bought large amounts of paper money at a low price, and this clause

was made for the purpose of securing payment in full. Henry
said that speculators had bought it up at one for a thousand.
The Eastern states were the chief speculators, he had been informed, and. vast quantities of paper money acquired for a
trifle were packed in barrels in the Northern states.[49] Madison
admitted there might be speculations.[50] Mason said individuals
had made great fortunes out of it, and both he and Henry
objected that the prohibition of ex post facto laws which would
impair the obligation of contracts, compelled payment of the
paper money at its nominal value in gold and silver. "We may
be taxed for centuries," said Mason, "to give advantage to a
few particular states in the Union, and a number of rapacious
speculators." The prohibition of ex post facto laws, they declared, tied the hands of both the state and federal governments,
and compelled redemption of the money at its nominal value.[51]
Were the members of the Federal Convention, as has been
charged, interested in the securities of the states and United
States, and did that lead them to frame such a Constitution
as would render those interests secure? Professor Beard, in
his Economic Interpretation of the Constitution, shows that
the majority of the members in the Convention were, directly
or indirectly, interested in the public securities, and if the results of his researches be applied to the vote on this clause,
it leads one almost irresistibly to conclude that these economic
influences and considerations were silently at work in the Convention. This appears in the affirmative vote on the clause
prohibiting the emission of bills of credit. Twenty-eight of the
thirty-five delegates from the eight states voting in the affirmative held securities.[52] All the delegates from four of these states,
and a majority from four others were holders of public paper.[53]
Williamson of North Carolina had a small trunk full.[54] Virginia voted in the negative. Maryland was divided.[55] The majority here held no securities. The New Jersey delegates were
apparently not present.[56] King who first proposed a prohibition against the states interfering in private contracts was a
large holder of government securities.[57] The new Constitution
would increase the holdings from six to twenty times.[58] The
temptation from a financial point of view was, therefore, very
strong. The records of the treasury department show that very
large amounts of the public securities were bought up by North-

ern speculators.[59]   All this would appear to justify Patrick Henry's charge that there was here "a contest for money." [60]

On the other hand, everybody was interested in trade and commerce, so that this group would of necessity be larger than that of the security holders. We may, therefore, give due credit to the statement made by Roger Sherman and Oliver Ellsworth in their letter to Governor Huntington of Connecticut, September 26, 1786, in which they declare that the restraint on the state legislatures regarding the "emitting of bills of credit, making anything but money a tender in payment of debts, or impairing the obligation of contracts by ex post facto laws, was thought necessary as a security to commerce, in which the interest of foreigners, as well as the citizens of different states may be affected." [61]

(7) "*Or grant any title of nobility.*"   For sources, see Art. I, Sec. 9, cl. 8).

No State to Lay any Imposts or Duties on Imports or Exports.   (Art. I, Sec. 10, cl. 2.)   This originated in the committee of detail on August 6, which reported a provision prohibiting the states from levying imposts or duties on imports without the consent of the United States.[62]   On August 28, King moved to insert the words "or exports," after "imports," to prevent the states from taxing either, which was done.   Langdon had suggested this on August 21.   Sherman moved to add after "exports" the clause "nor with such consent, but for the use of the United States," in order that all duties on imports or exports might go into the treasury of the United States.[63] Gouverneur Morris supported this on the ground that it would prevent the Atlantic states from taxing the Western states, and in their own interest "opposing the navigation of the Mississippi."   The resolution was adopted.[64]   On September 12, the committee on style reported the clause as in the Constitution, with the omission of the words, "except what may be absolutely necessary for executing its inspection laws." [65]   On the same day, the clause was reconsidered at the instance of Colonel Mason, who feared that it would prevent levying incidental duties necessary for inspection and safe-keeping of their produce, and be ruinous to the five staple Southern states.   He moved to add a clause providing that nothing in the provision should be construed to restrain any state from laying duties upon exports for the sole purpose of defraying the charges of inspecting, packing, storing, etc.[65] Madison, believing that it would restrain the states to bonafide inspection duties and expressly authorize such, seconded it. Next day, Mason renewed his proposition, and added a clause giving Congress revision and control in case of abuse, which was adopted.[66] This latter had been suggested by Dickinson to prevent states like New Hampshire, New Jersey, and Delaware from being oppressed by their neighbors through taxing them under the guise of inspection duties.[67]

The source of this clause is to be found in *American experience* under the Articles of Confederation. The Articles prohibited the states from levying any duties or imposts which would interfere with any treaties already proposed to France and Spain by the United States. Otherwise, they were left to levy duties as they pleased.[68] The Dickinson Draft also proposed that duties levied by the states on imports or exports must not interfere with any treaties made by the United States.[69] The result, we have seen, was that some states taxed the imports and exports of their neighbors.[70] The exporting states were naturally anxious to retain this power to tax. The states which had paid the duties feared that heavy taxes might be levied on their commodities by the other states "for their own exclusive emolument." [71] The clause was inserted to prevent that and to secure freedom of commercial intercourse for all the states. It is "calculated at once to secure to the states a reasonable discretion in providing for the conveniency of their imports and exports, and to the United States a reasonable check against the abuse of this discretion." [72]

No State to Lay any Duty of Tonnage, Keep Troops, or Ships of War in Time of Peace. This clause originated in the committee of detail which reported on August 6.[73] On September 15, McHenry and Carroll moved that no state be restrained from laying duties of tonnage for the purpose of clearing harbors and erecting light-houses. There was some uncertainty as to whether the states were restrained from laying tonnage duties by the power given Congress to regulate trade. McHenry's motion was, therefore, changed to read as follows: "That no state shall lay any duty on tonnage without the consent of Congress," which was agreed to six to four.[74]

The sources were:

(1) *The Articles of Confederation.* Article six prohibited the states from doing any of these things.[75] Massachusetts had violated the Articles by raising and keeping troops without consent of Congress. The Dickinson Draft contained the same provisions.[76]

(2) *The state constitutions.* Several of these declared against keeping standing armies in time of peace without the consent of the legislature, as Maryland, 1777; Virginia, 1776; [77] North Carolina, 1776; Pennsylvania, 1776; Massachusetts, 1780; and New Hampshire, 1784.[78] This was one of the principal grievances against George III—"he had kept among us, in time of peace, standing armies without the consent of our Legislatures." [79]

(3) *The English Constitution.* A standing army was organized in 1645, and authorized by the Instrument of Government, 1653. The army became the real ruler of England, a tyrant feared and hated by the people. Out of that came the legacy of fear and hatred of standing armies to the British race, strong and persistent in the colonies as in the home-land, and which resulted in Parliamentary opposition in the reigns of Charles II, and James II, and which created the provision against standing armies in the Bill of Rights, 1689. This made it illegal to keep "a standing army within the Kingdom in time of peace unless it be with consent of Parliament." [80] Parliamentary consent was given annually.[81] The Bill of Rights, 1689, is, therefore, the original source of the constitutional principle.

NOTES TO CHAPTER IX

1. Elliot, V, 381; Meigs, Growth of the Const. seq. 316 (V, 10).
2. Elliot, V, 381, 484, 485.
3. Elliot, V, 381; Id. 484, 485; Sherman's hatred of paper money, owing to his losses caused by it, doubtless influenced him.   Proc. Am. Antiq. Soc. 190-7, 214.
4. Journals of Cong. under date, article two.
5. Elliot, V, 485.
6. Some state constitutions prohibited this.   See Supra. Art. I, sec. IX, cl. 3.
7. Elliot, V, 488.
8. Elliot, I, 301; Id. 311; Id. V, 546.
9. Art. VI.
10. Elliot, V, 119, 208.
11. Id. 120, 208, 248, IV, 20.
12. Montesquieu, Spirit of Laws, Bk. IX, Chap. III.

13. Hart, Actual Government, 431, 439.
14. Art. 5, Am. Hist. Leaflets. No. 20, p. 8.
15. Com. I, 258, and Cooley's note in Cooley's Blackstone.
16. Acts and Resolves of R. I. 1776, p. 5.
17. Arts. VI, IX.
18. Journals of Cong. July 12, 1776.
19. Federalist No. 43 (Dawson ed.).
20. Art. VI; Federalist No. 43.
21. Blackstone, Com. I, 277; 110 U. S. 421.
22. Arts. of Confed. IX; Federalist No. 43.
23. Art. 18; Journals of Cong. July 12, 1776.
24. 9 Howard 560.
25. Federalist No. 43.
26. McClain, Const. Law. p. 31; Hart, Actual Govt. 496, 497.
27. Hutchinson, Hist. of Mass. I, 402.
28. Laws of R. I. P. 60, 79; Colonial Laws of N. Y. Vol. I, p. 666; Hening, Vol. 7, p. 18; Laws of Maryland, 1769. Chaps. XIV, Col. Laws of N. Y. I, 24; Statutes at Large, IX, 97.
29. Hart, Actual Government, 497; Cooley, Const. Law. Chap. IV, sec. VI.
30. Elliot, IV, 183.
31. Id. 335.
32. Id. 334; See Laws of Conn. 1709, 145; 1715, 152, 155, 157, 171, 183, 185, 189, 193, 199, 201.
33. Elliot, IV, 183.
34. Elliot, II, 486.
35. Elliot, II, 144.
36. Elliot, IV, 20.
37. Elliot, IV, 183, 184.
38. Elliot, IV, 183, 184.
39. Letter, Elliot, I, 376.
40. Madison's Letter to Chas. J. Ingersoll, Feb. 22, 1831. Writings, IV, 130. Farrand, Records, III, 495.
41. Elliot, IV, 333-335; III, 179.
42. Statutes of S. C. IV, 513, 560.
43. Laws and Resolves of Mass. 1786-7, p. 113.
44. Laws and Resolves of Mass. 1786-7, p. 576, 622. See also R. I. Acts and Resolves, 1780, p. 21.
45. 4 Wheat, 204.
46. Case of Trevett v. Weeden, James M. Varnum, Preface.
47. 4 Wheat, 206.
48. 4 Wheaton, 151.
49. Elliot, V, III, 474.
50. Id. 471.
51. Elliot, III, 471-474.
52. N. H.; Mass.; Conn.; Pa.; Del.; N. C.; S. C.; Ga.; Elliot, I, 271, 376, 377; III, 478; V, 485; Beard, Econ. Interpretation, Ch. V, 78, 130.
53. Id. Ch. V.
54. Id. 146.
55. Elliot, I, 271, V, 485.
56. Id. 484.
57. Econ. Interpretation, 120.
58. Econ. Interpretation, 256.
59. Beard, Econ. Interpretation, 287, 289.

60. Elliot, III, 475.
61. Elliot, I, 492.
62. Elliot, V, 381; Meigs, Growth of the Const. 316 (V).
63. Elliot, V, 486; Id. 454; Id. 486-7.
64. Elliot, V, 487.
65. Elliot, I, 301; The clause giving Congress revision and control was also adopted later.
Elliot, V, 538-9.
66. Id. 540; I, 312, 313.
67. Id. 539, 547, 548.
68. Art. VI.
69. Am. Hist. Leaflets, no. 20, p. 9.
70. As. N. Y., those of Conn., N. J., Mass. and Vt.; Conn. those of Mass.; Va. those of N. C.; Va. and S. C. the exports of N. C.; Pa. those of N. J. and Del.; N. Y. the exports of N. J.; R I. the exports of Conn. and Mass.; Elliot, III, 158; IV, 186, 224; 184; II, 227, 228, III, 192, V, 119; IV, 157; V, 112; III, 483, 184. McRee, Life and Corres. of Iredell, II, 227, 228.
71. Elliot, V, 454, 483.
72. Federalist, No. 43 (Dawson ed.).
73. Elliot, I, 381.
74. Elliot, V, 548, I, 313.
75. Art. VI.
76. Am. Hist. Leaflets No. 20, 9, 10; Elliot, V, 119, 120, 248.
77. Federalist No. 26; Poore, 819, 1909.
78. Poore, 1542, 959, 1282.
79. Decl. of Independence. See also Albany Plan, 1754; MacDonald Sel. Ch. 257.
80. Adams & Stephens, Sel. Doc. p. 464.
81. Blackstone, Com. I, 414; Medley, Eng. Const. Hist. 478, 479; MacDonald, Sel. Charters, 257.

CHAPTER X

THE PRESIDENTIAL OFFICE

1. *A Single Executive.* (Art. II, Sec. 1, cl. 1.) The Articles of Confederation made no provision for an executive. This worked badly in practice, and, therefore, Madison in his letter to Randolph, April 8, 1787, wrote, "A national executive will also be necessary." Accordingly, the Virginia Plan and Charles Pinckney's Draft provided for an executive. The New Jersey Plan provided for a plural executive "to consist of —— persons." [1] On June 1st, Wilson moved that the executive consist of a single person. Rutledge supported Wilson's motion on the ground that a single executive would "feel the greatest responsibility, and administer the public affairs best." Wilson declared that a single magistrate would give most energy, despatch, and responsibility to the office, and would be a safeguard against tyranny. [2] Randolph offered vigorous opposition, saying that unity in the executive was the fetus of monarchy which the people opposed. He could not see why the great requisites for the executive—vigor, despatch, and responsibility—could not be found in three men as well as one. He proposed an executive of three men drawn from different sections of the country. [3] Butler and Gerry pointed out that a General with three heads would be extremely inconvenient or fatal in military affairs. [4] On June 4, Wilson said that he could see no evidence of the antipathy of the people, and the fact that had great weight with him was that everyone of the thirteen states had a single executive. Three equal members would result in "nothing but uncontrolled, continued, and violent animosities," which would interrupt the public administration and diffuse their poison through all branches of the government, the states, and people. The reasoning of Wilson, Gerry, and Butler won, and the Convention agreed to a single executive, seven to three. [5] The sources were:

(1) *State experience.* The states all had single executives.

(2) *Colonial experience.* The Colonies had single execu-

165

tives.   The Colonial Charters provided for such.[6]   The Charter
of the East India Company provided for the same in the year
1600.[7]

(3) *English constitutional experience.*   Every man in the
Convention knew that "the executive power of the English nation" was "vested in a single person . . . for the sake of unanimity, strength, and despatch."   Wilson appears to have Blackstone's language in mind.[8]   Montesquieu had also said "the
executive branch of the government having need of despatch is
better administered by one than by many."[9]   Rutledge, apparently, had this in mind.

2. *The Title of the Executive.*   The title appears to have
originated in the committee of detail.   Randolph's draft has
the word "Governor" written on the margin by Rutledge.   Wilson's draft, later than Randolph's, also uses the title, "Governor," but Wilson cancelled it, and wrote "President" instead.[10]
In all the states represented on the committee, the title of "Governor" was used, except in Pennsylvania, Wilson's own state,
which used "President."[11]   It is quite evident, the committee
at first agreed on "Governor" as the title, and then changed it,
before reporting on August 6: "His style shall be, The President of the United States of America," and his title shall be
"His Excellency."[12]   Doctor Franklin was President of Pennsylvania.   The language of the report was apparently taken
from the constitution of Massachusetts,[13] which might indicate
Gorham's influence, while again, the report follows the constitution of New Hampshire in the *style,* "President," *title,* "His
Excellency" and *language.*[14]   The whole thing might have been
taken from the constitution of New Hampshire of 1784.   Pinckney's plan also used the title "President."[15]   The constitutions
of Delaware, New Jersey, and Pennsylvania used the titles
"President" and "Vice-President" while they had also been used
in the South Carolina constitution of 1776.[16]   "The President
and Vice-President," said Bowdoin in the Massachusetts convention, "answer to offices of the same name in some of the
states, and to the office of Governor and Lieutenant-Governor
in most of the States."[17]   The President also presided over the
Congress of Confederation.[18]   The presiding officers of some of
the Provincial Congresses, as those of New Jersey and Massachusetts, were called President and Vice-President or Secre-

tary.[19] The title was also to be found in some of the colonial charters as the Grant of New Hampshire, 1629, and the Commission for New Hampshire, 1680.[20] The first part of Art. II, Sec. 1, cl. 1 can be duplicated exactly from the state constitutions, namely, "That the executive authority be vested in the President." [21]

3. *The Length of the Presidential Term.* The Virginia Plan left the term of years blank to be settled later by the Convention. The Pinckney Plan, apparently, provided for a term of seven years. Wilson, on June first, proposed a three-year term on the supposition that provision would be made for the reeligibility of the President.[22] He was a great admirer of the constitution of New York, and took the idea of a three-year term from that.[23] Delaware also had a three-year term for its executive. South Carolina had a two-year term, and all the other states a one-year term.[24] Pinckney moved for seven years. Sherman supported a three-year term, and reeligibility on the ground that rotation threw out of office the men best qualified for the service.[25] Bedford of Delaware proposed a term of three years, and ineligibility after a third term. Impeachment would reach misfeasance, but not the incapacity of a President elected for seven years.[26] The Convention decided on a seven-year term with ineligibility. After an attempt to substitute an executive "during good behaviour," as in Hamilton's plan, had been defeated on the ground that it would simply be a life term and a hereditary monarchy, the Convention voted against the seven-year term and ineligibility.[27] A six-year term was agreed to, and then the seven-year term and ineligibility. This was referred to the committee of detail which reported similarly August 6. On August 24, it went to the committee on postponed and unfinished portions which recommended a Presidential term of four years.[28] If the Convention adopted a long term, it was felt that reeligibility must be abandoned, and many held with King that was too great an advantage to be given up,[29] therefore, a shorter term with eligibility was favored and adopted. The model was that of the Governor of New York. "There is a close analogy between him and a Governor of New York, who is elected for three years, and is reeligible without limitation." [30]

The Electoral College. (Art. II, Sec. 1, cl. 2, 3.) Lord Bryce regarded electors as "a faint reminiscence of the methods" used in electing the Doge of Venice and the Roman Emperor in Germany.[31] Others have seen resemblances to the Polish or cardinal electoral schemes. These were mentioned in the Convention of 1787, but as methods of election with dangerous or undesirable tendencies, weaknesses, and defects which ought to be avoided by the Americans.[32] It may be said, there are two views of the origin of the electoral college.

(1) *Bowdoin's view.* He regards the Maryland electoral scheme as the source. "This method of choosing," he said, "was probably taken from the manner of choosing Senators under the Constitution of Maryland." [33] Though Bowdoin was not a member of the Federal Convention, and he merely states a probability, and does not make a positive statement, his view has been universally accepted.

James Wilson of Pennsylvania was the man who first proposed the election of the President by means of electors. On June 1, 1787, he said he was almost unwilling to make known his method, as he was afraid that it might appear chimerical. He declared himself in favor of popular election of the President in theory at least, and pointed to the experience of Massachusets and New York as proving that the election of the executive by the people was both convenient and successful. On June 2, he moved that the Executive be elected by electors chosen by districts by the voters qualified to vote for members of the first branch of the national legislature.[34] A portion of Article XV of the Maryland constitution, and part of Wilson's resolution are identical. This reads: "That the said electors of the ——— meet at ——— and they, or any ——— of them, so met, shall proceed to elect by ballot." [35] It is clear he had the Maryland electors in mind. The use of the same, identical phraseology could not possibly be the result of chance or accident. It is probable that the term "electors" may have been suggested to Wilson by the Maryland constitution. However, he could have taken it from the constitution of his own state, which applied it to members of the General Assembly and Council when acting as electors of the President and Vice-President of Pennsylvania. Iredell applies the term to members of the state legislatures when choosing senators.[36] Gouverneur Morris applies it to members of Congress as prospective electors of the President.[37] The term was commonly applied to persons

acting in an electoral capacity, or performing electoral functions, and the name would naturally be given to anyone who
helped to elect the President, whether directly or indirectly,
immediately or intermediately.

(2) *Madison's view.* He says: "The President is indirectly
derived from the choice of the people, according to the example
in most of the States." [38] This "example" was found in eight
states in 1787, in which the executive was elected by joint ballot of both houses of the legislature. In Georgia, the house of
representatives elected.[39] The legislatures in those eight states
possessed and exercised both legislative and electoral powers, and
were legislatures or electoral colleges, according as they exercised
legislative or electoral functions. There were two sets of functions—electoral and legislative—performed by one set of men.
The committee of eleven in the Convention of 1787, separated
the functions, and provided two sets of men, or two Congresses,
namely, an electoral body and a legislative body of representatives. The Virginia plan provided for *legislative election* of the
President, or election by Congress.

That is, the plan retained the method of electing the President in the Congress of Confederation. James Wilson proposed
popular election of the executive, confessedly based on American experience, but the Convention believed both dangerous.[40]
On the one hand, they must guard against the dangers of a
legislative election. These would be intrigue, faction, cabal,
and corruption. The President would be the mere creature of
the House and Senate, as the one was to impeach him and the
other to try him. He would not dare even to exercise the veto
power. The only safeguard would be to make the President
ineligible, which they opposed. Legislative election must be rejected to secure the President's complete independence, and preserve inviolate the sacred doctrine of the separation of powers.
It would result in foreign influence and intrigue in Presidential
elections, as in Poland and Germany,[41] while Congress would be
so excited and divided into factions over elections that the national administration and public business would suffer through
neglect.[42] An insuperable objection to election by Congress was
that the electoral body would be a standing, permanent body
that could be approached at any time, courted and intrigued
with by the candidates, their partisans, and the ministers of

foreign powers. The electoral body must never be a standing, permanent, pre-existing body which could be found at any time, and intrigued and bargained with, and "tampered with beforehand to prostitute their votes," whenever opportunity offered.[43]

On the other hand, the dangers of popular election must be guarded against. If the people should elect the President, the unsophisticated voters would be duped and deluded by scheming political tricksters. It was unthinkable to suppose that the people would ever be able to unite on any one man, and simply preposterous to believe they could be capable of judging and voting intelligently on the subject. Utmost confusion and periods of interregnum would result. To the small states, a more terrible spectre loomed up—popular election would throw the power to elect the President into the hands of the large states.[44] The people would be sure to throw the President out of office for doing his duty, and dangerous riots, faction fights, and wild commotions would occur as in Poland. Popular election was utterly impracticable because of the vast extent of territory in the Union. The South would be placed at a decided disadvantage in the election as the negroes would not have a vote, and the Southern influence on elections would be disproportionate to her population. "To avoid the inconveniences already enumerated and many others that might be suggested," said James Wilson, "the mode before us was adopted." [45]

The great problem before the Federal Convention was, then, to devise such a method of election, as would get rid of the evils and dangers of both methods.[46] Legislative election, or election by Congress provided, as in the states, for two sets of functions—electoral and legislative—to be performed by one set of men. In that fact, lay all the dangers and difficulties of a legislative election. Therefore, to get rid of these dangers, or minimize them as far as possible, the committee of eleven separated the functions of Congress, and provided an independent body of representatives to perform the electoral work. This gave an *electoral Congress* and a *legislative Congress*. The electoral body is modelled after Congress, contains the same number of representatives apportioned in the same way, and is the exact counterpart and miniature of Congress.[47] Should the electors meet to elect a President, they would simply represent a joint session of both houses met for electoral purposes. It is a temporary body, called into existence for the sole purpose of taking over and doing the electoral work of Congress, meets, performs its work, and immediately becomes defunct. On September 6, it was moved twice "that the electors meet at the seat of the general government," but this was rejected.[48] The Convention then adopted the report of the committee of eleven, which broke up the electoral body into bodies of state electors to meet and ballot in their own states. Collectively, these state electoral colleges stand instead of, and represent a joint session of both houses of Congress met for electoral purposes. The breaking up into bodies of state electors, it was believed, would still further remove the dangers of a legislative election. It also gives the states a share in the selection of the President, and makes the election partly federal.[49] The Electoral College was, then, merely a second or substitutionary Congress created for the express purpose of taking over and doing the work originally intended to be done by Congress, because it was believed this substituted body could do the electoral work better and with greater safety to the nation. This was clearly understood by the members of the Federal Convention. General Pinckney pointed out in the South Carolina convention that instead of being elected by the Senate and House of Representatives, as was originally planned, the President was "to be elected by the people through the medium of electors chosen particularly for that purpose." This would secure executive independence.[50] Charles Pinckney said in the Senate of the United States on January 23, 1800, he remembered that the Convention had taken great care "to provide for the election of the President of the United States independently of Congress, and to take the business as far as possible out of their hands. The votes are to be given by electors appointed for that express purpose." On March 28, 1800, he said: "I well remember it was the object . . . to give Congress no interference or control over the election of the President." [51] Baldwin of Georgia, a member of the committee of eleven, appointed to deal with postponed and unfinished portions of the Constitution, said, on January 23, 1800, that the Constitution had directed "electors to be appointed throughout the United States, equal to the whole number of Senators and Representatives in Congress for the express purpose of entrusting the Constitutional branch of power to them." [52]   The Electoral College then appears to be simply the existing state institution mentioned by Madison, but modified, and adapted to meet the needs of the nation.

The Charter of New England, 1620, created a Council of forty persons, and confided the power of electing the President to them.   The Charter of Massachusetts Bay, 1629, provided for election of Governor and Deputy-Governor by the General Assembly.   The first general court held in Boston, October 19, 1630, decided the freemen should choose the Assistants, and the Assistants the Governor.   The Charter of the East India Company, December 31, 1600, gave the General Court power to elect the Governor and Deputy-Governor.   The General Courts exercised electoral functions.   The first state to adopt a constitution providing for legislative election of the executive was South Carolina, March 26, 1776.[53]   The principle of indirect election also appears in the English boroughs, where, in some cases, the freemen elected the delegates to the county court, and the delegates elected the representatives to Parliament.[54]   Out of such a background, English, colonial, and state, the Electoral College grew.   The electors are to be appointed by the states "in such manner as the Legislature thereof may direct." [55]

This was apparently suggested by the method provided for electing delegates to Congress from the states under Article V, Articles of Confederation, which required delegates to Congress to be appointed "in such manner as the legislature of each state shall direct."

No member of Congress "or person holding an office of trust or profit under the United States, shall be appointed an elector." [56]   This is the application to electors of the clause in the Constitution disqualifying officeholders as members of Congress.[57]   The same principle is found in the Articles of Confederation, the Dickinson Draft,[58] and in several state constitutions as New Hampshire, Pennsylvania, Maryland, North Carolina, and Georgia.[59]   Back of this, the principle is found in the Charter of Georgia, 1732, and the Concessions of West New Jersey, 1676.[60]   Identity of principle and phraseology of the Georgia Charter and state constitutions with the English Act of Settlement, 1701, and the Place Act of 1707,[61] shows them to have been the ultimate source of the principle. Part of the phraseology of the Place Act appears in the Constitution of the United States. The purpose, according to the Federalist (67), was to secure electors "free from any sinister bias."

Several important working principles of the Electoral College were evidently suggested by the constitution of Massachusetts of 1780.

(1) *The Electors "shall make a list of all persons voted for, and of the number of votes for each."* [62] The Massachusetts constitution provided that the town clerk with the assistance of the selectmen "shall . . . form a list of the persons voted for with the number of votes for each (person)." [63]

(2) *The Electors are required to "sign, certify, and transmit" the list "sealed to the seat of the Government, . . . directed to the President of the Senate."* [64] In general outline this follows the Massachusetts plan which provided for the clerk and selectmen sealing up copies of the list, attesting them, and transmitting the list to the sheriff who is to transmit it to the Secretary's office.[65]

(3) *"The President of the Senate shall in the presence of the Senate and House of Representatives" open the certificates and count the votes.* [66] The Massachusetts constitution provided for the counting of the votes "before the Senate and House of Representatives." [67] The Delaware constitution provided for counting the vote for President "by the Speakers of each house in the presence of the other members." [68] In Virginia, the vote was to be "examined jointly by a committee of each house." [69] It is the Massachusetts plan, or possibly that and the suggestion of Delaware regarding the Speakers presiding that is adopted. The language of Massachusetts is employed.

(4) *The Constitution provided that the person having the greatest number of votes, if "a majority of the whole number of Electors," should be President.* [70] The constitution of Massachusetts required "an election by a majority of all the votes returned." [71]

(5) *The Constitution gives eventual election to the House of Representatives.* [72] This was also suggested by the constitution of Massachusetts which gave eventual election to the legis-

lature.[73]   On July 17, James Wilson spoke in the Federal Convention in favor of the Massachusetts expedient giving eventual election to the legislature.   The committee of eleven, however, gave eventual election to the Senate, apparently on the ground that the large states would have the advantage in nominating the candidates, while ultimate election by the Senate would give the advantage to the small states.[74]   Gouverneur Morris gave a second reason.   Randolph asked: Why is eventual election given to the Senate instead of the legislature?   Gouverneur Morris replied: "The Senate was preferred, because fewer could then say to the President, 'You owe your appointment to us.' " [75] His answer shows that the committee had the Massachusetts plan under consideration, and that giving the Senate eventual election was merely a conscious adoption of part of the Massachusetts expedient for the whole.   On September 4 and 5, Wilson moved to strike out "Senate" and give eventual election to the legislature.[76]   That is, that the principle of Massachusetts be adopted.   However, it was felt that the Senate was too powerful already to have anything to do with eventual election,[77] and it was seen that the same advantages might be secured to the small states, if eventual election were given to the House of Representatives, and the vote taken by states.   On Sherman's motion, the Convention, therefore, adopted this expedient.[78]   In a letter to George Hay, August 23, 1823, Madison says, eventual election was given to the House as "an accommodation to the anxiety of the smaller States for their sovereign equality," and because of the jealousy of the larger states "towards the cumulative functions of the Senate."   The House was thought safer than the Senate, because it had a larger number of members, and would, therefore, present greater obstacles to corruption.   The arrangement, he declares, was a *compromise* between the large and small states, in which the former secured the advantage by selecting the candidates from the people, and the latter by selecting the President from the candidates.   Were it not for this, he says, a joint ballot of both houses would have been substituted.[79]   That is, the complete Massachusetts plan would have been adopted.   The Vermont constitutions of 1777 and 1786, both provided for eventual election of the Governor by joint ballot of both houses. The North Carolina constitution contained the same provision.[80]

King declared the small states would never have consented to the appointment of the President by electors, if the large states had not consented to eventual election, and an equal vote in the House.[81]

Congress Is to Determine the Time of Choosing Electors, and Casting the Electoral Vote. The report of the committee of eleven submitted by Brearly, September 4, contained this provision in germ. "And of their giving their votes" was inserted September 5, and "the election shall be on the same day throughout the United States" was added September 6.[82] Some slight verbal changes were made in the clause as reported by the committee on style on September 15.[83]

(1) *The purpose of the clause was to secure regularity and uniformity.* Spaight, a member of the Federal Convention, said in the North Carolina convention, it was felt that if the power to determine the day were left to the states, one would appoint one day and another another day, which would result in confusion.

(2) *Another purpose of the clause by requiring the electors to meet on the same day, was to prevent cabal, combination, corruption, and bargaining between the Electoral colleges of the different states.* Spaight said again: "And that the election being on the same day in all the States, would prevent combination between the electors." [84] Iredell pointed out that if the day of election had been different in different states, electors chosen in one state might have gone from state to state which would have left room for undue influence. The requirement of the same day, however, prevented any kind of combination or secret deals or intrigues between the electors of different states.[85] Governor Randolph, a member of the Convention, gave the same explanation, and Gouverneur Morris of the committee of eleven said: "As the electors would vote at the same time throughout the United States, and at so great a distance from each other, the great evil of cabal was avoided. It would be impossible also to corrupt them." [86]

The Qualifications of the President. (Art. II, Sec. 1, cl. 5.) On August 20, Gerry moved that the committee of detail "be instructed to report proper qualifications for the President." [87] On August 22, Rutledge reported from the committee, a clause providing that the President should "be of the age of thirty-

five years, and a citizen of the United States, and shall have
been an inhabitant thereof for twenty-one years." No action
appears to have been taken on this, and it went to the committee
of eleven, which reported the clause September 4, almost as it
stands in the Constitution.[88]

The President must be a "natural-born citizen." This is
the language of common law—birth within the King's allegiance
or jurisdiction constituting such persons natural-born subjects.
This likewise became the fundamental principle of American
citizenship.[89] Aliens were distrusted, and this requirement was
intended as a safeguard against alien danger.[90] The exception,
"or a citizen of the United States at the time of the adoption
of the Constitution," was inserted for the purpose of excepting
a number of men of foreign birth, who had taken a prominent
part in the Revolution and in American affairs, such as Wilson,
Hamilton, Davie, Butler, McHenry, and Robert Morris. Wilson himself was, doubtless, responsible for the exception. He
had said on August 9, he would be placed in a peculiarly em-
barrassing position if foreigners were disqualified for office, as
he would be incapacitated under the very Constitution "he had
shared in the trust of making," [91] This, no doubt, guided the
committee in framing the clause.

The New Hampshire constitution of 1784 required an age
qualification of thirty years for Governor.[92] The discussion on
the age of Senators, which was fixed at thirty years, shows some
members of the Convention held that a man was not mentally
or politically mature till at least thirty years of age. If so,
thirty-five for President would put it on the safe side.

Some of the states made constitutional provision for a residence qualification for the office of Governor, as Massachusetts,
1780, seven years. New Hampshire following Massachusetts
required seven years, and South Carolina, ten years.[93] If this
were considered necessary for a state executive, then fourteen
years would be none too long for the more important office of
Executive of the United States.

*The Vice-President to Succeed the President in Case of
Death, etc.* (Art. II, Sec. 1, cl. 6.) This provision originated
in the committee of detail which, however, proposed that the
President of the Senate succeed the President.[94] On August 23,
Gouverneur Morris objected to the President of the Senate as

successor, and suggested the Chief Justice. Madison objected also on the ground that the Senate might retard the election of a President in order to carry points, which could be carried only when the revisionary power was in the hands of their own President, and on motion further action was postponed. The clause went to the committee of eleven, which substituted the Vice-President for the President of the Senate in its report of September 4.[95] The sources of the clause are to be found:

(1) *In the state constitutions.* This section was modelled after the constitution of New York. Hamilton says in the Federalist: "We have a Lieutenant-Governor chosen by the people at large who presides in the Senate, and is the Constitutional substitute for the Governor in casualties similar to those, which would authorize the Vice-President to exercise the authorities and discharge the duties of President."[96] This refers to Article XX of the New York Constitution which uses the same words as the Constitution of the United States. In case of impeachment, death, resignation, absence, or removal from office, the Lieutenant-Governor was to succeed the Governor.[97] It will be noticed that the Constitution of the United States omits impeachment as one of the occasions on which the Vice-President succeeds to the Presidency. As a matter of fact, Rutledge and Gouverneur Morris moved "that persons impeached be suspended from their offices until they be tried and acquitted." This was in harmony with Rutledge's own state constitution, South Carolina,[98] as well as with the constitution of New York[99] from which it was evidently taken by South Carolina. Madison, instantly with wise foresight, pointed out what it took New York a century and a quarter to learn, namely, that intermediate suspension would place the President absolutely in the power of one branch of the legislature, which could at any moment unite to remove him. The proposal was, therefore, wisely defeated.[100] Other states made a similar provision, as South Carolina and Massachusetts.[101]

(2) *The colonial charters.* The Charter of Massachusetts Bay, 1691, provided that in case of the death, removal from office, or absence of the Governor, "the Lieutenant or Deputy-Governor" should succeed to the Executive office. The Charter of 1629, the Commission for New Hampshire, the Charter of Connecticut, 1662, and the Charter of Rhode Island, 1663, all

contained a similar provision.[102] The Albany Plan of 1754, provided that the speaker of the Grand Council should succeed the President General in case of death.[103]

(3) *The English trading charter.* This principle of succession is found, for example, in the charter to the East India Company, December 31, 1600, which empowered the Deputy-Governor to act in the absence, death, or removal from office of the Governor.[104]

The report of the committee of eleven provided that the Vice-President act "until the time of electing a President arrive." Madison objected that this would prevent the filling of a vacancy by an intermediate election, and suggested instead the phrase "or a President shall be elected," which was adopted.[105]

Compensation of the President. The Virginia Plan provided that the President should receive a fixed compensation which could not be increased or diminished.[106] The report of the committee of the whole, June 13, provided for a fixed stipend paid out of the national treasury. The Patterson Plan was similar to the Virginia Plan. The Convention agreed to the report of the Committee of the Whole, July 20 and 26. The committee of detail reported the clause almost as in the Constitution. The last clause, "and he shall not receive . . . them," was added on motion of Rutledge and Doctor Franklin.[107] There was no discussion on the subject in the Convention, hence the reasons for the clause must be sought elsewhere. James Wilson said: "In order to secure the President from any dependence on the legislature as to his salary," the Constitution provided it shall not be increased nor diminished during his term of office, and that he should not receive any other emolument from the United States.[108] This frees the President from any temptation to have his salary increased by Congress on the one hand, or pressure brought to bear on him on the other.

The President's Oath. (Art. II, Sec. 1, cl. 8.) The report of the committee of detail provided the form of oath to be taken by the President. This contained the first half of the oath, namely, "I do solemnly swear . . . States." On August 27, Colonel Mason and Madison moved to add what became the second half of the oath: "and will to the best . . . United States."

The Convention drew on the oath of Pennsylvania as a model. The phraseology is taken from the Pennsylvania oath with the changes and additions necessary to render it suitable for the President of the United States. "I do (solemnly) swear (or affirm) that I will faithfully execute the office of" is from the Pennsylvania Constitution.[109] The addition, as originally offered by Mason and Madison contained a whole clause from the Pennsylvania oath: "And will to the best of my judgment and (abilities)." The words "preserve, protect, defend the Constitution of the United States" seem to be an echo of the Governor's oath of Georgia and South Carolina which required him to take an oath to "support, maintain and defend" the Constitution. The state constitutions, the Charter of Massachusetts Bay, 1691, and the Charter of the East India Company, 1600, required an oath of office of the Governor. The British coronation oath required the King to promise to rule according to the Constitution and Laws.[110]

NOTES TO CHAPTER X

1. Elliot, V, 108; Elliot, V, 128; I, 148; Am. Hist. Assoc. Rep. 1902, I, 118; Am. Hist. Rev. IX, 742; Moore, Am. Eloquence, I, 364; Elliot, I, 176.
2. Elliot, V, 140, 141.
3. Id. 140, 141, 149.
4. Elliot, V, 149, 150, 151.
5. Elliot, V, 150, 151, 190, 376, 380, 472; I, 302.
6. Poore, Charters passim.
7. Prothero, Statutes, 450.
8. Blackstone, Com. I, 250; Comp. Elliot, V, 141, with Blackstone, I, 250.
9. Montesquieu, Spirit of Laws, Bk. XI, Chap. VI. American experience of a lack of an executive under Confederation also counted.
10. Meigs, Growth of the Constitution, 316 (VI), 200.
11. Poore, 1542.
12. Elliot, V, 380.
13. Poore, 964.
14. Poore, 1287.
15. Am. Hist. Rev. IX, 742.
16. Poore, 274, 1545, 1312, 1617, 1287.
17. Elliot, II, 127.
18. Art. IX, Arts of Confed.
19. Minutes of the Prov. Cong. of N. J. 170, 173, 198, 203; Journals of Prov. Cong. of Mass. 15, 16, 84.
20. Poore, 1272, 1275, 1278.
21. Poore, 1335, 1542, 1617, 1689.
22. Elliot, V, 128, 142; Am. Hist. Assoc. Rep. I, 1902, 118.
23. Poore, 1335.

24. Id. 274, 1621, 1622.
25. Elliot, V, 142.
26. Elliot, V, 143.
27. Id. 142, 143, 149, 190; I, 377; Id. I, 179; V, 205, 325, 326, 327.
28. Id. 339, 369, 370, Id. 380; Meigs, Growth, 316 (VI, seq.). Elliot, V, 507.
29. Id. 359.
30. Federalist, No. 68, 38 (Dawson ed.).
31. Am. Commonwealth, I, 40.
32. Elliot, Debates, V, 204, 205, 322, 323, 360.
33. Elliot, II, 127.
34. Elliot, V, 142.
35. Elliot, V, 143; Poore, Charters, 823.
36. Poore, Charters and Constitutions, 1546 (Sec. 32). Elliot, IV, 134.
37. Elliot, V, 323, 503, 506.
38. Federalist (Dawson ed.), no. 38, pp. 259, 260.
39. N. J. Poore, 274 (Lodge ed.), p. 234; Del. Id. 1312; Pa. Id. 1545; Md. Id. 824; Va. Id. 1910; N. C. Id. 1412; S. C. Id. 1617, 1621; Ga. Id. 378.
40. Elliot, V, 1, 192; III, 201; Elliot, V, 128; Id. 142, 143, Id. 142, 322; II, 511.
41. Elliot, V, 144, 322, 323, 337, 364, 508, 509. Id. 363, 364, 365. Id. 508, 512. Id. 304. Id. 361, 508, 519, 337, 360, III, 486, 490, 491.
42. Id. 363.
43. Elliot, V, 364; Federalist no. 67 (Dawson ed.).
44. Elliot, V, 323, 337, 367. Id. 322, 323, 337, 367. Id. 323, 324, 365.
45. Elliot, V, 337, 322-4, 365; Id. II, 511; Id. II, 512.
46. Farrand, Records, II, 404; III, 150; Elliot, V, 357, 358; III, 494. Dropped because of (1) Inconvenience (2) Expense.
47. Farrand, Records, III, 461.
48. Elliot, V, 518; I, 288.
49. Elliot, V, 364; III, 486; IV, 304, 305; II, 512; Federalist no. 67 (Dawson ed.).
50. Elliot, IV, 304.
51. Annals of Cong. (sixth sess.). Vol. 10, p. 29. Federalist 67; Farrand III, 386.
52. Annals of Congress (sixth sess.), Vol. 10, p. 29.
53. Poore, 924, 925; Poore, 937; Elliot, New Eng. Hist. 179; Prothero Statutes, 450; Poore, 1615.
54. Taswell-Langmead, Eng. Const. Hist. p. 278.
55. U. S. Const. Art. II, cl. 2.
56. Const. U. S. Art. II, Sec. I, cl. 2.
57. Const. U. S. Art. I, Sec. VI, cl. 2.
58. Art. V, Art. 18.
59. Poore, 1291, 1543, 824, 825, 1414, 380. So. Carolina, Poore, Charters, 1618, 1624
60. Id. 372; MacDonald, Sel. Charters, 182.
61. Adams and Stephens, 479, 483, 484.
62. Const. U. S. Art. II, sec. 1, cl. 3.
63. Poore, 964.
64. Const. U. S. Art. II, Sec. I, cl. 3.
65. Poore, 965.
66. Const. U. S. Art. II, Sec. I, cl. 3.
67. Poore, 965.
68. Poore Charters, 274.

69. Id. 1910.
70. Const. U. S. Art. II, sec. I, cl. 3.
71. Poore, 965.
72. Const. U. S. Art. II, sec. I, cl. 3.
73. Poore, 965.
74. Elliot, V, 323; Elliot, V, 503, 513.
75. Elliot, V, 510.
76. Id. 509, 513.
77. Id. 513, 514, 515, 516, 517.
78. Elliot, V, 519.
79. Farrand, Records, III, 458.
80. Poore, 1862, 1870, 1417.
81. Farrand, Records, III, 461.
82. Elliot, V, 507; Id. 515, 158.
83. Id. 302, I, 314.
84. Elliot, IV, 105.
85. Elliot, IV, 105.
86. Elliot, IV, 486; Id. V, 508.
87. Id. V, 447.
88. Elliot, V, 462; Id. 507.
89. Blackstone Com. II, 250, 251; 11 St. Tr. 106; Prothero, 446; Blackstone I, 366, 374; U. S. v. Wong Kim Ark, 169, U. S. 649; Calvin's Case, 7 Coke 1, 4b, 6a, 18a, b.
90. Elliot, V, 397-8; 411-412.
91. Elliot, V, 399.
92. Poore, 1287.
93. Poore, 964; Id. 1287; Id. 1621.
94. Elliot, V, 380.
95. Id. 480, 481, 520, 521, I, 302, V, 549, for further history.
96. Federalist. no. 67 (Dawson ed.).
97. Poore, Charters & Constitutions, 1336.
98. Poore, 1621.
99. Poore, 1336.
100. Elliot, V, 541, 542.
101. Poore, 1618, 1621, 1622, Poore, 967.
102. Id. 953, 937, 1278, 253, 1598.
103. MacDonald, Sel. Charters, 257.
104. Prothero, Statutes, 450.
105. Elliot, V, 520, 521, I, 302; V, 549. See Succession Laws of 1792 and 1786.
106. Elliot, V, 128.
107. Elliot, V, 190, 192, 370, 376, 380, 302, I, 302, 314; Id. 549.
108. Elliot, II, 446.
109. Id. V, 380, 481.
110. Poore, 1547, 381, 950, 1620.
Prothero, 450, 392.

CHAPTER XI

The Powers of the President

He is Commander-in-chief and May Grant Reprieves and Pardons. (Art. II, Sec. 2, cl. 1) The Pinckney Plan provided that the President should "be commander-in-chief of the army and navy of the United States, and of the militia of the several states." [1] In the Patterson Plan, he was "to direct all military operations." [2] Hamilton's plan gave him "the direction of war when authorized or begun." [3] Rutledge wrote on the margin of the Randolph draft, the words of the Pinckney draft above,[4] and "his pardon shall not however be pleadable to an impeachment." [5] This was reported from the committee of detail, August 6, by Rutledge,[6] and "except in cases of impeachment" substituted on August 25.[7] On August 27, Sherman moved to amend by adding: "when called into the actual service of the United States," after "states," which was adopted.[8]

The clause providing that the President might require the opinion in writing of the heads of the executive departments, grew out of the idea of furnishing the President with an executive council. Gerry on June 1, suggested giving the executive a council, and Sherman pointed out there was a council in all the states, and the British King had a council. Rutledge suggested on July 21 that the President could advise with the officers of state as of war, finance, and avail himself of their information and opinion,[9] and Ellsworth on August 18 proposed that the council consist of the President of the Senate, Chief Justice, and the heads of foreign and domestic affairs, war, finance, and marine "who should advise but not conclude the President." [10] Charles Pinckney asked that the question be permitted to lie over which was done, and on August 20, Gouverneur Morris and Pinckney submitted a plan for a council of state to be referred to the committee of detail. This was to consist of the Chief Justice and six secretaries as foreign affairs, war, state, and provided the President "may require the written opinion of any one or more of the members," but left him free to adopt their advice or not as he pleased.[11] Rutledge reported from the committee August 22, recommending a Privy Council and adding the President of the Senate and Speaker of the House to its members, "but their advice shall not conclude him nor affect his responsibility for the measures which he shall adopt." [12]   No action was taken on this, by the Convention, and it went to the committee of eleven on postponed and unfinished portions of the Constitution which reported the clause, as it stands, on September 4.   Rutledge's suggestion of July 21, and a portion of the plan of Gouverneur Morris and Pinckney were combined in the clause.[13]   Gouverneur Morris explained that the committee had rejected a council because it believed that a President who could persuade his council to consent to wrong measures, "would acquire their protection for them." [14]   This arrangement was intended to take the place of a council, and was such that it could scarcely result in anything but a cabinet.

The pre-convention origins of the clause were as follows:

1. *The President is Commander-in-chief.* This had its source:

(1) *In the state constitutions.* The Massachusetts Constitution of 1780 made the executive commander-in-chief of the army and navy.[15]   New Hampshire followed Massachusetts word for word. New York, North Carolina, and New Jersey made the governor commander-in-chief of the militia.   The other states also made the executive commander-in-chief, but worded the provision differently.   The constitutional provision combines the statements of Massachusetts, New York, North Carolina, and New Jersey.[16]

(2) *The colonial charters.* The Charter of Massachusetts Bay, 1691, made the governor commander-in-chief of the militia. The constitution of Massachusetts simply repeated the language of this charter.[17]   The charter of Georgia, 1732, Virginia, 1609, New England, 1620, Massachusetts Bay, 1629, Connecticut and Rhode Island, 1662 and 1663, and the Grant of the Province of Maine, 1664, all contained the principle.[18] The North West Ordinance made the Governor commander-in-chief of the militia.[19]   The British executive was also declared

by statute to be commander-in-chief of the militia and all the forces by sea and land.[20]

2. *The Executive May Require the Opinion in Writing of Heads of Departments.* Departments were already in existence when the constitution was framed.[21] The Convention refused to give the President a council, because it would divide and destroy responsibility. The desire was to have the President alone responsible.[22] In the American republic it would serve to destroy, or would greatly diminish the intended and necessary responsibility of the Chief Magistrate himself." [23] In England the King was not responsible, the Council was. In America the executive himself was responsible, impeachable, and punishable. There was not, therefore, the same need for a council as in England, but it was very desirable that he should have advisors to assist him in discharging his arduous duties. The advice of experienced heads of departments has, therefore, been placed at his disposal. The opinions are to be given in writing because that will make them more cautious as to the kind of advice they give, will deepen their sense of responsibility and act as a check upon them, since all opinions are to be preserved. The Convention substituted this arrangement for a council.[24] The suggestions for this came from three sources:

(1) *The state constitutions.* The governors were supplied with councils to advise them on executive business. The constitution of New Hampshire provided a council of five to advise the governor.[25] Massachusetts, New York, Pennsylvania, Virginia, North Carolina, South Carolina, and other states had councils.[26] It was difficult for the framers to think of a government without a council.

(2) *The colonial charters.* The colonial governors had their councils provided by the charters, as Massachusetts, Rhode Island, Pennsylvania, Virginia, and Georgia.[27] The idea of a council was an inseparable part of American political experience.

(3) *The example of England.* The Convention had the English council specially in mind. Pinckney called the proposed council "a cabinet council." The model proposed was similar to that of England.[28] Speaking of this Iredell said: "It is very difficult immediately on our separation from Great

Britain, to disengage ourselves entirely from ideas of government we had been used to. We had been accustomed to a council under the old government, and took it for granted we ought to have one under the new." It has been the opinion of many gentlemen, that the President should have a council. This opinion, probably, has been derived from the example of England. "Even in Great Britain," said Sherman, "the King has a council." [29] The arrangement of the Constitution was, therefore, an intentional substitution for an executive council.

3. *The President's Power to Grant Reprieves and Pardons.* The sources of this are threefold:

(1) *The state constitutions.* The Governor of Massachusetts could grant reprieves and pardons with the advice of his council except in cases of impeachment.[30] The New Hampshire constitution gave the Governor the same power.[31] The New York Governor could grant reprieves and pardons even for impeachment, and except in cases of treason and murder.[32] In Delaware, Virginia, and North Carolina, the executive could grant reprieves and pardons except in impeachment cases.[33] In Pennsylvania, the executive and council could grant pardons in all cases "except in cases of impeachment," and reprieves in all cases except treason and murder till the end of next session of Assembly.[34]

(2) *The colonial charters.* The Charter of New England, 1620, gave the council and Governor power to pardon in all cases, civil and criminal.[35] The Charter to Sir Walter Raleigh, 1584, the Massachusetts Charter of 1629, the Charter for the Province of Pennsylvania 1681, the Grant of the Province of Maine, 1684, and the New Jersey Concession and Agreement 1665, all gave the same or similar power.[36] The colonial governors had exercised the power from early times.

(3) *The English constitution.** The English Kings had exercised the prerogative of mercy, and the members of the committee of detail had in mind Danby's Case and the Act of Settlement, and apparently had Blackstone's account before them.[37] Danby, on being impeached in 1679, pleaded the King's pardon in bar of the impeachment. The Commons declared this "was illegal and void, and ought not to be allowed in bar of the impeachment of the Commons of England," [38] and they

demanded judgment. Settlement of the case was prevented by prorogation of Parliament, but on June 6, 1689, the Commons voted "that a pardon is not pleadable in bar of an impeachment." [39] The question was not finally settled till 1701 by the Act of Settlement which declares: "That no pardon under the great seal of England be pleadable to an impeachment by the Commons in Parliament." [40] So when Rutledge wrote on the margin of Randolph's committee draft, "His pardon shall not however be pleadable to an impeachment," he used the phraseology of the Act of Settlement, while the report of the committee of August 6, used the exact phraseology of the vote of the Commons on June 6, 1689.[41]

"By the act of settlement," said the Supreme Court of the United States in Ex Parte Wells, "12 and 13 Will. III, c. 2, Eng., no pardon under the great seal is pleadable to an impeachment by the Commons in Parliament, but after the articles of impeachment have been heard and determined, he may pardon. The provision in our Constitution, excepting cases of impeachment out of the power of the President to pardon, was evidently taken from that statute, and is an improvement upon the same." On the other hand, the phraseology of the Constitution closely resembles that of *the state constitutions*— "except in cases of impeachments" being the exact language of Pennsylvania.[42]

The Treaty-making and Appointing Power. (Art. II, Sec. 2, cl. 2.) Hamilton's plan gave the executive power to make all treaties "with the advice and approbation of the Senate." [43] The report of the committee of detail, August 6, gave the Senate power to make treaties.[44] Objection was made by Mason to the treaty-making power of the Senate on the ground that it might alienate territory and dismember the union,[45] and Madison urged that the President should be an agent in treaties, since, the Senate represented the states alone.[46] No further action was taken and the clause went to the committee of eleven on postponed and unfinished portions which reported September 4, giving the President power to make treaties "by and with the advice and consent of the Senate," provided two-thirds of the members present concurred.[47] When the clause was discussed on September 7, Wilson objected that two thirds would put it in the power of a minority to control the will of a majority, but all attempts on the part of Wilson and others to change this were defeated and the Convention agreed to the clause as reported.[48]

The Pinckney plan gave the President power to nominate, and, with the consent of the Senate, appoint all other officers of the United States except "ambassadors, other ministers, and judges of the Supreme Court." [49] The resolution of the committee of the whole gave the executive power to appoint to offices "not otherwise provided for." The New Jersey Plan followed the resolutions, and Hamilton's plan gave the President the sole appointment of the heads of the departments of finance, war, foreign affairs, and the nomination of all other officers subject to the approbation or rejection of the Senate. On July 17 the Convention agreed to the provision of the committee of the whole and the New Jersey Plan. It was agreed on July 21 that the judges should be appointed by the second branch. The report of the committee of detail gave the appointment of judges and ambassadors to the Senate and to the executive the appointment of officers not otherwise provided for by the Constitution.[50] The clause was referred to the committee of detail [51] and the whole subject went to the committee of eleven on postponed and unfinished portions which reported on September 4, giving the President power to appoint ambassadors, "other public ministers, judges of the Supreme Court, and all other officers of the United States whose appointments are not otherwise herein provided for";[52] "and consuls" was added on September 7. "And which shall be established by law" was added on September 15. On Gouverneur Morris' motion, the clause "but the Congress may by law vest . . . departments," was added on the ground that it was too necessary to be omitted.[53]

1. *Treaties.* The sources were:

(1) *The state constitution.* The Constitution of South Carolina furnished a precedent for requiring that treaties be made with the consent of the legislature. The President, according to the constitution of 1776, could not make a final treaty without the consent of the General Assembly and legislative Council and the constitution of 1778 required the consent of the Senate and House of Representatives.[54] The Randolph draft shows that the committee of detail adopted this at first

and Wilson proposed it on September 7 in the Convention but it was rejected.[55]   Only part of the South Carolina provision was adopted because the Senate represented the states, "that thereby," said Spaight in the North Carolina Convention, "the interest of every state" might be "equally attended to in the formation of treaties." [56]   The small states absolutely refused to enter the union "without an equal voice in the formation of treaties."   Without this, they believed their interests would be neglected or sacrificed in treaty making.   "This difficulty," said Davie, "could not be got over. . . . Every man was convinced of the inflexibility of the little states on this point. It, therefore, became necessary to give them an absolute equality in making treaties.[57]

Hugh Williamson testifies that the requirement that "two thirds of the Senators present concur" was expressly intended to prevent a majority from giving up the Mississippi.[58]

(2) *The English Constitution.*   All were familiar with the fact that the King or Executive "made treaties . . . with foreign states and princes." [59]

General Pinckney quoted from Blackstone's Commentaries in the South Carolina Convention to prove that it was the King's prerogative to make treaties.[60]   Accordingly, some members of the Convention desired to lodge the treaty-making power in the President alone.   "Political caution and republican jealousy rendered it improper for us to vest it in the President alone," and as a result, it was deemed safest to vest the power in the President and Senate—the President to have the power of proposing treaties and the Senate "the power of agreeing or disagreeing with the terms proposed." [61]   Congress had made treaties under the Articles of Confederation,[62] and this power is in part continued in the Senate which is a continuation of the old Congress.

2. *Appointments.*   The portion of the section dealing with appointments has its source.

(1) *In the state constitutions.*   On July 18, Gorham suggested that the Convention adopt the provision of the constitution of Massachusetts for the appointment of judges which provided that "all judicial officers . . . shall be nominated and appointed by the Governor by and with the advice and consent of the Council."   The New York Constitution of 1777

also provided for a Council of appointment composed of Senators, and the Governor appointed the officers "with the advice and consent of the said Council." [63] It is, however, the phraseology of Massachusetts that was adopted. The House of Representatives was excluded from having any voice in appointments, because the small states would not hear of it. On the other hand, "the extreme jealousy of all the states would not give it to the President alone," consequently, it was given to the President and Senate which preserves the federal principle and was believed to be safer, said Davie.[64] Gouverneur Morris, in a letter to Lewis Morris December 10, 1803, said, the Senate's negative on appointments to office was simply a share of the ancient executive power exercised by the old Congress of Confederation.[65]

(2) *The Charter of Massachusetts Bay 1691.* This provided that the "Governor with the advice and consent of the Councill or Assistants" was "from time to time to nominate and appoint judges." [66] The constitution of Massachusetts, 1780, retained this provision which passed in this way to the Constitution of the United States. The Charter of Georgia provided for appointments by the Council.[67]

(3) *The English Constitution.* (a) *Indirect influence.* Roger Sherman said on June 18, 1789, in the House of Representatives that the Convention knew that the crown of Great Britain had, by exercising the prerogative of making appointments, been able to swallow up the whole administration and subject both houses of the legislature to its will and pleasure, therefore, the members thought it would tend to secure the liberties of the people if they prohibited the President from the sole appointment of all officers. This shows the indirect influence on this section of the Constitution of a defect in the English system.

(b) *Direct influence.* The *enacting words of British statutes* appear twice in the clause. Gerry called attention to this in the House of Representatives on June 16, 1789. "If we observe the enacting style of the statutes of Great Britain," he said, "we shall find pretty near the same words as what are used in the Constitution with respect to appointments: "*Be it enacted* by the King's most excellent majesty, *by and with the advice and consent of Parliament.*" [68]

The King also appointed and sent ambassadors to foreign states,[69] and in 1311, the New Ordinance provided for the appointment of certain officers—the Chancellor, two Chief Justices, the treasurer, comptroller and others—by the King "by the counsel and assent of his baronage and that in Parliament." That is by the executive and upper house or what became the upper House as in the Constitution of the United States.[70]

The President May Fill Vacancies During a Recess of the Senate. (Art. II, Sec. 2, cl. 3.) This clause was introduced on motion of Spaight of North Carolina on September 7 and agreed to immediately by the Convention.[71] He took it from the constitution of his own state which gave the Governor power to fill vacancies during the recess of the General Assembly with the advice of the council of state "by granting a temporary commission which shall expire at the end of the next session of the General Assembly.[72]

The President is to Advise Congress, Convene Extraordinary Sessions, Adjourn Them in Case of Disagreement, Receive Ambassadors, and Execute the Laws. (Art. II, Sec. 3.) This section originated in the committee of detail which reported it on August 6 almost as it stands in the Constitution. The words "other public ministers" were added on August 25, the purpose of which is obvious.[73] On September 8, McHenry called the attention of the Convention to the fact that the President had not been given power to convene the Senate in extraordinary session without the lower house, and moved to substitute: "He may convene both or either of the Houses on extraordinary occasions," for the clause simply giving power to "convene them on extraordinary occasions," which was agreed to by the Convention. Some slight changes were made in phraseology by the committee on style.[74]

1. *The President's Message to Congress.* This took its origin:

(1) *From the Constitution of New York, 1777.* This made it the duty of the Governor to "inform the Legislature at every session of the condition of the state, so far as may respect his department; to recommend such matters to their consideration as shall appear to him to concern its good government, welfare and prosperity." The method was not prescribed.

(2) *The colonial system or constitution.* The colonial legislative system was modelled closely after the English Parliamentary system. The colonial Governor stood in place of the King. The Council represented the House of Lords, and the General Assembly, the English House of Commons. On the opening of Parliament the King delivered a speech from the throne. The Governor of New York followed this custom, so long and so well known to the people, and communicated with both houses by spoken message. This custom of delivering a speech, or spoken message at the opening session of the legislature was followed by the Governors of the State of New York from 1777 to 1821, the date of the adoption of New York's second constitution.[75] Washington adopted the practice and communicated with Congress by spoken message. Adams followed Washington, but Jefferson, being a poor speaker, adopted the written message, which continued to be the custom down to President Wilson who made a return to the custom of spoken message.

(3) *The English Parliamentary practice.* Parliamentary custom required the King to deliver a speech at the opening of Parliament.[76] This became the custom in Colonial New York. It was adopted by the constitution of 1777 and passed to the Constitution of the United States as shown above.

2. Extraordinary Sessions. The clause giving the President power to call extraordinary sessions of Congress was taken from the constitution of New York.[77] Other state constitutions provided for calling extraordinary sessions of the legislature,[78] but it is the phraseology of New York's constitution that is used. The Ordinance of Virginia 1621, also gave the Governor power to call the Council or General Assembly together "for very extraordinary and important occasions."[79] In England, no Parliament could be convened by its own authority. It must be called by the King's writ [80] and only on two occasions did it meet without the royal summons, 1660 and 1688. These meetings were called Conventions or Convention-Parliaments and their action legalized by succeeding Parliaments.[81] The executive was given power to call the Senate in extraordinary session because it had a concurrent power with the executive in making treaties, and it was believed it might be necessary to call the Senate together for this purpose, when it would be utterly unnecessary to convene the House of Representatives.[82]

3. *Power to Adjourn Congress.* This idea was taken from the constitution of Massachusetts 1780 which gave the Governor with the advice of the Council power to adjourn the General Court.[83] Governor Randolph testified that the constitution of Massachusetts was produced in the Federal Convention, as an example in favor of giving this power to the President.[84]

4. *The President to Recei.e Ambassadors.* The executive "sends or receives embassies," s., ,s Montesquieu in describing the British Constitution.[85] "The King, therefore, considered as the representative of his people, has the sole power of sending ambassadors to foreign states and receiving ambassadors at home," says Blackstone.[86] The American executive is given the same powers.

5. *The President to Execute the Laws.* This clause was taken from the constitution of New York 1777, which makes it the duty of the Governor "to take care that the laws are faithfully executed." [87] The exact phraseology of the Constitution of the United States appears in the constitution of Pennsylvania 1776, but in this case the duty or obligation is laid on the Governor and Council conjointly.[88] The Pennsylvania Frame of Government, 1683, contains a similar provision,[89] while the constitutions of Vermont, 1777 and 1786 similarly provide for the Governor and Council.[90]

6. *The President to Commission All Officers of the United States.* The state constitutions gave the executive or executive and council power to commission all state officers. In New York, New Jersey, North Carolina, Virginia, and Georgia the Governor commissioned all state officers,[91] while in Pennsylvania and South Carolina the same duty was performed by the President and Council.[92]

The President, Vice-President, and Civil Officers Removable by Impeachment. (Art. II, Sec. 4.) The Virginia Plan provided for impeachment of national officers by the national judiciary.[93] Pinckney's plan provided for the impeachment of the President.[94] On June 2, Williamson and Davie moved that the executive "be removable on impeachment and conviction of malpractice or neglect of duty" which was adopted.[95] The New Jersey Plan provided for the removal of the executive by

Congress on the application of a majority of the state executives and impeachment of federal officers to be heard by the Supreme Court.[96] On July 20, the discussion and vote in the Convention favored the idea of making the executive impeachable as a safeguard against incapacity, negligence, or perfidy.[97] The resolutions referred to the committee of detail on July 26, contained the motion of Williamson and Davie, and the report of the committee on August 6, provided that the President "shall be removed from his office on impeachment by the House of Representatives, and conviction in the Supreme Court of treason, bribery, or corruption." [98] Gouverneur Morris declared the Supreme Court an improper tribunal for trying the President, and on his motion the question was postponed, August 27.[99] The clause went to the committee on postponed and unfinished portions which reported on September 4, substituting the Senate for the Supreme Court, and cutting out the word "corruption." [100] On September 8, Mason said that treason as defined by the Constitution would not reach many dangerous offences. Hastings was not guilty of treason. Attempts to subvert the Constitution might not be treason as defined above. Bills of attainder had saved the British Constitution. As these were forbidden, it was necessary to extend the power of impeachments. He moved to add "or maladministration." Madison pointed out that this was so vague, the executive would simply hold office at the pleasure of the Senate. Mason then substituted "other high crimes and misdemeanors against the State" which was adopted.[101] The word "state" was stricken out and "United States" inserted to remove ambiguity [102] and the following clause added: "The Vice-President and other civil officers of the United States, shall be removed from office on impeachment, and conviction as aforesaid." [103] The committee on style reported the clause as in the Constitution.[104] The sources were:

(1) *The state constitutions.* These provided for impeachment of state officers for offences committed in office, as Massachusetts, New York, Pennsylvania, Delaware, and New Hampshire.[105]

(2) *The English Constitution.* Impeachment originated in England in 1376. "Treason, bribery, or other high crimes and misdemeanors" are terms very familiar to students of

English constitutional history and law. Howell's State Trials show that the most common offence for which men were impeached was treason. Bribery also appears as an impeachment offence, as for example, in the case of Sir John Bennet 1621 who was impeached for "bribery and corruption." [106] These were the terms contained in the resolutions of the committee of detail. "High crimes and misdemeanors," says Roger Foster, was a "technical term used by the Commons at the bar of the Lords for centuries before the existence of the United States." [107] The phrase was used in 1624 as appears from Howell's State Trials, in the trial of Lord Treasurer Middlesex, and it was employed almost as frequently as the term treason.[108] The purpose of the Constitution was to make the President personally responsible for any abuse of his great powers and thus safeguard the people of the United States. "It will not only be the means of punishing misconduct but it will prevent misconduct," said Iredell.[109]

NOTES TO CHAPTER XI

1. Moore, Am. Eloquence, I, 364.
2. Elliot, V, 192.
3. Id. 205.
4. Meigs, Growth of the Const. 316 (VI seq.).
5. Id. 316, VII, seq.
6. Elliot, V. 380.
7. Id. 480.
8. Elliot, V, 480.
9. Id. 141, 150, 349.
10. Elliot, V, 442.
11. Id. 446.
12. Elliot, V, 462.
13. Id. 349, 446, 526.
14. Id. 525.
15. Poore, 965.
16. Id. 1288, 1335, 1412, 1312, 275, 381, 1517, 1621, 1863, 1545, 825, 1911; Federalist, No. 68, p. 480, 481 (Dawson ed.).
17. Poore, 953, 965.
18. Id. 377, 1396, 1901, 927, 941, 785, 256, 1600.
19. McClain, Const. Law, App. of Docs. p. 400.
20. 13 Car. II, c. 6; 30 Geo. II, c. 25.
21. See J. F. Jameson, Essays in Const. Hist. or Journals of Congress, Index, war, treasury, etc.
22. Elliot, V, 525.
23. Federalist, No. 69, Elliot, IV, 110.
24. Elliot, IV, 108, 109.
25. Poore, 1289.

26. Poore, 967, 1332, 1542, 1544, 1910, 1412, 1617, 1621.
27. Id. 949, 955, 1597, 1527, 1898, 1905, 1906, 371.
28. Moore, Am. Eloquence, I, 364; Elliot, V, 442, 446, 522, 525.
29. Elliot, IV, 108; Federalist, No. 69, p. 493-4 (Dawson ed.), Elliot, V, 150.
30. Poore, 966.
31. Poore, 1288.
32. Poore, 1335; Federalist No. 68.
33. Poore, 274, 1911, 1412.
34. Id. 1545.
35. Id. 925.
36. Poore, 1381, 932, 1511, 784, 786; MacDonald, Sel. Charters, 145.
37. Blackstone, Com. IV, 261.
38. Cobbett, Parl. Hist. IV, 1129; Blackstone, Com. IV, 261; Adams and Stephens, 439.
39. Com. Jour. under date.
40. Adams and Stephens, p. 479.
41. Com. Jour. under date.
* See Ex. parte Wells, 18 Howard 307 and Ex. parte Grossman, Adv. Sheets, Apr. 1, 1925, p. 332.
42. Adams and Stephens, Sel. Docs. of Eng. Const. Hist. 479, Poore, Charters 1545, Blackstone, Com. IV, 261.
43. Elliot, V, 205.
44. Id. 379.
45. Id. 428.
46. Id. 469.
47. Elliot, V, 507.
48. Id. 525, 526, 527, 528; I, 303.
49. Moore, Am. Eloquence, I, 364.
50. Elliot, V, 190, 192, 205, 325, 351, 380, 379.
51. Elliot, V, 470.
52. Id. 507, 524, 550.
53. Id. I, 314, 303.
54. Poore, 1619, 1626.
55. Meigs, Growth of the Constitution, p. 316 (plate V). Elliot, V, 523.
56. Elliot, IV, 27, 123, 124.
57. Elliot, IV, 120.
58. Farrand Records, III, 306, 307.
59. Blackstone, I, 256.
60. Elliot, IV, 278.
61. Id. 264, 265. Gen. Pinckney in S. C. Convention.
62. Art. IX.
63. Poore, 966, 1336; Elliot, V, 328.
64. Elliot, IV, 122, 123; In early Va., the Governor and Council appointed judges. Hening, I, 132, 168.
65. Farrand, Records, III, 405.
66. Poore, 949.
67. Id. 376.
68. Elliot, IV, 392, Annals of Cong. I, 537. Adams and Stephens, p. 485, 488, 490, 491, 477, 472 or
69. Blackstone, I, 253.
70. Adams and Stephens, p. 94; Federalist, 68.
71. Elliot, V, 524.
72. Poore, 1413.

73. Elliot, V, 380; Meigs, Growth of the Constitution, 316 (VI). Elliot, V, 479.
74. Elliot, V, 530; Id. I, 303.
75. See Messages from the Governors, Ed. by Chas. Z. Lincoln, Vol. I, passim; Id. II, 2.
76. Prothero, Statutes, p. 282 for example.
77. Poore, 1335.
78. Poore, 275, 965, 1545, 1624; Hening, I, 112; Laws of R. I. 1719, p. 1, 2.
79. MacDonald, Sel. Charters, p. 35.
80. Blackstone, Com. I, 150.
81. Id. 151, 152.
82. Federalist, No. 76, p. 537 (Dawson ed.).
83. Poore, 965.
84. Elliot, III, 367, 368.
85. Spirit of Laws, Bk. XI, Chap. VI.
86. Com. I, 253.
87. Poore, 1335.
88. Id. 1545.
89. Id. 1521, 1528.
90. Id. 1863, 1871.
91. Poore, 1336, 1312, 1412, 1911, 380.
92. Id. 1545, 1619, 1625.
93. Elliot, V, 128.
94. Id. 131.
95. Id. 149.
96. Elliot, V, 192.
97. Id. 340-342, 343, 376, 149.
98. Id. 380, Meigs, Growth of the Const. 316 (Plot VI, seq.).
99. Elliot, V, 480.
100. Elliott, V, 480.   For reasons see Art. I, sec. 3, cl. 6.
101. Elliot, V, 528.
102. Elliot, V, 529.
103. Id.
104. Elliot, I, 303.
105. Poore, 963, 1337, 1545, 277, 1286; See Art. I, Sec. 2, cl. 5 and Sec. 3, cls. 6, 7.
106. Howell, St. Tr. II, 146, St. Tr. (Table of Contents).
107. Roger Foster, The Constitution, 586, Blackstone, Com. IV, 5, 29, 121, 259; Adams and Stephens, 394.
108. St. Tr. II, 1182 IV, 42, 119, 151, 167, 174, etc.
109. Elliot, Debates, IV, 32; Federalist, No. 76 (Dawson ed.), 537-8.

CHAPTER XII

THE JUDICIARY

Origin of Supreme Court: Term of Office and Compensation of Judges. (Art. III, Sec. 1.) The Virginia Plan provided "that a national Judiciary be established; to consist of one or more supreme tribunals, and inferior tribunals; to be chosen by the national legislature; to hold their offices during good behaviour, and to receive punctually, at stated times, fixed compensation for their services, in which no increase or diminution shall be made so as to affect the persons actually in office at the time of such increase or diminution." [1] Pinckney's plan also provided for federal courts. [2] On June 4, the first clause was adopted, [3] and the words "to consist of one supreme tribunal, and of one or more inferior tribunals" [4] added. The words "one or more" were stricken out on June 5. [5] Rutledge moved to strike out the clause for establishing inferior tribunals on the ground that it would encroach on the jurisdiction of the states. Though opposed by Madison and Wilson, this was done, [6] but they immediately moved "that the national legislature be empowered to institute inferior tribunals." They distinguished between absolute establishment of such tribunals, and giving the legislature discretionary power to establish them or not as they saw fit. This was adopted. [7] On June 13, Madison moved that the judges be appointed by the Senate because being a less numerous and more select body, it would be more competent to elect than the whole legislature. This was also adopted. [8] The New Jersey Plan provided for one supreme court with appointment of judges by the executive. On August 27, Doctor Johnson said the judicial power ought to extend to *equity* as well as law, and moved to add "both in law and equity" which was agreed to, but these words were stricken out on September 15, as Section 2, cl. 1, contained them. [9] On July 18, on motion of Gouverneur Morris, the words "no increase" were stricken out on the ground that it might be necessary to increase salaries because the value of money,

197

social conditions, and the amount of business might change.[10]
The sources of the Supreme Court were various.

(1) *Hamilton's view*. This was that the Supreme Court
was not a new and original creation, but taken from a similar
system which existed in a majority of the states at the time.
He says: "These considerations teach us to applaud the wisdom of those states, who have committed the judicial power,
in the last resort, not to a part of the Legislature, but to
distinct and independent bodies of men. Contrary to the supposition of those who have represented the plan of the Convention, in this respect, as novel and unprecedented, it is but a
copy of the constitutions of New Hampshire, Massachusetts,
Pennsylvania, Delaware, Maryland, Virginia, North Carolina,
South Carolina, and Georgia; and the preference which has
been given to those models is highly to be commended." [11]
Delaware organized a supreme court, and then organized a second court of seven persons appointed "during good behaviour,"
and called the "Court of Appeals." An appeal was allowed
to this court from the supreme court in matters of law and
equity.[12] Delaware felt the need of a court to take the place
of the King in Council, and modelled its court of last resort,
in some degree, after the Supreme Court of the Empire as a
precedent.

(2) *The Court of Appeals in cases of capture*. Professor,
Jameson, H. L. Carson, and J. C. Bancroft Davis regard this
as "one of the origins of the Supreme Court of the United
States." [13]   Professors Willoughby and Channing think this
is a mistake.[14]   The Revolution destroyed the colonial admiralty courts, and courts were substituted which culminated
in the Court of Appeals in Cases of Capture.[15]   Several courts
were established till, finally, on January 15, 1780, Congress
passed a resolution establishing a court for the trial of all
appeals from the courts of admiralty in the United States in
cases of capture. The court was to consist of three judges
appointed and commissioned by Congress, any two of whom
could hold court for the despatch of business.[16]   Their commission empowered the judges to hear and determine appeals
"according to the law and usage of nations, and the Acts of
Congress." [17]   The court was, therefore, to apply both federal
and international law, as the Supreme Court of the United

States does.   On May 24, 1780, Congress adopted a resolution naming the court: "The Court of Appeals in Cases of Capture." [18]   H. L. Carson holds that one hundred and eighteen
cases could scarcely be appealed from the state courts of
admiralty to the federal court without familiarizing the people
with a federal judicature in federal matters.[19]   J. C. Bancroft
Davis says, "The idea of a federal court with a jurisdiction
coextensive with the limits of what were then the United Colonies and Provinces of Great Britain in North America, originated with Washington," who wrote to Congress November 11,
1775, urging that a prize court be established under its
authority.   H. L. Carson shows that Elbridge Gerry proposed
the establishment of such a court as early as June, 1775, in
the Second Continental Congress.[20]   Professor Jameson points
out that trial by committee was taken "from the example of
the appellate prize Courts of England." [21]   Acts of Parliament
provided for an appeal from the admiralty courts of the colonies to the commissioners for hearing such appeals appointed
under the Great Seal of Great Britain,[22] the "same as appeals
are allowed to such commissioners from the court of admiralty
within this Kingdom." [23]   The American court, then, according
to this view, finds its origin in the English commissioners of
appeals, or appellate committee of the Privy Council.   Even
this points to the Privy Council as the source of the American
court.

    (3) *Congress under the Articles of Confederation.*   H. L.
Carson says the power vested in Congress to establish judicial
tribunals by Article IX, Articles of Confederation, was "the
germ of our national judiciary—the seminal principle which
subsequently unfolded itself in the Constitution of the United
States." [24]   This gave Congress power to appoint "courts for
the trial of piracies and felonies committed on the high seas,
and establishing courts for receiving and determining finally
appeals in all cases of captures."   Congress also exercised the
function of a national court of final jurisdiction "in all disputes and differences" between the states, "concerning bound-
ary, jurisdiction, or any other cause whatever."   Commissioners
were appointed to try such causes.   It is held that all this
had an educative influence on the people of the United States
in leading them to the idea of the necessity of creating a suc-

cessor—the Supreme Court of the United States. Professor
Jameson thinks the organization of this court was taken from
the English Act of 1770, for settling disputed elections.[25]

(4) *The King in Council.* To speak of the courts under
Confederation as if they accustomed Americans to the idea of
a Supreme Court for the first time, is very short-sighted. There
never was a time when American colonists were not familiar
with the idea. The English King in Council had always been
a court of last resort to which appeals were carried from the
colonial courts or laws sent over "for approbation or disallowance." Professor Edward Channing, Herbert D. Hazeltine,
and others adopt the view that the King in Council was the
predecessor of the Supreme Court of the United States.[26] The
Charter of Carolina, 1663, the Grant to the Duke of York,
1664, and 1674, the New Hampshire Commission of 1679,
the Charter for the Province of Pennsylvania, 1681, the Commission ,of Governor Dongan of New York, 1686, the commission of Andros, 1686,[27] and the Charter of Massachusetts
Bay, 1691, all provided for appeals to the Supreme Court of
the Empire—the King in Council. The colonies passed laws
regulating appeals from their superior courts to the King in
Council.[28] Some of the cases carried to the Council on appeal
created a great stir in the colonies. Among these were Winthrop v. Lechmere, 1727, the Torrey case, Phillips v. Savage,
and Clark v. Tousey.[29] Many cases were carried from Rhode
Island and other colonies. Professor Channing mentions a score
of cases between 1760 and 1765.[30] It was impossible that all
this could take place without familiarizing the people with the
idea of one Supreme Court for all the colonies or people of
America. The Revolution cut them off from this court, and
the Articles of Confederation furnished nothing to take the
place of the Privy Council, and though the states established
superior courts, there was no common tribunal to which appeals
in cases in law or equity could be carried from all the state
courts as before the Revolution. The Court of Appeals in
Cases of Capture was modelled after the Lords Commissioners
of the Privy Council, which heard appeals from the admiralty
courts of the colonies, and the court created by Congress was
a substitute for the Privy Council which had formerly settled
disputes between the colonies.[31] The state of Delaware felt

the need of a court to take the place of the King in Council
so strongly that they not only created a supreme state court,
but also a court of appeals to "have all the authority and
powers heretofore given by law in the last resort to the King
in Council under the old government." [32] It is not going far
enough to say that the Court of Appeals in Cases of Capture
was the origin of the Supreme Court, because that Court was
itself based on the Privy Council which appears to be the real
source of the Supreme Court of the United States.

(5) *American experience.* The lack of such a court forced
the people to see the necessity of creating one to remedy so
serious a defect, and caused a unanimous demand for the establishment of a Supreme Court. Under the Articles of Confederation, Congress could not do anything but appeal to the states
and state courts to enforce its will. A good example is seen
in the case of counterfeiting dealt with in connection with Art.
I, Sec. 8, cl. 6, above. All Congress could do was to appeal
to the states. Hamilton in his "Resolutions for a General
Convention," 1783, declared among other things that the Confederation was defective, "Thirdly: in want of a Federal
Judicature, having cognizance of all matters of general concern
in the last resort." [33] This lack caused national treaties to be
infringed and the national faith to be violated.[34] Randolph
in enumerating the defects of Confederation declared Congress
could not cause "infractions of treaties or the law of nations to
be punished." Among the proposed amendments to the
Articles of Confederation was one for the establishment of a
federal judiciary.[35] Charles Pinckney, who was a member of
the Grand Committee which proposed an amendment to establish a Supreme Court, gave expression to the general feeling or
experience of America when he said: "The institution of a
federal judiciary upon the principles mentioned in this Article
(10th) has long been wanting." [36] James Wilson, speaking of
the controversy between Pennsylvania and Connecticut, said
that though Pennsylvania secured from the court a decree in
her favor, it was useless, because, "The Congress had no power
to carry the decree into execution." "Ought the government
then to remain any longer incomplete? I hope not. No person
can be so insensible to the lessons of experience as to desire
it." Hamilton said the crowning defect of the Confederation

was "the want of a judiciary power. Laws are a dead letter, without courts to expound and define their true meaning and operation." [37] Experience, therefore, dictated the necessity of establishing a federal judiciary.

(6) *American political philosophy.* Montesquieu's great principle of the separation of powers was adopted by the Americans as a political first truth. The state constitutions had adopted the principle, and attempted to apply it, by establishing an independent judiciary. The doctrine had been violated by the nation under the Articles of Confederation. The requirements of this political philosophy impelled the statesmen to endeavor to realize it, as an actual thing in the nation by establishing an independent national judiciary. Experience taught the need, and political philosophy pointed out the way.[38]

The Judicial Term of Office. (Art. III, Sec. 1, cl. 1.) The Federalist gives the origin of this principle as:

(1) *The state constitutions.* Hamilton said: "According to the plan of the convention, all judges who may be appointed by the United States are to hold their offices during good behaviour; which is conformable to the most approved of the State Constitutions, and among the rest, to that of this State." . . . "Upon the whole there can be no room to doubt that the convention acted wisely in copying from the models of those constitutions which have established good behaviour as the tenure of their judicial offices, in point of duration." [39] The principle was found in the constitutions of Delaware, Maryland, Massachusetts, New Hampshire, New York, North Carolina, South Carolina, Vermont, and Virginia. The phraseology is exactly that of Massachusetts and New Hampshire.[40] While the ordinance for establishing a court of appeals in cases of capture, was being debated in Congress June 25, 1781, it was proposed "that the judges of the said court shall hold their commissions during good behaviour," but further consideration was postponed after the motion was defeated.[41]

(2) *The British Constitution.* The Act of Settlement, 1701, provided "that the judge's commissions be made quam diu se bene gesserint." [42] They had formerly been made durante bene placito.[43] A statute of the reign of George III, also enacted that the judges hold office during good behaviour notwithstanding the demise of the King which formerly vacated

their offices.[44] "The experience of Great Britain," wrote Hamilton, "affords an illustrious comment on the excellence of the institution." [45] The purpose of the provision in the English Acts, as well as in the state and Federal Constitutions, was to secure the independence of the judges.

3. *The Compensation of the Judges.* The salary of a judge may be increased, but cannot be reduced while he holds office. The purpose was to secure the complete independence of the judges. Wilson said in the Pennsylvania Convention: "To secure to the judges this independence (i.e. of the legislature) it is ordered that they shall receive for their services a compensation that shall not be diminished during their continuance in office." "In the general course of human nature," said Hamilton, "a power over a man's subsistence amounts to a power over his will." [46] They must not be left where the legislature could deter them from their duty by threats of reduction in salary, or "by the apprehension of being placed in a less eligible situation." [47]

The state constitutions provided for "adequate" salaries, "adequate and fixed" salaries, or fixed salaries. Massachusetts provided for permanent salaries established by law, and for their enlargement from time to time if found insufficient. This principle is similar to that in the Constitution of the United States. No provision is made for diminution or reduction of salaries, though provision is made for an increase. The words "during their continuance in office," are found in the constitutions of New York and Delaware.[48] These with Massachusetts apparently furnished the precedent. The Constitution of the United States is more definite than the state constitutions, for the purpose of precluding legislative evasions.[49]

The root of the principle was to be found in the English Act of Settlement, 1701, which provided that the salaries of judges shall be "ascertained and established." [50] The constitutions of Massachusetts and New Hampshire use the word of the Act of Settlement—"established." [51] Grayson recognized in the Virginia convention that the root of the principle lay in the English Constitution.[52] Fluctuations in the value of money and the state of society rendered it inexpedient to fix a definite amount.[53]

The Jurisdiction of the Federal Courts. (Art. III, Sec. 2, cl. 1.)   The Virginia Plan proposed that the national judiciary be given jurisdiction over six classes of cases. The inferior courts were to hear and determine such cases in the first instance, and the Supreme Court in the dernier resort. The Convention agreed to strike out all the powers given, and Randolph and Madison moved a clause giving the national judiciary power over national revenue, impeachments, and questions involving the national peace and harmony, included in the Virginia Plan. The Committee of the Whole reported a resolution giving such jurisdiction.[54] The New Jersey Plan included ambassadors, construction of treaties, and regulation of trade in addition to the classes of cases included in the Virginia Plan. The resolutions referred to the committee of detail gave the national judiciary jurisdiction over two classes of cases:

(1) "To all cases arising under the national laws." (2) To questions involving the national peace and harmony.

These were proposed by Madison and agreed to on July 18. The report of the committee of detail, August 6, practically gave the Supreme Court jurisdiction over the same classes of cases as in Art. III, Sec. 2, cls. 1, 2, except that original jurisdiction was given in impeachments.[55] On August 27, Madison and Gouverneur Morris moved to add "to which the United States shall be a party," after 'controversies.' Doctor Johnson moved that "this Constitution and the," be inserted before "laws"; Rutledge that "and treaties made or which shall be made under their authority" be added after 'United States'; Dickinson that "both as to law and fact" be added after "appellate"; and Sherman that the words "between citizens of the same State claiming lands under grants of different States" be inserted, all of which was agreed to nem con.[56]

The jurisdiction extends:

(1) *To all cases in law and equity arising under the Constitution, laws, and treaties of the United States.* Courts of law and courts of equity were established in England, the latter probably about 1290.[57] Blackstone, speaking of the house of peers as the Supreme Court of Judicature says: "Lastly, there presides over all one great court of appeal, which is the last resort in matters both of law and equity."[58] Dr. Johnson, August 27, suggested that the Supreme Court of the United States be given the same powers, which was agreed to by the

Convention.[59]   The colonial and state governments had established courts of law and equity.   In 1657, the county courts of Virginia were given jurisdiction of all causes of common law and equity.   The state constitutions retained the distinction and provided for courts of equity in the majority of cases. The North Carolina constitution provided for a "Supreme Court of Law or Equity." [60]   The Superior Court of Connecticut was, by statute, given jurisdiction of all suits in Equity.[61] The framers of the Constitution, therefore, simply retained a distinction with which they were familiar in colonial, state, and the English practice of that day.[62]

The purpose was to secure *uniformity* in interpretation and decision.   "The mere necessity of uniformity in the interpretation of the National laws, decides the question.   Thirteen independent courts of final jurisdiction over the same causes, arising upon the same laws, is a hydra in Government, from which nothing but contradiction and confusion can proceed." [63]   The Federal law and Constitution would "be interpreted and applied one way in one state, and another way in another," and "would cease to be a law for the United States, because the decisions would establish no rule for the United States," and "the Constitution would lose its uniform force and obligation."   The result would be disaster and dissolution of the Union.[64]

As to cases "arising . . . under treaties made, or which shall be made, under their authority," the Convention had in mind the violation of treaties, especially the British treaty of peace, by the states, and the utter helplessness of Congress to secure a performance of the treaty, or prevent the states from violating it.   The purpose of giving cases arising under treaties to the federal courts was to secure enforcement of treaties made by the United States, and prevent the states from wantonly breaking the plighted bond of the Union.   James Wilson explained, in the Pennsylvania Convention, the reason for giving the federal judiciary control over such cases.   "But it is highly proper," he says, "that this regulation should be made; for the truth is—and I am sorry to say it—that, in order to prevent the payment of British debts, and from other causes, our treaties have been violated, and violated too, by the express laws of several States in the Union.   Pennsylvania— to her honor be it spoken—has hitherto done no act of this kind; but it is acknowledged on all sides that many states in the Union have infringed the treaty; and it is well known that, when the minister of the United States made a demand of Lord Carmarthen of a surrender of the western posts, he told the minister, with truth and justice, 'The treaty under which you claim these possessions has not been performed on your part; until that is done, those possessions will not be delivered up.' This clause, Sir, will show the world that we make the faith of treaties a constitutional part of the character of the United States; that we secure its performance no longer nominally, for the judges of the United States will be enabled to carry it into effect, let the legislatures of the different States do what they may." Madison declared that if uniformity were necessary anywhere, it was in the exposition of treaties, and this could only be secured by establishing "one revisionary superintending power," [65] and giving this Supreme Court authority to decide all controversies regarding the construction of treaties.

The Report on Trade and Revenue of August 14, 1786, provided for an appeal from the state courts to the federal judicial court "in all causes wherein questions shall arise on the meaning and construction of treaties entered into by the United States with any foreign power." [66] The principle in question, and even the phraseology, is to be found in the identical laws sent down by Congress to the States in April, 1787. In this, the courts of law and equity "in all causes and questions cognizable by them respectively and arising from or touching the said treaty," shall decide and adjudge according to the true intent and meaning of the same.[67] That is, the courts shall decide all cases in law and equity arising under a treaty—the British treaty. The framers applied this principle for the purpose of securing uniformity in interpretation, and enforcement of treaties. Hitherto, Congress could simply recommend in case of a broken treaty, but under the Constitution, Congress was given power to enforce treaty obligations by means of the federal judiciary.

(2) *The judicial power of the United States extends to* "*cases affecting ambassadors, other public ministers, and consuls.*" The persons mentioned above have both a national, and an international character, and, therefore, it is fitting that

any cases connected with them should be dealt with by the national courts rather than by state courts. Madison pointed out in the Virginia convention that this was the only way in which uniformity could be secured in such cases.[68] Congress in 1779, claimed that authority to execute the law of nations was vested in it, and that control by appeal was necessary "in order to compel a just and uniform execution of the law of nations."[69] On November 23, 1781, Congress recommended the state legislatures to provide punishment for offences against the law of nations, and erect courts to try such cases.[70] Then Connecticut, for example, enacted a law giving the county courts and Superior Court jurisdiction to try such offences.[71] This meant that Congress without national courts was helpless to punish infractions of the law of nations and appealed to the states for aid. All Congress could do was to recommend that the states erect courts for punishing such offences. The nation was responsible in such cases, but had no courts with which to mete out justice. The states were not responsible, and could regard or disregard the pleadings of Congress as they saw fit. An actual case arose in 1784 in Pennsylvania in connection with the Consul General of France, M. Marbois, which created a great stir, and showed the need of national courts to deal with offences against the law of nations.[72] Foreign representatives can have official dealings only with the government to which they are accredited, and, therefore, cases involving them ought to be dealt with by the nation, not by the states.[73] The nature of the cases, and the experience of Congressional helplessness under the Articles of Confederation, caused the Convention to give jurisdiction over such cases to the federal judiciary.

(3) *Admiralty and maritime cases.* "Such cases necessarily belong to national jurisdiction."[74] Courts of admiralty existed in the colonies and states.[75] On June 5, Wilson, in reply to Rutledge's statement that state courts ought to try cases in the first instance, said that admiralty jurisdiction ought to be given wholly to the national government, because it related to cases not entirely within the jurisdiction of separate states, and to a scene in which controversies with foreigners would be likely to happen.[76] The states had no jurisdiction over such cases, and only the national government could deal

with controversies with foreign nations. Again, Madison and Randolph said the purpose was to secure uniformity in admiralty decisions. No uniformity could be secured if thirteen separate and independent state courts exercised jurisdiction over the same cases; and what would be the effect on foreign relations? [77]

The germ of the provision is in Article IX, Articles of Confederation. Out of this grew two courts—the Court of Appeals in Cases of Capture, which dealt with prize cases coming on appeal from the state admiralty courts, and a court for the trial of piracies and felonies committed on the high seas, established April 5, 1781.[78] The Convention by this provision simply transferred jurisdiction from these courts to the Supreme Court of the United States. As Mason said: "This is a power which existed before, and is a proper subject of federal jurisdiction." [79]

The phraseology used is "a technical term of the law of nations," said Madison, "that we should find ourselves authorized to introduce it into the laws of the United States." "Piracy and felony," the words of the Articles of Confederation, are not used. "Felony" was from British law and unknown to the law of nations.[80] Madison had proposed in a letter to Randolph, April 8, 1787, that the federal judiciary be given exclusive jurisdiction in admiralty cases. This enabled the federal courts "to exercise the powers of admiralty courts in England." [81]

(4) *"Controversies to which the United States shall be a party."* Madison and Gouverneur Morris moved the insertion of these words, and gave as the reason that "controversies affecting the interest of the United States ought to be determined by their own judiciary, and not be left to partial local tribunals." [82] The state courts might be partial or prejudiced. "The universal practice of all nations," says Wilson, "has and unavoidably must have admitted of this power." The phraseology appears to be taken in part from the Report on Trade and Revenue submitted to Congress August 14, 1786, in which Art. 19, proposed that the federal judicial court extend to questions where "the United States shall be a party." [83]

(5) *To controversies between two or more states."* This was taken from Article IX, Articles of Confederation. "Pro-

vision is made for this by the existing Articles of Confederation," said Madison in the Virginia convention. "This power is vested in the present Congress," said Wilson in the Pennsylvania convention. Charles Pinckney pointed out the same thing. The Dickinson and Franklin Drafts also contained the provision.[84] The report of the committee of detail had made the Senate, instead of Congress, the court of last resort for this purpose, because the Senate corresponded to the old Congress.[85] This was stricken out because Rutledge and Wilson urged that the judiciary could do the work better.[86]

The principle originated in colonial days, when the English Privy Council exercised original jurisdiction in disputes between the American colonies "as concerning the extent of their charter and the like"—boundaries, and other causes.' The Charter of Rhode Island, 1663, provided that in all controversies between the colony and other New England colonies, an appeal might be carried to the King in Council.[87]

American experience also contributed something to the idea by showing wherein the old method of settling disputes failed. Governor Randolph mentioned several cases in the Virginia convention which had actually occurred, to prove the necessity of giving power to the federal judiciary to decide controversies between the states, namely, the disputes between Pennsylvania and Connecticut, Rhode Island and Connecticut, Virginia and Pennsylvania, and the Nathan Case. So bitter was the feeling between Pennsylvania and Virginia that reprisals were made. The state courts were incompetent to settle such controversies. The national judiciary must be given jurisdiction over such cases, and further, Wilson pointed out that Congress could not enforce the decisions. So the federal judiciary is given the additional power of carrying their decrees into effect.[88]

(6) *"To controversies . . . between a State and citizens of another State,"* Madison in his letters to Washington, April 16, 1787, and Randolph, April 8, 1787, declared it necessary to provide for an appeal to a national tribunal in all cases which concern the inhabitants of other states. He held that the effect would be to compel states to bring suits against citizens in the federal courts.[89] Wilson held the power was necessary to secure impartial justice and conserve the interests of both parties. "When a citizen has a controversy with another

State," he said, "there ought to be a tribunal where both parties may stand on a just and equal footing." Madison agreed with Wilson that the provision originated in the desire to provide for impartial trial by an impartial tribunal in such cases.[90] There was one case under Confederation where a citizen of another state sued a state. Simon Nathan brought suit in the court of Common Pleas, Philadelphia County, against the state of Virginia in 1781, and a quantity of clothing belonging to Virginia was seized in Philadelphia. The Virginia delegates in Congress protested to the Executive Council of Pennsylvania that this was a violation of the law of nations, and the court ordered the sheriff to surrender the goods seized.[91] This case created a great stir, and was known to all the statesmen of that day. Many of the members of the Federal Convention were in Congress at the time.[92] Madison, Randolph, Jones, and Bland were the delegates from Virginia in Congress, who protested against the suit to the Executive Council of Pennsylvania.[93] Randolph mentioned the case in the Virginia convention and said: "In the case of Mr. Nathan, they (the Virginia legislature) thought the determination of the dispute ought to be out of the State for fear of partiality." [94] The committee of detail evidently discussed the case, and the result is seen in Rutledge's writing on the margin of the Randolph draft: "In disputes between a state and a citizen, or citizens of other states." [95] Madison, evidently, had the case in mind when he wrote to Washington and Randolph, and when he discussed the provision in the Virginia convention.[96]

(7) *"To controversies . . . between citizens of different states."* This provision originated in the purpose to secure an impartial trial in cases where bias or prejudice might exist against citizens of other states, because of the existence of claims held by them. "We know what tardy, and even defective administration of justice has happened in some states," said Madison. "A citizen of another state might not chance to get justice in a state court, and at all events he might think himself injured." [97] The jurisdiction of the United States will be exercised impartially, because the judges are independent, said Wilson, and any verdict obtained by local prejudices will be corrected by another trial.[98] Citizens of one state who are creditors of citizens of another state "might be either entirely

denied or partially granted" justice, or payment of debts prevented,[99] said Madison and Wilson. "This is no imaginary evil," said Madison, "before the war New York was to a great extent a creditor of Connecticut." The laws and regulations of Connecticut withheld payment. "There were reasons to complain. These illiberal regulations and causes of complaint obstruct commerce." [100] American experience had actually found, therefore, that justice was not always obtainable in state courts, hence, the Convention transferred controversies between citizens of different states to the jurisdiction of the federal courts, which it was believed would be more impartial.[101]

(8) *"To controversies . . . between citizens of the same state claiming lands under grants of different states."* On August 27, Sherman moved to insert these words "according to the provision in the 9th Article of the Confederation, which was agreed to nem. con." [102]

(9) *"To controversies . . . between a State or the citizens thereof, and foreign states, citizens, or subjects."* American experience had found the Confederation defective in not providing for the settlement of disputes between citizens and foreigners. This lay with the state courts, and from 1783, the claims of an alien, especially a British subject, were not likely to be dealt with impartially, or even honestly by the state courts. "We well know, Sir, that foreigners cannot get justice done them in these courts," said Madison.[103] The states passed laws sequestrating or preventing the collection of British debts,[104] and stay and tender laws, and installment laws preventing payment of debts. All this destroyed confidence and impaired public and private credit.[105] There were no *national courts* to which aliens could appeal for justice. Congress was helpless. All it could do was to take its usual impotent course of action, namely, resolve and recommend, which it did.[106] Hamilton, in his "Resolutions for a General Convention," June 3, 1783, pointed out that the Confederation was defective: "In want of a Federal Judicature, having cognizance of all matters of general concern in the last resort, especially those in which foreign nations and their subjects are interested." [107] Madison, in his letter to Edmund Randolph, April 8, 1787, wrote: "It seems at least essential that an appeal should lie to some national tribunals in all cases which concern foreigners." [108] This

experience of the inability or unwillingness of state courts to do justice in such cases resulted in the clause in the Virginia Plan giving foreigners the right of appeal to the Supreme Court.[109]

The law of nations also appears to have contributed something to the idea. Madison said in the Virginia convention that he did not think any controversy between an American state and a foreign state could ever be decided in the federal courts without the consent of the parties. "If they consent, provision is here made. The disputes ought to be tried by the national tribunal. This is consonant to the law of nations." [110]   That is, Madison, who, we have seen was responsible for having the provision inserted in the Virginia Plan, declares they are but following the law of nations in adopting this clause.

The clause also originated in a purpose to restore credit with foreign states. James Wilson, commenting on the provision, in the Pennsylvania convention, asked if it were not necessary if they meant to restore either public or private credit, "that foreigners, as well as ourselves, should have an impartial tribunal to which they may resort?" [111]   He continues that in the Federal Convention, "it was thought proper to give the citizens of foreign states full opportunity of obtaining justice in the general courts, and this they have by its appellate jurisdiction; therefore, in order to restore credit with those foreign states, that part of the article is necessary." [112]

A fourth contributing influence was the desire to make such an arrangement, as would enable the nation to avoid controversies and preserve peace with foreign nations.[113]   By giving jurisdiction to the national judiciary in these cases, it was believed that justice would be done, and that it would not be in the power of any member of the Union to drag the whole nation into war by perpetrating injustice.[114]   The United States is accountable for injuries to foreign states or their citizens. "If the United States are answerable for the injury, ought they not to possess the means," said Wilson, "of compelling the faulty state to repair it? They ought; and this is what is done here." [115]

THE ORIGINAL AND APPELLATE JURISDICTION OF THE SUPREME COURT

1. *Original Jurisdiction Is Given.* (Art. III, Sec. 2, cl. 2.)
(1) *"In all cases affecting ambassadors, other public ministers and consuls."* Original jurisdiction was given here, because, says Hamilton, "Public ministers of every class are the immediate representatives of their sovereigns. All questions in which they are concerned are so directly connected with the public peace, that, as well for the preservation of this, as out of respect to the sovereignties they represent, it is both expedient and proper, that such questions should be submitted in the first instance to the highest judiciary of the Nation." Cases involving "the safety, peace, and sovereignty of the nation," require a grant of original jurisdiction to the national courts.[116]

(2) *"Those in which a State shall be a party."* This was not new. Disputes between the colonies were heard by the King in Council in England, thus bringing the colonies under the jurisdiction of a court of justice and making them parties to a suit.[117] The Franklin and Dickinson Drafts gave Congress power to settle all disputes between the colonies. The Articles of Confederation provided an awkward arrangement by which a state could seek justice in a federal court. This provision of the federal Constitution seems never to have been intended to make states dependents at the suit of individual citizens.[118]

2. *Appellate Jurisdiction in All Other Cases.* The King in Council and the Court of Appeals in Cases of Capture had exercised appellate jurisdiction in the colonies and states, and the same powers are given the Supreme Court. The provision was necessary to secure "uniformity of decisions throughout the United States." "If there were no revising authority to control" "jarring and discordant judgments and harmonize them into uniformity," the Constitution, laws, and treaties of the United States would be, in all probability, different in different states.[119]

3. *"Both as to law and fact."* In the Convention, on August 27, Gouverneur Morris asked whether the appellate jurisdiction of the Supreme Court "extended to matters of fact as well as law, and to cases of common law as well as to civil law." He spoke as a member of the committee of detail, and added

that the jurisdiction of the federal court of appeals had been so construed. Dickinson then moved to add the words above, which was done.[120]

The provision grew out of American experience of the Court of Appeals in Cases of Capture. Wilson stated this very definitely. "We find it essentially necessary," he said, "from the ample experience we have had in the courts of admiralty with regard to captures." Had the Court of Appeals not had authority to set aside the *verdicts of juries*, many owners of vessels would have had a poor share in the late war. "The jurisdiction as to fact may be thought improper; but those possessed of information . . . see that it is *necessary*." [121]

4. *"With such exceptions and under such regulations as the Congress shall make."* This was introduced for the purpose of enabling Congress to remedy defects without having to wait for an amendment of the Constitution by the people. Wilson said it was better that Congress be left with power to regulate cases as they arose from time to time as soon as discovered. Anything done by the Convention must remain unalterable until amended by the people in the manner prescribed by the Constitution.[122]

Criminal Trials to Be by Jury in the Vicinage. (Art. III, Sec. II, cl. 3.) Charles Pinckney urged trial by jury in both civil and criminal cases.[123] The committee of detail reported on August 6, a provision providing for criminal offences being tried by jury (except cases of impeachment) in the states where committed.[124] On August 28, the Convention added: "but when not committed within . . . directed." The purpose of this was to provide for a jury trial in cases where the offence was committed outside the bounds of any state, as on the high seas.[125] This principle of a legislative change of venue is found in the constitution of New Hampshire.[126]

Some of the state constitutions had adopted the common law principle of trial in the vicinage as Massachusetts, New Hampshire, Maryland, and North Carolina.[127] The clause "except in cases of impeachment," [128] simply follows the English practice as in sec. 39, of Magna Carta, which refers to proceedings in the ordinary courts of justice, and had no reference to, or connection with impeachment trials.[129]

Treason: Definition, Conviction, and Punishment. (Art. III,

Sec. 3, cls. 1, 2, 3.) This originated in the committee of detail, which reported the provision on August 6, defining treason as: (1) Levying war against the United States. (2) Adhering to the enemies of the United States. Two witnesses were required to convict, and no attainder of treason was to work corruption of blood or forfeiture except during the life of the person attainted.[130] On August 20, Dickinson wanted to know whether "the testimony of two witnesses" meant to the same overt or to different overt acts, and someone moved to insert "to the same overt act," which was adopted.[131] Colonel Mason moved to add the words of the British Statute, "giving them aid and comfort," which was done, to remove indefiniteness.[132] Luther Martin then moved to add "or on confession in open court," which was adopted.[133]

(a) *This definition of treason was taken from the Statute of Edward III, 1352.* Madison, Mason, Gouverneur Morris and others declared that they wished to follow the British Statute on the subject.[134] Although this was British law, it was also

(b) *American law—colonial and state.* The colonies in enacting treason laws adopted the treason law of Edward III. Connecticut, for example, 1715, and 1750, enacted such laws.[135] The law of Massachusetts, 1678, and 1696, was that of Edward the Third's Treason Act.[136] The Convention of Maryland passed a resolution on July 4, 1776, defining treason as in the English Statute.[137] The Virginia treason act of October, 1776, defines treason in the same way,[138] as does also the Massachusetts law of 1777.[139] Others might be cited.[140] In urging the adoption of the British Statute, Madison, Mason, Randolph, Gouverneur Morris, Ellsworth, and others were simply urging the adoption of their own state law on the subject.

(c) *"Two witnesses to the same overt act," or "confession in open court," required to convict.* This goes back to "the Evidence Act of Edward VI," or "An act for the punishment of divers kinds of treason" which provided that no person could be convicted of treason unless on the testimony of two lawful witnesses brought face to face with the accused, "unless he shall willingly and without violence confess the same." [141] The Treason Trials Act of 1696, also required the "testimony of two lawful witnesses, either both of them to the same overt act,

or one of them to one, and another of them to another overt
act of the same treason unless the party indicted . . . in open
court confess the same." [142] We have here the exact phraseology of clause two of the Constitution. The Virginia treason
act of 1776, and the Massachusetts law of 1777, contained the
same provisions. [143] The Massachusetts laws of 1678, and 1696,
also contained the same requirements—the latter declaring
treason trials were to be regulated by the English Treason
Trials Act of 1696. [144] The colonial laws of Connecticut and
Delaware made use of the same provision. [145]

(4) *Congress to declare the punishment of treason; but no
attainder shall work corruption of blood.* By defining treason,
the Convention guarded against constructive treasons, and oppression of the people. [146] By this clause, the Convention guards
against barbarous or unjust punishments for treason, such as
those described in Blackstone. The English Parliament had
declared the punishment of treason. [147] The state legislatures,
for example, Virginia, Massachusetts, and Pennsylvania, had
also done so. [148] The Virginia Act of 1776, enacted "that no
such attainder shall work any corruption of blood." [149] The
laws of Pennsylvania and Massachusetts laid down the same
doctrine. The constitution of New York, 1777, also provided
"and that such acts (i.e., acts of attainder) shall not work a
corruption of blood." [150] The same limitation is placed on Congress by the Federal Constitution.

The doctrine of corruption of blood came into English law
from continental feudalism at the Norman conquest. Saxon
law knew no "corruption of blood for felony or any other
cause." The land was forfeited to the King but no corruption
of blood ensued. [151] The Long Parliament, 1641, [152] passed an
act to prevent corruption of blood in Stratford's Case.

An act of 1650, declaring what offences should be adjudged
treason under the commonwealth, laid down the doctrine of the
Constitution of the United States. [153] Other English statutes
provided there should be no corruption of blood for certain
treasons and crimes. [154] This idea was a survival from the ancient Saxon law. Blackstone says that "by the Statute of 7.
Ann. c. 21 (the operation of which is postponed by statute 17.
Geo. II. c. 39.), after the death of the sons of the late pretender, no attainder for treason will extend to the disinheriting

any heir, nor the prejudice of any person, other than the offender himself, which virtually abolishes all corruption of blood for treason." [155] This is clearly the doctrine of clause three of the Constitution of the United States. The Act of Parliament reversing the attainder of Jacob Leisler and others, 1694, declared that no corruption of blood should be incurred by the said attainders.[156] The Convention of 1787, therefore, went back to the ancient Saxon law on the subject, and adopted that as the law of the Constitution.

NOTES TO CHAPTER XII

1. Elliot, V, 128.
2. Moore, Am. Eloquence, I, 367.
3. Elliot, V, 155.
4. Id.
5. Elliot, V, 155.
6. Id. 159.
7. Elliot, V, 159, 160.
8. Id. 188.
9. Id. I, 303, 314.
10. Elliot, V, 330.
11. Federalist, No. 81, p. 562 (Dawson ed.), Poore, Charters, passim.
12. Poore, 276.
13. Jameson, Essays on the Const. Hist. of the U. S. p. 44; Am. Hist. Assoc. Papers, V, 3, p. 392.
14. Sup. Ct. p. —, Hist. of U. S. III, 526.
15. See Journals of cont. cong. I, 367, 370, 394, 419, 447, 480.
17. Id. 342, IV, 487, 521, 554, 586.
18. Id. VI, 75.
19. The Supr. Court of the U. S. pp. 63, 64; Journals, IV, 593, 605, 614, 617, 619.
20. 131 U. S. App. XIX; Supreme Court of the U. S. p. 40.
21. Essays in Const. Hist. of U. S. p. 13, 14.
22. 17 Geo. II, c. 34, Sec. VIII; 29 Geo. II, c. 34, sec. VIII.
23. Acts cited above and Blackstone, Com. III, 69.
24. Supreme Court of U. S. p. 53; See Art. IX.
25. Art. IX, H. L. Carson, The Supreme Court of the U. S. p. 63, 11 Geo. III, c. 42, sec. VIII.
26. Hist. of U. S. III, 502; Am. Hist. Assoc. Rep. 1894, p. 350.
27. Poore, 1389, 784, 786, 1276, 1511, 951; N. Y. Col. Docs. III, 379.
28. Laws of R. I. 1719, 1745, p. 80, 106, 192; Laws of 1730; Acts and Res. of R. I. 1771, p. 36. Id. 1775, p. 73.
29. Am. Hist. Assoc. Rep. 1894, p. 307; Hist. U. S. III, 3-27.
30. In N. Y. appeals were provided for from the Supreme Court of the Colony to the King in Council, where the value of the matter in controversy exceeded £300. See Tryon's answer, Lincoln's Const. Hist. of N. Y. I, 1-3, 7.
31. Arts. of Confed. Art. IX, Hart, Actual Government, p. 312.
32. Poore, Charters, 276.

33. Hamilton, Works I, p. 289 (Lodge ed.).   Am. Hist. Leaflets, No. 28, p. 16.

34. Am. Hist. Leaflets, No. 28, p. 16; 2 Elliot, V, 128.

35. Am. Hist. Leaflets, No. 28, p. 29.

36. Moore, Am. Eloquence, I, 367.

37. Elliot, II, 462; Federalist no. 22 (Dawson ed.).

38. Federalist, 46, 47; Poore, State Constitutions.

39. Federalist, No. 78 (Lodge ed.) 483, 490.

40. Poore, Charters, 275, 819, 960, 968, 1290, 1336, 1412, 1619, 1625, 1864, 1911.

41. Journals (Hunt ed.), V, XX, 695-6.

42. 13 W. III, c. 2.

43. Blackstone, Com. I, 268.

44. 1 Geo. III, c. 23; Adams and Stephens, No. 243, p. 479.

45. Federalist, No. 78 (Lodge ed.), 491.

46. Elliot, II, 446; Federalist No. 79 (Dawson ed.).

47. Federalist, no. 79 (Dawson ed.).   The income tax reduces it, Evans v. Gore, 253, U. S. 245.

48. Poore, 1413, N. Y. 1545, 1627, 1711, 967, 1413.

49. Federalist, no. 79 (Dawson ed.).

50. 12 and 13, Wm. III, c. 2.

51. Poore, 967, 1289; Elliot, II, 564.

52. Elliot, III, 564.

53. Fed. no. 79, p. 491.

54. Elliot, V, 128, 187, 188, 190.

55. Elliot, V, 192; 332, 376, 380.

56. Elliot, V, 482, 483.

57. Medley, Eng. Const. Hist. 385-389; Blackstone Com. III; 45 seq. Ch. XVII. Taswell-Langmead, Eng. Const. Hist. 141-146.

58. Com. III, 60.

59. Elliot, V, 481.

60. Hening, I, 303; Poore, Del. 275, 383, 827, 828, 1336, 1625, 1863, 1911, 1413.

61. Acts and Laws of Conn. 1784, p. 29; Idem. 1786, p. 29.

62. Stimson, Fed. and State Constitutions, 24; McClain, Const. Law. 230, 252.

63. Federalist, No. 80.

64. Cooley, Const. Law. Ch. VI.

65. Elliot, II, 499, 490.

66. Am. Hist. Leaflets, No. 28, p. 29.

67. Journals of Cong. V, 12, p. 33; 21 Howard, 484.

68. Elliot, III, 532.

69. Journals (Hunt ed.), V, 88.

70. Id. XXI, 1136, Vol. 7, p. 234, 235.

71. Acts and Laws of Con. 1782, p. 602.

72. 1 Dall. 111-118; His assailant Chas. J. Longchamp was convicted in the Court of Oyer and Terminer at Philadelphia for threatening, and committing assault and battery on the person of M. Marbois, and fined £200, and required to furnish £2,000 security to keep the peace.

73. Federalist, No. 81 (Dawson ed.), p. 566; Vattel, 148; Blackstone, Com. I, 253, 254.

74. Dall. 419, seq.

75. Hening, I, 466-7, 537-8, Acts & Res. of R. I. 1780, p. 13, 9.   In the Colonies, appeals lay from their vice-admiralty courts to the courts

of admiralty in England, or to the King in Council. Blackstone Com. III, 69-70.

76. Elliot, V, 159.

77. Id. III, 532, 571. The Supreme Court of the U. S. in Waring v. Clark, said: "There was but one opinion concerning the grant, and that was the necessity to give a power to the U. S. to relieve them from difficulties which had arisen from the exercise of admiralty jurisdiction by the states separately." 5 How. 441; McClain, Cases, 641.

78. Journals of Cong. XIX (Hunt ed.), p. 354.

79. Elliot, III, 523.

80. Id. 531.

81. Elliot, V, 108; Also in letter to Washington, April 16, 1787; McClain Const. Law, 233; Blackstone, Com. III, 69-70.

82. Elliot, V, 482, Id. III, 532; 4. Id. II, 490. The necessity is seen from the fact Connecticut, for example, passed a law giving the United States the right to sue in the Courts of the State "for recovery of their common rights and interests."—Acts and Laws of Conn. 1782, p. 609.

83. Am. Hist. Leaflets, no. 28, p. 29.

84. Elliot, III, 532; Id. II, 490; Moore, Am. Eloquence, I, 367; Art. 18; Art. V.

85. Elliot, V, 379.

86. Elliot, II, 490.

87. Blackstone, Com. I, 232; Hart, Actual Government, 312; Poore, 1603; MacDonald, Sel. Charters, 132.

88. Elliot, II, 491.

89. Elliot, V, 108; Id. III, 533.

90. Id. II, 491; Id. III, 533.

91. 1 Dall. 77-80.

92. Madison, Randolph, Ellsworth, Wilson, Rutledge, Clymer, Jenifer, Carroll, and others.

93. Journals of Cong. V, 7, 192.

94. Elliot, III, 571.

95. Meigs, Growth of the Const. p. 316; Plate VII, seq.

96. Elliot, III, 533.

97. Elliot, III, 533.

98. Elliot, II, 491; Id. III, 535.

99. Elliot, III, 535; II, 491, 492.

100. Id. III, 535, 543.

101. Id. II, 491, 533.

102. Elliot, V, 483; Art. IX, Arts of Confed.

103. Elliot, III, 583.

104. See State Laws 1783-1789. Index "British debts" in the several state statutes.

105. Elliot, II, 491, 492.

106. Journals of Cong. V, 12, p. 32-33, and under date of Apr. 13, 1787.

107. Am. Hist. Leaflets. No. 28, p. 16. Hamilton, Works, I (Lodge Ed.), p. 288.

108. Elliot, V, 108.

109. Id. 128.

110. Elliot, III, 533; Elliot, V, 355.

111. Vattel, Law of Nature and of Nations, Bk. II, Ch. VIII, 103; Elliot, II, 492, 493.

112. Elliot, II, 492.

113. Id. 493; III, 533, 534.

114. Elliot, III, 534.
115. Elliot, II, 493.
116. Federalist No. 81, p. 566 (Dawson ed.), 1 Wheat, 315.
117. McClain, Cases, 693; Hart, Actual Government, 312.
118. Am. Hist. Leaflets, No. 20, pp. 4, 11, 12; Art. IX; Elliot, III, 573.
119. McClain, Cases, p. 758.
120. Elliot, V, 483.
121. Id. II, 493; Federalist, no. 81, p. 570 (Dawson ed.).
122. Elliot, V, 494.
123. Moore, Am. Eloquence, I, 369.
124. Elliot, V, 381.
125. Id. 484; 1 U. S. Stat. at Large, p. 114.
126. Poore, 1282.
127. Poore, 817, 818, 959, 1282, 1409.
128. Adams and Stephens, p. 47.
129. Amendment VI.
130. Elliot, V, 379.
131. Elliot, V, 449.
132. Elliot, V, 450.
133. Id. 450, 451; 4 Sawyer, 457.
134. Elliot, V, 447, 448, 449; Adams and Stephens, p. 121; McClain, Cases, p. 541; 25 ed. III, c. 2.
135. Laws of Conn. 1715, p. 14 Id. 1750, p. 244.
136. Ancient Charters and Laws of Massachusetts, p. 62, 294.
137. The Conventions of Md. 1774-6, p. 191.
138. Hening, IX, 168.
139. Laws of Mass. 1780-1807, V, II, p. 1047.
140. In the New York law of Feb. 16, 1787, there appears all that is in the law of the U. S., even to the exact phraseology (Greenleaf) Laws of N. Y. Vol. 1, p. 346.
141. 5 & 6 Ed. VI, c. 11; Prothero, Statutes, p. 60; 13 Eliz. c. I, 9; Blackstone, IV, 351, 352.
142. 7 & 8 Wm. III, c. 3; Adams and Stephens, 473.
143. Hening 9, 168; Laws of Mass. 1780-1807, V, II, 1047.
144. Anc. Charters & Laws of Mass. p. 62, 294.
145. Laws of Conn. 1715, 1759, pp. 14, 244; Laws of Delaware, I, 352.
146. Elliot, II, 488, 489.
147. Adams and Stephens, p. 307-8; Blackstone, Com. IV, 93, 384-5, seq.
148. Hening, V, 9, 168, 691.
149. Id.
150. Laws of Mass., 1780-1807, V, II, 1051; Stats. at Large of Pa. V, 10, 112; Poore, 1339.
151. Blackstone, Com. IV, 388, 413.
152. Adams and Stephens, p. 362.
153. Adams and Stephens, 402.
154. 1 Jac. 11; 21, Jac. c. 26; 5 & 18 Eliz.; 28 Hen. 8, c. 15; Hale, Historia, Placitorum Coronae, Vol. I, 353; IV, 389.
155. 6 and 7 Wm. and Mary; Journal Gen. Assembly, N. Y. Vol. 1, 1691-1743. Appendix.

CHAPTER XIII

The States and the Nation: Adoption of Amendments

The Rule of Comity. (Art. IV, Sec. 1.) The first half of the section was reported by the committee of detail. On August 29, Randolph moved a proposition making state acts, whether legislative, executive, or judicial, "binding in every other State," provided they be properly attested under the seal of the state. Gouverneur Morris then moved the commitment of the proposition in the Constitution. He added the second half of the section to the report of the committee of detail.[1] Rutledge, Randolph, Gorham, Wilson, and Johnson were appointed a committee to which the propositions of Randolph and Morris were committed. On September 1, Rutledge reported the section from the committee practically as it appears in the Constitution.[2]

The source of the first half of the section was Article IV, Articles of Confederation, which had been adopted by the Continental Congress, November 11, 1777.[3] Of the second half, Madison says: "The power of prescribing by general laws, the manner in which the public acts, records and judicial proceedings of each state shall be proved, and the effect they shall have in other States, is an evident and valuable improvement on the clause relating to this subject in the Articles of Confederation. The meaning of the latter is extremely indeterminate."[4] The *purpose* was to remedy the inconvenience of retrying a case which had been once fairly tried in a competent court of justice, and also to do away with the uncertainty and confusion which prevailed in England and America as to what credit and effect should be given to the judgments of foreign tribunals. . Some courts held that such judgments should be accepted as final, and "others that they should be regarded as only prima facie binding."[5]

Interstate Privileges and Immunities of Citizens. (Art. IV, Sec. 2, cl. 1.) The committee of detail reported this as it appears in the Constitution.[6]

(1) *The immediate source of the clause was the Articles of Confederation.*[7] The word "free" was stricken out by the committee of detail. Charles Pinckney claims the honor of having been the original drafter of the provision, and says he knew at the time there did not exist a colored citizen in the union, nor could he have conceived that such a thing would be possible. The Dickinson Draft contained the same provision.[8]

(2) *The colonial charters.* The principle is found in the Charter of Sir Walter Raleigh, 1584.[9] The Charter of Virginia, 1606, gave all subjects everywhere within the colonies or "Dominions" of England "all liberties, franchises, and immunities within any of our Dominions."[10] The charters of Virginia, 1609, 1611-12, of New England, 1620; Massachusetts Bay, 1629 and 1691, Connecticut, 1662, Rhode Island, 1663, Carolina, 1663, and 1665, and Georgia, 1732, all contained the provision, even to the phraseology of the Constitution.[11]

(3) *The English Constitution.* It was a well-known principle of the law of England that a subject was entitled to all the rights, privileges, and immunities of the inhabitants of every other colony or dominion regardless of his place of residence in the Empire. There was an imperial citizenship which of right enjoyed all the rights, liberties, privileges, and immunities of citizenship in all parts of the British Empire. Lord Chancellor Ellesmere in the case of the Post-nati, or Calvin's Case, 1608, held that by the law of England, all the Scotch post-nati were natural born subjects of the King of England, and entitled, as such, to all the rights and privileges of English subjects.[12] The Act of Union with Scotland, 1707, contained the same principle.[13] "The object of the clause," said the Supreme Court in Paul v. Virginia, "was to place the citizens of each State upon the same footing with citizens of other States, so far as the advantages resulting from citizenship in those States are concerned. It relieves them from the disabilities of alienage in other States." Without this, the Republic would have been a mere league of states, and "would not have constituted the Union which now exists."[14] After the Revolution, when the colonies "became independent and sovereign States, the citizens of each State would have been under all the

disabilities of alienage in every other State," but for this provision in the Articles of Confederation. This was inserted in the Constitution "substantially as it stood in the Articles," and was "intended to guard against a State discriminating in favor of its own citizens." [15]

Extradition of Criminals. The New Jersey Plan contained an arrangement for the punishment of criminals fleeing into other states,[16] but the clause in the Constitution was reported by the committee of detail.[17]

The immediate source was the Articles of Confederation.[18] The provision in Wilson's draft, and the report of the committee of detail were taken from Article IV.[19] This was originally introduced in Congress on November 11, 1777.[20] In the Articles, it contained the phrase "high misdemeanor," which was stricken out on August 28, and the words "other crime" inserted for the purpose of including all proper cases, it being doubtful whether "high misdemeanor" had not a technical meaning which was too limited.[21] Connecticut in 1786, 1784, and 1620, passed laws for the rendition of fugitives from justice.[22] A Virginia extradition law of 1779 follows the Articles of Confederation,[23] while Pennsylvania, New Jersey, Maryland, and Delaware possessed an arrangement whereby offenders were returned for trial.[24] Even before the Revolution, criminals who fled were arrested and returned for trial to the colonies where they had committed the crime.[25] The New England Confederation, 1643, provided for the extradition of criminals. They were to be surrendered to the person pursuing them, on a warrant issued by the magistrates of the jurisdiction from which they escaped, upon a certificate from "two magistrates of the jurisdiction where he escaped from." [26] Charles II of England made an extradition treaty with Denmark in 1661, and with the States General in 1662. The earliest mention in English history of the extradition of criminals is contained in a treaty between Henry II and William the Lion of Scotland. This provided that those charged with felony in England and fleeing to Scotland should be surrendered to the English authorities, or else tried for their crime in Scotland and vice versa.[27]

Fugitive Slaves. (Art. IV, Sec. 2, cl. 3.) On August 28, during the discussion on the clause providing for the extradition of criminals, Butler and Charles Pinckney moved to re-

quire "fugitive slaves and servants to be delivered up like criminals." Wilson objected that the executive would be obliged to
do it at public expense, and Sherman said there was no more
propriety in the public seizing and surrendering a slave than a
horse. Butler then withdrew his proposition for the purpose
of securing an independent provision on the subject. Next
day, he moved to insert the proposition which appears in the
Constitution. The committee on style changed Butler's proposition to read: "No person *legally* held to service or labor in
one State," etc. On September 15, the word "legally" was
stricken out, because some members of the Convention believed
it implied that slavery was legal from a moral point of view.[28]

The Northwest Ordinance of 1787 provided for the rendition
of fugitive slaves. Butler's proposition, and the report of the
committee on style bear the earmarks of the ordinance.[29] The
New England Confederation of 1643 also provided that if any
servant ran away from his master into any other of the Confederated territories, he should be surrendered upon the proper
proofs being made.[30]

Iredell, in the North Carolina convention, begged leave to
explain the reason for the clause. "In some of the Northern
States," he said, "they have emancipated all their slaves." If
any Southern slaves should go there and remain a certain time
they would, under the existing laws, be free, and their masters
could not get them again. "This would be extremely preju-
dicial" to the Southern States, and to prevent it, this clause
was inserted in the Constitution. This is the meaning, though
the word slave is not mentioned, owing to the scruples of the
Northern delegates on the subject of slavery.[31] General Pinckney said in the South Carolina convention, "We have obtained
a right to recover our slaves in whatever part of America they
may take refuge, which is a right we had not before. In short,
considering all the circumstances, we have made the best terms
for the recovery of this species of property it was in our power
to make. We would have made better if we could, but, on the
whole, I do not think them bad." [32] It is clear the Southern
members insisted on some provision of the kind, and that it was
a compromise between North and South, in which the South
secured the best terms they could from the Northern members.

The Admission of New States. (Art. IV, Sec. 3, cl. 1.)

The Virginia Plan provided "for the admission of States lawfully arising within the limits of the United States whether from a voluntary junction of government and territory, or otherwise, with the consent of a number of voices in the national legislature less than the whole." This was agreed to June 5, in committee of the whole.[33] Charles Pinckney's Plan, and the Patterson Plan also provided for the admission of new states to the Union.[34] The committee of detail reported as Article XVII, a provision admitting new states on terms of equality with the original states on a two-thirds vote of both houses, requiring the consent of the legislatures to the formation of new states within the limits of old states, and giving Congress power to make conditions with new states concerning the public debt.[35] On August 29, Gouverneur Morris moved to strike from the section the clauses for the admission of new states, on terms of equality with the original states and concerning the public debt. He did not wish Congress to be bound to admit the western states on equal terms, as it would throw power into their hands. Madison declared emphatically that the western states neither would nor ought to submit to any union which degraded them from an equal rank with the other states, but Morris' motion was adopted.[36] He then moved a substitute for Article XVII which became the clause in the Constitution. It read: "New states may be admitted by the legislature into the Union; but no new states shall be erected within the limits of any of the present states, without the consent of the legislature of such state, as well as of the general legislature." The first part to "Union" was adopted unanimously.[37] Morris said he thought the proposition would please the small states because it held up the idea of dismembering the large states. Doctor Johnson had suggested that the resolution of Morris would subject Vermont to New York, contrary to the faith pledged by Congress, and Gouverneur Morris moved to strike the word "limits" from his resolution, and to insert the word "jurisdiction" instead, which was done. This was intended to guard the case of Vermont—"the jurisdiction of New York not extending over Vermont, which was in the exercise of sovereignty, though Vermont was within the asserted limits of New York." Dickinson then offered a proposition similar to Morris' which was adopted as the second half of the clause.[38]

The clause originated in American experience of the defects of the Articles of Confederation. No provision was made for the admission of new states to the Union. Canada was to be admitted on "joining in the measures of the United States," and other British Colonies if nine states consented.[39] When the states ceded their Western territory, then Congress found it necessary to provide for the organization and government of such territory, or see anarchy prevail there. So the Ordinance of 1787 provided for the organization and government of the territory, and the admission of not less than three, nor more than five states on an equality with the original states. Congress, however, had no constitutional power to make any such arrangement. "All this has been done; and done without the least color of constitutional authority," says the Federalist.[40] When the Convention of 1787 met, expectation that a number of new states would soon seek admission to the Union was general.[41] The clause was, therefore, inserted in the Constitution to meet an actual situation with which Congress had no power to deal under the Articles of Confederation. "With great propriety, therefore, has the new system supplied the defect." [42]

Again, there appears to have been an impression that the small states would annex themselves to the larger states, or unite to form larger states, and this was intended to facilitate such action.[43]

The provision requiring the state legislatures to consent was inserted, because it would be "inconsistent with the rights of free and independent states to have their territory dismembered without their consent." This "quiets the jealousy of the larger states; as that of the smaller is quieted by a like precaution, against a junction of states without their consent." [44]

An interesting touch is added by Gouverneur Morris as to the *motive*, in a letter to Henry W. Livingston, December 4, 1803, which shows that one purpose Gouverneur Morris had was to so word this clause as to exclude Canada and Louisiana from the Union. If so, it was not due to accident or oversight that no constitutional power existed in 1803 for the annexation of Louisiana. In reply to Livingston's question, as to whether or not Congress could admit as a new state, territory which did not belong to the United States when the Constitution was framed, Morris wrote: "In my opinion they cannot. I always thought that when we should acquire Canada and Louisiana, it would be proper to govern them as provinces, and allow them no voice in our councils. In wording the third section of the fourth article, I went as far as circumstances would permit to establish the exclusion. Candor obliges me to add my belief, that, had it been more pointedly expressed, a strong opposition would have been made." [45]

The Government of Territories. (Art. IV, Sec. 3, cl. 2.) Gouverneur Morris offered the resolution almost as it stands in the Constitution, on August 30.[46] Morris, Carroll, and Madison all contributed to the clause—Morris suggesting the first part, Carroll the second, and Madison the proviso "or of any particular state." [47] Carroll had intimated that Maryland would probably reject the Constitution unless the claims of the United States to the "back lands" were secured. The phrase "to dispose of" was part of a proposition offered by Madison on August 18. "The proviso . . . was probably rendered absolutely necessary by jealousies and questions concerning the Western territory, sufficiently known to the public." [48]

The clause originated in American experience under the Articles of Confederation. Congress had no power to make rules and regulations for the territories, and as a consequence found itself in the difficult position of either usurping power, or of seeing anarchy prevail there. It chose to usurp power, and passed the North West Ordinance carving the North West into states, abolishing slavery, providing for the establishment of temporary governments, and ultimate admission of the states into the Union on a footing of equality with the original states —all done without the constitutional power to act. The states, not Congress, retained power over the territories—the absurd power of thirteen different governments passing laws for the same territories. Both experience and necessity, therefore, dictated this provision of the new federal Constitution giving Congress control over the territories.

The germ of territorial control appears in the Albany Plan of 1754 which gave the central government power to regulate and govern the territories till formed into states.[49]

The principles of the American territorial system were simply continued from the Old Colonial System in operation before the Revolution.[2]

The Guarantee of a Republican Form of Government. (Art. IV, Sec. 4.)　The Virginia Plan contained a resolution guaranteeing "a republican government and the territory of each state" by the United States. Read objected to guaranteeing territory, because it abetted the idea of distinct states which would be a perpetual source of discord. This could be avoided only by consolidating the states. This resulted in the resolution being amended to read: "A republican Constitution, and its existing laws, ought to be guaranteed to each State by the United States." [50] Gouverneur Morris objected to guaranteeing such laws as Rhode Island had, and Houston objected to the constitution of Georgia. Wilson said the *purpose* was to secure the states against dangerous commotions, insurrections, and rebellions, to which Randolph added, to secure a republican government. Mason declared emphatically that if the general government could not suppress rebellion against particular states, it must remain a passive spectator of its own destruction. Gorham said without this power an enterprising citizen might establish monarchy in a state, and set up a tyranny over the whole Union, while the government of the United States would be compelled to remain an inactive witness of its own destruction. Carroll believed the question whether Congress could crush rebellion in a state or not ought to be placed beyond doubt. Wilson then moved, "that a republican form of government shall be guaranteed to each State; and that each State shall be protected against foreign and domestic violence." This was agreed to nem. con.[51] The committee of detail reported it almost as in the Constitution, except that the word "foreign" was struck out on August 30, as being implied in the word "invasion," and therefore superfluous. Dickinson moved to insert "or executive" after "legislature," because the disturbance might hinder the legislature from meeting, which was adopted. A part of Article VII of the report of the committee of detail gave Congress power "to subdue rebellion in any state on the application of its legislature." On August 17, this was amended by adding "or without it when the legislature cannot meet," on motion of Ellsworth. This was added as the clause in brackets, September 15.[52]

This section originated in *American experience* of the defects of the Articles of Confederation and Shays's rebellion in

Massachusetts. One defect of the Articles was that they gave the federal government no power to suppress a rebellion in any state, "not having constitutional power, nor means to interpose according to the exigency," said Randolph. The reference was to Shays's rebellion in Massachusetts which he expressly mentions, and which Madison cites as "among the ripening incidents preparing the way for the new Constitution." During that crisis, the government of the United States was helpless. Congress began to raise troops as "an ostensible preparation against the Indians." [53] They did not dare say it was to protect federal property or aid Massachusetts. The whole nation was alarmed. "The flames of internal insurrection were ready to burst out in every quarter . . . from one end to the other of the continent, we walked on ashes, concealing fire beneath our feet; and ought Congress to be deprived of power to prepare for the defence and safety of our country?" said Wilson in the Pennsylvania convention.[54] Madison in his speech on the Patterson Plan in the Federal Convention on June 19 asked: "Will it secure the internal tranquillity of the states themselves? The insurrections in Massachusetts admonished all the states of the danger to which they were exposed. Yet the plan of Mr. Patterson," he said, "contained no provisions for supplying the defect of the Confederation on this point." [55] In his letter to Randolph, April 8, 1787, Madison wrote: "An article ought to be inserted expressly guaranteeing the tranquillity of the States against internal as well as external dangers." [55] This dangerous defect must be remedied by giving Congress constitutional power to protect the states, hence, this section grew out of American experience of danger, helplessness, and need.

Madison explained the republican form of government as necessary in a government founded on republican principles "to defend the system against aristocratic or monarchical innovations." He quoted Montesquieu's illustration: "Greece was undone as soon as the King of Macedon obtained a seat among the Amphictyons." [56] To Abbot's question in the North Carolina Convention as to what the clause meant, Iredell replied that "it was essential to the existence and harmony of the Confederacy" that each of the thirteen governments should remain republican, "and that no State should have a right to establish an aristocracy or monarchy." The purpose was to prevent any state from changing its government, and working mischief by endeavoring to subvert the freedom of the other states. He also recalled, as a warning, how the King of Macedon subverted the Confederate States of Greece.[57]

As to republican governments, the colonial governments of Rhode Island and Connecticut were republican. The resolution of Congress of October 10, 1780, provided for the unappropriated lands being "formed into distinct republican States."[58] Jefferson's plan for the government of the western territory, 1784, and the North West Ordinance of 1787 provided for republican governments. To secure harmony and permanence, all must conform to the republican governments of the original states.

The latter half of section 4 seems to have been taken from, or suggested by, the New York Act to regulate the militia of April 4, 1786, which gave the commander-in-chief power to call out the militia in case of invasion or other emergency, or on application of the executive of any of the United States, to order the militia to such state.[59]

The Amending Power. (Art. V.) The Virginia Plan provided for amending the Constitution without consent of the legislature. Pinckney's plan apparently proposed an arrangement by which the Constitution might be amended on proposal by the federal government and ratification by a certain number of the state legislatures, though he opposed this on June 5.[60] Opposition developed to making the consent of the national legislature unnecessary, and Mason answered that this was done because it might abuse its power, and then refuse consent for that very reason. The convention agreed to the first report of the resolution of the Virginia Plan, June 11, but postponed the second part requiring the consent of the national legislature. The committee of detail proposed a provision for amending the Constitution by Congress calling a convention on application of two thirds of the state legislatures. On August 30, Gouverneur Morris suggested that Congress be left free to call a convention whenever they pleased. Hamilton said Congress would be the first to see the need for amendments, and ought to be given power to call a convention whenever two thirds of each branch should concur.[61] Sherman then proposed such an amendment, and Wilson moved to insert the "three fourths" requirement for consent which the convention agreed to nem. con. Madison then moved to postpone consideration of the amended proposition in order to take up one offered by himself, which practically corresponded to Article V, down to "proposed by the Congress." Rutledge declared he could never agree to give a power which would enable the states not interested in slave property and prejudiced against it to alter the articles relating to slaves. He then offered the proviso that no amendment prior to 1808 could affect the first and fourth clauses of Art. I, Sec. 9. The Convention agreed to Madison's proposition as amended by Rutledge.[62] On September 15, Sherman expressed fears that three fourths of the states might undertake to do things which would be fatal to particular states, as depriving them of their equality in the Senate, and moved "that no State shall, without its consent, be affected in its internal police, or deprived of its equal suffrage in the Senate." This was rejected. Gouverneur Morris moved to annex the last half of Sherman's motion which was done.[63] Mason pointed out that as it stood, the plan for amending the Constitution was dangerous, because both the proposed methods depended on Congress, and the people would never be able to secure proper amendments if the government became oppressive. As a result, Gouverneur Morris moved to amend the article so as to require a convention on application of two thirds of the states, which was done.[64]

The sources were:

(1) *American experience under the Articles of Confederation.* This forced the nation to see that some convenient and practicable method must be devised, whereby it would be possible to amend the Constitution when found absolutely necessary to do so. One great defect was that the Articles gave Congress no power to secure a permanent revenue, and any amendment must be agreed to by Congress, and then "confirmed by the legislatures of every State." All attempts to amend the Articles of Confederation failed. Rhode Island blocked the Five-percent Amendment in 1781, and New York the Revenue Amendmentment of 1783. Madison, in reply to Patrick Henry's objection to the three fourths requirement in Article V,[65] said: "Could anything in theory be more perniciously improvident

and injudicious then this submission of the will of the majority to the most trifling minority? Have not experience and practice actually manifested this theoretical inconvenience to be extremely impolitic? . . . the smallest state in the Union has obstructed every attempt to reform the government; . . . Twelve states had agreed to certain improvements . . . thought absolutely necessary to preserve the existence of the general government; but as these . . . could not, by the Confederation, be introduced into it without the consent of every State, the refractory dissent of that little State prevented their adoption. The inconveniences resulting from this . . . in the Confederation must be known to every member of this Convention. . . . Is it not self-evident that a trifling minority ought not to bind the majority? . . . Would the honorable gentleman agree to continue the most radical defects in the old system, because the petty state of Rhode Island would not agree to remove them?" This experience suggested a different method of amending the Constitution, whereby it could be done without the concurrence of all the legislatures or state conventions. [66]

(2) *American constitutional precedents—chiefly state and colonial.* The Articles of Confederation and the Dickinson Draft contained the same provision for amendment.[67] The Franklin Draft provided that Congress might propose amendments to be ratified by a majority of the colonial legislatures.[68] This principle found its way into the Constitution. The state constitutions provided for their amendment, and the Convention had this in mind. The states of Delaware, Georgia, Maryland, Pennsylvania, Vermont, New Hampshire, and Massachusetts provided for amendment. None of them made the mistake of the Articles of Confederation by requiring unanimous consent. Maryland required the concurrence of two thirds of each branch of the legislature to amend, and Pennsylvania and Vermont two thirds of the Council of Censors to call a convention.[69] The Pennsylvania Charter of Privileges, 1701, the Pennsylvania Frame of 1696, and the Frame of Government of 1683 for Pennsylvania provided for their own amendment with the consent of the Governor and six parts in seven of the legislature. The last also required the consent of the Proprietary.[70] An amendment was framed and submitted to the

people for ratification for the first time in America in 1660 in Connecticut. It was proposed by the legislature and confirmed or ratified by the people.[71]

(3) *English precedents.* Conventions originated in England, and are traced to the right of the people to assemble. The "conventus publicos proprie authoritate" is mentioned as early as the twelfth century.[72] The American convention, however, finds its origin in the English revolutionary conventions of 1660 and 1689.

In both these cases, no legal Parliament could be called, because no King existed to issue the writs; therefore conventions or convention Parliaments were summoned composed of members chosen by the electors. These revolutionary conventions exercised the function of a provisional government for England, and undertook to reconstruct the constitution. These conventions were the models and originals on which all American conventions were based.[73] The first revolutionary convention in America was called in 1689, in connection with "the tyranny of Andros." Fifty-four towns sent delegates and it was modelled after the English convention of 1660, as was the English one of 1689.[74] The American constitutional convention originated in the adaptation of the English revolutionary convention of 1660 and 1689, to American needs during the Revolution and afterwards. The states or colonies borrowed the revolutionary convention during the Revolution, and carried on the war against England by that means. The Provincial Congresses and Conventions and the Continental Congresses were simply revolutionary conventions. In England, the convention had settled the constitution by drawing up the Bill of Rights. The states or colonies likewise used the revolutionary convention to settle the constitution and draw up bills of rights, as Virginia.[75] The constitutional convention is an adaptation of the revolutionary convention to constitutional purposes. The American colonists felt that they had been oppressed by the English Parliament which framed the laws. Might their legislatures not do the same thing, if permitted both to legislate and frame the constitution or organic law? American statesmen, therefore, sought some solution of the problem, and this led them to turn to the convention idea. This convention would be modelled after the revolutionary convention, but entrusted with but a single delegated function, namely, to frame the constitution. It ceased to be a revolutionary body as thus used, and became a constitutional convention called to "recommend and make improvements in the fundamental law." [76] The first colony to call a convention or Provincial Congress was New Hampshire in 1775.[77]

The principle of excepting certain clauses or parts of the constitution from the ordinary amending power is found in the Pennsylvania Charter of Privileges, 1701, and in the Delaware Constitution, 1776. That in regard to slaves was a compromise insisted on by South Carolina and Georgia in order that they might replenish their supply of slaves lost during the war.[78] That in regard to "equal suffrage in the Senate," was insisted on by the small states to prevent a consolidation of the states, and was probably meant as a palladium to their residuary sovereignty. Madison says South Carolina and Georgia united with the small states in securing slavery and equality in the Senate.[79]

NOTES TO CHAPTER XIII

1. Elliot, V, 381.
2. Elliot, V, 488, 504.
3. Journals of Cong. (Ford ed.), Vol. IX, 887-889; Elliot, V, 488.
4. Federalist, no. 41, p. 296 (Dawson ed.).
5. McClain, Cases, 847; 11 How. 165, 176.
6. Elliot, V, 381.
7. Art. IV.
8. Meigs, Growth of the Const. 257; Annals of Cong. 16, 1134; See Curtis in Dred Scott Case, Am. Hist. Leaflets, no. 20, p. 9; Journals of Cong. p. 887 (Ford ed.). Secret Journals, Vol. 1, 329-331.
9. Poore, 380; Bryce, The Am. Commonwealth, I, 19.
10. Poore, 1891.
11. Poore, 1901, 1905, 930, 944, 255, 950, 1602, 1385, 1393, 374; Caldwell, Am. Hist. Studies, No. 3, p. 54.
12. 11 St. Tr. 106; 169 U. S. 649.
13. 5 Ann. c. 8; Adams and Stephens, 481 (Art. IV).
14. 18 Wall. 168.
15. 20 N. Y. 607, 608-9, 627, Lemmon v. The People of New York.
16. Elliot, IV, 192.
17. Id. V, 381; Meigs, Growth of the Const. p. 258.
18. Art. IV; Meigs, 258.
19. Id. Elliot, V, 381.
20. Journals IX, 887 (Ford ed.), Secret Journals, Vol. I, 329, 330.
21. Elliot, V, 487.
22. Statutes and Laws, 160, 1786, 1784; Moore, Extradition, I, 824.
23. Hening, Vol. 10, p. 130.

24. Moore, Extradition, I, 824.
25. Hurd, Habeas Corpus, 592.   See Blackstone, IV, 121, 122, for common law meaning.
26. MacDonald, Sel. Charters, 99; Winthrop, Hist. of Mass, II, 101.
27. Moore, Extradition, I, 10.
28. Elliot, V, 487, 492, 550.
29. Ordinance of 1787 (last article).
30. MacDonald, Sel. Charters.
31. Elliot, IV, 176; Willoughby, I, 32.
32. Elliot, IV, 286.
33. Id. V, 128, 155, 156, 190.
34. Moore, Am. Eloquence, I, 364.
35. Elliot, V, 381; Meigs, Growth of the Const. p. 316 (plate VIII, seq.).
36. Elliot, V, 492, 493.
37. Id. 493.
38. Elliot, V, 493, 495, 496.
39. Art. XI; Federalist no. 37; Elliot, V, 281.
40. Federalist, no. 37 (Dawson ed.); Elliot, V, 281.
41. Id. 250, 256, 279, 356, 281, 492; I, 383, 493, 495, 496.
42. Federalist, No. 42; 13 Wall. 441; Elliot, V, 439; Journals of Cong. Vol. 6, p. 213; Jefferson's Works, IV (Ford ed.); 251 seq., 275 seq. Pickering, I, 457, 546.
43. Moore, Am. Eloquence, I, 368.
44. Elliot, I, 384; 394; Federalist, no. 42.
45. Farrand, Records, III, 404.
46. Elliot, V, 497.
47. Id. 496.
48. Id. 496, 494, 439; Federalist no. 42.
49. MacDonald, Sel. Charters, 256.   2 Blackstone, Com. I, 107-8.   May, Const. Hist. of Eng. Vol. II, ch. XVII.   Cooley, Const. Law. Ch. II, p. 35. "The Territories."   101 U. S. 129; McClain, Cases on Const. Law, 831, 835; Evans, Cases on Am. Const. Law, 74, 75; 182 U. S. 244; Willoughby, Const. Law. Chaps. 23, 24, Vol. I, Compare Declaratory Act.
50. Elliot, V, 128, 182.
51. Elliot, V, p. 332, 333.
52. Id. 381, 499, 379, 485, 551.
53. Elliot, V, 127, 126, 119, 94, 95, 99; Id. II, 521; Secret Journals of Congress, Oct. 21, 1786; A. C. McLaughlin, Confed. Const., 164-167.
54. Elliot, II, 521; III, 180.
55. Id. V, 209.
Elliot, V, 108; Id. I, 384; Federalist, Nos. 21, 42.
56. Federalist, No. 42.
57. Elliot, V, 195.
58. Journals of Congress, VI, 213.
59. Jefferson, Works, IV (Ford ed.), 251; Art. V, N. W. Ord. Laws of New York, 1786 (Greenleaf), p. 232.
60. Elliot, V, 128, 157; Moore, Am. Eloquence, I, 368-9.
61. Elliot, V, 182, 190, 376, 381, 498, 531.
62. Elliot, V, 531, 552.
63. Elliot, V, 551, 552; Madison says, this was "dictated by the circulating murmurs of the small states." Elliot, V, 552. It is clear they feared the possibility of their being deprived of their equal suffrage in the Senate, and Sherman, as the representative of Connecticut, a small State, was foremost in advocating this proviso.

64. Elliot, V, 551.

65. Art. XIII; Am. Hist. Leaflets, No. 28, 1781-9; Federalist, No. 42; above Leaflet, Elliot, III, 49, 50.

66. Elliot, III, 88, 89; See also Hamilton's statement, Elliot, V, 531, and Mason, Id. 182.

67. Art. XIII; Am. Hist. Leaflets, no. 20, p. 16.

68. Am. Hist. Leaflets, no. 20, p. 6.

69. Elliot, V, 157; Poore, 278, 383, 828, 1548, 1865, 1874-5, 1293, 972.

70. Poore, 1539, 1536, 1530.

71. Colonial Records of Conn. I, 346. See account of this case.

72. Jameson, Const. Conventions, pp. 5, 6. The first suggestion for a constitutional convention seems to have come from Sir Harry Vane in a letter to Cromwell, 1656, in which he recommended that conventions "chosen for that purpose by the free consent of the whole body" be called to draw up a Constitution for England. Such a convention would represent the sovereignty of the people. Foster, Commentaries on the Constitution, p. 35.

73. J. A. Jameson, Const. Conventions, p. 45. See any English Constitutional History. Jameson, Const. Conventions, p. 7.

74. Jameson, Const. Conventions, pp. 8, 9.

75. Jameson, Const. Conventions, p. 11, 12.

76. Jameson, Const. Conventions, p. 10-15.

77. Poore, 1279; Poore, 1539, 278.

78. Elliot, IV, 178.

79. Federalist, No. 42; Elliot, V, 552; Id. IV, 177; Farrand, III, 436.

CHAPTER XIV

National Debts Secured and the Supreme Law of the Land

Debts Contracted Under Confederation Secured. (Art. VI, Sec. 1, cl. 1.) The Virginia Plan proposed "the completion of all engagements of Congress" and this was adopted June 5. Several resolutions were offered which secured the debts of the states and United States and among them was one by Gouverneur Morris offered as an amendment, namely, "The legislature shall discharge the debts, and fulfill the engagements of the United States." This was agreed to unanimously. On August 23, Butler expressed dissatisfaction with the clause, lest it compel payment to the bloodsuckers, and gave notice of reconsideration. When the question came up on August 25, Randolph moved to postpone the clause in favor of one he offered, which became the clause in the Constitution. This was adopted ten to one.[1]

The *purpose* of the clause was to assure the public creditors of the United States that the change in government made by the new Constitution did not destroy the claims of creditors against the government. Such claims would be valid under the new, as under the old government.[2] This "may have been inserted, among other reasons, for the satisfaction of foreign creditors of the United States, who cannot be strangers to the pretended doctrine, that a change in the political form of civil society has the magical effect of dissolving its moral obligations," said Madison.[3]

It appears that the leading members of the Convention were personally interested, as the holders of public securities, in the assumption of state debts by the United States, and in securing the debts of the United States. It is a noteworthy fact that the delegates from every state voting for the Rutledge resolution August 21 (on assumption of state debts) were holders of public paper, while in the states voting against it, the holdings were in most cases small.[4] Gerry thought it necessary to disclaim any interest in the question as he held no more of the securities than would, by the interest, pay his taxes.[5] Professor Beard says Gerry "modestly underestimates the amount" of securities he held, or else "his taxes were rather high" for the Massachusetts loan office records show that the interest paid Gerry "pursuant to the act of Congress of April 28, 1784" amounted to about $3,500 a year.[6] Gerry had, therefore, some personal interest, in spite of his attempt to hide it, in working so strenuously in the Federal Convention to confer on the government both the power and the obligation to pay the holders of public securities. A study of other cases reveals the same thing.

Randolph, the author of the clause in the Convention, based it on Article XII of the Articles of Confederation. As first introduced, his resolution read: "All debts contracted . . . by or under the authority of Congress." [7] Both the phraseology and the principle of Article XII were borrowed by Randolph.

The Supreme Law of the Land. (Art. VI, cl. 2.) The Virginia Plan gave the national legislature power to negative all state laws contravening any treaty or the Articles of Union, and provided a council of revision composed of the executive and a convenient number of the national judiciary with power to examine every act of a state legislature before a negative thereon should be final. Charles Pinckney's plan also seems to have provided for a congressional negative on state laws contravening the Constitution.[8] The resolution of the Virginia Plan was, on motion of Doctor Franklin, agreed to on May 31, without debate or dissent.[9] On June 8 Pinckney moved that the national legislature be given "authority to negative all laws which they shall judge to be improper." [10] Pinckney and Madison appealed for support to American experience of the violation by the states of acts of Congress and treaties with foreign nations, and spoke of the British negative as beneficial to the colonies. It would not have been inconvenient, Madison declared, had the supreme power possessed the necessary information, and acted in the interests of America. The proposition was rejected.[11] During the discussion on July 17, Sherman said the negative was unnecessary, as the state courts would not consider valid any law contravening the Articles of Union,[12] and Gouverneur Morris declared such a negative would disgust the states: "A law that ought to be negatived will be set aside in the judiciary department" or repealed by national law.

Madison replied that the states would pass laws accomplishing their injurious object before Congress could repeal them, or the federal courts declare them void. It was taken for granted that both state and federal courts were to declare laws void. The negative was finally rejected because it was believed to be impracticable among so many states passing so many laws (Madison) because it was held that the plan would throw sufficient power into the hands of Massachusetts, Pennsylvania, and Virginia to enable them to negative the laws of the other ten states at pleasure, and because it was clearly seen that a state law contrary to the Federal Constitution would be void. Sherman pointed this out just before the vote was taken on July 17.[13] They had been thinking of the British King's negative as the model for the negative in the Federal Constitution. A colonial law contrary to the British Constitution had always been void. The same would be true of a state law contrary to the Federal Constitution. State judges had already declared state laws contrary to the state constitution void. For the purpose of realizing the same end as the Congressional negative of state laws was intended to secure, Luther Martin, immediately after the vote of rejection, moved: "That the legislative acts of the United States, made by virtue and in pursuance of the Articles of Union, and all treaties made and ratified under the authority of the United States, shall be the supreme law of the respective states, as far as those acts or treaties shall relate to the said states, or their citizens and inhabitants; and that the judiciaries of the several states shall be bound thereby in their decisions, anything in the respective laws of the individual states to the contrary notwithstanding." This was agreed to nem. con.,[14] and was referred to the committee of detail. The committee reported the provision on August 6, in slightly altered phraseology. On August 23, Rutledge moved to amend the article so as to read: "This Constitution and the laws of the United States made in pursuance thereof etc." instead of "the acts of the United States made in pursuance thereof . . . "[15] On motion of Madison and Gouverneur Morris, the clause was further amended by adding the words, "or which shall be made" after the words "all treaties made." The purpose of this was to obviate all doubt concerning the force of treaties preexisting, by making the words "all treaties made" refer to them, while the newly inserted clause would cover future treaties.[16] The committee on style then made two changes. The words "shall be the supreme law of the several states" were changed to read "shall be the supreme law of the land." "Anything in the Constitutions or laws of the several states" was changed to read "anything in the Constitution or laws of any state."[17] This left the clause as in the Constitution.

The immediate source of Luther Martin's proposition was resolution six of the New Jersey Plan. A comparison shows the phraseology to be nearly identical.[18] Luther Martin had participated in drawing up the resolutions of the New Jersey Plan for the Convention.[19]

(1) *The Constitution and laws are to be the supreme law of the land.* There seems to be an evident connection between this provision and the Bayard v. Singleton case, decided in the May term of the Superior Court at Newbern, North Carolina, 1787. The report of the committee of detail read: "The acts of the legislature of the United States made in pursuance of this Constitution etc." On August 23, Rutledge of South Carolina moved to amend the article by striking out the above words and substituting: "This *Constitution* and laws of the United States made in pursuance thereof," which was unanimously done.[20] He was chairman of the committee of detail, and this change was in accordance with the decision in the case of Bayard v. Singleton, in which the judges declared the Articles of Confederation to be of paramount authority "as a part of the law of the land, unrepealable by any act of the General Assembly."[21] Jefferson wrote to John Adams in 1787: "It has accordingly been the decision of our Courts that the Confederation is a part of the law of the land, and superior in authority to the ordinary laws, because it cannot be altered by the legislature of any state."

In the South Carolina convention, Rutledge declared the Articles of Confederation were paramount law,[22] and in the Federal Convention he applied the idea to the new Constitution, as well as to acts of the legislature. It is not known just when news of the decision reached the Convention. Davie, one of the delegates from North Carolina, was associated with Iredell as counsel and would naturally receive word as soon as possible. Spaight wrote his letter to Iredell denying the authority of the judges to declare a law void, August 12.[23] There was, therefore, plenty of time for the whole Convention to learn what the decision had been before August 23.

Further, the members of the Federal Convention knew that the state courts had declared the new state constitutions to be the supreme law of the several states, and had set aside laws opposed to the constitution.[24] Laws repugnant to the Constitution were held by the courts to be void. The constitutions of Massachusetts and New Hampshire were declared "to be a part of the laws of the land." [25] In certain states, the judges had declared the state constitutions to be the supreme law of the land, and the Convention follows the decisions of the courts in making the Federal Constitution the supreme law of the land. The phrase "the law of the land" is a Magna Carta phrase.[26]

Again, the colonists had always been familiar with the idea of a supreme law of the land—with the idea that the Constitution and laws of the central government were the supreme law of the land. The English Common law, sometimes modified by act of Parliament, was the supreme law common to all the colonies, the supreme law of the several colonies. The charters provided that the Constitution, laws, and statutes of England should be the supreme law in the colonies [27]—the supreme law of the land. If any of the colonial courts failed to respect this law, or refused to be bound thereby in their decisions, anything in the acts or laws of any colony to the contrary notwithstanding, then their decisions might be set aside on appeal to the Supreme Imperial Court—the King in Council.[28] James M. Varnum, in the Trevett v. Weeden case, argued that the Revolution had not changed this; that the Constitution and laws of England still remained the supreme law of the land, and as the King in Council set aside laws of the colonies repugnant or contrary thereto, so the courts of Rhode Island must henceforth do the same thing.[29] The Americans were, therefore, always familiar with the idea of the Constitution and laws being the supreme law and binding on the judges in every colony, anything in the acts or laws of any colony to the contrary notwithstanding. It was a principle familiar to all under the colonial governments.

American experience under the Articles of Confederation also contributed something to the idea. There was no method by which the supremacy of the national Constitution could be enforced over the state constitutions. Neither was there any method by which the government could single out and punish guilty individuals. "The great and radical vice in the construction of the existing Confederation," said Hamilton, "is the principle of legislation for states or governments in their corporate or collective capacities, and as contradistinguished from the individuals of which they consist . . . the United States have no definite discretion to make requisitions for men and money; but they have no authority to raise either, by regulations extending to the individual citizens of America. The consequence of this is, though in theory their resolutions concerning those objects are laws, constitutionally binding on the members of the Union, yet in practice they are mere recommendations, which the states observe or disregard at their option." [30]   There was not even an express provision giving Congress power to use force to compel the states to discharge their duty. The violations of the Federal Articles were "numerous and many." New Jersey, for example, expressly refused to comply with a requisition of Congress.[31] Davie said in the North Carolina Convention: "Another radical vice in the old system . . . was that it legislated on states, instead of individuals; and that its powers could not be executed but by fire or by sword—by military force, and not by the intervention of the civil magistrates . . . the most dreadful consequences would ensue. . . . It was therefore absolutely necessary that the influence of the magistrate should be introduced, and that the laws should be carried home to individuals. . . . Every member saw that the existing system would ever be ineffectual, unless its laws operated on individuals, as military coercion was neither eligible nor practicable." The Convention, therefore, was led by such considerations to depart from that solecism in politics, "the principle of legislation for states in their political capacities," and to establish the government on the people.[32]

Charles Pinckney gave similar testimony in the South Carolina convention. When the convention met, every delegate present, he says, saw that it was indispensably necessary to establish the government upon different principles, which "should operate upon the people in the first instance," "instead of requiring the intervention of thirteen different legislatures between the demand and the compliance." [33] This unanimity on the part of the convention was the result of bitter experience under the Articles of Confederation, ending in the blocking by the states of every attempt on the part of Congress to amend the Articles [34] in order to remedy this radical defect. The result was that in the Federal Convention, there was no question as to the necessity of either coercion or force. The only question was: Should it be a coercion of *arms*, or a coercion of *law?* That is, should force be applied to states, or to individuals? The Virginia Plan provided for calling forth the force of the Union to coerce a delinquent state. [35] As early as May 30, Colonel Mason argued against providing for coercion and punishment of delinquent states as impossible in the nature of things, and urged the establishment of such a government as could operate directly on individuals "and would punish those only whose guilt required it." [36] On June 6, he said that under the Confederacy, Congress represented the states, and not the people of the states, but that this would be changed in the new plan of government. Congress would operate on the individuals, not on the states. Madison declared the use of force would be visionary, impracticable, and a declaration of war against a state which would dissolve the Union.[37] Hamilton also declared that the use of force would be impossible, because it would be war between the parties.[38] Randolph pronounced coercion to be "impracticable, expensive, cruel to individuals." "We must resort, therefore, to a national legislation over individuals." Wilson, with clear, comprehensive grasp, outlined the plan still further on June 25. Every citizen, he pointed out, would stand in a two-fold relation to government under the new Constitution, "first, as citizens of the general government; and, secondly, as citizens of their particular state. The general government was meant for them in the first capacity: the state governments in the second." [39]

The Convention was, therefore, prepared by bitter experience to establish a government operating on individuals rather than on the states. In the winter of 1784-85, Noah Webster, known to the public by his valuable political writings, had proposed the establishment of a government which should act directly on individuals instead of on the states, and in which Congress should be given the same power to compel obedience to its laws as the state legislatures had in the states.[40]

This apparently left its impress on Madison,[41] who also pointed out in the Convention that a precedent existed under the Articles of Confederation for the idea of a government which operated on individuals instead of on states, namely, in cases of piracies and felonies, the government operated immediately on individuals. The Patterson plan also proposed to do so in many instances.[42] Hamilton, the day before, had also mentioned that the government exercised its power over individuals "among ourselves in cases of piracy" and that the Patterson plan was "to operate eventually on individuals." [43] It was clear to the Convention that this principle must be adopted, and embodied in their scheme of government. The Constitution must provide for a coercion of law, and not for a coercion of arms.[44]

On July 17, during the discussion on the negative on state laws, which Article VI of the Virginia Plan proposed to give the national legislature, Sherman, adopting the principle of declaring laws contrary to the Constitution void, which had been laid down by the state courts, pointed out that the negative was quite unnecessary, as the state courts would refuse to consider "as valid any law contravening" the national Constitution. The idea of such a negative was wrong in principle anyway, because it assumed that a state law contrary to the Federal Constitution would, if not negatived by the national government, be a valid and binding law, whereas it would be ipso facto null and void—no law, and not binding on the citizens. The state judges would declare it so.[45] Then Luther Martin offered the resolution of the New Jersey Plan, making acts of Congress and treaties the supreme law of the several states, binding on state officers, and enforceable by state judges. This, when perfected, becomes the supreme law clause which provides for a coercion by law—a coercion which acts upon delinquent individuals only.[46]

The effect and importance of this in solving one important problem of the Convention was well stated by Governor Johnston in the North Carolina convention: "The Constitution must be the supreme law of the land, otherwise it would be in the power of any one state to counteract the other states, and withdraw itself from the Union. The laws made in pursuance thereof by Congress ought to be the supreme law of the land; otherwise, any one state might repeal the laws of the Union at large. Without this clause, the whole Constitution would be a piece of blank paper." [47]

(2) *Treaties are made the supreme law of the land.* How did the idea of making treaties the supreme law originate? *First, American experience.* One of the pressing problems under the Articles of Confederation had been, how was the Federal government to compel the states to observe treaties made by the United States, especially the treaty of peace with Great Britain, which had been violated by the states. Though treaties were the law of the land, yet Congress was powerless to enforce obedience, if the states chose to violate them. All Congress could do was to recommend the repeal of acts violating such treaties. The result was, Madison declared in convention on June 19, that "the files of Congress contain complaints already, from almost every nation with which treaties have been formed." [48]

The existing Confederacy did not effectually provide against a rupture with other nations on these grounds. [49] Treaties made by the United States with France and Holland had also been violated by the states. Every treaty had been violated by some of the states. [50] Rhode Island, "the home of the otherwise minded," absolutely refused to comply with a request of Congress to repeal all laws repugnant to the treaty of peace with Great Britain, on the ground that it would be calling in question the propriety of their former measures. [51] The disastrous results to the United States were forcibly set forth by Madison in the Virginia convention, 1788. Foreign nations were entirely unwilling to make any treaties with the United States, because the government was powerless to secure obedience to the treaty on the part of the states, as they could violate treaties at pleasure. "Our violation of treaties already entered into proves this truth unequivocally. No nation will, therefore, make any stipulations with Congress conceding any advantages of importance to us." [52] The British, as a result of violations of the treaty of peace by the states, held the western posts, much to the chagrin and annoyance of the United States. Something must be done which would enable Congress to compel the states to obey its treaties; hence the Virginia Plan proposed to give Congress power to veto any state law contravening a treaty made by Congress. The principle of the New Jersey Plan which made treaties the supreme law of the states and enforceable by the state courts, was substituted for the Congressional veto. This compelled the states to obey the national treaties. "Have we not seen, in America, that Treaties were violated though they are in all countries considered as the supreme law of the land? Was it not, therefore, necessary to declare in explicit terms that they should be so here?" said George Nicholas in the Virginia convention. [53]

American experience under the Articles of Confederation, therefore, dictated the necessity of making treaties the supreme law of the land to secure obedience by the states.

Secondly, the provision originated in part in the resolutions of Congress of March 21, 1787, and the recommendation for identical laws sent down to the states April 13, 1787. Congress recommended the states to enact these identical laws for the purpose of repealing their acts which contravened the British treaty of peace. On March 21, 1787, Congress unanimously agreed to the following: "Resolved, That the legislatures of the several states cannot of right pass any act or acts for interpreting, explaining or construing a national treaty, or any part or clause of it, nor for restraining, limiting or in any manner impeding, retarding or counteracting the operation and execution of the same, for that on being constitutionally made, ratified, and published, they become in virtue of the Confederation, part of the law of the land, and are not only independent of the will and power of such legislatures, but also binding and obligatory on them."

"Resolved, That it be recommended to the several states . . . to pass an act declaring in general terms, that all such acts and parts of acts repugnant to the treaty of peace between the United States and his Britannic majesty, or any article thereof, shall be and thereby are repealed, and that the courts of law and equity in all causes and questions cognizable by them respectively, and arising from or touching the said treaty, shall decide, and adjudge according to the true intent and meaning of the same, anything in the said act or parts of acts to the contrary thereof in any wise notwithstanding." [54]

On April 13, 1787, Congress sent along with the resolutions a letter to the states recommending that the states pass identical laws repealing their acts opposed to the treaty of peace. It declared that Article IX of the Articles of Confederation gave Congress sovereign power in the matter of treaties and continued: "When, therefore, a treaty is constitutionally made, ratified and published by us, it immediately becomes binding on the whole nation, and superadded to the laws of the land without the intervention of state legislatures." [55] " . . . The treaty of peace is a law of the United States which cannot by any or all of them be altered . . . and further that the courts of law and equity within their state be, and they hereby are directed and required in all causes and questions cognizable by them respectively, and arising from or touching the said treaty, to decide and adjudge according to the tenor, true intent and meaning of the same, anything in the said acts or parts of acts to the contrary thereof in any wise notwithstanding. . . . By repealing in general terms all acts and clauses repugnant to the treaty, the business will be turned over to its proper department, viz., the judicial, and the courts of law will find no difficulty in deciding whether any particular act or clause is or is not contrary to the treaty." [56]

The connection here is clear. We find it stated: (1) Treaties are part of the law of the land, superadded to the laws of the land, independent of the will and power of state legislatures, binding and obligatory on them and the whole nation. (2) State courts are to be bound by treaties, as the law of the land, in their decisions, anything in the state laws to the contrary notwithstanding. (3) The *treaty of peace* with Great Britain is the law of the United States, which cannot be altered by any or all of the states.

This is the source—the immediate source—of the principle making treaties the supreme law of the land and binding on the state judges. The provision of the New Jersey plan was taken from the above resolutions and letter of Congress. Comparison presents indisputable evidence on this point. Gorham, King, Madison, Blount, Few, Pierce, and Johnson of Connecticut, who had aided in drawing up the New Jersey Plan, were all present in Congress in 1787, and shared in the discussion and adoption of the resolution recommending identical laws. Charles Pinckney was also present up to February 21, when his term expired.[57] The identical laws were sent down to all the states and were, therefore, known to every member of the Federal Convention.

The connection between Congress and the Convention is clearly seen in the action of the committee on style. Three members of that committee—Johnson, Madison, and King [58]— had been in Congress, March 21 and April 13, 1787, and their influence is seen in the change they made in the phraseology. The report of the committee of detail read: "All treaties . . . shall be the supreme law of the several states, and of their citizens and inhabitants." The committee on style changed this by substituting the phrase they had used in Congress March 21 and April 13, 1787, namely, "the supreme law of the land." Then, on June 18, 1788, Madison shows that he was fully conscious of the existence of a causal relation between the resolutions and identical laws recommended by Congress, and the Constitution by declaring in the Virginia convention that: "Many of the states have recognized the treaties of Congress to be the supreme law of the land. Acts have passed within a year, declaring this to be the case. I have seen many of them." [59]

Third, treaties had been recognized as the law of the land under the Articles of Confederation. In the South Carolina convention, General C. C. Pinckney declared that the treaty of peace with Great Britain "had been adjudged in a variety of cases, to be part of the law of the land, and had been admitted to be so whenever it was pleaded." [60] He mentioned other instances where the treaty of peace with Great Britain was considered by the courts as part of the law of the land. "The judge who held the court at Ninety-six discharged upwards of one hundred recognizances of persons committed for different crimes, which fell within the meaning of this treaty." A man named Love, accused of murder, was liberated, though the people, enraged at him, lynched him soon after. Another murderer, who had conducted General Pickens' brother into an Indian ambuscade where he was captured and killed, was allowed to plead the treaty in bar.[61] "I contend that the article in the new Constitution, which says that treaties shall be paramount to the laws of the land, is only declaratory of what treaties were, in fact, under the old compact. They were as much the law of the land under that Confederation, as they are under this Constitution."[62]

John Rutledge said emphatically that "every treaty was law paramount . . . this treaty is binding in our courts as in England. In that country, American citizens can recover debts due to them under the treaty." Davie and Maclaine also stated in the North Carolina convention that the treaty of peace was the supreme law of the land.[63]

Fourth, Blackstone's Commentaries.[64] In the Virginia Convention, Patrick Henry objected vigorously that "treaties were to have more force here than in any part of Christendom." Treaties rested on the laws and usages of nations. "To say that they are municipal is, to me, a doctrine totally novel. To make them paramount to the Constitution and laws of the states is unprecedented. I would give them the same force and obligation they have in Great Britain, or any other country in Europe."[65] To this, Madison replied that Blackstone's Commentaries would inform him that treaties were the supreme law of the land in England.[66] Nicholas said, "If a treaty was to be the supreme law of the land here, it was so in England," and he quoted a passage from Blackstone, Book I, 257, to prove that treaties were the supreme law of the land there. He declared that treaties made by the President and Senate have the same force and validity in the United States. "They are the supreme law of the land here. This book shows us they are so in England."[67] Corbin said in the convention that the honorable gentleman had said treaties were not the supreme law of the land in England. "My honorable friend proved the contrary by the Commentaries of Blackstone."[68] On January 17, 1788, General Pinckney, in the South Carolina convention, also quoted from Blackstone's Commentaries to prove that treaties were the supreme law of the land according to the laws and constitution of England.[69]

It is quite evident that the Congress of 1787 modelled its identical laws upon Blackstone's doctrine. Madison was a leader in Congress at the time. Blackstone said a treaty, when constitutionally made, was "binding upon the whole community." [70] Congress said a treaty constitutionally made "becomes binding on the whole nation." Blackstone said that in England the law of nations was "adopted in its full extent by the common law, and is held to be a part of the law of the land." He also said that the statute law of England interposed in certain cases "to aid and enforce the law of Nations, as part of the common law." It thus becomes part of the law of the land. Congress in its resolution of March 21 said that a national treaty on being constitutionally made, ratified and published became "part of the law of the land." [71] This use of Blackstone's exact phraseology was not accidental, but a conscious, intentional adoption and following of Blackstone's doctrine with which all the statesmen of 1787 were familiar. They were simply following the greatest authority on English law. This legal principle was everywhere accepted as law, and, therefore, it was adopted for the purpose of securing and guaranteeing enforcement of treaties in America. By following Blackstone in making treaties the supreme law of the land, and requiring the courts to enforce them as paramount law, the states would be compelled to obey them.

Fifthly, it was a well-known international law doctrine that treaties were the law of the land. Madison declared in the Virginia Convention on June 18, 1788, that treaties were the supreme law of the land in every country.[72] Nicholas said the law of nations was superior to any act or law of any nation and was mutually binding on all. "Have we not seen in America that treaties were violated, though they are in all countries considered as the supreme law of the land " [73] Maclaine in the North Carolina convention said treaties were the supreme law of the land in all countries, or else they could have no validity.[74] Davie, a member of the Federal Convention, said in the North Carolina convention, "By the law of *nations*, they are the supreme law of the land to their respective citizens or subjects." [75] The work on international law that was studied and quoted by all the statesmen of 1787 was Vattel's Law of Nature and of Nations. It declared treaties "binding on the whole nation" and "obligatory on the whole state." [76] General

Pinckney quoted both Vattel and Burlamaqui in the South Carolina convention on January 17, 1788, to prove treaties the law of the land.[77] After quoting Burlamaqui's words: "Ils ont force de loi a l'Egard des sujets, considérés comme tels," he says: "It is remarkable that the words made use of by Burlamaqui establish the doctrine, recognized by the Constitution, that treaties shall be considered as the law of the land." [78] The Federal Convention simply applied this principle of the law of nations to the case in hand.

The phrase "in pursuance thereof" excludes all laws not made in pursuance thereof from the effect of the clause; that is, excludes them from being the supreme law of the land. The phrase was evidently taken from the Articles of Confederation, where it reads "in pursuance of the present Confederation." [79] This, in Luther Martin's resolution, was changed to "in pursuance of the Articles of Union." [80] The committee of detail changed it to "in pursuance of this Constitution," [81] while Rutledge's change on August 23, by which "This Constitution" was introduced in the first part of the clause, rendered change necessary to prevent the awkward reading: "This Constitution and the laws of the United States made in pursuance of this Constitution." So the word "thereof" was substituted for the phrase "in this Constitution" by Rutledge's amendment.

The phrase "the law of the land" runs back to Magna Carta and beyond,[82] through English statutes and legal phraseology. The immediate source of the phrase was found in the resolutions of Congress passed March 21, 1787. Treaties were spoken of there as "part of the law of the land." [83] The letter of April 13, 1787, accompanying the resolutions, spoke of a treaty as "superadded to the laws of the land," and as "part of the law of the land." [84] When the article went to the committee on style, it read, "law of the several states, their citizens or inhabitants." For this, the committee substituted "law of the land." [85] Four members of the committee on style had been in Congress on March 21 and April 13, 1787, and had taken part in the proceedings which had declared a treaty part of the law of the land, namely, Madison, Hamilton, King and Johnson. Congress took the phrase from Blackstone's Commentaries.[86]

Again, it was to be found in every state constitution except that of New Jersey and Georgia,[87] and it is clear that the framers had Magna Carta in mind, because in nine of the state constitutions the phrase is quoted along with other phraseology from Chapter Thirty-nine of Magna Carta. New York and Delaware are the only states that do not do this. In another state, Rhode Island, both courts and legislature recognized the existence of a law of the land. The statute involved in the case of Trevett v. Weeden provided for the trial of offenders under it "without any jury by a majority of the judges present according to the laws of the land." [88] Varnum denied such a law could be a law of the land. [89] General Varnum was in Congress, and had participated in the proceedings of March 21 and April 13, 1787. The meaning was that there was a law of the land for each state, and not one law for the whole of the United States. [90]

The phrase runs back to the lex terrae of England and la ley de la terre of France. In England any form of judicial trial or test was called a lex, such as the ordeal, compurgation, or trial by combat. So that lex terrae stood originally for a method of judicial procedure, and was also used in the popular sense of the present day. In Magna Carta it may be used in both senses. Later, the popular meaning came to control and the technical meaning was dropped. Coke's interpretation finally prevailed, namely, as equivalent to "due process of law." [91] "In the old Germanic law," says Thayer, "there were many of these leges, or modes of trial. Trial by battle was the lex ultrata; by the ordeal, the lex appareus, manifesta, or parabilis; by the single oath, the lex simplex; by the oath with compurgators, the lex probabilis or the lex disraisinae; by record, the lex recordationis. Our phrase 'law of the land' comes down out of the midst of all this. . . . 'By the lex terrae is meant,' says Brunner, 'the procedure of the old popular law.' " [92] Due process of law has now a very definite meaning and requires: (1) Notice of the charge against a person. (2) The right to defend in court, or opportunity to defend. (3) The right to counsel and witnesses for defense.

NOTES TO CHAPTER XIV

1. Elliot, V, 128, 157, 440, 441, 451, 464, 469, 476; I, 305.
2. Elliot, III, 472, 473; V, 451, 463, 471, 475; Cooley, Const. Law, 62.
3. Federalist, No. 42.

4. Beard, Economic Interpretation of the Constitution, 81, 89, 90, 97, 120, 138, 127; Elliot, V, 441.
5. Elliot, V, 476.
6. Econ. Interp. of the Const., 97.
7. Elliot, V, 476; comp. Art. XII, Arts. of Confed.
8. Elliot, V, 127, 132; Moore, Am. Eloquence, I, 365, 366.
9. Elliot, V, 139.
10. Id. 170.
11. Id. 171-173, 174.
12. Id. 321.
13. Elliot, V, 321, 322, 348, 349.
14. Elliot, V, 322.
15. Id. 467.
16. Id. 478.
17. Elliot, I, 305.
18. Elliot, V, 192, 322.
19. Elliot, I, 349, V, 191.
20. Elliot, V, 379.
21. Martin's Reports, p. 48-52, 2nd Ed., I, 42-48.
22. Adams, Works, IV, 579; Elliot, IV, 267.
23. McRae, Life of Iredell, II, 169.
24. Elliot, V, 151: viz., Holmes v. Walton, N. J., Trevett v. Weeden, R. I., and perhaps others.
25. Poore, Constitutions and Charters, 973, 1293.
26. Mag. Carta, Ch. 39. Blackstone, I, 143.
27. Poore, 255, 374, 940, 951, 1277, 1278, 1384, 1385, 1392, 1600.
28. Baldwin, Two Centuries Growth of Am. Law, p. 19, 20. Poore above.
29. Varnum, case of Trevett v. Weeden, p. 23, 29, 12.
30. Federalist, No. 15 (Dawson Ed.).
31. Elliot, V, 207; Federalist, No. 21 (Dawson Ed.).
32. Elliot, IV, 21, 22.
33. Elliot, IV, 256.
34. A. C. McLaughlin, Confed. and Constitution, Chaps. IV, V, XI; Am. Hist. Leaflets, No. 28.
35. Elliot, V, 128.
36. Elliot, V, 133.
37. Id. 161, 140, 171.
38. Elliot, V, 200.
39. Elliot, V, 198.
40. Sketches of Am. Policy, p. 30, 48.
41. Am. Hist. Leaflets, No. 28, p. 21-22. Elliot, V, 118.
42. Elliot, V, 206.
43. Id. 199.
44. Elliot, II, 197.
45. Elliot, V, 321, 322.
46. Elliot, II, 197.
47. Elliot, IV, 187, 188.
48. Elliot, V, 207.
49. Elliot, V, 207; II, 144.
50. Elliot, IV, 119, 120; Moore, Am. Eloquence I, 365.
51. Elliot, V, 577; Secret Journals of Congress, Oct. 13, 1786.
52. Elliot, III, 135.
53. Elliot, III, 506, 507.

54. Journals of Congress, Vol. 12, p. 32-33.
55. Journals of Congress, Vol. 12, p. 46 (April 13, 1787).
56. Id. p. 32-46.
57. Journals of Congress, Vol. 12, p. 31, 40, 41, 42, 54, 10, 14.
58. Elliot, V, 530.
59. Elliot, III, 514.
60. Elliot, IV, 266.
61. Elliot, IV, 270, 272.
62. Elliot, IV, 278, 267.
63. Elliot, IV, 120, 164.
64. Elliot, III, 500. Blackstone was "in every man's hand," Madison said.
65. Elliot, III, 500.
66. Id. 501.
67. Id. 502, 506-7.
68. Id. 510.
69. Elliot, IV, 278.
70. Com. I, 257; Elliot, IV, 506.
71. Journals of Congress, Vol. 12, p. 33. Blackstone, I, 73; Blackstone, IV, 78, 79; Journals of Cong., Vol. 12, p. 32.
72. Elliot, III, 501.
73. Id. 502, 507.
74. Elliot, IV, 28.
75. Elliot, IV, 119.
76. Vattel, Book II, Ch. XII, 154, 186.
77. Elliot, IV, 278, 279.
78. Id. 279.
79. Art. XII.
80. Elliot, V, 322.
81. Id. 379.
82. Id. 379, 467; Mag. Carta, Chap. 39.
83. Journals of Con., Vol. XII, p. 23, 24, or see under date April 13, 1787.
84. Journals of Congress under date April 13, 1787, or Vol. 12, p. 32-36.
85. Elliot, V, 467.
86. Vol. IV, Ch. V.
87. Pa. Poore 1542, Del. 277, Md. 818, Va. 1909, N. C. 1410, S. C. (1778) 1627, Vt. (1777 and 1786) 1860, 1868, N. Y. 1337, N. H. 1282, 1293, and Mass. 958, 973. N. J. uses an equivalent phrase "part of the law of this Colony," Poore, 1313, and Georgia uses "according to the laws of this State," Poore, 380.
88. Varnum, cases of Trevett v. Weeden, p. 2, 3.
89. Id. p. 11, 35.
90. Coxe, Judicial Power, etc., p. 287-290, 321, 322.
91. For the meaning, see W. S. McKechnie, Magna Carta, 379-382, G. B. Adams, Origin of the Eng. Const., 379-382, Stephens Hist. Criminal Law, I, 162, 163, Coxe, Judicial Power, etc., 287-290, 321-322; Murray v. Hoboken Land and Improvement Co., 18 How. 272; Hall, Cases in Const. Law, 263; McClain, Cases, 896-7; Coke 2, Inst. 50.
92. Thayer, A Preliminary Treatise on Evidence at Common Law, p. 200, 201.

CHAPTER XV

The Origin of the Doctrine of Judicial Review

The Supreme Court of the United States declared an act of Congress void for the first time in 1803. The state courts had declared state laws void over twenty years before that date. Several converging lines of influence contributed to bring about this result. There were:

(1) *The influence of legal writers.* They stated the law, and the state judges, who first declared acts void, simply applied that law to actual cases coming before them for decision. This law was found chiefly in the works of three famous law writers—Coke, Blackstone, and Vattel. James Otis, in the Writs of Assistance case, quotes Coke's famous statement in Doctor Bonham's case as indisputable law: "And it appears in our books that in many cases the common law will control acts of Parliament and adjudge them to be utterly void; for where an act of Parliament is against common right and reason, or repugnant, or impossible to be performed, the common law will control it and adjudge such act to be void." Otis has also Lord Hobart's dictum in mind: "An act of Parliament made against natural equity . . . is void." [1] This was English law, as stated in Bacon's Abridgment, 1735, Viner's Abridgment, 1751, and Comyn's Digest, 1762, while behind these were older authorities. Otis quoted from Viner's Abridgment, so that his argument had the legal support of the greatest names in English law. [2] There was nothing new in his defense, for the very good reason that, as a lawyer, he was not at liberty to create law, but was restricted to pleading the actually existing law. The Massachusetts House of Representatives said in 1764 that they hoped it would not be considered a new doctrine that acts of Parliament against natural equity or the fundamental principles of the British Constitution are void. [3] The Massachusetts House accepted the doctrine as law.

Coke's doctrine was a favorite and widely accepted doctrine in the Colonies long before the American Revolution. As early

255

as 1688, "the men of Massachusetts did much quote Lord Coke" on the subject.[4] Hutchinson in 1765 said the chief cause of opposition to the Stamp Act was that the Act of Parliament was held to be contrary to Magna Carta, and therefore null and void, according to Lord Coke.[5] In a letter to Jackson in which Governor Hutchinson speaks of the Stamp Act, he says: "Our friends to liberty take advantage of a maxim they find in Lord Coke that an act of Parliament against Magna Carta or the peculiar rights of Englishmen is ipso facto void. This . . . seems to have determined *a great part of the Colonies* to oppose the execution of the act with force, and to show their resentment against all in authority who will not join them."[6] In 1776, John Adams wrote to William Cushing, who became Chief Justice of Massachusetts, and later a Justice of the Supreme Court of the United States: "You have my hearty concurrence in telling the jury the nullity of Acts of Parliament."[7] This shows that the belief in this legal doctrine was widespread and regarded as positive law.

Blackstone lays down the doctrine that "Acts of Parliament that are impossible to be performed are of no validity; and if there arise out of them collaterally any absurd consequences, manifestly contradictory to common reason, they are with regard to those collateral consequences void. I lay down the general rule with these restrictions, though I know it is generally laid down more largely, that acts of Parliament contrary to reason are void."[8] This is spoken of as Blackstone's Tenth Rule for Construing Statutes,[9] and is deduced from Coke's account of the case in Fitzherbert's Abridgment, Annuitie, 41.

Vattel, in his Law of Nature and of Nations, discusses the question whether legislative authority extends so far as the fundamental laws, so "that it could change the Constitution." He lays it down that "the authority of these legislators does not extend so far, "unless the state has in very express terms given them the power to change them. "For the Constitution of the state ought to be fixed . . . the fundamental laws are excepted from their commission. . . . In short, these legislators derive their power from the Constitution. How, then, can they change it without destroying the foundation of their authority?"[10]   Vattel is stating a well-known principle of the Roman law—the rule that "the act of a delegated authority contrary to the commission under which it is exercised, is void. Therefore, no legislative act contrary to the Constitution can be valid."[11]   Bowyer quotes from the Digest (lib. 17, tit. 1, 1, 5): "Diligenter fines mandate custodiendi sunt; nam qui excessit aliud quid facere videtur."[12]

This was also a rule of the English common law with which American jurists and statesmen of the period were familiar. Hamilton, for example, in discussing the ground or authority on which a statute might be declared void, says: "There is no position which depends on clearer principles, than that every act of a delegated authority, contrary to the tenor of the commission under which it is exercised, is void.   No legislative act, therefore, contrary to the Constitution, can be valid."[13]   John Marshall expresses the same idea, when he asks in the Virginia convention: "Can they (Congress) go beyond their delegated powers?"[14]   Ellsworth laid down the same rule of law in the Connecticut convention.[15]   To the American statesmen of that time, *this was law, not mere theory.*

Did the courts apply this law?   The law was actually applied and appealed to time and time again.   In Trevett v. Weeden, 1786, Varnum quoted Vattel's complete passage, Blackstone's passage, and from Bacon's Abridgment to prove the acts of the Rhode Island legislature unconstitutional and void, and as legal authority for the right and duty of the judges to declare them so.[16]   When the judges were summoned by the legislature to give "their reasons for adjudging an act of the general assembly to be unconstitutional and so void," Judge Howell defended his action in the legal language of Coke, and Attorney-General Channing on being consulted declared the decision of the judges "conformable to the principles of constitutional law."[17]

In the North Carolina case of Bayard v. Singleton, 1787, the Superior Court laid down Vattel's doctrine as part of the law of the land, and based its decision upon it.[18]   Iredell, afterwards a Justice of the Supreme Court, in reply to a letter from Spaight, a member of the Convention, of August 12, 1787, attacking the decision, wrote two letters dated August 17, and August 26, 1787, in which he lays down the legal doctrines of

Vattel, Coke, and Blackstone in defense of the decision.[19]   In
Kamper v. Hawkins, 1793, the judges quoted Vattel, Coke,
Blackstone, and the Roman law of mandate or common law
rule as authority for declaring a law void.[20]   In Van Horne
v. Dorrance, 1795, Justice Patterson quotes Vattel's doctrine
approvingly in charging the jury, and in Luther v. Borden
Justice Woodbury combines the views of Patterson and Vattel
in his dissenting opinion.[21]   Chief Justice Marshall quotes Coke
as authority in Marbury v. Madison,[22] though not by name,
and accepts and applies the common law rule laid down by
Hamilton in the Federalist, and expressed in his own question
in the Virginia convention. *The judges believed that was good
law*, and when cases involving the application of the principle
came before them, they simply applied that law and decided
accordingly.   It was not a theory or a philosophy they were
applying, but the law as stated by the greatest legal authorities.

(2) *The belief that the English Courts had declared acts
of Parliament void.*   There was a widespread belief that the
English courts had actually declared laws void. Coke mentions
several such cases. In Edward First's reign, the statute of
Carlisle had been adjudged void.[23] He also cites Tregor's case,
and quotes Chief Justice Herle: "Some statutes are made
against law and right, which those who made them perceiving,
would not put them in execution." [24] Coke also cites a case
where a writ of Cessavit was refused by Justice Willoughby
because the act W. 2, C. 21, was against common right and
reason, and, therefore, the common law adjudged the act of
Parliament void.[25]   An act of 1 E. 6, C. 14, was adjudged
void in Strowd's Case in the reign of Elizabeth.[26]   In Dr.
Bonham's case judgment was entered for the plaintiff on Coke's
arguing that an act against reason was void.[27]   The case of
The City of London v. Wood is also noted in Coke's reports.
Chief Justice Holt quotes Coke in Dr. Bonham's case approvingly, and Chief Justice Hobart in Day v. Savadge declared
"an act of Parliament made against natural equity so as to
make a man judge in his own case was void." [28]

Otis quotes from these cases in support of the idea that
acts of Parliament were, under certain circumstances, void,
and says the judges of England have declared them so.
"When such mistake is evident and palpable . . . the judges

of the executive courts have declared the act of the whole Parliament void." [29]   In 1764, the Massachusetts House of Representatives said the English judges have declared themselves in favor of these sentiments when they expressly declare that "acts of Parliament against natural equity are void, that acts against the fundamental principles of the British Constitution are void." [30]   The American judges believed this and applied the doctrine in the courts.   In England, the theory died, and the doctrine of the legislative omnipotence of Parliament took its place.   In America, the theory lived on, and became a fundamental principle of American constitutional law. This was due to the separation of political thought in the American Colonies from that of the mother land by the Revolution. [31]

(3) *Colonial experience.*   The King in Council had declared colonial laws or acts repugnant to the Constitution and laws of England void.   The Charters provided for this. [32]   Colonial laws contrary to or repugnant to the laws of England were declared void time and time again.   This furnished an actual precedent.   By a statute of 7 & 8 W. III, C. 12, any colonial law repugnant to the above act, or four acts of the reign of Charles II, or any future Act of Parliament "relative to the said plantations shall be utterly void." [33]   The most famous of the cases in which colonial laws were declared void was that of Winthrop v. Lechmere, 1727, in which the King in Council set aside four decisions of the Superior Court of Connecticut, and declared two acts of the legislature void because repugnant to the laws of England. [34]   The colonists became accustomed to the idea of having their laws declared null and void because repugnant to the Constitution and laws of England.   There never was a time when they were not familiar with the practice.   It became firmly imbedded in the American mind. [35]   The Albany Plan of Union made similar provision for declaring the laws of the colonies void. [36]

It would appear, therefore, to be the most natural thing in the world for the Americans to continue doing what had always been done for them.   If the Supreme Court of the Empire declared laws null and void before the Revolution, why should the Supreme Courts of the sovereign states not do the same thing after the Revolution?   The states were the heirs of the Crown, and this is just what they did—adopt and follow the English custom of disallowing colonial laws.[37] This is seen in the fact that the constitutions of Massachusetts, New Hampshire and others embodied the principle of the charters on the subject, and made use of the same language.[38] They were imbued with the idea that an act or law contrary to, or repugnant to the constitution, could not be a law. It had always been so in their experience, and Chief Justice Marshall in the case of Marbury v. Madison simply declared what had always been the law in the colonies.[39]

The influence of the custom by which the King in Council set aside colonial laws, is clearly seen as a precedent in the case of Trevett v. Weeden. Varnum quotes the Charter of Rhode Island that laws may be made by the legislature, "but not contrary and repugnant unto, but as near as may be agreeable to the laws of England." Then, he says: "This grant . . . expressly limits the legislative powers; and by invariable custom and usage, they are still so confined, that they cannot make any laws repugnant to the general system of laws, which governed the realm of England at the time of the grant. The revolution hath made no change in this respect." According to James M. Varnum, the Revolution made no change in the principle and practice of declaring laws void. The "invariable custom and usage" of disallowing laws repugnant to the Constitution and laws existed unchanged and unimpaired by the Revolution. The Supreme Court must still declare laws void as did the Supreme Court of the Empire. This connects the case of Trevett v. Weeden with the usage of the King in Council in declaring colonial laws null and void.[40] It would have been a greater wonder had the Americans not given their courts this power, than to find that they did so. The practice was always known to colonial experience.

(4) *American state experience.* The state courts had actually declared laws void in several cases. J. B. Cutting's letter to Jefferson, dated London, July 11, 1788,[41] says that the Supreme Court of Massachusetts declared a statute unconstitutional.[42] The same thing was done in the cases of Holmes v. Walton, 1780, in New Jersey; Trevett v. Weeden in Rhode Island, 1786; and Bayard v. Singleton, May, 1787, in North Carolina.[43] Here we have the thing actually done by the state

courts, namely, a legislative act declared void because repugnant to the constitution.

This was the result of three converging lines of influence—legal writers, the belief that the English Courts had done so, and the actual practice of the King in Council—meeting in the state courts. This furnished the national judiciary with actual American precedents and practice which made it easy and natural for the Federal courts to adopt the same procedure.

(5) *Several state constitutions provided for declaring laws void or for judicial review.* Historical and legal writers tell us that prior to the framing of the Constitution of the United States in 1787 there was nothing in any of the state constitutions or other American documents, either directly or indirectly giving the courts authority to declare laws void. This appears to be a hasty and an unwarranted conclusion. The charter of Massachusetts, 1691, granted the

"Governor and the General Court or Assembly . . . full power and authority from time to time to make ordaine and establish all manner of wholesome and reasonable orders Laws Statutes and Ordinances Directions and Instructions either with penalties or without (soe as the same be not repugnant or contrary to the Laws of this our realm of England) as they shall judge to be for the good and welfare of our said Province or Territory." [44]

Laws repugnant or contrary to the laws of England were transmitted to the King in Council in England where they were either declared valid or disallowed and declared "utterly void and of none effect." In 1695, for example, fifteen acts of the legislature of 1692 were declared void by orders in council while a total of two decimal nine per cent of the laws of Massachusetts were declared void under the charter. In 1780, the framers of the constitution of Massachusetts inserted this provision of the charter of 1691 in the constitution, word for word, except that in the constitution it read "soe as the same be not repugnant or contrary to this constitution" instead of "soe as the same be not repugnant or contrary to the Lawes of this our realme of England." [45] This was a change necessitated by the Revolution and the adoption of the state constitution. It is self-evident that as under the charter any law of the legislature repugnant or contrary to the laws of England was void, so any law repugnant to the constitution of Massachusetts was also void. It is unreasonable to suppose that the framers of the constitution of 1780 knowing the meaning and effect of the provision deliberately inserted it in the constitution for the purpose of making it mean something entirely different and with the intention of having it operate in an entirely different way. They knew what the practice was under the charter. They intended it to have the same result under the constitution, otherwise the provision has no place there and is absolutely devoid of meaning or purpose.

In the case of Supervisors of Elections 1873 the supreme judicial court of Massachusetts, after quoting the language of the provision said:

"Whenever application is made to the judiciary to carry into effect any statute in a particular case and the statute in question appears to be clearly repugnant to the constitution, it is the duty of the judges to obey the constitution and disregard the statute."

This was as true in 1780 as in 1873. "It is a canon of construction that when the words of a statute, fundamental or ordinary, are brought forward into a new one there comes with it the meaning which it then has." [46] It cannot surely be said that the language authorized the courts to do this in 1873, but that the same provision did not authorize the courts to disregard a repugnant statute in 1780. It was as much the duty of the judges under the provision to disregard a statute clearly repugnant to the constitution in 1780 as in 1873. The convention of 1780 intended that laws repugnant should be dealt with in the one case as in the other. Every judge in Massachusetts took an oath to perform his duties "agreeably to the rules and regulations of the constitution and the laws of the commonwealth." Before he could do this, he must determine what the law was, and that required him to make careful examination of statutes for the purpose of deciding whether or not any given law was repugnant to the constitution and if in his judgment it was such an act, he must "obey the constitution and disregard the statute." The constitution of New Hampshire, 1784, contains the same provision,[47] so that what is said of Massachusetts applies to New Hampshire with equal force.

Article seven of the constitution of Georgia, 1777, gives the legislature power to make laws "provided such laws and regulations be not repugnant to the true intent and meaning of any rule or regulation contained in this constitution." Back of this, was a provision in the charter of Georgia, 1732, giving the corporation power to make laws "not repugnant to the laws and statutes of England," and providing as in Massachusetts that such laws be presented to the King in Council for approbation or disallowance.[48] The result was that nine and two-fifths per cent of Georgia's laws were disallowed by the Council. This was a very high average as the percentage of laws declared void was only five and one-half per cent for all the colonies.[49] Prior to the framing of the constitution, the people of Georgia had become quite accustomed to having their laws declared void. It had become part of their constitutional experience, and when the statesmen of Georgia framed a state constitution at Savannah, that experience inserted a provision limiting the legislative power in the future as it had been limited in the past by providing that the legislative power could not make a law repugnant to the constitution. Such laws are specifically named as exceptions to legislative authority. The first constitution of Georgia was, therefore, a limited constitution, one which limited legislative power. "Limitations of this kind," said Alexander Hamilton, "can be preserved in practice no other way than through the medium of courts of justice, whose duty it must be to declare all acts contrary to the manifest tenor of the constitution void." Further, article seven of the constitution of 1777 was carried into the constitutions of 1789 and 1798 with but little change in the phraseology. Suppose the Georgia legislature had enacted a law repugnant to the constitution, as for example, an act depriving accused persons of the right of trial by jury, then this section (art. VII) of the constitution authorized and required the courts in any case involving the application of the law to refuse to administer it as null and void. No citizen of Georgia could be deprived of his constitutional right to a jury trial, guaranteed by article sixty-one of the constitution, by such a law.[50] In the later case of Cooper v. Telfair, E. Tilghman argued for the plaintiff that if the law involved was contrary to the state constitution, it was void and the judicial authority either of the state or of the United States may pronounce it so. Ingersoll and Dallas for the defendant conceded that if a law plainly and obviously violated the constitution of Georgia, it was void and never was a valid rule of action. Justice Cushing declared: "I am of opinion that this court (the Supreme Court of the U. S.) has the same power that a court of Georgia would possess to declare a law void." [51] This recognizes that an act contrary to the constitution was void and that the courts of the state had power to declare such acts invalid. The courts were authorized to do this under section seven of the constitution of 1777 as much as under section twenty-two of the constitution of 1798. The language gave the courts power to declare an act of the legislature unconstitutional in 1777 as much as in 1798. It could not mean one thing in 1777 and quite another in 1798, or 1800.

Again, article twenty-two of the New Jersey constitution of 1776 provided that the common law of England and so much of the statute law as have been heretofore practised in the colony, shall remain in full force until altered by the legislature, such parts only excepted as are repugnant to the rights and privileges contained in this charter; and that the inestimable right of trial by jury shall remain confirmed as a part of the law of this colony, without repeal, forever. Article twenty-three required New Jersey legislators to declare on oath they would never assent to any law annulling or repealing the provision respecting trial by jury. This was trial by a common law jury of twelve men. Suppose the legislature of New Jersey to enact a law providing for the trial of accused persons by a jury of six men, then such a law would be repugnant to the constitution and void, because it deprived accused persons of their right to trial by a common law jury of twelve men which is made part of the law of New Jersey, without repeal, forever. It would deprive men of a right guaranteed by the constitution, and in such a case article twenty-two would authorize the courts to declare the law void. This is what took place in New Jersey in the case of Holmes v. Walton in 1779.[52] On October 8, 1778, the New Jersey legislature passed a law authorizing the seizure of any goods which were being conveyed to the British. Persons violating the law were to be taken before a justice of the peace of the county and tried according to the law of February 11, 1775, which provided for a jury of six men. Major Walton seized a quantity of goods in possession of John Holmes and Solomon Ketcham who were charged under the statute with having brought them within the lines of the enemy. They were tried before John Anderson, Justice of the Peace of Monmouth county, May 24, 1779. The jury of six men brought in a verdict in favor of Walton, and Anderson gave judgment accordingly. While the case was pending, the defendants had applied to the Supreme Court and the chief justice issued a writ of certiorari to Anderson returnable at the next session of the court. William Willcocks, attorney for the plaintiffs in certiorari, argued that the jury consisted of six men only, contrary to the law of New Jersey.

"For that the proceedings and trial in the said plaint in the court below, and the judgment thereon given were had and given contrary to the constitution, practices and laws of the land."

The Supreme Court reversed the judgment of Anderson and ordered a new trial before the justice. In the course of this, Willcocks argued: "As a trial by six men is unconstitutional there is no law by which this cause could be tried." Chief Justice Brearly declared the act unconstitutional and void. Speaking of this case in State v. Parkhurst the court said:

"There it had been enacted that the trial (arising on the seizure laws) should be by a jury of six men; and it was objected that this was not a constitutional jury; and so it was held; and the act upon solemn argument was adjudged to be unconstitutional and in that case inoperative. And upon this decision the act, or at least that part of it which relates to the six men jury, was repealed and a constitutional jury of twelve men substituted in its place." [53]

In Holmes v. Walton, Willcocks argued that the act was contrary to the constitution and the court adopting this view held the act unconstitutional. Section twenty-two authorized and required the court to do this. This was not a case like Ham v. McClaws and wife in South Carolina in 1788 in which it was held that a statute was void because, in a particular case, it operated against the principles of common right and reason. The New Jersey statute was held void because contrary to the constitution of the state. [54]

The Delaware constitution of 1776 provided for the erection of a supreme court from which an appeal could be taken in law and equity to the "court of appeals," a court of seven judges which was to "have all the authority and powers heretofore given by law in the last resort to the King in Council under the old government." [55]

Did this provision confer power on the Delaware Court of Appeals to declare laws void? The authority and powers of the King in Council included the power to disallow colonial laws. Can it be said that the Delaware court possessed all the authority and powers of the King in Council under the old government, if it could not disallow or declare the laws of Delaware void? Such a court would certainly not possess all the authority and powers of the King in Council under the old government in any true sense. If this language conferred on the court all the powers of the King in Council under the old government, it conferred power to disallow acts of the legislature.

Rhode Island and Connecticut retained their charters as state constitutions. Connecticut enacted a law providing that the form of civil government contained in the charter of Charles II, 1662, "shall be and remain the Civil Constitution of this State." This remained as the constitution of the state till 1818, and empowered the legislature to enact laws "not contrary to the Laws of this Realm of England." The Rhode Island charter, 1663, gave the general assembly power to pass laws "soe as such lawes . . . bee not contrary and repugnant unto, but, as neare as may be, agreeable, to the lawes of this our realme of England." [56] There was no express provision in either charter requiring the submission of laws to the King in Council as in the Massachusetts charter, but as this was insisted on by the government of the Empire, they were sent over for review and in some cases disallowed.[57]

This system of law and this practice remained unchanged after the Revolution as part of the law of the land in Connecticut and Rhode Island. Consequently, in the Superior Court of Judicature James M. Varnum argued in the case of Trevett v. Weeden, 1786, that the Revolution had made no change, therefore, an act of the legislature repugnant to the constitution was, as before, void. The act involved in this case provided for trial without a jury by a majority of the judges present and denied the right of appeal from such decision. In his address to the court, Varnum, after quoting the above passage from the charter, said:

"This grant . . . expressly limits the legislative powers; and by invariable custom and usage they are still so confined that they cannot make any laws repugnant to the general system of laws which governed the realm of England at the time of the grant. The revolution has made no change in this respect." [58]

The judiciary had taken the place of the King in Council and it was the duty of the judges to decide when the legislature had violated the constitution and to declare such an act void. They were under obligation to obey the principles of the constitution in preference to any acts of the general assembly wherever they were in conflict. The act of Rhode Island deprived citizens of a fundamental right under the constitution and was, therefore, unconstitutional and void. The judges adopted Varnum's view as correct law and declared the act void holding "the information was not cognizable before them." The act of the legislature being void they had no jurisdiction. In their memorial to the legislature, signed by Judges Hazard, Howell, and Tillinghast, the judges in defence of their action claimed that the entire power of construing and judging of the acts of the legislature was, in the last resort, vested solely in the supreme judiciary of the state. The Attorney-General, Channing, told the legislature the decision of the judges in this case was "conformable to the principles of constitutional law." [59]

As the highest court known to the law declared repugnant laws void before the Revolution, so the highest court known to the law—the superior court of judicature of Rhode Island—declared a repugnant law void after the Revolution and the attorney-general of the state held that procedure to be in harmony with the constitutional law of the state. The same procedure would have been authorized by the constitution of Connecticut, had the occasion arisen. What was constitutional for Rhode Island would also have been constitutional for Connecticut. It is clear that at least some of the first state constitutions placed express limitations on the power of the legislatures so that they could not enact a law repugnant to the constitution. If they enacted such a law through inadvertence or otherwise, it was void from the beginning and this gave the courts power to declare such an act void. No court could administer justice in accordance with a law that never was law, and a repugnant law was, under all these state constitutions, null and void ab initio.

(6) *The action of the Federal Convention of 1787.* One difficult problem which the Convention was called to solve was, how were the states to be prevented from nullifying Federal laws and treaties. The first idea of the Convention was to give Congress a negative on all state laws contravening treaties or the Articles of Union.[60] This was suggested by the negative of the King in Council. On April 8, Madison wrote to Randolph: "Let it (Congress or the national government) have a negative in all cases whatsoever on the legislative acts of the states, as the King of Great Britain heretofore had."[61] Again, he says: "This negative on the laws of the States was suggested by the negative in the head of the British Empire which prevented collisions between the parts and the whole, and between the parts themselves." "Its utility is sufficiently displayed in the British system," he said on July 17 in the Convention.[62]

This negative was abandoned because not practicable among so many states enacting so many laws, and "instead of the proposed negative, the objects of it were left as finally provided for in the Constitution."[63] That is, Madison declares, the purpose of the negative was not abandoned but realized in another way, namely, by the adoption of a judicial negative instead of a legislative negative vested in Congress, by making the Constitution, laws, and treaties of the United States the supreme law of the land, and requiring the state courts to declare null and void anything in the Constitution or laws of any state contrary thereto. This secured obedience on the part of the states, because the state judges were thus "bound" to declare void any state law repugnant to the treaties, laws, or Constitution of the United States.

Luther Martin's resolution, then, of July 17, which was agreed to instead of the negative by Congress was intended to realize and did realize the same end by judicial means. During the discussion Sherman declared the legislative negative unnecessary as the state courts would veto any laws contravening the authority of the Union, and Gouverneur Morris said a law that ought to be negatived would be set aside in the judiciary department.[64] Immediately on rejection of the legislative negative by the Convention, Luther Martin offered the supreme law clause as a substitute. There was no debate on the resolution, no opposition, and it was unanimously and immediately adopted instead of the legislative negative which had been rejected.[65] This is also clearly seen from the debate on August 23, when Charles Pinckney again attempted to have the Convention adopt the legislative negative on state laws. Williamson, referring to the adoption of the supreme law clause as a substitute, said *the question had been decided already,* and a revival of it was a waste of time, and Wilson added that the firmness of judges was not sufficient. "Something further is requisite. It will be better to prevent the passage of an improper law, than to declare it void when passed." [66]

Wilson, thus, expresses his preference for the legislative negative, but recognizes that the judicial negative had been adopted as a substitute by the Convention. It is clear from this that all the members were not satisfied with the judicial negative as a substitute because they feared it would not afford a sufficient safeguard as compared with the legislative negative. Therefore, the function of the King in Council, in declaring laws void under the Old Colonial System, was purposely and with full knowledge transferred to the courts by the Convention, and became under the Constitution a judicial function as it had been before the Revolution. Thus, "the objects of it were left as finally provided for in the Constitution," namely, in the hands of the judiciary where it had always been.

Luther Martin's resolution was, of course, based on resolution six of the New Jersey Plan, while resolution six was based on the draft of identical laws proposed by Congress to the states, April 13, 1787, requiring state courts to decide all cases coming before them involving the treaty "according to the tenor, true intent, and meaning of the same, anything in the said acts, or parts of acts, to the contrary thereof in any wise notwithstanding." [67] Congress required state courts, under this, to declare laws void. No Federal courts existed. Luther Martin's resolution was likewise intended to give state courts power to declare state laws and constitutions void when they were contrary to Federal laws and treaties.[68]

Further, every member of the convention knew that state courts had in actual practice declared laws void in a number of cases. On June 4, Gerry mentioned that in some "*states*" the judges had declared laws void because contrary to the Constitution. This had been "done too with general approbation." He used the plural "states," so that he had more than one case in mind, and not merely, as has been suggested, the case of Holmes v. Walton.[69] On July 17, Madison in the Convention mentioned the case of Trevett v. Weedon.[70] Brearly, the Chief Justice of New Jersey, Livingston the Governor, and Patterson the Attorney-General were members of the Convention. The case of Holmes v. Walton had been argued before the Chief Justice, and the Governor had approved the decision. These men had taken a prominent part in drawing up the New Jersey Plan, and Patterson had presented it to the Convention. In 1782, Blair and Wythe had been judges in the case of Commonwealth v. Caton.[71] In 1785, Gouverneur Morris had cited the case of Holmes v. Walton in an address to the legislature of Pennsylvania.[72] Another member, Davie of North Carolina, had been counsel for the plaintiffs in the case of Bayard v. Singleton. Spaight wrote to Iredell from the Convention about the case on August 12.[73] It was, therefore, known to every member of the Convention that the state courts had already in some cases declared laws void, and the Convention created a fundamental law requiring every state court to do so wherever the state constitution or laws violated the Federal Constitution, laws, or treaties.

(7) *The Federal courts.* All the preceding lines of influence finally converged on the Federal courts, and they, perhaps hesitatingly at first, followed the precedents of the state courts and the supreme law clause of the Constitution. In Hayburn's case, 1792, the judges are said to have expressed individual opinions that an act of Congress was unconstitutional. In United States v. Yale Tod, 1794, the Supreme Court held an act of Congress unconstitutional, though the record is not clear.[74] In Vanhorne v. Dorrance, 1795,[75] the United States Circuit Court declared an act of Pennsylvania void, and in 1803, in the case of Marbury v. Madison, an act of Congress was declared void by the Supreme Court.[76]

This decision established the power of the Supreme Court to

pass judgment on a federal act of doubtful constitutionality. Before the Supreme Court actually ventured to apply the doctrine, it had found widespread acceptance by the leading minds of the country. This is evident from the answers of the state legislatures to the Kentucky and Virginia Resolutions, 1799. The states replied that the power to decide on the constitutionality of acts and laws of Congress resided in the federal judiciary exclusively "and in the Supreme Court of the United States ultimately." [77] The state legislatures, therefore, in several cases declared the right of the Supreme Court to declare laws void before it actually did so. In 1786, the Rhode Island legislature had opposed the judges for declaring an act of the legislature void. In 1799, the legislature declared that the federal courts have such power. In 1795, Swift in his "System of the Laws of Connecticut," though arguing against the power, says that the contrary opinion "is very popular and prevalent." [78] So far as the record goes, at least twenty-five members of the Federal Convention of 1787 favored judicial control.[79] This included all the leading members. The doctrine was held by large numbers of statesmen and lawyers throughout the country. Justice Chase said in 1800 in the case of Cooper v. Telfair that it was a "general opinion expressly admitted by all this bar" that the Supreme Court can declare an act of Congress unconstitutional.[80]

In the same case, Justice Patterson declared the Supreme Court had power to pronounce a law void when it involved "a clear and unequivocal breach of the Constitution." [81] The influence of the state courts, as precedents, is seen in the statement of Justice Cushing in the same case. "I am of opinion that this court has the same power that a court of the state of Georgia would possess to declare a law void," he said.[82] John Marshall held in 1788 that the Supreme Court would declare any act of Congress void if it infringed the Constitution.[83]

This opinion prevailed because it had the stronger support. This does not mean that there was no opposition. That was very strong in some quarters, but like many political opinions, it failed to win general support. The state courts are expressly mentioned in the Constitution, because it was the states which had violated the treaty of 1783 and others. It was not necessary to expressly mention the Federal courts or judges, because, the Constitution being the supreme Federal law, it would bind them anyway.

(8) *Was this power of the courts to declare laws void granted intentionally, or was it usurped?* It is fair to conclude that if the men who framed the Constitution expected it to be done, then they intended it; otherwise, one most important problem which the Convention was called to solve remained unsolved and the Convention was a failure. That problem was, how was the United States to secure obedience by the states to acts and treaties made by the national government. Oliver Ellsworth said in the Connecticut convention, January 7, 1788: "If the United States go beyond their powers, if they make a law which the Constitution does not authorize, it is void; and the judicial power, the national judges, who, to secure their impartiality, are to be made independent, will declare it to be void. On the other hand, if the states go beyond their limits, if they make a law which is a usurpation upon the general government, the law is void; and upright, independent judges will declare it to be so." [84] There can be no question as to what Ellsworth expected the Federal courts to do. It is not possible to quote at length here from the speeches of all the framers of the Constitution of the United States, but a careful study shows that the members understood the Federal judiciary was to declare both state and United States laws void.[85] Among these were Davie, Dickinson, Mason, Gerry, Hamilton, King, Luther Martin, Gouverneur Morris, Madison, Patterson, Edmund Randolph, John Rutledge, Roger Sherman, Hugh Williamson, and James Wilson.[86] All these men held firmly to the idea that the Constitution required the federal courts to declare state and national laws void, if they contravened the Constitution of the United States. These were the men who framed the Constitution, and they all expected the federal courts to exercise judicial control over legislation. It is a contradiction in terms to say or hold that they all expected the courts to do this, and yet never intended the judiciary to exercise such power. They expected it only because they framed the Constitution with that end in view. To say that the Convention had no intention of conferring such power, is simply to say that the legislative negative was voted down,[87] and then no other method

provided by which the United States could secure obedience to the Union on the part of the states, and the Convention signally and intentionally failed to accomplish the great end for which it was called.

The argument from *silence* is also worth something. When the doctrine of judicial control was presented in the Convention over and over again as an accomplished fact, it was never contradicted, but was always silently accepted as correct.[88] This does not mean that nobody in the Convention was opposed to the doctrine. Mercer declared himself opposed to it,[89] but that simply recognized its existence. By its tacit consent or acceptance, the Convention, however, recognized the existence of the power. Nobody denied it. The same is true of the ratifying conventions of Connecticut, New York, Pennsylvania, Maryland, and Virgihia.[90] They accepted the fact as established without any attempt to deny or question its existence.

Is it quite accurate to say that *"no question was voted upon which squarely raised the issue"* of judicial control in the Convention of 1787? Was the vote of July 17 in the Convention not such a vote, when the legislative negative was rejected by a vote of seven to three, and judicial control adopted instead "unanimously in the affirmative?"[91] Even more emphatic was the vote of August 23. Though technically a vote to commit the proposition, it was really a vote on the question of the adoption of a legislative negative versus judicial control.[92] Wilson shows that it meant they were to vote on two plans of control, legislative versus judicial. By a vote of six to five, they rejected the former and adopted the latter.[93]

The *Constitution* grants the Federal courts judicial control: the state courts are to be bound by the Constitution, laws and treaties of the United States as the supreme law, in their decisions.[94] Then, the Supreme Court is given appellate jurisdiction in the above cases—in all cases in law and equity arising under the Constitution, laws, and treaties of the United States.[95] This provides for appeals in such cases from the state courts to the Supreme Court of the United States. The twenty-fifth section of the Judiciary Act of September 24, 1789, authorized reexamination upon a writ of error of the final judgment or decree in law or equity of the highest court of a state, where the validity of a treaty or statute of the United

States, or statute of a state was questioned, and the decision of the state court declared the Federal statute void but the state statute valid. The Supreme Court may reverse or affirm the decisions of the highest state courts in such cases. This simply means that the Supreme Court is given jurisdiction to declare statutes void or valid in these cases. Without such power, the Supreme Court could not decide such cases—reverse or affirm them—and appeals would be useless. The Federalist recognizes this.[96] In such cases, the Supreme Court must decide which of two contradictory laws is void and which valid in order to decide the case, and that power is given by the Constitution of the United States, which confers jurisdiction on the court.

NOTES TO CHAPTER XV

1. Rights of the Colonies Asserted and Proved, 41; Quincy, Mass. Reports, 521; Coke, Reports, Vol. 4, Bk. VIII, 375.
2. Quincy, Mass. Reps. 256.
3. Otis, Rights of the Colonies, 70.
4. Quincy, Mass. Reps. 527.
5. Id. Coke, Inst. I, Proeme.
6. Quincy, Mass. Reps. 441.
7. Id. 528.
8. Blackstone, Com. I, 91.
9. Coxe, Judicial Powers and Unconstitutional Legislation, 179.
10. Vattel, Law of Nature and of Nations, Bk. I, Ch. III, sec. 34.
11. Quoted by Coxe in Judicial Power and Unconstitutional Legislation from Bowyer, Univ. Pub. Law, 443, 433-4.
12. Coxe, 114.
13. Federalist, 78 (Lodge ed.), p. 485.
14. Elliot, III, 553.
15. Id. II, 196.
16. Jas. M. Varnum, Trevett v. Weeden, 24-5.
17. Jas. M. Varnum, Trevett v. Weeden, 37, 38, 51.
18. Coxe, Judicial Powers and Unconstitutional Legislation, 251.
19. Id. 257, 260, 259.
20. Virginia Cases, I, 20, 29, 32, 75, 76, 81.
21. Coxe, p. 120.
22. Cranch, 137; McClaine Cases, 816.
23. Coke's Reps. Vol. IV, 377 (118, a); C. H. McIlwaine, The High Court of Parliament, Chap. IV.
24. Coke, Reports, Vol. IV, Bk. VIII, p. 376 (118, a).
25. Id. 376.
26. Id. 277.
27. Id. 376.
28. Coke, Rep. IV, Bk. VIII, 376.
29. Hobart's Rep. 87; Coxe, Judicial Powers, etc., 173; Quincy, Mass. Reps. App. I, 474; Otis, Rights, 73, 74.

30. Otis, Rights, etc., p. 70. Note: John Lilburne is regarded as the first man to argue in a court of law that a statute against the fundamental law was void. One copy of the Agreement of the People provided that laws contrary to it were null and void. He, therefore, had the doctrine in mind when he wrote that Constitution for England. Foster, Constitution, 34, 53, 59; Howell, St. Tr. IV, 1363; V, 438, 439, 446-450, 443, 444.

31. Lowell, Gov. of Eng. II, 48, 481.

32. As Mass. 1629, 1691; Poore, 937, 952; Georgia, 1732, Poore, 374; N. H. 1680, Poore, 1277.

33. Statutes of the Realm, VII, 105. It was a well-known principle of the English common law that any act of a corporation was ultra vires and, therefore, null and void if in excess of the powers granted by the charter; and that corporation by-laws were void if contrary to the laws of England. The Colonies were political or trading corporations.

34. Pub. Records of the Colony of Conn. VII, 571. For other cases, see Am. Hist. Assoc. Rep. 1894; Edward Channing, Hist. of U. S. III, 501 (n. 1). "The Hardwicke Papers"; Foster, Com. on the Const. 634; Mass. His. Soc. Proceedings, First Series, 1860-62, p. 64-80, 164-171.

35. Baldwin, Two Centuries of Am. Law, 19, 20.

36. MacDonald, Sel. Charters, 257.

37. Hart, Actual Government, 316.

38. Poore, 937, 957, 961, 1284.

39. 1 Cranch, 137.

40. Varnum's Pamphlet, Trevett v. Weeden, 22, 23.

41. See Harvard Law Rev. VII, 415.

42. Bancroft, Hist. of the Const. II, 473.

43. Am. Hist. Rev. IV, 456; Varnum, Trevett v. Weeden, Pamphlets, 22; Martin's Reports, 48 seq. Second Ed. I, 42 seq.

44. Poore, Charters, 951, 952.

45. Poore, 961; Const. Mass. Ch. I, sec. 1; Art. IV.

46. 114 Mass. 247, p. 114, McClain, Cases; Ellingham v. Dye, 99 N. E. 10; 97 N. E. 113; 8 CYC. 739.

47. Poore, Charters, 1284; 14 Dall, 514.

48. Poore, Charters, 379, 374.

49. E. B. Russell, Rev. of Am. Colonial Legislation by the King in Council, 103-4.

50. Poore, Charters, 383; Const. of Ga. LX, LXI, LXII.

51. 4 Dall. 14.

52. Am. Hist. Rev. IV, 458.

53. 9 N. J. Law, 427.

54. I Bay (S. C.) 93, 98.

55. Poore, Charters, 276, 278.

56. Poore, Charters, 257-8, 1598, 255.

57. E. B. Russell, Rev. of Am. Col. Legislation, 103-4.

58. Trevett v. Weeden, Varnum, Pamphlet, 4, 11, 12, 22-3, 27-9, 38, 45. Thayer, Cases, I, 74.

59. Chandler, Criminal Trials, 335, 347.

60. Elliot, V, 127.

61. Id. 108.

62. Id. 121, 321.

63. Id. 121.

64. Elliot, V, 121.

65. Id. 322, 468.

66. Id. 468.

67. Elliot, V, 192; Journals of Cont. Cong. Vol. 12, p. 35.
68. Coxe, Judicial Power and Unconst. Legislation, 315.
69. Elliot, V, 151, 429; Am. Hist. Rev. IV, 456 seq.
70. Elliot, V, 321.
71. Id. 191.
72. Sparks, Life of Morris, III, 438, 464.
73. McRee, Life and Correspondence of Iredell, II, 169-70.
74. 131 U. S. (app.).
75. 2 Dall. 304.
76. 1 Chanch, 137.
77. See answer of R. I., Mass., N. Y., N. H. and Vt. legislatures, Elliot, IV, 533, seq.
78. Harvard Law Rev. VII, 134.
79. C. A. Beard, The Supreme Court and the Constitution, Chap. II.
80. 4 Dall. 19.
81. Id. 19.
82. Id. 20.
83. Elliot, III, 553.
84. Elliot, II, 196.
85. See Beard, Supr. Court and the Const. Chap. II.
86. Elliot, IV, 157, 160, 155-160; Id. V, 429, 346; Id. 347, III, 521-523; Farrand, Record, II, 299; Elliot, V, 151, IV, 361, 386, 393; Federalist, 16, 78, 81, pp. 541, 561 (Dawson Ed.); Elliot, V, 151, 468, 469; Farrand, I, 109; Id. III, 286, 287; Elliot, I, 380; Id. V, 321, 485, 429, 121; Benton's Abridgment, II, 550; Elliot, V, 121, 321, 356; IV, 382; Beard, The Supreme Court and the Const. 35, 36; 2 Dall. 309; 4 Dall. 19; Elliot, V, 317, 380, 580; Meigs, Growth of the Constitution, p. 316, seq. (plate VI); Elliot, III, 570; comp. Elliot, IV, 446, 447, with Federalist No. 78; Elliot, V. 159, 349, 481; IV, 446, 447; III, 553; Id. V, 321, 322, 191, 192; Id. V, 463, 468, 322; Id. V, 151, 153, 155, 164, 344, 429, 468, 344; II, 445, 446, 489.
87. Elliot, V, 322.
88. Id. 346.
89. Id. 429.
90. Elliot, II, 196, 445, 446, 489; I, 380; III, 553; Federalist, No. 78.
91. Am. Hist. Rev. Jan. 1913, 380, 381; Elliot, I, 207; V, 321, 322.
92. Id. 260; V, 468.
93. Id. 468, 469; Coxe, Jud. Power and Unconst. Legis., 334.
94. Art. VII, 2.
95. Art. III, sec. II, cl. 2.
96. Fed. No. 82, p. 574-5 (Dawson Ed.), No. 78, Lodge ed.

CHAPTER XVI

THE NON OBSTANTE CLAUSE; NO RELIGIOUS TEST FOR OFFICE;
RATIFICATION AND ATTESTATION

(Art. VI, Sec. 2.) The immediate source of the non obstante clause is found in the resolution of Congress of March 21,
1787, and the letter of Congress sent with the resolution to the
states, in which Congress proposed a non obstante clause to be
embodied in all state legislation on the subject of the treaty of
peace. The courts were then to decide all cases arising under
the treaty according to the true intent and meaning of the same
"anything in the said acts or parts of acts to the contrary
thereof in anywise notwithstanding." [1] That is, the treaty was
made the supreme law of the land for state courts, and the non
obstante clause repealed all laws to the contrary.

New York, for example, acting on the suggestion of Congress, passed an act repealing her acts repugnant to the treaty
with Great Britain, "anything in the said act . . . notwithstanding." [2] Brinton Coxe held the device was suggested to
Congress by the case of Rutgers v. Waddington. It was feared
that a conflict between a statute of New York and the treaty
of peace, 1783, would result and one or other would be void.
The court, however, side-stepped the issue and concluded there
was nothing in the statute repugnant to the treaty, if properly
interpreted, or repealing any part of the law of nations; that
there was no intention on the part of the legislature to interfere with the law of nations because the statute did not contain
the common non obstante clause, "and it is an established maxim
that where two laws are seemingly repugnant, and there be no
clause of non obstante in the latter, they shall if possible have
such construction that the latter may not repeal the former
by implication." This opinion is based on Dyer's Reports,
348. Had the New York statute contained a non obstante
clause, the court would have been compelled to decide in accordance with the statute, because the non obstante would have been
an express repeal of the treaty. The absence of such a non

obstante enabled the court to say it was not expressly repealed and they had no right to imply that it was. This suggested to Congress the idea of using the non obstante for the
purpose of repealing all state laws contrary to the treaty of
peace.[3] The use of the non obstante runs back through colonial and English history for over five hundred years before the
statesmen of 1787 gave it such an important place in the Constitution of the United States. The original source of the
non obstante goes back apparently to the bulls of the popes
who issued de plenitudine potestatis bulls "non obstante any
law to the contrary." Matthew Paris mentions the fact that
Henry the Third justified his use of the non obstante clause
on one occasion by quoting the authority of the Pope.[4] "The
power and prerogative of dispensing with laws and granting
non obstantes," says the writer of Bacon's Abridgment, "hath
always been looked upon with a jealous eye, and are said to
have been first invented in Rome and brought into this Kingdom by the pope and clergy."[5] The famous bull of Alexander
VI, partitioning America, 1493, contains a non obstante clause
as does also the bull Clericos Laicos, 1296.[6] The English Kings
then began to imitate this practice about the middle of the
thirteenth century in their secular documents. It is believed
Henry the Second was the first to do this. Other kings followed suit and soon the non obstante clause became common
in statutes, letters patent, writs, grants, and proclamations.
It denoted a license from the sovereign to do something which
would otherwise be contrary to the law.[7] The effect of the
doctrine on the prerogative was to set it above the law. The
clause is found in the Charters of the City of London in Edward
Third's reign, 1327. It then appears regularly from time to
time in the charters. It also appears in the Proclamation of
Richard the Third, 1383, concerning liberties granted to the
citizens of London.[8] The Bill of Rights, 1689, destroyed the
power in England.[9]

The colonial charters also made use of the non obstante
clause. The Charter to Sir Walter Raleigh, 1584, and the
First Charter to the East India Company, December 31, 1600,
make use of it. It is found in the majority of colonial charters
as Carolina, Connecticut, Delaware, Georgia, Maine, Massachusetts, Maryland, Pennsylvania, and Rhode Island.[10]

The colonies employed the non obstante clause in their legislation, as for example, New York in the "Act Against Forging, Counterfeiting and Clipping of Foreign Coyn." The non obstante appears for the first time in New York legislation in its first Colonial Assembly held at Fort James, the City of New York, October 17, 1683. On October 30, the Charter of Libertyes and Privileges granted by the Duke of York contains the first non obstante used in the colony. It reads "Any Laws, Customs or usage to the contrary in anywise Notwithstanding." It also appears in an Act of November first, 1683, and is then used right through New York legislation.[11] At the time of the framing of the Constitution of the United States the usage was definitely and widely established.

The Oath to Support the Constitution, and No Religious Test for Office. (Art. VI, Sec. 3.) The Virginia Plan proposed to bind the state legislative, executive, and judiciary powers by oath to support the Articles of Union. Randolph said this was necessary to prevent competition between the national constitution and laws on the one hand, and those of the states on the other in case of a contest between the two.[12] Gerry moved to amend on July 23 by inserting a provision including the national government, to prevent the officers of the two governments from considering them as distinct from, and not as parts of the general system. In all cases of interference preference had been given to the state governments. The proposed oath would cure that error.[13] Wilson said oaths were but "a left handed security" anyway, but the resolution was adopted. The committee of detail reported it substantially as it appears in the Constitution. On August 30, the words "or affirmation" were added after 'oath,' and Charles Pinckney moved to add the clause prohibiting a religious test as a requirement for office. Sherman said this was unnecessary as the prevailing liberality would be a sufficient security, but it was agreed to nem con.[14]

The state constitutions provided an oath for office-holders. In South Carolina, they were required by the constitution of 1776 to take an oath "to support, maintain, and defend the Constitution." The Georgia Constitution of 1777 required the Governor to take an oath to "support, maintain, and defend the State of Georgia and the Constitution."[15] The state constitutions also provided for the making of an affirmation instead of an oath in the case of those with conscientious scruples against oath taking. The constitution of Maryland, for example, allowed Quakers, Dunkers, and Mennonites to make an affirmation. In New Hampshire, Quakers and those "scrupulous of swearing," might make an affirmation.[16] In New York, Massachusetts, and Vermont, an oath or affirmation was permitted.[17] The Constitution of the United States permits the same classes to make an affirmation instead of making an oath.

Why was this provision adopted? Why are state legislators, Governors, and judges required to take an oath to support the Federal Constitution while Federal officers are not required to take an oath to support the state constitutions? Madison answers this question by saying: "The members of the Federal Government will have no agency in carrying the State Constitutions into effect. The members and officers of the State Governments, on the contrary, will have an essential agency in giving effect to the Federal Constitution. The election of the President and Senate will depend, in all cases, on the Legislatures of the several States, and the election of the House of Representatives will equally depend on the same authority in the first instance; and will probably, forever be conducted by the officers, and according to the laws of the States."[18]

"No religious test" was ever to be required as a qualification for office.

The state constitutions provided, in most cases, for a religious test. Delaware, 1776, required faith in the triune God, and in the Divine inspiration of the Scriptures; Maryland, a declaration of belief in the Christian religion; Georgia, New Jersey, and South Carolina required the Protestant belief; North Carolina and Pennsylvania required, in addition to the above, belief in a future state of rewards and punishments.[19] Luther Martin says that this provision "was adopted by a great majority of the Convention, and without much debate."[20] Some, however, desired to adopt (1) belief in the existence of a Deity and (2) belief in a State of future rewards and punishments as security for the good conduct of the rulers.[21] That is, some in the Convention desired to adopt the religious test to be found in some of the state constitutions, notably those of North Carolina, and Pennsylvania. The reason why a religious test was rejected is to be found in the bitter history of such religious tests in England. The Corporation Act of 1661 required all holding municipal office to take the sacrament according to the rites of the Church of England. The Test Act of 1673 excluded from office all who refused to take the sacrament according to the rites of the English Church. Dissenters took the sacrament once a year, which qualified them to hold office. Americans denounced these laws as making men arrogant, persecutors, and hypocrites, while at the same time they failed to accomplish any useful purpose and degraded and profaned a sacred rite.[22] The only effect was to exclude from office honest men, who were well qualified to serve their country, while the dishonest and unprincipled and unscrupulous were left free to fill the public offices. Therefore, America determined to secure the country from the very possibility of such oppression as had resulted in England from the test laws. "This article is calculated," said Iredell, a Justice in the Supreme Court, later, "to secure universal religious liberty *by putting all sects on a level*—the only way to prevent persecution." [23]

Ratification and Attestation. (Art. VII.) On April 8, 1787, Madison wrote to Randolph: "To give the new system its proper energy, it will be sensible to have it ratified by the authority of the people, and not merely by that of the legislature." [24] The Virginia Plan, accordingly, provided for ratification by conventions chosen by the people.[25] On June 5, Sherman argued ratification by the people was unnecessary because the Articles of Confederation provided for ratification of any changes by the state legislatures. Madison replied this was defective because in many states the Articles rested on legislative sanction only, with the result that in conflicts between state and congressional acts, the judges in the decisions of state courts were either uncertain what to do, or else favored state authority. If the people did not ratify the Constitution, it might be regarded as a mere treaty, and the doctrine advocated that a breach of one article by any of the parties absolved the others from obligation. To prevent this, it was indispensable that the new Constitution be ratified by the supreme authority of the people. Wilson supported Madison, and said he hoped a provision for ratification would be adopted which would admit of a partial union with the door open for the accession of the rest. "This hint," says Madison, "was probably meant in terrorem to the smaller states of New Jersey and Delaware." [25]   The Convention adopted the resolution, June 12, providing for ratification by "the people of the United States." On August 20, Wilson proposed to fill the blank in the resolution with "seven" namely, "the ratification of the Conventions of seven States." This, he said, would be a majority of the states, and sufficient for the commencement of the plan.[26]   Sherman suggested ten states and Randolph nine, which, he said, was a respectable majority of the whole, and a number made familiar to everybody by the Articles of Confederation. Carroll moved to fill the blank with thirteen, as unanimity was necessary to dissolve the existing Confederation. This was correct law, but Madison proposed to fill the blank with a proposition requiring a concurrence of both the states and people, the fountain of all power, who could alter constitutions as they pleased.[27]   The Convention agreed to 'nine,' the number required in all important questions under Confederation, preferable for that very reason, said Colonel Mason. In the Virginia convention, Randolph said: "What number of States ought we to have said? Ought we to have required the concurrence of all the thirteen? Rhode Island in rebellion against integrity; Rhode Island plundered all the world by her paper money; and notorious for her uniform opposition to every federal duty, would then have it in her power to defeat the union; and may we not judge with absolute certainty from her past conduct that she would do so? Therefore, to have required the ratification of all thirteen states would have been tantamount to returning without having done anything. To have required twelve, would have left it in the power of one State to dissolve the union. . . . A majority of the whole would have been too few. Nine states, therefore, seem to be a most proper number." [28]   On August 31, on agreement of nine states, the words "between the said states" were added to the end of the article on motion of King for the purpose of confining the operation of the government to those states ratifying the Constitution. The committee on style changed it to "between the states so ratifying the same." Maryland refused to consent because her delegates, correctly enough, believed that the dissolution of the existing Confed-

eracy required the unanimous consent of the states.[29]   This
made the Constitution *revolutionary* because adopted in violation of the existing law.   Congress was not asked to approve
the new Constitution because it was believed that would practically destroy all chances of ratification.[30]

The causes of the Convention's adoption of this method of
ratification were:

(1) *The legislatures had no power to ratify the Constitution of the United States.*   Such a ratification by state action
would make it but a league or treaty between states, and succeeding legislatures having equal power could undo the acts of
their predecessors.

(2) *The Convention also feared that some of the states
would vote against the new Constitution, and, therefore, a
unanimous vote could not be secured.*   The result would be
that one or two states would prevent union.   The rejection of
the Five-per-cent Amendment of 1781, and the Revenue Amendment of 1783 by Rhode Island and New York was fresh in
their minds.

(3) *It was believed that only the consent of the people,
the sovereign power, could give validity to the Constitution,
and establish it beyond power to question its authority.*   In
some states, as Virginia, the government was not derived from
the clear and undisputed authority of the people, and many
regarded the constitution as established by an assumed authority.   The Constitution of the United States must not be left
open to such criticism, nor must it be a mere compact resting on
legislative sanction only, so that it could be regarded as a
mere league or treaty, the violation of any one article of which
rendered the whole null and void, and released all the parties
from obligation.   It must be founded on the solid basis of the
consent of the people, so that the heretical claim could not
be made that a party to the compact had the right to revoke it.

(4) *Conventions would secure the attendance of the ablest
men in the states, many of whom were excluded from the state
legislatures.*

(5) *It was feared that even in states favorable to the new
plan, the state legislatures might reject the Constitution
through fear of losing power and importance.*   This danger
could be avoided by calling conventions of the people.[31]

The Attestation. The Convention agreed to the Constitution, September 15, 1787.[32] On September 17, Doctor Franklin urged every member who had objections to "doubt a little of his own infallibility," and to sign the Constitution. He offered the following as a convenient form: "Done in Convention by the unanimous consent of the States present. . . . In witness wherof we have subscribed our names." This ambiguous form was drawn up by Gouverneur Morris for the purpose of winning the dissenting members of the Convention, and persuading them to sign. Instead of presenting it himself, he thought it would have a better chance of being accepted if presented by the shrewd, diplomatic, conciliatory Franklin.[33] Gouverneur Morris pointed out that the proposed form simply declared that the *states present* were unanimous, and this won over Blount of North Carolina who had said he would not sign the instrument.[34] This did not imply that all the individual delegates approved the Constitution. Doctor Franklin's motion was adopted by the vote of ten states. South Carolina was divided because General Pinckney and Pierce Butler, disliking the ambiguous, equivocal form of ratification, voted in the negative.[35]

NOTES TO CHAPTER XVI

1. Journals of Cong. Vol. 12, p. 33 (Mch. 21 and April 13).
2. Laws of N. Y. 2, p. 679.
3. Brinton Coxe, Judicial Power and Unconstitutional Legislation, 268, 267-8, 278-9, 223, 28.
4. Taswell-Langmead, Eng. Const. Hist. 252.
5. Bacon's Abridgment, Vol. VIII (Bouvier ed.), p. 66.
6. Fiske, Discovery of America, I, app. Hart, Am. Hist. Told by Contemporaries. Halsey, Great Epochs in Am. Hist. I, 44. Adams and Stephens, Doc. p. 85.
7. As 1391, 15 Rich. II; 1 Henry V.
8. Adams and Stephens, 80, 68, 150, 174, 473, 537. Stephens, Com. on Laws of Eng. II, 678. Walter de Gray Birch, Hist. Charters and Const. Docs. of the City of London, 52, 56, 62, 64, 84, 86, 93, 73.
9. 7 Coke, 14. Encyclopaedia of Laws of Eng. Vol. 10, p. 44.
10. Poore, Charters, 1379, 1380, 1381, 1382. Prothero, Statutes, p. 451. The following Charters use the clause: *Va.* 1606, 1609, 1611-12, Poore, 1893, 1902, 1908; *Mass.* 1629, 1691, 1726, Poore, 938, 940, 942, 948, 952, 954, 955, 956; *Md.* 1632, Poore, 814, 815, 816; *Maine,* 1639, 1664, 1674, Poore, 779, 783, 785, 788; *Conn.* 1662, Poore, 256, 257; *R. I.* 1663, Poore, 1597, 1603; *Carolina,* 1663, 1665, Poore, 1385, 1386, 1387, 1393, 1394, 1395, 1396; *Pa.* 1681, 1696, 1701, Poore, 1514, 1515, 1536, 1540; *Del.* 1701, Poore, 273; *Ga.* 1732, Poore, 377.

11. Colonial Laws of N. Y. I, 521, 525, 526, 527, 116, 124.
12. Elliot, V, 128, 157, 183.
13. Elliot, V, 352, 376, 381; I, 305.
14. Id. 498. See also Id. 446, and Moore Am. Eloquence, I, 369.
15. Poore, 1620; 381.
16. Id. 820, 1291.
17. Id. 1334, 971, 1864.
18. Federalist, No. 43, p. 317 (Dawson ed.).
19. Poore, 276, 820, 379, 1313, 1623, 1413, 1418, 1543.
20. Elliot, I, 385.
21. Elliot, I, 385.
22. Elliot, II, 118-119; III, 93; IV, 192, 193.
23. Elliot, II, 118; IV, 192, 193, 200; IV, 196.
24. Elliot, V, 108.
25. Elliot, V, 128, 157, 183.
    Elliot, V, 157, 158.
26. Elliot, V, 183, 498.
27. Elliot, V, 498, 499, 500, 501.
28. Elliot, V, 500, 501; III, 28.
29. Elliot, V, 499; I, 386, 305.
30. Elliot, V, 534.
31. Elliot, V, 128, 157, 158, 353-356, 363, 376; IV, 207; Federalist, no. 22, 149, 306.
32. Elliot, V, 553.
33. Id. 555.
34. Elliot, V, p. 555.
35. Id. 557, 558; I, 125.

CHAPTER XVII

THE FIRST TEN AMENDMENTS

In ratifying the Constitution, a number of states had recommended the adoption of amendments to guarantee the inherent rights of the people. Professor Ames says seven states proposed one hundred and twenty-four amendments, while Professor Thorpe mentions one hundred and forty-five. Madison speaks of one hundred and twenty-six. The first ten amendments are known as "The Bill of Rights" and the Supreme Court has held that they are binding on the United States but not on the states.[1]

The great objection urged against the ratification of the Constitution was, "there is no bill or declaration of rights" to guard "the fundamental guarantees of life, liberty, and property against the unwarranted exercise of power by the national government." [2] North Carolina and Rhode Island had refused to ratify the Constitution till amendments were adopted. The arguments of Wilson and Hamilton that a bill of rights was unnecessary, and the Constitution itself was a Bill of Rights entirely failed to allay popular fear and satisfy the public mind.[3] *The first ten amendments originated in fear and grew out of the demand for a bill of rights to limit the federal government.* The New York convention had sent out a circular letter earnestly requesting the state legislatures to unite in calling a convention for the purpose of securing the adoption of amendments to the Federal Constitution.[4] Virginia, acting on this request, presented a petition to Congress on May 5, 1789, requesting Congress to call a convention for the purpose of considering the amendments proposed by the state conventions.[5] Madison, after an exhaustive study of the amendments recommended by the states, introduced the subject in Congress June 8, 1789.[6] The motives given for this action were: (1) To satisfy the minority opposed to the Constitution that their liberties were not in danger. (2) To bring North Carolina and Rhode Island into the union. (3) To guard against abuse of power by the central government. (4) To unite and strengthen the nation which had been divided over the Constitution.[7]

The First Amendment. Livermore of New Hampshire was in some measure responsible for the phraseology of amendment one. It provides:

(1) *For freedom of religion.* This principle of religious freedom originated in the controversy which arose in several of the colonies and states where an attempt was made to legislate "respecting an establishment of religion." This culminated in Virginia where each male over sixteen years of age was taxed ten pounds of tobacco, and one bushel of corn annually for the support of the church. Dissenters were compelled to contribute even though they had their own church and minister.[8] The result was a bitter contest in Virginia for religious freedom and the abolition of the established church. Jefferson and Madison led the dissenters in this fight. On October 22, 1776, the dissenters from the Church of England in the counties of Albemarle, Amherst, and Buckingham presented a petition to the Virginia House of Delegates setting forth that being compelled by law to contribute to the support of the established church, they did not enjoy equal religious privileges, and praying that every religious denomination be given equal rights.[9] On October 24, the Presbytery of Hanover presented a memorial to the House asking the repeal of all laws countenancing religious establishments; the protection of every religious sect in their several modes of worship, and exemption from compulsory payment of taxes for the support of any church.[10] On October 25, two petitions were presented by dissenters complaining of the hardship of being obliged to support the established church contrary to the dictates of conscience, and praying that the ecclesiastical establishment be suspended or laid aside.[11] On November 1, the dissenters of the counties of Amherst and Albemarle presented a second petition declaring that they "are exposed to great hardships as being obliged to contribute to the support of the established church contrary to the dictates of their conscience," and praying that all religious denominations be put upon an equal footing.[12] On November 9, a similar petition was presented from Augusta county. In opposition to these, on November 8, 1776, the

clergy of the established church presented a memorial to the legislature setting forth the excellency of the religious establishment, and praying that final action be deferred till the sentiment of the people could be collected, as they believed a majority of the people desired to see the church establishment continued. The petitions were referred to the committee on religion, but on November 9, the committee was discharged and the petitions referred to the Committee of the Whole House on the state of the country.[13] Jefferson championed the views of the dissenters, and he characterizes the struggle of 1776 in the Virginia legislature as the most severe in which he had been engaged.[14] A bill exempting dissenters from punishment for non-attendance on Episcopal services, and from contributing to the support and maintenance of the established church was introduced and read a second time, December 2, 1776, ordered to third reading December 4, and passed December 5, 1776. This act established "equal liberty as well religious as civil" for all people in Virginia.[15] In 1784, another attempt was made to establish the Episcopal Church permanently in Virginia. A bill for the purpose, "establishing provision for teachers of the Christian religion" was introduced in the legislature, and excited tremendous opposition. James Madison prepared a "Memorial and Remonstrance" against the bill which was widely circulated among the people and largely signed.[16] The bill was defeated in the legislature, and Thomas Jefferson drafted another. "The Act for Religious Freedom," which was passed, December 16, 1785. When the Convention of 1787 met, Jefferson was in France, and on seeing the Constitution wrote expressing disappointment that it contained no declaration insuring religious freedom.[17] In ratifying the Constitution, North Carolina, Virginia, Maryland, and New Hampshire requested a provision either in a bill of rights, or as an article of amendment providing for religious freedom. "Accordingly, at the first session of the first Congress, the amendment now under consideration was proposed with others by Mr. Madison." [18]

In addition to the precedents already cited, the state constitutions and colonial charters furnished additional precedents against an establishment of religion, as Virginia, North Carolina, Pennsylvania, Delaware, and New Jersey, 1776, Vermont and Georgia, 1777 and 1786, Massachusetts, 1780, and New Hampshire, 1784.[19] In 1786, Connecticut had passed a law granting freedom of worship, and freedom from taxation for support of other churches.

Some of the *charters* had also granted religious liberty. The charter of Rhode Island, 1663, prohibited any religion from being established by law and granted liberty of religion.[20] In 1674, Governor Andros was instructed to permit the free exercise of religion in New York.[21] The Pennsylvania Frame of Government, 1683, and the Charter of Massachusetts Bay, 1691, the Charter of Delaware, and the Charter of Privileges of Pennsylvania, 1701, and the Charter of Georgia, 1732, granted religious liberty.[22] Catholics were excepted in Massachusetts and Georgia because the existing English law made such an exception.[23] The statesmen of that day were well aware of the bitterness, bad blood, and persecution caused by the Test and Corporation Acts in England, and drew from that history a practical lesson for America.[24]

(2) *Congress shall make no law abridging the freedom of speech, or of the press.* The Virginia Declaration of Rights asked by the ratifying convention contained these two guarantees. The amendments recommended by North Carolina in convention contained an identical provision in article sixteen of the Declaration of Rights. As first introduced by Madison, the phraseology was that of Virginia and North Carolina.[25] The Maryland Convention also recommended the adoption of an amendment guaranteeing freedom of the press.[26] In the Federal Convention, August 20, 1787, Charles Pinckney submitted a proposition guaranteeing freedom of the press, to be referred to the committee of detail. This was taken from the South Carolina constitution of 1778. The draft of the Pinckney plan seems to have contained a similar provision.[27]

The state constitutions provided for free speech and a free press, as Maryland, North Carolina, Pennsylvania and Virginia, 1776, Georgia and Vermont, 1777, South Carolina, 1778, Massachusetts, 1780, New Hampshire, 1784, and Vermont, 1786.[28]

Back of this again, lies the history of the struggle for freedom of the press in England. After the invention of printing, the church assumed control, and then the crown after the

Reformation. Under Elizabeth, a strict censorship was enforced. Under the first Stuarts, the press was muzzled by the licenser, torture, mutilation, and the pillory. The Licensing Act of 1662 gave the government entire control of the press. It expired 1679, but was renewed and continued in force till 1695, when, owing to the resistance of Parliament, it expired again, and the press was, henceforth, legally free.[29]

The *purpose* of this part of the amendment has been stated by the courts. In the case of Commonwealth v. Blanding, 1825, C. J. Parker of Massachusetts said: "It is well understood that it was intended to prevent all such previous restraints upon publications as had been practised by other governments and in early times here, to stifle the efforts of patriots towards enlightening their fellow subjects upon their rights and the duties of rulers." This language was repeated by the Supreme Court of the United States in the case of Patterson v. Colorado.[30] The persecution of the press in England was evidently in mind.

(3) *Congress shall make no law abridging the right of assembly and petition.* This amendment did not create the right. It is simply declaratory of existing rights and affirmative of existing law. The right existed long before the Constitution was framed.[31] The sources are found:

(a) *In the amendments recommended by the conventions called to ratify the Federal Constitution.* Virginia and North Carolina recommended an identical proposition to Congress providing for the right of assembly and petition.[32] The words in the North Carolina Declaration are those of Virginia, and as the Virginia Declaration was dated June 27, 1788, and the North Carolina one August 1, 1788, the latter was obviously taken from the former.[33]

(b) *In the state constitutions.* In 1787, the rights of petition and assembly were guaranteed by the constitutions of North Carolina and Pennsylvania, 1776, Massachusetts, 1780, New Hampshire, 1784, and Vermont, 1777, and 1786. The constitution of Maryland, 1776, secured the right of petition for redress of grievances.[34] Consternation was produced in the colonies by the Massachusetts Act of 1774, by which the British Parliament abridged these rights, so vigorously asserted by the Resolves of the Virginia House of Burgesses, May 16, 1769, and by the Declaration of Rights of October 19, 1765.[35] These may also be regarded as precedents.

(c) *In the English Constitution.* The right of petition existed from earliest times in England. The amendment provides that the people must assemble peaceably. This is a limitation on the right. To check tumultuous demonstrations connected with the presenting of petitions, an act was passed in England in 1661, providing that petitions should not be presented by more than ten persons and should not be signed by more than twenty persons unless approved by three justices or a majority of the grand jury of the county. The Bill of Rights of 1689 enacted: "That it is the right of the subjects to petition the King and all commitments and prosecutions for such petitioning are illegal." [36] Blackstone says, "the right of petitioning the King or either house of Parliament for redress of grievances appertains to every individual." [37]

Amendment II. This guarantees to the people the right to keep and bear arms. The "arms" mentioned are those of the soldier to be used for defence, and do not include knives, daggers, sling-shots, or other such weapons. Neither is there any reference to the secret carrying of arms to be used for "deadly individual encounters." The carrying of concealed weapons may, therefore, be prohibited by law under the police power.[38] The sources were:

(1) *The amendments of the ratifying conventions.* The state conventions, called to ratify the Federal Constitution, which requested the adoption of an amendment on the subject were those of North Carolina and Virginia. They stated their proposed amendments almost in the same words as the amendment in the Federal Constitution.[39]

(2) *The state constitutions.* The constitutions of North Carolina, Pennsylvania, and Virginia, 1776, Massachusetts, 1780, and Vermont, 1777 and 1786, contained a provision guaranteeing the right to keep and bear arms.[40]

(3) *The British Constitution.* The Assize of Arms, 1181, compelled all freeman to equip themselves with arms in proportion to their wealth. The Statute of Winchester, 1285, provided that "every man between fifteen years of age and sixty years, shall be assessed and sworn to armor according to the quantity of their land and goods." The English Bill of

Rights, 1689, guaranteed, "That the subjects which are Protestants may have arms for their defence suitable to their conditions and as allowed by law." The fifth and last auxiliary right of the subject," says Blackstone, "is that of having arms for their defence, suitable to their condition and degree, and such as are allowed by law, which is also declared by the same statute, 1 W & M st 2. C 2." [41]

Amendment III. No Quartering of Soldiers. The sources of this guarantee are:

(1) *The amendments asked by the ratifying conventions.* Among the states recommending the adoption of this amendment were Virginia, North Carolina, and Maryland.[40] The North Carolina provision was clearly taken from Virginia, and both are almost identical with the provision in the Constitution of the United States. In the Federal Convention, on August 20, Charles Pinckney submitted a proposition providing that "no soldier be quartered in any house in time of peace without consent of the owner." [41]

(2) *The state constitutions.* The amendment was to be found in the state constitutions of New Hampshire, 1784, Massachusetts, 1780, New York, 1777, and Maryland, 1776. Gerry attempted to secure the insertion of the phrase, "by a civil magistrate" from the Massachusetts constitution for the purpose of giving civil officers power to quarter soldiers, but his effort failed.[42]

(3) *American experience.* One of the grievances of the Declaration of Independence was that George III kept standing armies among the colonists in times *of peace without consent* of their legislatures, and quartered large bodies of armed troops among them. In 1772, Samuel Adams complained that fleets and armies had been introduced to support the unconstitutional officers in collecting the unconstitutional revenue, and says: "Introducing and quartering standing armies in a free country without the consent of the people either by themselves or by their representatives is, and always have been deemed a violation of their rights as freemen; and of the charter or compact made between the King of Great Britain and the People of this Province, whereby all the rights of British Subjects are confirmed to us." [43] Out of the remembrance of this grievance, caused by the English Quartering

acts, came the third amendment. "Such oppressions were fresh in the minds of the people when the Declaration of Independence was made, and they then denounced what they prohibited by this amendment." [44]

During the war with France the colonial legislatures provided by law for the quartering or billeting of troops. The New York legislature, for example, on December 1, 1756, passed an act providing for the billeting of troops by the civil officers —Mayor, Deputy-Mayor and two aldermen." This act expired at the end of the year, but was continued or reenacted by the legislature from year to year during the war, on the principle of the Mutiny Act. [46] Then, during the Revolution, the state legislature in 1778 provided by statute for the billeting of soldiers on the inhabitants by the justices of the peace. [47] New York, therefore, prescribed by law the manner of quartering troops in time of war. The Constitution of the United States simply follows this colonial and state experience and practice, in providing that soldiers shall not be quartered in any house "in time of war, but in a manner to be prescribed by law." [48]

(4) *The English Constitution.* Charles I by way of punishment, billeted soldiers and sailors on those who refused to pay his illegal exactions, or forced loans, 1627. [49] This practice became an intolerable grievance in England, with the result that Parliament led by Coke drew up the Petition of Right, which, amongst other things, made the quartering of soldiers in private houses without consent of the owner illegal. [50] This is the original source of the fourth amendment, though a law of the reign of Charles II, 1677, provided that soldiers could not be quartered or billeted by any officer, military or civil, on any inhabitant of the realm without his consent. The influence of this English Act is seen in the fact that the state of New York, January 26, 1787, passed a law prohibiting the quartering or billeting of soldiers, and the act simply repeats the exact phraseology of the English Statute of 1677 on the subject. It was a common law notion that every man's house was his castle. The abuse of billeting or quartering soldiers was as old as King John's reign. [51]

Amendment IV. General Warrants Declared Illegal. A general warrant is one which either does not give the name of the person to be apprehended, or does not specify any particular place to be searched. In 1763, Wilkes declared a warrant for his arrest, but which did not contain his name, "a ridiculous warrant against the whole English nation." The sources of amendment IV are:

(1) *The amendments recommended by the ratifying conventions.* The conventions of Virginia, Maryland, and North Carolina asked for such an amendment.[52] The reason given by Maryland for requiring this amendment as indispensable was that Congress had "the power of laying excises (the horror of a free people) by which our dwelling houses, those castles considered so sacred by the English law, will be laid open to the insolence and oppression of office," and, therefore, "there could be no constitutional check provided that would prove so effective a safeguard to our citizens."[53]

(2) *The state constitutions.* The following states had adopted a provision in their constitutions prohibiting the issuing of general warrants—Vermont, 1786 and 1777, New Hampshire, 1784, Massachusetts, Pennsylvania, Maryland, Virginia, and North Carolina in 1776.[54] Blackstone declared general warrants illegal, and it is interesting to see his influence on the state constitutions. They use his phraseology, and Maryland repeats a considerable part of his language in her declaration on the subject.[55]

(3) *American experience.* In the colonies, especially in New Hampshire and Massachusetts, writs of assistance were issued to the revenue officers authorizing them to search for smuggled goods. In Boston, the legality of the writs was challenged by James Otis in 1761, representing the Boston merchants.[56] There was nothing either startling or "novel" in the argument of Otis. He was a lawyer making a lawyer's plea for his clients. His argument was legal, not political, and based not on abstract grounds, but on English law and English precedents. He made no claim that he was stating anything new in law. That would have been to lose his case, so he argued that general warrants were illegal, and in that he was supported by the great legal writers of England—Hale, Coke, and Hawkins. General warrants were illegal by the common law of England, and Otis, therefore, argued that the writ mentioned in 13 and 14 Car. 2. was a special writ according to 12 Car. 2. This was in all probability correct as Lord Hale gives

no hint that they are general, says Horace Gray.[57] There is no reason to believe that his speech attracted much attention at the time, or that it had anything to do with the Revolution except in the mind of John Adams. But the use of general warrants in the shape of writs of assistance in the colonies caused considerable stir, and roused intense opposition to the practice. In 1772, Samuel Adams included general warrants in the list of infringements and violations of the rights of the colonists, and declared: "These officers are by their commission invested with power altogether unconstitutional, and entirely destructive to that security which we have a right to enjoy." This abuse of general warrants was fresh in the memory of the men who framed the state and Federal Constitutions, and that caused them to insert in the fundamental law of state and nation a guarantee against the use of such warrants in time to come.[58]

(4) *The English Constitution.* General warrants appear to have originated in the acts for regulating the press. The Star Chamber gave general warrants to their messenger of the press for the arrest of unnamed authors of libels. Lord Camden in the case of Entick v. Carrington, 1765, said he believed they originated in a decree of the Star Chamber of 1636, which cited as its authority an older decree of the 28th Elizabeth. After the abolition of the Star Chamber, the practice was revived by the Licensing Act of Charles II, and was continued after this Act expired in 1695.[59]

General warrants were not legal by the common law of England. Sir Matthew Hale in his Pleas of the Crown declares general warrants void and illegal, and mentions the case of a justice who issued a warrant to apprehend all persons suspected of a robbery, and the court held the warrant void "in the case of Justice Swallowe." A warrant, he holds, is void in law unless it expresses the name of the party to be taken. A general warrant to search all places is void. Coke also declared general warrants illegal in his Institutes.[60] Hawkins, in his Pleas of the Crown, lays it down that general warrants are illegal. "I do not find any good authority," he says, "that a justice can justify sending a general warrant to search all suspected houses in general for stolen goods."[61] A general warrant, he holds, to search for felons or stolen goods seems to be illegal on the very face of it. A justice cannot grant such a general warrant. Otis had these great English authorities behind him on which to base his legal argument.[62] Blackstone, in his Commentaries, also declares general warrants illegal. The influence of Blackstone on the provision in the constitution of Maryland has already been mentioned. A comparison of Blackstone with Amendment IV shows that it uses the phrase "particularly describing," which is Blackstone's. He says: "A general warrant to apprehend all persons suspected, without warning or particularly describing any person in special is illegal and void for its uncertainty; for it is the duty of the magistrate and ought not to be left to the officer, to judge of the ground of suspicion. And a warrant to apprehend all persons guilty of a crime therein specified is no legal warrant. . . . It is in fact no warrant at all."[63] The men of 1776 and 1787 followed their greatest legal·authority in adopting a constitutional provision prohibiting the issuing of general warrants. Blackstone simply follows Hale, Hawkins, and Lord Coke.

Then, a series of English cases in which the courts declared general warrants illegal, had a great influence on the men of the Revolutionary period. In the case of Wilkes, 1763, Lord Halifax, Secretary of State, issued a general warrant for the arrest of the publishers of No. 45 of the North Briton. Armed with this warrant, forty-nine persons were arrested, many of whom were innocent, and Wilkes' house was entered and ransacked, his escritoire broken open, his private papers and even his pocket book seized and carried off. Wilkes and the printers brought actions against the messengers who had made the arrests. In the first action, the printers were awarded £300 damages. In Wilkes v. Wood (the under-secretary of State) the jury awarded the plaintiff £1,000 damages. Lord Camden declared general warrants "illegal, and contrary to the fundamental principles of the Constitution," 1763.[64] In the case of Leach v. Money and Three of the King's Messengers in 1763, Leach secured a verdict for £400. A bill of exceptions was tendered, and the case argued before the Court of King's Bench in 1765. Lord Chief Justice Mansfield said: "The last point is, whether this general warrant be good . . . But here, it is not contended that the common law gave the officer authority to apprehend; nor that there is any act of parliament which warrants this case. Therefore, it must stand upon principles of common law." But general warrants were unknown to the common law, for, "as to authorities—Hale and all others hold such an uncertain warrant void; and there is no case or book to the contrary." James Otis had, therefore, good law behind him for his argument against general warrants. Justice Wilmot declared that he had never had any doubt that these warrants were "illegal and void." With this, the other two justices, Yates and Aston agreed. "They were clear and unanimous in opinion that this warrant was illegal and void." [65]

In Entick v. Carrington, 1765, general search warrants were declared void. In November, 1762, Halifax, Secretary of State, issued a warrant directing certain messengers to take a constable and search for John Entick, concerned in the writing of the "Monitor or British Freeholder," and to seize him, his books and papers. The name of the person against whom the warrant was directed was specified in this case so that it differed in this respect from Wilkes' case. It was not a general warrant in that sense, but it was a general search warrant since no papers to be seized were specified. All books and papers were to be seized at discretion. [66] Lord Camden again declared such a general search warrant illegal. He said: "If it is law, it will be found in our books. If it is not to be found there, it is not law. . . . The case of searching for stolen goods crept into the law by imperceptible practice. It is the only case of the kind that is to be met with. No less a person than my Lord Coke denied its legality (4 Inst. 176.) . . . That the right to search, seize and carry away all the papers of the subject" "should have existed from the time whereof the memory of man runneth not to the contrary, and never yet have found a place in any book of law, is incredible." [67]

Another thing which influenced the men of 1789 was the ransacking of Algernon Sidney's house and the seizing and carrying away of his papers for the purpose of convicting him of treason. [68]

The English Parliament took up the subject of general warrants and debated their legality at length. Pitt declared there was not a man to be found "of sufficient profligacy to defend this warrant upon the principle of legality." On April 25, 1766, Parliament adopted a resolution declaring all general warrants for the seizure of persons or papers illegal.[69] These court decisions and exciting events of English history constituted "the immediate occasion for this constitutional provision." [70]

The law as expounded by Lord Camden "has been regarded as settled from that time to this," said Mr. Justice Bradley in Boyd v. U. S., 1886. He says he believes that the men who framed this amendment relied on the language of Lord Camden "as expressing the true doctrine on the subject of searches and seizures, and as furnishing the true criteria of the reasonable and unreasonable character of such seizures." Chief Justice Waite and Justice Miller adopted the same view as to the origin of the amendment in their dissenting opinion.[71]

Amendment V. This amendment divides itself naturally into four parts:

1. *"No person shall be held to answer for a capital or otherwise infamous crime, unless on a presentment or indictment of a grand jury, except . . . danger."* The sources were:

(1) *The Massachusetts Convention of 1788 called to ratify the Federal Constitution.* It was submitted to the convention as a series of propositions on January 31, 1788, by John Hancock, the president, and referred to a committee which reported them later to the convention. As recommended by the convention, it read: "Sixthly, That no person shall be tried for any crime, by which he may incur an infamous punishment or loss of life, until he be first indicted by a grand jury, except in such cases as may arise in the government of the land and naval forces." [72] Madison changed it to read: "In all crimes punishable with loss of life or member, presentment or indictment by a grand jury shall be an essential preliminary." [73] The committee to which it was referred, and of which Madison was a member, reported it back to the House substantially as it stands in the Constitution." [74]

(2) *The state constitution of North Carolina, 1776.* This was the only one of the state constitutions which provided for such a constitutional rule. Article VIII reads: "That no free-

man shall be put to answer any criminal charge but by indictment, presentment, or impeachment." [75]

(3) *The English common law.* The law of England did not permit informations for capital crimes by the Attorney-General without indictment by a grand jury. The same legal principle applied to other felonies. So the fifth amendment merely affirms a rule of the common law.[76] A grand jury consisted of at least twelve men, and not more than twenty-three, so that twelve might always be a majority.[77] Blackstone says that in common law, the King could only prosecute a case, or give his sanction for such prosecution, after "a grand jury had informed him on their oaths that there was sufficient ground for instituting a criminal suit." "Whenever any capital offence is charged, the same law requires that the accusation be warranted by the oath of twelve men before the party shall be put to answer it." [78] The grand jury in criminal cases is mentioned for the first time in the Constitutions of Clarendon, 1164, the Assize of Clarendon, 1166, and Assize of Northampton, 1176, though it may go back to the Jury of Presentment known to Ethelred's law.[79] A statute of Edward III provided that "none shall be taken by petition or suggestion made to our lord the King, or to his council, unless it be by indictment or presentment of good and lawful people of the same neighborhood where such deeds be done, in due manner, or by writ original at the common law." [80] Such was the law embodied in this clause of the fifth amendment.

An infamous crime, according to the Supreme Court of the United States, is a crime punishable by imprisonment for a term of years at hard labor.[81]

The *purpose* of the exception, "in the land and naval forces," was to prevent conflict between the civil and military authorities. As a matter of fact, military offences had been subject to punishment by court-martial since September 20, 1778, when Congress adopted Articles of War.[82]

2. *Nor Shall Any Person for the Same Offence be twice put in jeopardy of life or limb.*" The sources of this are to be found:

(1) *In the recommendation of the Maryland Convention.* This was practically the only state convention which asked for this amendment. The convention stated it as follows: "And that there be . . . no second trial after acquittal." [83]

(2) *The state constitution of New Hampshire,* 1784. This constitution was the only one which contained the proviso Article XVI provided, that "no subject shall be liable to be tried, after an acquittal for the same crime or offence."[84]

(3) *The colonial laws and charters.* The Massachusetts Body of Liberties, 1641, provided that "no man shall be twice sentenced by Civill Justice for one and the same crime, offence or trespasse." The Fundamental Constitutions of Carolina, 1669, drawn up by John Locke, provided that "no cause shall be twice tried in any one court, upon any reason or pretence whatsoever." [85]

(4) *The English common law.* It was a very ancient maxim of the common law that no man should be tried twice for the same offence—"non bis in idem." In the case of The People v. Goodwin, tried in the Supreme Court of New York, 1820, Chief Justice Spencer said, "the principle is a sound and fundamental one of the common law, that no man shall be twice put in jeopardy of life or limb for the same offence." [86] He quotes Blackstone as the authority on the subject. Justice Miller in Ex Parte Lange after stating that it was a common law principle that no man can be twice lawfully punished for the same offence, quoted Coke: "No one ought to be twice punished for the same offence." (4 Rep. 480), and Hawkins: "No one can be twice punished for the same crime." (2 Hawkins, Pleas of Crown, 377). The common law, he declared, prohibited both a second punishment and a second trial for the same offence. "Hence, to every indictment, or information charging a party with a known and defined crime or misdemeanor, whether at the common law, or by statute, a plea of autrefois acquit, or autrefois convict is a good defence." [87]

Blackstone lays it down as "a universal maxim of the common law of England that no man is to be brought into jeopardy of his life more than once for the same offence." Hence, when upon any indictment a man has been once acquitted or found not guilty before any court having competent jurisdiction to try the offence, such acquittal may be pleaded by him "in bar of any subsequent accusation for the same crime." [88] In fact, this maxim is so ancient that it appears to be from an old Gothic custom or constitution.[89] The same legal principle is laid down by Hawkins who says: "The plea of autrefois acquit is grounded on this maxim, that a man shall not be brought into danger of his life for one and the same offence more than once." So that "*all the books* say that where a man has been once found not guilty on an indictment or appeal free from error, he may by the common law plead such acquittal in all cases in bar of any subsequent indictment or appeal for the same crime." [90] Bracton mentions this rule of the common law in the thirteenth century. Archbishop Becket objected to Henry Second's Constitutions of Clarendon, 1164, on the ground that delivering a degraded ecclesiastic to the secular power for punishment was to try a man twice for the same offence. That is, would violate a fundamental maxim of the common law.[91]

In 1788, loss of limb was not inflicted as a punishment by the laws of any state, and the same was true of the law of England for a long time before that. It is intended to denominate offences formerly punished by dismemberment, and refers to felonies. The meaning is that no man shall be tried twice for the same offence.[92]

3. *"Nor Shall Any Person be Compelled in Any Criminal Case to be a Witness Against Himself."* The sources are:

(1) *The state ratifying conventions.* The Virginia convention recommended the adoption of a provision reading as follows: "Nor can he be compelled to give evidence against himself." The convention of North Carolina urged an identical provision.[93] North Carolina evidently followed the Virginia convention which met and completed its work before the North Carolina convention assembled, August 1, 1788. The provision is repeated in the state constitutions, and is clearly copied from the Virginia Bill of Rights, adopted June 12, 1776. All the states repeat the words of Virginia.

(2) *The state constitutions.* The identical provision is found in the constitutions of Virginia, North Carolina, Maryland and Pennsylvania, 1776, Vermont, 1777 and 1786, Massachusetts, 1780, and New Hampshire, 1784.[94]

(3) *The English common law.* This clause is a common law principle, the purpose of which was to prevent the very possibility of using the inquisitorial methods of questioning accused persons in vogue in continental Europe and in England till the Revolution of 1688.[95] The common law, as well as the

Roman law, permitted unforgivable cruelties to be inflicted on persons suspected of crime, for the purpose of compelling them to confess their guilt or to reveal their accomplices. Witnesses were browbeaten, bullied, tortured, entrapped in contradictions often the mere result of fear or timidity. Under the humane influence of Christianity, and the notorious odiousness of such trials as those of Sir Nicholas Throckmorton and Udal in England, the system was universally condemned, and a demand made for the total abolition of the inhuman system. "The change in the English criminal procedure in that particular seems to be founded upon no statute and no judicial opinion, but upon a general and silent acquiescence of the courts in a popular demand. But, however adopted, it has become firmly imbedded in English, as well as in American jurisprudence. So deeply did the iniquities of the ancient system impress themselves upon the minds of the American colonists that the states, with one accord, made a denial of the right to question an accused person a part of their fundamental law, so that a maxim, which in England was a mere rule of evidence, became clothed in this country with the impregnability of a constitutional enactment." So the common law maxim, "nemo tenetur seipsum accusare," had its origin in a universal protest against an odious method of examining witnesses, and persons suspected of crime.[96] Justice Bradley said, what Congress had in mind may be inferred from the 15th section of the Judiciary Act of 1789 which gives the courts of the United States power to require parties to produce books and papers in cases, and under circumstances where they might be compelled to produce the same by the ordinary rules of proceeding in chancery. One "cardinal rule of the court of chancery is never to decree a discovery which might tend to convict the party of a crime or to forfeit his property." Any "compulsory discovery made by extorting the oath" of the party "or compelling the production of his private books and papers to convict him of crime or to forfeit his property, is contrary to the principles of free government." It is abhorrent to the instincts of both an Englishman and an American.[97]

4. *No Person "Shall be Deprived of Life, Liberty, or Property Without Due Process of Law."* The sources are:

(1) *The state ratifying conventions.* The convention of

Virginia recommended the adoption of an amendment with this provision which was taken from the Bill of Rights of the state constitution. The phraseology of Magna Carta (ch. 39) was used. The North Carolina convention simply followed Virginia.[98]

(2) *The state constitutions.* The following state constitutions had adopted the provision—Vermont, 1777 and 1786, New Hampshire, 1784,[99] Massachusetts, 1780, South Carolina, 1778, Maryland, 1777, North Carolina, Pennsylvania, and Virginia, 1776. The North West Ordinance, 1787,[100] also contained the provision. In all the precedents enumerated here the phraseology of Magna Carta is used. Neither the North West Ordinance nor the state constitutions use the words, "due process of law."

(3) *The English Constitution.* The provision is borrowed from Magna Carta, Chapter 39, though the legal principle is clothed not in the language of Magna Carta, but in the language of English statutes, which paraphrased or interpreted the language of Magna Carta—"the law of the land"—by substituting the phrase, "due process of law." The language first appears in 1354, in a statute of Edward III, which reads "Item, That no man of what estate or condition that he be, shall be put out of land or tenement, nor taken, nor imprisoned, nor disinherited, nor put to death, without being brought in answer by due process of law." Another statute of Edward III paraphrases "the law of the land," by using the words, "without due process of law." [101] while another paraphrases it by using the phrase, "by the course of the law." The statute of 42 Ed. III interprets it by using the words "or by due process and writ original according to the old law of the land." [102]

The English House of Commons and English courts also interpreted the Magna Carta phrase to mean "due process of law."

Lord Coke interprets the words "by the law of the land" as meaning "due process of law," and says they were so interpreted by the statutes.[103] Sir Matthew Hale says that lex terrae of Magna Carta means the common law, and declares this is seen from "the exposition thereof in several subsequent statutes, and particularly in the statute of 28 Edward III (ch.

3), which is but an exposition and explanation of that statute. Justice Selden said the expression "due process of law" first appeared in a statute of Ed. III as a paraphrase of the words "by the law of the land" in Magna Carta, and from that day to this, both had "been held to refer to the common law as distinguished from statutory enactment." [104]

The American jurists accepted and adopted this English interpretation as laid down by Coke and other English jurists, namely, that "the law of the land," means the same thing as "due process of law." Sir Matthew Hale, Selden, and Coke are quoted by the judges as authorities on whom they rely for the interpretation adopted. [105] At the time the colonists emi- grated to America, this was the accepted interpretation, and Coke is the man who is responsible for this clause being in the Constitution of the United States, as all refer to him as authority for the interpretation in question. His statement found universal acceptance. The state constitutions followed the language of Magna Carta or Blackstone. [106] The Federal Constitution follows the language of the statute 28 Ed. III, and Coke's interpretation. Why did they refuse to follow the precedents found in the state constitutions? Let the Supreme Court of the United States answer the question. Justice Curtis in Murray's Lessee v. Hoboken Land and Improvement Co., said: "The Constitution of the United States, as adopted, con- tained the provision, that 'the trial of all crimes, except in cases of impeachment, shall be by jury.' When the fifth article of amendment containing the words now in question was made, the trial by jury in criminal cases had thus already been provided for. By the sixth and seventh articles of amendment, further special provisions were separately made for that mode of trial in civil and criminal cases. To have followed, as in the state constitutions, and in the Ordinance of 1787, the words of Magna Carta, and declared that no person shall be de- prived of his life, liberty, or property but by the judgment of his peers or the law of the land, would have been in part superfluous and inappropriate. To have taken the clause, 'law of the land' without its immediate context, might possibly have given rise to doubts, which would be effectively dispelled by using those words which the great commentator on Magna Carta had declared to be the true meaning of the phrase 'law of the land' in that instrument, and which were undoubtedly then received as their true meaning." [107]

The *purpose* was to protect the individual by placing a limitation on governmental power, and it applies to both common and statute law. Justice Denio in Westervelt v. Gregg said: "The provision was designed to protect the citizen against all mere acts of power, whether flowing from the legislature or executive branches of government." It was originally intended, says McKechnie, to prohibit John from placing execution before judgment. It "hears," said Webster, "before it condemns," "and renders judgment only after trial." [108]

5. *"Nor Shall Private Property be Taken for Public Use Without Just Compensation."* This is the right of *eminent domain* which is inseparable from sovereignty unless denied to the state by its fundamental law. The sources of this are:

(1) *The Virginia ratifying convention may be regarded as furnishing a precedent.* It requested a clause providing that "no freeman ought to be deprived of his property but by the law of the land."

(2) *The state constitutions and the North West Ordinance.* The constitution of Pennsylvania, 1776, contains a clause identical in principle; Vermont, 1777 and 1786,[109] and Massachusetts, 1780, contain similar provisions. Massachusetts repeats the exact language of article ten of the Declaration of Rights of 1765 on the subject. The North West Ordinance of 1787 also contains a clause which in part follows the phraseology of the Massachusetts constitution and the Declaration of Rights of 1765.[110]

(3) *The Massachusetts Body of Liberties of 1641.* This provides that "no man's cattell or goods of what kinds soever shall be pressed or taken for any public use, or service, unless it be by warrant upon some act of the general court, nor without such reasonable prices and hire as the ordinarie rates of the countrie do afford." [111] That is, the market value must be paid for such property, or just compensation made to the owner.

(4) *The English common law.* Blackstone, in his Commentaries, lays down the common law on the subject. The right of property, he says, was an absolute and an inherent right of every Englishman. Magna Carta and other statutes se-

cured this right to the subject, and only the legislature had power to interpose and compel the individual to acquiesce in alienating his property for the general good of the whole community. It does this, not by stripping the subject of his property in an arbitrary manner, but by giving him a full indemnification and equivalent for the injury thereby sustained. "All that the legislature does is to oblige the owner to alienate his property for a reasonable price." [112] The constitution of New York of 1777 did not contain any provision guaranteeing compensation for private property taken for a public use. The Court of Appeals has, however, held that though no provision on the subject was inserted in the constitution till 1821, nevertheless, the people of the state were protected in the interval from 1777 to 1821 by the *common law of England* which had been adopted by the constitution of 1777 as the law of New York.[113] Grotius in his Rights of War and Peace, 1625, stated the law of "eminent domain," and was the first writer to use the term. It was adopted from his work.[114]

Amendment VI. 1. "*In all criminal prosecutions, the accused shall enjoy the right to a speedy and public trial by an impartial jury*" *of the district.* This is a principle of the common law, and precedents were to be found:

(1) *In the amendments of the state ratifying conventions.* In the amendments offered by Virginia and North Carolina the provision was to be found, and a similar provision was recommended by the Maryland convention.[115]

(2) *The state constitutions.* A provision practically identical with the amendment was to be found in the state constitutions of Virginia, Maryland, Pennsylvania, Massachusetts, New Hampshire, and Vermont. The Maryland convention stated that one of the great objects of amendment was to secure "the boasted birthright of Englishmen," trial by jury in all cases.[116]

(3) *Assertions of the principle during the revolutionary and colonial periods.* One of the great grievances of the American colonies against Great Britain was in the words of the Declaration of Independence "transporting us beyond the seas to be tried for pretended offences." [117] An ancient English statute of Henry Eighth's time was revived giving colonial Governors power to send persons accused of treason in the

colonies to England for trial. The colonists resisted and complained of this as an invasion of their rights under the English Constitution.[118] The First Continental Congress complained that both houses of Parliament have resolved that, "Colonists may be tried in England for offences alleged to have been committed in America by a statute passed in the 38th year of Henry VIII." This deprived the colonists "of a trial by their peers of the vicinage." [119] Colonists guilty of violating the trade laws and Stamp Act were to be tried by the Admiralty Courts without a jury. Samuel Adams complains of the extension of the powers of the courts of vice-admiralty so enormously as to deprive the colonists of their inestimable right of trial by jury.[120] In the address to Quebec, the Continental Congress declared one of their rights under the English Constitution was trial by a jury of peers of the vicinage.[121] On October 4, 1774, the Continental Congress resolved that the colonies were "entitled to the common law of England and more especially to the great and inestimable privilege of being tried by their peers of the vicinage according to the course of that law." On October 21, Congress resolved "that the seizing or attempting to seize any person in America in order to transport such person beyond the sea for trial of offences committed within the body of a county in America, being against law, will justify, and ought to meet with resistance and reprisal." [122] Jefferson in his Summary View, and the Virginia House of Burgesses, May 16, 1769, also complained and protested against trial beyond the sea as derogatory to the rights of British subjects.[123] The Resolutions of the Stamp Act Congress laid claim to trial by jury as the inherent and inalienable right of every British subject in the colonies. The result of all these discussions, declarations, complaints, claims and resolutions of the colonists was the safeguarding of this "inestimable privilege" by means of provisions in the fundamental law of the states guaranteeing the common law right of trial by jury in the district. As early as 1623, the Plymouth Colony adopted an ordinance declaring that all criminal facts should be tried by a jury of twelve honest men.[124]

(4) *The English common law.* The amendment confers no rights on the criminal beyond those conferred by the common law. Article III, Sec. 2, cl. 3, of the Constitution required

that all crimes be tried by jury, but it did not require the accused to be tried in the district of the crime where a state was divided into two districts, nor did the terms require a jury drawn from the vicinage.[125]   The jury is a common law jury composed of twelve men, and a unanimous verdict is required in all Federal Courts.[126]   Blackstone said when a prisoner on arraignment pleaded not guilty, "the sheriff of the County must return a panel of jurors, liberos et legales homines, de vicineto," that is "freeholders of the visne or neighborhood, which is interpreted to be of the county where the fact is committed."   This bulwark of the Englishman's liberties is secured by Magna Carta, Sec. 39, from which he quotes as guaranteeing trial by jury.[127]   Story, and Justice Harlan of the Supreme Court of the United States quoted Magna Carta as the foundation of the right of trial by jury.   Doctor McKechnie declares this to be "a persistent error" "hard to dispel" and a belief "now held by all competent authorities to be unfounded." [128]   (For the origin of trial by jury, see Taswell-Langmead, Eng. Const. Hist. 1911, Chap. V; J. B. Thayer, Evidence at Common Law; Haskins, Am. Hist. Rev. VIII, The Early Norman Jury.)   It matters little whether this idea of Magna Carta was unfounded or not, for men insisted on the fact that it guaranteed jury trial, and because they believed it, and insisted on it, they made it guarantee jury trial, and in this way, it actually did guarantee jury trial whether originally intended to do so or not.

2. *"To be Informed of the Nature and Cause of the Accusation."*   This information is furnished by the indictment, a copy of which must be given the accused.   The sources of this provision are found:

(1) *In the ratifying state conventions.*   The Virginia convention, recommended an identical provision in Sec. 8 of the proposed Declaration of Rights though the phraseology was slightly different.   It read, "a man hath a right to demand the cause and nature of his accusation," and was taken from the state constitution.   The North Carolina convention recommended the identical provision of Virginia.[129]

(2) *In the state constitutions.*   The provision of the Virginia constitution of 1776 is quoted above.   North Carolina, Pennsylvania, and Vermont followed Virginia.   Massachusetts, 1780, and New Hampshire, 1784, used the same lan-

guage. The Maryland constitution of 1776 declared: "Every man hath a right to be informed of the accusation against him." [130] By inserting the words "cause and nature" reversed, after the word informed, we have the clause as it stands in the Constitution. The clause of the constitutions of Virginia, Pennsylvania, and Vermont supplied the words "nature and cause."

(3) *The English common and statute law.* "This is a reaffirmation of the essential principles of the common law," said Circuit Judge Putnam in the case of United States v. Potter. [131] The Treason Trials Act of 1696 required that persons accused of treason, or misprision of treason, "shall have a true copy of the whole indictment" at least five days before the trial. By another statute, all persons indicted for treason or misprision of treason were required to be given a copy of the indictment at least ten days before the trial. [132]

3. *"To be Confronted With the Witnesses Against Him."* The precedents for this were:

(1) *The recommendations of the state ratifying conventions.* The convention of Virginia requested a bill of rights, one clause of which read: "To be confronted with the accusers and witnesses." North Carolina followed Virginia. [133]

(2) *The state constitutions.* The Virginia constitution of 1776 contained the identical clause recommended by the ratifying convention of 1788. Madison introduced in Congress what was practically the Virginia proposition. The word "accusers" was used in this but was dropped by the committee of eleven. The Maryland constitution of 1776 read: "To be confronted with the witnesses against him." The constitution of Pennsylvania, 1776, Vermont, 1777 and 1786, Massachusetts, 1780, and New Hampshire, 1784, contained practically the same provision, "To meet the witnesses against him face to face." [134] The Congress of 1789 adopted and recommended to the states the clause used by Maryland, Pennsylvania, and Vermont.

(3) *The First Continental Congress.* In the address to Quebec, the Continental Congress declared that neither life, liberty, nor property could be taken from the possessor without trial by jury in the vicinage held face to face with the witnesses in open court. [135] This is similar to the phraseology of Massachusetts and New Hampshire.

(4) *The English common law.* This is merely a recognized

common law rule of procedure—a settled rule of the common law. Hawkins in his Pleas of the Crown said: "It is a settled rule, that in case of life, no evidence is to be given but in presence of the prisoner." The Statute of 5 and 6 Edward VI provided that no person should be indicted for treason, unless on the testimony of two lawful witnesses who should be brought face to face with the accused in court.[136] This became the foundation of the rule of procedure which has given the subject "a mighty safeguard against oppressive prosecutions." Udal, who was tried for felony in 1590, claimed the legal right of meeting a witness against him face to face. If it be his testimony, "why is he not present," he said, "to verify it face to face according to the law?"[137]

4. *"To have compulsory process of obtaining witnesses."* The sources of this are found:

(1) *In the ratifying conventions and state constitutions.* The conventions of Virginia and North Carolina suggested amendments giving the accused the right "to call for evidence."[138]

The state constitutions of Virginia, Pennsylvania, and Vermont contain the same provision. The constitution of Maryland declared the criminal had the right "to have process for his witnesses." New Jersey provided that "all criminals shall be admitted to the same privileges of witnesses . . . as their prosecutors." Massachusetts and New Hampshire said: "Every subject shall have a right to produce all proofs that may be favorable to himself." The constitution of North Carolina contained a general provision on the subject.[139]

(2) *The charters.* The Charter of Delaware, 1701, provided "that all criminals shall have the same privileges of Witnesses . . . as their Prosecutors." The Charter of Privileges for Pennsylvania, 1701, contained the same provision.[140]

(3) *The English Constitution.* This provision did not come from the common law. Such a rule was unknown to it. In treason and felony no witnesses were allowed to accused persons though witnesses were heard against them. Still later, the accused were allowed witnesses, but they could not be sworn before giving testimony. The result was that the government witnesses were believed by the jury rather than the witnesses for the defence.[141] In Throckmorton's case, 1554—a trial for

treason—John Fitzwilliams appeared as a witness for Throckmorton who insisted on his being heard in his defence, but
"John Fitzwilliams departed the court" (on being ordered to
do so) "and was not permitted to speak." In 1565 Sir Thomas
Smith gives an account of a capital trial in his Commonwealth
of England, but says nothing whatever of witnesses for the
accused. But in 1589, a statute provided that any person
charged with felony under the act should be permitted "to
make any lawful proof that he can, by lawful witness or otherwise, for his discharge and defence." [142] In 1590, Udal, on
being tried for felony, offered witnesses in his defence, but the
witnesses were told "that because their witness was against the
Queen's majesty, they could not be heard." [143] In 1606, the
English House of Commons, in opposition to the Crown, the
Lords, the practice of the English courts, and the express law
of Scotland, insisted on inserting a provision in the act abolishing hostility between England and Scotland, granting Englishmen the right to be defended by witnesses in trials held in the
Northern Counties for felonies committed in Scotland. Coke
in speaking of this law and 31 Eliz. says: "To say the truth,
we never read in any act of Parliament, ancient author, book
case, or record, that in criminal cases the party accused should
not have witnesses sworn for him; and therefore there is not
so much as scintilla juris against it." [144] Sir Matthew Hale,
however, states the actual practice: "Regularly, the evidence
for the prisoner in cases capital is given without oath."
From this rule, a departure occurred in 1632 in Tyndall's case
—a case of felony. Witnesses were heard in his defence, and
some of these were sworn. Gradually it became the practice
in capital cases for the witness to be heard on oath in behalf
of the accused. This was done in a series of cases. [145] But a
reversion occurred in 1679 in Whitebread's Case. Chief Justice Scroggs refused, saying that in no capital case could witnesses be sworn against the King. One of the accused persons
cited Coke, as above, on the law, but the Lord C. J. said:
"You argue against the known practice of all ages" and L. C.
J. North agreed, saying: "There was never any man in a
capital case sworn against the King." [146] But the Treason
Trials Act of 1695 provided that persons on trial for treason
had the right to make any proof that he or his counsel could

"produce by lawful witness or witnesses, who shall then be upon oath" for their defence. All persons indicted for treason were to "have the like process of the court . . . to compel their witnesses to appear for them at any such trial or trials as is usually granted to compel witnesses to appear against them."[147]   Then, an act of 1701 provided that all witnesses for prisoners on trial for treason or felony, shall before they give evidence take an oath "to depose the truth, the whole truth, and nothing but the truth in such manner as the witnesses for the Queen are by law obliged to do."[148]

5. "To Have the Assistance of Counsel for His Defence." The sources for this were:

(1) The ratifying state conventions. The Virginia Convention recommended a provision in its proposed bill of rights which allowed the criminal "counsel in his favor." North Carolina proposed an identical provision.[149]   Neither of their state constitutions contained the clause.

(2) The state constitutions. The constitution of Maryland, 1776, stated that accused persons were "to be allowed counsel." The New Jersey constitution stated that all criminals shall be admitted to the same privileges . . . of counsel as their prosecutors are entitled to." Massachusetts, 1780, and New Hampshire, 1784, used the same provision, while Pennsylvania and Vermont used what was an identical provision, though differing slightly from Massachusetts.[150]

(3) The charters. The Charter of Delaware and the Charter of Privileges for Pennsylvania, 1701, gave all criminals the same privileges of counsel as their prosecutors.[151]

(4) The English Constitution. Douglas Campbell tells us that though this principle was established in Delaware and Pennsylvania in 1701, and introduced into the Constitution of the United States in 1791, yet "it was not introduced into England until 1836, and then only after a bitter struggle extending over many years."[152]   This is partially correct, partially incorrect.

Originally, a person on trial for felony or treason in the English criminal courts was not allowed counsel.[153]   Hale in his Pleas of the Crown states the common law rule as follows: "Neither is counsel allowed to give evidence to the fact, nor in any case, unless matter of law doth arise" in cases capital or misprision of treason. Blackstone also states the law clearly: "It is a settled rule at common law, that no counsel shall be allowed a prisoner upon his trial, upon the general issue in any capital crime, unless some point of law shall arise to be debated." He condemns this as not being of a piece with the humane treatment of prisoners by the English law,[154] but he says, the judges are so sensible of the defect that they never scruple to allow counsel to a prisoner "to instruct him what questions to ask or even to ask questions for him with respect to *matters of fact;* for as to *matters of law,* arising in the trial, *they are entitled to the assistance of counsel."* [155] The Treason Trials Act of 1696 gave persons accused of treason and misprision of treason the right to be represented "by counsel learned in the law," who should "make their full defence" and "to whom such counsel shall have free access at all seasonable hours." In case an indicted person desired counsel, the judge was *required* immediately to assign counsel to such person "not exceeding two." [156] It was not, however, till 1836, after a bitter struggle, that Ewart succeeded in securing for prisoners indicted for felony the right to be defended by counsel, "which the cruelty of our jurisprudence," says Erskine May, "had hitherto denied them." [157] So, while the principle of allowing criminals to be defended by counsel became a part of English jurisprudence in 1696, it was not granted as a right in the case of all criminals till 1836. While, therefore, the principle was of English origin, America in the case of two charters, the state constitutions, and the Constitution of the United States had given it a wider application to criminal cases.

Amendment VII. Jury Trial in Civil Cases Guaranteed. The amendment divides itself into two parts:

1. *"In Suits at Common Law, Where the Value in Controversy Shall Exceed Twenty Dollars, the Right of Trial by Jury Shall be Preserved."* Some charged Americans with a glaring inconsistency in framing a constitution which failed to give the people a great right denied by the British King, and for which the colonists had revolted and fought—the right of trial by jury.[158] The amendment originated:

(1) *In the insistent objection that the Federal Constitution made no provision for a jury trial in civil cases.* Why did

the Convention omit a right for which Americans had shed their blood? On September 15 in the Federal Convention, Pinckney and Gerry, a signer of the Declaration of Independence, moved to annex to the end of Article III, Sec. II, of the Constitution, the clause, "and a trial by jury shall be preserved as usual in civil cases." Gorham immediately raised the objection that the constitution of juries was different in different states. King urged the same objection and General Pinckney declared the clause would result in embarrassments. The clause was, therefore, disagreed to nem con.[159] Spaight said in the North Carolina convention that the reason why the convention did not provide for a jury trial in civil cases was because "it was impossible to make a uniform regulation for all the states, or that would include all cases." [160] In some states, jury trials were used in equity and maritime cases, while in others they were not used. It would have involved these cases, if the Convention had made all cases triable by jury.[161] Such a vehement storm of protest arose against the omission that it had resulted in the proposal of the amendment to the states by Congress.

(2) *In the recommendations of the ratifying conventions.* The Massachusetts convention proposed what most resembled the amendment, so far as the language is concerned. "In civil actions between citizens of the different states, every issue of fact, arising in actions at common law, shall be tried by a jury, if the parties or either of them request it." Maryland recommended a similar provision. Virginia, North Carolina, and New Hampshire also provided for jury trial in civil cases.[161a]

(3) *The state constitutions.* The state constitutions secured the right of trial by jury in civil cases by using different language. Pennsylvania, 1776, for example, declared trial by jury "ought to be held sacred." North Carolina that it "ought to remain sacred and inviolable"; Georgia and New York that trial by jury "ought to remain inviolable forever." Massachusetts, New Hampshire, New Jersey, Vermont and Virginia all contained provisions guaranteeing the right in civil actions. The North West Ordinance of 1787 provided for "trial by jury and judicial proceedings according to the course of the common law." [162]

(4) *The English common law.* Justice Gray in the case of

Capital Traction Co. v. Hof said the jury required by the seventh amendment was a common law jury.[163]

2. *"No Fact Tried by Jury Shall be Otherwise Re-examined in Any Court of the United States Than According to the Rules of the Common Law."* This grew out of the objections urged against the want of any guarantee of a jury trial in civil cases in the Constitution. Patriotic alarmists like Patrick Henry declared emphatically that the Constitution introduced and established the civil law, and set aside or "left the common law altogether." In the Pennsylvania convention, Smilie said the Federal convention intended to give up trial by jury in civil cases, and to introduce the civil law instead. Wilson indignantly denied this,[164] and quoted Blackstone to disprove Smilie's assertion "that appeals are unknown to the common law; that the term is a civil law term, and with it the civil law is intended to be introduced." He showed that Blackstone in his chapter entitled "Of Proceeding in the Nature of Appeals," points out that the principal method of redress for erroneous judgments in the King's courts of record was by writ of error to some superior "court of appeal." This refuted the assertion that appeals were unknown to the common law.[165] The enemies of the Constitution had much insisted on this objection, and by inserting this second clause in the amendment, it destroyed the force of the objection, for facts were to be re-examined in United States Courts by the rules of the common law only. The civil law was entirely excluded.

Hamilton in number 81 of the Federalist made a suggestion which, through Madison, found its way in principle into this amendment. He said that no general rule could be fixed upon by the Convention which would suit all the states. He suggested that Congress had power to provide that in appeals to the Supreme Court there should be no re-examination of facts where they had been originally tried by juries. If this should, however, be "thought too extensive, it might be qualified with a limitation to such causes only as are determinable at common law in that mode of trial." Madison acted on this suggestion by proposing on June 8, 1789, to amend the Constitution by adding to the clause dealing with the appellate jurisdiction of the Court, the words: "nor shall any fact, triable by a jury, according to the course of the common law, be otherwise re-examinable than according to the principles of the common law." That is, upon a *new trial only*, either granted by the trial court or ordered by an appellate court for error in law. (Capital Traction Co. v. Hof, 174 U. S. 1.)

Amendment VIII. Excessive Bail, Excessive. Fines, and Infliction of Cruel and Unusual Punishment Prohibited. Precedents for this are to be found:

(1) *In the proposals of the ratifying conventions.* The Virginia convention urged the adoption of such a provision in a bill of rights. North Carolina recommended the adoption of the same clause, and New York included it among the rights which "cannot be abridged or violated." [166]

(2) *The state constitutions.* The constitutions of Virginia, North Carolina, Maryland and Pennsylvania, 1776, Georgia and Vermont, 1777, Massachusetts, 1780, and New Hampshire, 1784, all contained the provision. [167]

(3) *The English Constitution.* By the common law, it was an offence against the liberty of the subject for any magistrate to delay or refuse to admit to bail any person charged with a bailable offence. It was also a violation of the statute law of England. Section twenty of Magna Carta provided that excessive fines should not be imposed. The Statute of Westminster the First, 1275, made it an offense for sheriffs to refuse to set persons free who were charged with bailable offenses. Heavy penalties were provided in such cases. [168] In the reign of Henry VI, 1444, the English Parliament passed an act requiring that "Sheriffs and other officers shall let out of Prison all Manner of Persons upon reasonable sureties of sufficient Persons." The Habeas Corpus Act of 1679 required persons imprisoned for bailable offenses to be set free on bail, so that the King's subjects could no longer be "detained in prison in such cases where by law they are bailable." [169] However, one of the defects of the Act was that it placed no limit on the amount of bail which the judge might demand. He was left free to fix the bail in any sum according to his discretion. By demanding unreasonable bail for the prisoner's appearance, the law was easily evaded. "And lest the intention of the law should be frustrated by the justices requiring bail to a greater amount than the nature of the case demands, it is expressly declared by Statute, 1 W. & M. St. 2, c. 1, that excessive

bail ought not to be required." [170] The real origin of the clause was, therefore, the English Bill of Rights.[171] The Stuart Kings had committed many grievous wrongs against, and inflicted severe punishments on the people. Illegal imprisonment was common. Therefore, when the Revolution of 1688 came, and the Convention Parliament undertook to confer the crown on William and Mary, they determined to adopt safeguards which would forever prevent the English sovereign from violating the constitution by committing outrages against the liberties of the people. A committee, of which Somers was chairman, was appointed. It drew up the Declaration of Right which recited the violations of "the laws and liberties" of England by James II, and then stated the constitutional principles which he had disregarded. This declaration, accepted by William and Mary, was passed as an act of Parliament, known as the Bill of Rights. Among the constitutional principles enacted as the law of the land was the eighth amendment to the Constitution of the United States: "That excessive bail ought not to be required, nor excessive fines imposed, nor cruel and unusual punishments inflicted." [172]

Amendment IX. This amendment grew out of Hamilton's defence of the Constitution against the objection that it contained no bill of rights. He met the objection by saying, amongst other things, that a bill of rights would not only be unnecessary because the people surrender nothing and retain everything, but even dangerous because such a bill "would contain various exceptions to powers not granted; and on this very account would afford a colorable pretext to claim more than were granted." [173] On June 8, 1798, Madison said in Congress: "It has been objected against a bill of rights that by enumerating particular exceptions to the grant of power, it would disparage those rights which were not placed in that enumeration, and it might follow by implication, that those rights which were not singled out, were intended to be assigned into the hands of the General Government, and were consequently insecure." [174] Madison declared, he had attempted to guard against this. That is, the purpose of introducing this amendment was to guard against the very danger which had been pointed out by Hamilton in number 84 of the Federalist. As first introduced by Madison this purpose is clearly seen. It read: "The exceptions here or elsewhere in the Constitution, made in favor of particular rights shall not be construed as to diminish the just importance of other rights retained by the people, or as to enlarge the powers delegated by the Constitution; but either as actual limitations of such powers, or as inserted for greater caution." The committee of eleven changed it to read as in the constitution, except that the words "deny or" between "to" and "disparage" added by the special committee of three were omitted.[175]

Amendment X. "In this article," said Jefferson Davis, "provision was deliberately made for the secession of a part of the States from the Union." Was this the purpose of the amendment? Judge Cooley says, the Union possessed the powers enumerated in the Constitution. "But lest there might be any possible question of this in the minds of those wielding any portion of this authority, it was declared by the tenth article of the amendments that "The powers . . . people."[176] Chief Justice Marshall said it was framed for the purpose of quieting the excessive jealousies which had been excited.[177] The purpose was, then, to safeguard the reserved rights of the states, and mark the line between the powers of the states and those of the United States.

The precedents for the amendment were found:

(1) *In the state ratifying conventions.* Massachusetts, on February 7, 1788, proposed among the amendments to the Constitution, "I. That it be explicitly declared that all powers not expressly delegated by the aforesaid Constitution are reserved to the several states, to be by them exercised."[178] Next, South Carolina on May 23, declared "that no section or paragraph of the said Constitution warrants a construction that the states do not retain every power not expressly relinquished by them, and vested in the general government of the Union."[179] On June 21, New Hampshire recommended the proposed amendment of Massachusetts, except that the words "and particularly" were inserted after "expressly."[180] On June 27, Virginia recommended a somewhat similar amendment. On the 26th of July, New York followed the Virginia convention in recommending an almost identical proposition.[180] On April 28, Maryland had proposed the simple proposition: "That Congress shall exercise no power but what is expressly dele-

gated by this Constitution." On August 1, North Carolina proposed the adoption of the same amendment as Virginia. Governor Randolph proposed on June 21 in the Virginia convention to put in the ratification these words: "And that all authority not given is retained by the people, and that it may be resumed when perverted to their oppression." [181] In the form of ratification reported by Governor Randolph on June 25, it was declared "that every power not granted thereby remains with them, and at their will." [182] That is, remains with the people.

(2) *The state constitutions.* Pennsylvania made the declaration of rights a part of the state constitution never to be violated on any pretence whatever. The constitution of Massachusetts, 1780, declared: "The people of this commonwealth have the sole and exclusive right of governing themselves as free, sovereign, and independent state, and do and forever hereafter shall exercise and enjoy every power, jurisdiction, and right which is not, or may not hereafter be, by them expressly delegated to the United States of America in Congress assembled." [183] The constitution of New Hampshire, 1784, adopted the Massachusetts provision, except that it used "state" for "commonwealth," and added "pertaining thereto," after the word "right." [184]

(3) *The Articles of Confederation.* The state conventions simply followed the phraseology of Article II, Articles of Confederation, in their proposed amendments, while the constitutions of Massachusetts and New Hampshire merely adopt and repeat the words of Article II. Samuel Adams said of the proposed amendment in the Massachusetts convention: "It is consonant with the second article in the present Confederation." [185] Spencer said in the North Carolina convention, if the Confederation clause had been inserted in the Constitution, there would have been no need for a bill of rights, and it ought to be inserted to secure the rights of individuals. North Carolina, therefore, proposed such an amendment taken word for word from the Articles of Confederation. [186]

(4) *The English Constitution.* There seems to have been a clear and well defined belief among American statesmen that the doctrine of reserved powers was of British origin and a maxim of the British Constitution. In the address to the

Inhabitants of the United Colonies of New Hampshire, Massachusetts, etc. from their Delegates in Congress, February 13, 1776, Congress declares: "That all power was originally in the people—that all the powers of government are derived from them—that all power, which they have not disposed of still continues theirs—are maxims of the English Constitution, which we presume will not be disputed." [187]   Thus, the whole American Congress declared the doctrine of reserved powers a maxim of the British Constitution, which was so generally accepted that no one would think of disputing it.

Richard Henry Lee in a letter to Governor Edmund Randolph, of Virginia, October 16, 1787, objected that the Constitution contained "no restraint in the form of a bill of rights, to secure (what Doctor Blackstone calls) *that residuum of human rights* which is not intended to be given up to society, and which, indeed, is not necessary to be given for any social purpose." [188]   Lee's reference is to Blackstone's Commentaries where he speaks of Magna Carta, Confirmatio Cartarum, the Petition of Right, the Bill of Rights, and Act of Settlement as "the declaration of our rights and liberties," which consist either in "that residuum of natural liberty which is not required by the laws of society to be sacrificed to public convenience," or those civil privileges which society hath engaged to provide in lieu of the natural liberties so given up by individuals.[189] Blackstone is quoted, then as an authority on and as a source of the doctrine of reserved rights.

Samuel Adams seems to refer to Blackstone in the Rights of the Colonies, 1772. "Every natural Right," he says, "not expressly given up, or from the Nature of a Social Compact necessarily ceded remains." He refers to Blackstone on the subject, attributes reserved rights to the British Constitution, and mentions the natural rights which no man or body of men can for themselves give up, or take away from others.[190] "These are some of the first principles of natural law and justice, and some of the great Barriers of all free States, and the British Constitution in particular," he says. In stating these rights, Adams quotes the words of John Locke. The Declaration of Independence also lays down the doctrine of reserved rights. Men are endowed by their Creator with "certain unalienable rights." In Book II, Chap. XI, Two Treatises on Civil Government, Locke teaches that there are certain rights men cannot give up to government. They cannot be conveyed by compact. They are unalienable rights, though Locke does not use this phrase in Chapter XI. There are certain rights that must be reserved—*reserved rights*. The Declaration of Independence also lays down that there are certain rights men cannot transfer to the control of the government—*reserved rights*. The Declaration of Rights hold back these rights, as did the great English constitutional documents which declared the rights reserved to the people.[191] Then, again, John Lilburne in his Agreement of the People, 1647, expressly reserved certain rights to the people.[192] The Agreement of the People expressly declared "the rights which the nation, reserved to itself, and which no authority might touch with impunity." The power of the government extended only to what was not expressly or impliedly reserved to the people.[193]

NOTES TO CHAPTER XVII

1. Ames, Amendments, 19; Const. Hist. U. S. II, 198; Farrand, Records, III, 489; 7 Pet. 243.
2. Elliot, II, 532; III, 657; IV, 243, 337; 176 U. S. 606.
3. Elliot, II, 452, 453; Federalist, no. 84.
4. Elliot, III, 413, 414.
5. Annals of Cong. I, 258-9.
6. Id. 431; Life and Work of Ames, I, 52.
7. Annals of Cong. I, 432, 445, 727, 436, 704.
8. Howison, Hist. of Va. II, 149.
9. Journal Va. House of Delegates, 1776, 27-28.
10. Id. 35.
11. Journal, House of Delegates, 1776, 35.
12. Journal, House of Delegates, 1776, p. 40, 46.
13. Journal, Va. House of Delegates, 1776, pp. 64, 63-64, 28, 32, 35, 40, 46, 64, 65.
14. Works, I, 32.
15. Journal, Va. House of Delegates, 1776, p. 106, 108, 110; Hening, Statutes, Vol. 9, p. 164. Howison, Hist. of Va. II, 190-194.
16. Semple, Va. Baptists, App.
17. Hening, Statutes at Large, Vol. 12, p. 86. 98 U. S. 145, McClain, Cases, 884.
18. Elliot, IV, 244, III, 659, II, 553; Doc. Hist. II, 143; 98 U. S. 145 seq.; McClain, Cases on Const. Law, p. 884.
19. Poore, Charters, 1909, 1410, 1413, 1541, 277,' 1868, 383, 957, 1281, 1868.
20. Id. 1596, 1597; Annals of Cong. I, 730.
21. N. Y. Col. Docs. III, 218.
22. Poore, Charters, 1526, 950, 271, 1537, 375.

23. Blackstone, Com. IV, 55.

24. Elliot, IV, 193.

25. Elliot, III, 659; Elliot, IV, 244; Annals of Cong. I, 447.

26. Elliot, II, 552.

27. Id. V, 445; Farrand, Records, III, 609; Article 43.

28. Poore, Charters, 820, 1410, 1542, 1547, 1909, 1860, 383, 1627, 959, 1282, 1283, 1869.

29. Prothero, Statutes, 168-172, 188-189; Medley, Const. Hist. of Eng. May, Const. Hist. of Eng. II, ch. IX; Blackstone Com. Vol. IV, p. 189 note (Hammond ed.).

30. Mass. Rep. 20 (3 Pick.) 313-314; 205 U. S. 454.

31. McClain, Cases, 34, 35; 92 U. S. 542.

32. Elliot, III, 658-9; IV, 244; II, 553.

33. Elliot, III, 657; IV, 240.

34. Poore, Charters, 1542, 1410, 959, 1283, 1869, 1860, 818.

35. Journal, Va. House of Burgesses under date; MacDonald, Sel. Charters; Journal of Cong. under date.

36. 13 Car. II, 1 c, 5; Adams and Stephens, Sel. Docs. 464.

37. Com. I, 152.

38. Cooley, Const. Law, Ch. XIV, sec. IV; Robertson v. Baldwin, 165 U. S. 275; Hall, Cases, 155; U. S. v. Cruickshank, 92 U. S. 542; 116 U. S. 252; 35 Tex. 473.

39. Elliot, IV, 244; III, 659.

40. Poore, Charters, 1410, 1542, 1909, 959, 1860, 1869.

40. Adams & Stephens, Sel. Docs. 23, 79, 465; Blackstone, Com. I, 154. Elliot, III, 659; IV, 244; II, 552.

41. Elliot, V, 445.

42. Poore, Charters, 1283, 959, 1331, 819; Cong. Register, 2nd Lloyd, 223-4.

43. Adams, Writings, II (Cushing) 362. See the Quartering Acts in MacDonald, Sel. Charters.

44. Cooley, Const. Law. Ch. XIII, Sec. II.

45. Colonial Laws of N. Y. Vol. IV, 123.

46. Col. Laws of N. Y. Vol. IV, 191, Dec. 16, 1758; Dec. 24, 1759, V, 24, etc.

47. Laws of N. Y. Vol. I, 59-60, 134.

48. Amendment IV.

49. Medley, Eng. Const. Hist. 480; Taswell-Langmead, 434.

50. Adams & Stephens, Sel. Docs. 340, 341.

51. Statutes at Large, Vol. 8, 432, or 31 Car 2, c. 1; McClain, Cases, 312. McKechnie, Magna Carta, 333. Pollock, I, 252, 267.

52. Elliot, III, 658; II, 551; IV, 244.

53. Elliot, II, 551.

54. Poore, 1868, 1860, 1282, 959, 1542, 819, 1909, 1409.

55. Blackstone, Com. IV, 351; Md. Const. Decl. of Rights, XXII; Poore, 819.

56. See Quincy, Mass. Rep. app.

57. Quincy, Mass. Rep. app. 532, 1. Hale, P. C. 580, 2 Hale 113, 114, 150. 2 Hawk, c. 13, 10.

58. Writings (Cushing) II, 361. McClain, Cases, 887, 888.

59. 19 St. Tr. 1068; Medley, Const. Hist. 447; May, Const. Hist. II, ch. XI, 251.

60. Pleas of the Crown, II, 150, 111, 112, 114; II, 577, 580; 4 Inst. 176, 177, 591.

61. Hawkins, Pleas of the Crown, II, 133, Ch. XIII, sec. 17.
62. Hawkins, Pleas of the Crown, II, 130 (Curwood Ed.). Quincy, Mass Rep. App. Justice Bradley in Boyd v. U. S. said Coke denied the legality of general warrants. 116 U. S. 628. This was English Common law.
63. Blackstone, Com. IV, 351.
64. 19 St. Tr. 1067; May, Const. Hist. II, Ch. XI. Medley, Const. Hist. 448.
65. 19 St. Tr. 1027.
66. May, Const. Hist. II, ch. XI, p. 250.
67. 19 St. Tr. 1066, 1067, 1068.
68. 19 St. Tr. 919.
69. 19 St. Tr. 1075; Jour. Com. Apr. 25, 1766; Parl. Hist. XV, 1393-1418, XVI, 6, 209.
70. Cooley, Const. Law (Second Ed.) 220.
71. 116 U. S. 630 seq.
72. Elliot, II, 177, 122, 123, 130-132, 138, 141, 162.
73. Annals of Cong. I, 452.
74. Annals of Cong. 435, 760.
75. Poore, 1409.
76. 114 U. S. 423.
77. Blackstone, Com. IV, 302; Stephen, Criminal Law, I, 254.
78. Blackstone, Com. IV, 309, 310.
79. Adams and Stephens, Sel. Docs. 12, 14, 15, 20, 21.
80. 25 Ed. III, c. 4; Stat. at Large, II, 53 (1350).
81. Ex Parte Wilson, 114 U. S. 417.
82. Journals of Cong. Sept. 20, 1778, Art. VI.
83. Elliot, II, 550.
84. Poore, 1282.
85. Sec. 42, MacDonald, Sel. Charters, 80; Poore, 1404; MacDonald, Sel. Ch. 160, 1524, 1534.
86. 18 Johnson (N. Y.) 200.
87. 18 Wall. 168, 169.
88. Blackstone, Com. IV, 335, 259, 349; 25 Ed. III, St. 5, c. 4.
89. Blackstone, Com. IV, 315.
90. Hawkins, Pleas of the Crown, II, ch. 35, 315-316; Hale, P. C. II, ch. 31.
91. Coxe, Judicial Power and Unconstitutional Legislation, 138. The Habeas Corpus Act provided that a person once delivered should not be recommitted for the same offence.
92. 18 Johnson (N. Y.) 200, 202.
93. Elliot, III, 658; IV, 243.
94. Poore, 1909, 1409, 818, 1542, 1860, 1868, 958, 1282; 211 U. S. 78; Evan's Cases, 115.
95. Cooley, Const. Law, Ch. XV, Sec. VI.
96. Justice Brown in Brown v. Walker, 161 U. S. 591; McClain, Cases on Constitutional Law, 991, 992.
97. 116 U. S. 631, 632.
98. Elliot, III, 658; IV, 243.
99. Poore, 1860, 1868, 1282.
100. Poore, 958, 1627, 818, 1410, 1542, 1909. Art. 2.
101. 28 Ed. III, c. 3, or Stat. at Large, Vol. II, 97; 37 Ed. III, c. 18 (Vol. I, 167).
102. 25 Ed. III, c. 4; 42 Ed. III, c. 3.

103. 3 St. Tr. 152; 2 Inst. 45, 46, 50; 18 N. Y. 416, 445; 11 Mich. 129; 18 Howard 276; McClain, Cases, 897.

104. Hale, Hist. Com. Law. 128. 18 N. Y. 445.

105. 18 N. Y. 445; 11 Mich. 129; 5 R. I. Rep. 506; 18 N. Y. 416; McClain, Cases, 896, 897; 18 Howard 276.

106. 110 U. S. 516; McClain, Cases, 907; Com. IV, 424; Pet. of Right 1628, sec. III.

107. McClain, Cases, 897; 18 Howard, 272, seq.

108. Cooley, Const. Law, Ch. XIII, sec. 4; 12 N. Y. 212; Magna Carta, 377. 4 Wheat, 508. Due process involves (1) notice (2) opportunity to defend (3) the right to counsel and witnesses for defence, Twining v. N. J. 211 U. S. 78.

109. Poore, 1541, 1859, 1868; 91 U. S. 367.

110. Poore, 958; Arts. 10, 12.

111. Mass. Body of Liberties, sec. 8; MacDonald, Sel. Charters, 75.

112. Com. I, 148, 149; IV, 139.

113. Const. of N. Y. 1777, sec. 35; Id. 1821, sec. 7; 206 N. Y. 289.

114. Grotius, Rights of War and Peace, Bk. III, c. 20, 27.

115. Elliot, III, 658; Elliot, IV, 243; Elliot, II, 550.

116. Poore, 818, 1909, 1541, 958, 959, 1282, 1860, 1868; Elliot, II, 550.

117. Decl. of Indep.

118. 38 Hen. VIII. Samuel Adams, Writings (Cushing), II, 367.

119. Journals, I, 64.

120. Stamp Act. sec. 112; Works, II, 366 (Cushing).

121. Journals of Cong. I, 64.

122. Elliot, I, 44; Journals, I, 53.

123. Am. Hist. Leaflets, no. 11, 12; Caldwell, Am. Hist. Studies, no. 3.

124. Wm. MacDonald, Sel. Charters, 315; Maxwell v. Dow, 176 U. S. 609.

125. Cooley, Const. Law, Ch. XV, sec. VI.

126. Justice Peckham, Maxwell v. Dow, 176, U. S. 586.

127. Blackstone, Com. IV, 350; III, 379.

128. 176 U. S. 610, 611; McKechnie, Magna Carta, 134-5, 392-3.

129. Elliot, III, 658; IV, 243.

130. Poore, 1909, 1409, 1541, 1860, 1868, 818.

131. 56 Fed. Rep. 88, 89, 90.

132. 7 Wm. III, c. 3; 7 Ann c. 21. See also Blackstone, IV, 352.

133. Elliot, III, 658; IV, 243.

134. Poore, 1909, 818, 1542, 1860, 1868, 958, 1282; Annals, I, 452, 782, 785.

135. Journals of Cong. I, 57.

136. Hawkins, Pleas of the Crown, II, 590; 5 & 6 Ed. VI, c. 11.

137. Foster, Crown Law, 258; 1 Howell, St. Tr. 1281.

138. Elliot, III, 658; IV, 243.

139. Poore, 1909, 1542, 1860, 1868, 818, 1313, 1282, 1409, 958.

140. Poore, 272, 1538.

141. Thayer, A Preliminary Treatise on Evidence at Common Law, 157.

142. 1 Howell, St. Tr. 884, 885; Thayer, Evid. at Com. Law, 157, note 4. 31 Eliz. c. 4, a 2.

143. 1 Howell, St. Tr. 1281.

144. 4 Jac. 1, c. 1, a 2; Blackstone, Com. IV, 360.

145. Hale, P. C. II, 283; Thayer, Evidence, 160; note; Laud's Case, 4 How. St. Tr. 342; Love's Case, 5 Howell, 136, Vane's Case and others, How. 6, 152; 3 How., 1428.

146. 7 Howell, St. Tr. 359.

147. 7 & 8, W. III, c. 3, §§ 1, 7.

148. Ann. Stat. 2; c. 9, a 3.
149. Elliot, III, 658; IV, 243.
150. Poore, 818, 1313, 958, 1282, 1541, 1860, 1868.
151. Poore, 272, 1538.
152. Papers of the Am. Hist. Association, V, 170.
153. McClain, Const. Law, 327.
154. P. C. II, 253; Com. IV, 355.
155. Com. IV, 356.
156. 7 & 8 W. III, c. 3, a 1.
157. Erskine May, Const. Hist. of Eng., Vol. II, ch. XVIII, 558.
158. Elliot, II, 113; IV, 143.
159. Elliot, II, 110, 111, 113, 515; III, 537, 540, 541, 546, 557, 558; IV, 143, 150, 154, 155.
160. Elliot, V, 550.
161. Elliot, IV, 144, 145. See also Chas. Pinckney, IV, 260; Farrand, III, 250.
161ª. Elliot, II, 177, 550; III, 658; IV, 243; Doc. Hist. II, 143.
162. Poore, 1542, 1410, 383, 959, 1282, 1313, 1860, 1869, 1909; Art. II.
163. 174 U. S. 38, 39; 170 U. S. 343.
164. Elliot, II, 515, 518; III, 540.
165. Elliot, II, 518, 519; Blackstone, Com. III, 406.
166. Elliot, III, 658; IV, 244; I, 328, 329.
167. Poore, 1909, 1409, 818, 1546, 383, 1864, 959, 1283.
168. Adams and Stephens, Sel. Docs. 45; 3 Ed. I, c. 15; Blackstone, Com. IV, 297.
169. Cobbett, Parliamentary Hist. V, 110; 31 Car. II, c. 2; Adams and Stephens, Sel. Docs. 440.
170. Adams and Stephens, 442; Blackstone, Com. IV, 297; I, 135.
171. 136 U. S. 446; 119 N. Y. 576.
172. H. D. Traill, William III, ch. V; I. W. & M., secs. 2, c. 2, or Adams and Stephens, Sel. Docs. 462. 119 N. Y. 576; 136 U. S. 446.
173. Federalist, No. 84.
174. Annals of Cong. I, 439.
175. Annals, I, 452; Thorpe, Const. Hist. of U. S. II, 226, 258.
176. Rise and Fall of Confed. Government, I, 100; Cooley, Const. Law, ch. II, 29.
177. 4 Wheat, 406, McCulloch v. Maryland.
178. Elliot, I, 322; II, 177; see same by John Hancock, II, 122, 123, 131.
179. Elliot, I, 325.
180. Elliot, I, 326, 327; III, 659.
181. Elliot, II, 550; IV, 244; III, 576.
182. Elliot, III, 656.
183. Poore, 1548, 958.
184. Poore, 1281.
185. Elliot, III, 661; IV, 244, 249; II, 550; I, 326, 327; Poore, 958, 1281.
186. Elliot, IV, 152, 163, 249.
187. Journals of Cong. (Ford Ed.) IV, 135.
188. Elliot, I, 503.
189. Blackstone, Com. I, 129.
190. Works, II (Cushing ed.) 352, 355.
191. Decl. of Indep. preamble, Elliot, IV, 151.
192. Roger Foster, Constitution, 49-50.
193. Borgeoud, Adoption and Amendment of Constits. p. 6.

CHAPTER XVIII

The Amendments: Eleven to Fifteen

The eleventh amendment was adopted for the purpose of overruling or reversing a decision of the Supreme Court of the United States in the case of Chisholm v. Georgia in 1793. Alexander Chisholm, a citizen of North Carolina, sued the state of Georgia, and when Justice Wilson said: "The action lies," and Chief Justice Jay said: "It is plain, then, that a state may be sued,"[1] the whole country was alarmed because the states regarded the decision as a denial of their sovereignty, and a violation of the legal rule that a sovereign (state) could not be sued without his consent. The decision "created such a shock of surprise throughout the country that at the first meeting of Congress thereafter the Eleventh Amendment to the Constitution was almost unanimously adopted and was in due course ratified by the legislatures of the states."[2]

On February 20, 1793, a motion was made in the Senate to adopt a resolution proposing an amendment to the Constitution of the United States which read: "The judicial power of the United States shall not extend to any suits in law or equity, commenced or prosecuted against one of the United States by citizens of another state, or by citizens or subjects of any foreign state."[3] On January 2, 1794, the amendment was taken up again. It read as it now stands in the Constitution. It was debated on January 13, and adopted by a vote of twenty-three to two in the Senate.[4]

The House considered the resolution in Committee of the Whole on March the fourth and passed it by a vote of 89 to 9. After its introduction on February 20, 1793, the only change in the phraseology was made by inserting the words "be construed to" before "extend" on January 2, 1794.

Its effect was to reverse or set aside the decision of the Supreme Court in Chisholm v. Georgia.[5]

It is quite possible that the Convention of 1787 never intended Article III, Section 2, clause 1 of the Constitution of

326

the United States: "The judicial power shall extend to controversies—between a state and citizens of different states"—
to mean that a sovereign state could be sued without its consent by a citizen of another state. This, at least, was John Marshall's idea when he said: "It is not rational to suppose that the
sovereign power should be dragged before a court. The intent
is, to enable the states to recover claims of individuals resid-
ing in other states." [6]   James Madison was in a position to
know and his statement is entitled to great weight. "It is not
in the power of individuals to call any state into court," he
said. "The only operation it can have is that if a state should
wish to bring a suit against a citizen, it must be brought before
the Federal court." [7]   Hamilton in No. 81 of the Federalist
presented the same view. Since "the suability of a state without its consent was a thing unknown to the law," it is very
doubtful if the framers of the Constitution ever intended the
clause to be given the literal interpretation given it by the
Supreme Court in Chisholm v. Georgia. In fact, the Supreme
Court itself has said that, looking at the subject from the
point of view of history and experience, the views of Hamilton, Madison, Iredell, and Marshall were clearly right.[8]

The precedent for the amendment was found in the third
amendment proposed by the ratifying convention of Rhode
Island on May 23, 1790, and transmitted to Congress on June
16, 1790, which read: "It is declared by the Convention that
the judicial power of the United States, in cases in which
a State may be a party, does not extend to authorize any
suit by any person against a State." [9]

Ratification by the required number of states was announced
on January 8, 1798, by President Adams.

Amendment XII. This amendment was the result, indirectly, of the election of 1796, and directly of the election of
1800. The first resulted in the election of a Federalist President—Adams—and a Republican Vice-President—Jefferson.
The second resulted in the crooked scheme to elect Jefferson as
Vice-President instead of President, and Burr President instead
of Vice-President, when it was found that they had each received an equal number of votes—seventy-three. Only after
thirty-six ballots extending over the period from February 11
to February 17 had been taken, was Jefferson elected.[10]   Both

Federalists and Republicans saw the necessity for amending the Constitution in order to prevent the recurrence of the scandal of 1800-1801. This could be done by requiring the electors to designate the person who was to be President, and the person who was to be Vice-President in separate ballots. The amendment, then, was designed to prevent the evils that occurred at the last Presidential election.[11]

On January 6, 1797, soon after the election of 1796, William Smith of South Carolina proposed in the House of Representatives a resolution to amend the Constitution providing for the election of President and Vice-President. The alteration required the electors to designate the persons intended for President and Vice-President respectively. The reasons given for the change were: (1) The discovery that great inconvenience might arise from the existing method. (2) The real intention of the electors could not always be carried into effect by it.[12]

Many attempts were made to secure an amendment on the subject, including two by Vermont and North Carolina, but all failed. Finally, on October 21, 1803, Dewitt Clinton of New York offered a resolution in the Senate for the purpose of settling the vexed question of the election of the President and Vice-President.[13] It proposed to expunge Art. II, Sec. 1, cl. 3, of the Constitution, and insert a new paragraph which became Amendment XII. The number from which the House was to choose the President was at first left blank. Senator Smith moved to fill the blank with "three highest" which was carried by a vote of 18 to 13. The question of filling the blank with five or three was reconsidered on the 29th, and three again adopted by a vote of 21 to 10. The purpose of inserting *three instead of five*, as in the original clause, was to prevent a man of a small electoral vote from being elected President or Vice-President over men with a large electoral vote. John Jay, it was pointed out, might be elected over Adams with sixty-five electoral votes, or over Jefferson with seventy-three, although he had only one electoral vote.[14]

It was also said in Congress that *the people wished for* three. On November 24, Bradley moved to amend by inserting "the Senate shall choose the Vice-President from the two highest on the list," and also that "in choosing the President, the votes shall be taken by States, the Representatives from each State having one vote." In the meantime, the House had been considering an amendment in Committee of the Whole on October 24 and October 28, but nothing was done, though Amendments were suggested by Messrs. Clay and Clapton.[15]

On December 1, 1803, Pickering offered an amendment as follows: "But if within twenty-four hours no election shall have taken place, then the President shall be chosen by law." This was offered as a remedy to avoid civil war, which had been threatened in debate. Senator Tracy asked, "What does 'by law' mean?" and Pickering replied: "The States might choose by lot, or by ballots in a box, or a number of names might be put in a box from which the Speaker might draw one." "Suppose," said Senator Smith, "they were to throw the dice for the Executive Chair? It would be equally wise with any of the expedients offered, and the candidate's names might be written, and the highest throw have it." [16]

On December 2, 1803, the question was put and carried in the Senate by a vote of 22 to 10, and it was ordered that the Secretary request the concurrence of the House. The House considered the subject on December 7, 1803, and was inclined to be rebellious. Many amendments were suggested—one proposing to insert "five" for "three highest" was negatived by 85 to 22 votes. On December 8, after a long, tedious, dreary debate in which the participants mostly had nothing to say, but insisted on saying it, the House agreed to the Senate resolution by a vote of 42 to 42. The amendment was then sent down to the states, after having been given to the country by the casting vote of Nathaniel Macon, the Speaker.[17] It became part of the Constitution on September 25, 1804.[18]

The *objections* urged during debate against the amendment by opponents were:

(1) *The principle of designation introduced would enable the large states to combine and four and a half states could elect the President against the will of the remaining twelve and a half states.* It would undermine the Confederacy, Thatcher declared, by throwing the whole power of election into the hands of a few states exclusively. This would place the small states in jeopardy, and men there would have about as many rights as the Helots of Greece.[19] The principle of voting by

states and the fact that a majority of states was made necessary to a choice obviated this objection. Rivalry and jealousy between large and small states was very prominent in debate.[20]

(2) *The amendment would render the Vice-President less respectable.* He will not need the qualifications requisite for supreme command, and the result will be that a man of moderate talents who will help to elect the President will be chosen.[21]

(3) *The danger of making innovations in the Constitution.* The great *object* of the amendment ought to be to prevent the person voted for by the electors as Vice-President becoming President, said Sanford.[22] It was declared in debate that the object was to prevent the election of a Federal Vice-President, and it was frankly acknowledged that would be the effect.[23] Smith, however, said the real effects would be (1) to guard against the dangers of intrigue and corruption; and (2) to place the choice in the power of the people, by securing to the majority the selection of the Chief Magistrate.[24]

Amendment XIII. 1. *The Legislative History of the Thirteenth Amendment.* On December 14, 1863, James M. Ashley of Ohio introduced a bill in the House of Representatives "to provide for the submission to the several states, of a proposition to amend the National Constitution prohibiting slavery, or involuntary servitude, in all the States and Territories now owned or which may be hereafter acquired by the United States." [25] On the same date, Wilson of Iowa offered a joint resolution in the House, providing that an amendment be submitted to the legislatures of the states as follows:

"Section 1. Slavery being incompatible with a free government, is forever prohibited in the United States; and involuntary servitude shall be permitted only as a punishment for crime.

"Section 2. Congress shall have power to enforce the foregoing section of this article by appropriate legislation." [26]

Both were referred to the Judiciary Committee, but before the Committee reported, Senator Henderson on January 11, 1864, asked, and by unanimous consent obtained leave to introduce a joint resolution (S. No. 16) proposing an amendment to the Constitution of the United States, which was read twice by its title and referred to the Committee on Judiciary. It read:

"Art. 1. Slavery or involuntary servitude, except as a punishment for crime, shall not exist in the United States."

On February 8, 1864, Senator Sumner proposed in the Senate the following joint resolution as an amendment: "Article——. Everywhere within the limits of the United States, and of each State or territory thereof, all persons are equal before the law, so that no person can hold another as a slave." This was suggested by the first French constitution, and after discussion was also referred to the Judiciary Committee,[27] which reported two days later through Senator Trumbull, the chairman. The committee had amended Senator Henderson's resolution so as to read:

"ARTICLE XIII

Sec. 1. Neither slavery nor involuntary servitude, except as a punishment for crime, whereof the party shall have been duly convicted, shall exist within the United States, or any place subject to their jurisdiction.

Sec. 2. Congress shall have power to enforce this article by appropriate legislation."[28]

On March 3, 1864, Senator Davis proposed to amend the amendment of the Judiciary Committee by inserting in lieu:

"That no negro, or person whose mother or grandmother is or was a negro, shall be a citizen of the United States, or be eligible to any civil or military office, or to any place of trust or profit under the United States."

The Davis amendment was voted down by a vote of 28 to 6.[29]

The amendment as it came from the Senate judiciary committee contained the clause "or any place subject to their jurisdiction." Why was this inserted? Senator Henderson simply used the words "United States," because he knew that Congress had power to abolish slavery in the territories where states had not been formed, and which were subject to the jurisdiction of Congress. The Senate Judiciary Committee, however, knew that was a disputed constitutional question, and resolved to take no chances on the subject of constitutional interpretation. They very cautiously added the clause covering not merely the United States, but all places under control of American sovereignty. Senator Trumbull, chairman of the Judiciary Committee, made this clear on February 17, when he said the committee had "proposed an amendment to the Constitution of the United States, so as to prohibit slavery throughout the United States and in all places within its jurisdiction." [30] This covered the territories and the District of Columbia, as well as the United States, and left no room for cavilling. This same purpose is clearly evident in the resolutions offered by Senator Sumner and Thaddeus Stevens. The former employed the language: "Everywhere within the limits of the United States or Territories thereof." Stevens used the words "in the United States and all its Territories." [31] This shows clearly that Senator Trumbull's words, "or any place subject to their jurisdiction," were intended to cover the territories or any place subject to the exclusive jurisdiction of Congress.

Why was section two added to the amendment? Senator Sherman of Ohio explained this in a speech in the United States Senate on December 13, 1865. The reason, he said, why this power was given Congress was to be found in the history of Art. IV, Sec. 2, cl. 1, of the Constitution. There never was any doubt about the construction of this clause, but the trouble was in enforcing it. He cited the celebrated case of "Mr. Hoar," who went to South Carolina, and was driven out though he had a perfect constitutional right to be there. This constitutional provision was in effect a dead letter to him. The reason was that there was no provision in the Constitution by which Congress could enforce the right. The Constitution guaranteed that the citizens of each should have the rights of citizens in all the states, yet there was no express power conferred upon Congress to secure these rights. "To avoid this very difficulty, that of a guarantee without a power to enforce it, this second section of the Constitutional amendment was adopted, which does give to Congress in clear and express terms the right to secure by appropriate legislation, to every person within the United States, liberty." If necessary, Congress may under authority of this clause pass enforcement legislation.

The Senate passed the joint resolution, April 8, 1864, by a vote of 38 to 6.[32]

In the House of Representatives, Windom of Minnesota had on February 15, 1864, moved the Senate resolution. On March 28 Stevens offered the following resolution in the House, and moved the previous question: "Article 1. Slavery and involuntary servitude, except for the punishment of crimes whereof the party shall have been duly convicted, is forever prohibited in the United States and all its territories."

The joint resolution (S. No. 16) was discussed on June 14 and 15, and rejected by a vote of 93 to 65, twenty-three not voting. During the roll-call, Ashley of Ohio, seeing that defeat was certain, changed his vote from the affirmative to the negative for the purpose of submitting a motion to reconsider at the proper time.[33] On the same day, he rose to a privileged question, and moved a reconsideration of the vote on the constitutional amendment. He did not, however, call up the motion that session, because he found that enough votes to pass the constitutional amendment could not be secured, and it was January 6, 1865, before he called up the motion for reconsideration.[34] On January 31 he moved the previous question, and the joint resolution (S. No. 16) was passed by 119 yeas to 56 nays, eight not voting.

When the Speaker announced that the required constitutional majority of two-thirds had voted in the affirmative, the Republicans sprang to their feet, and regardless of Parliamentary rules applauded, threw their hats in the air, and cheered wildly. In the crowded galleries men waved their hats and "cheered loud and long," while the hundreds of ladies present rose and waved their handkerchiefs amidst a scene of tremendous excitement and enthusiasm.[35]

2. *The Motives for the Thirteenth Amendment.* Why did Congress undertake to destroy slavery by means of an amendment? Senator Trumbull in submitting his report gave the reasons. The great reason was because all previous laws and proclamations were ineffectual to the destruction of slavery. Even if the laws of Congress were faithfully executed, the slaves of loyal masters would remain, and this would be no inconsiderable number, as many slaves are held by children and females not engaged in rebellion. Then, the President's Eman-

cipation Proclamation "excepts from its provisions all of Delaware, Maryland, Kentucky, Tennessee, Missouri, and a good portion of Louisiana and Virginia—almost half the slave states." So that, if we are to rid ourselves permanently of the institution of slavery, "we must have some more efficient way of doing it." Petitions have been sent to Congress asking it to abolish slavery by an Act of Congress. But it has been an admitted axiom among all parties from the foundation of the government that Congress had no authority to interfere with slavery in the states where it existed. We have authority to slay the enemies of the country, or to confiscate their property, because it is necessary, but that gives no authority to slay the friends of the country, to confiscate their property, or to free their slaves. "Then, Sir, in my judgment, the only effectual way of ridding the country of slavery" so that it can never be re-established, "is by an amendment to the Constitution forever prohibiting it within the jurisdiction of the United States." [36] The Senator was careful not to use the phrase "within the United States," but "within the jurisdiction of the United States."

The adoption of this amendment not only destroyed slavery, "but it can never be re-established by state authority, or in any other way than by again amending the constitution," whereas if slavery should be abolished by an Act of Congress, or proclamation of the President, "assuming that either has the power to do it," there is nothing whatever in the constitution to prevent any state from again re-establishing slavery, if it so desires.[37] The object in view, he said, was "to abolish slavery and prevent its existence hereafter." Messrs. Sherman, Wilson, Clark and Johnson gave similar testimony.[38]

3. *The Origin of the Thirteenth Amendment.* The precedent for the amendment was found in the anti-slavery clause of the North West Ordinance of 1787. The phraseology was repeated in Enabling Acts and state constitutions on the admission of the western states to the union.[39] Senator Trumbull, chairman of the Judiciary Committee, said in the Senate on April 8, 1864, that the Committee had both the Sumner and Henderson propositions before them. "There was some difference of opinion in the committee as to the language to be used; and it was upon discussion and examination of both these prop-

ositions . . . that the committee came to the conclusion to adopt the form which is reported here . . . a majority of the committee thought they were the best words; they accomplish the object." "The Committee considered this subject and deliberately agreed upon this form." Senator Howard said it was "the language employed by our fathers in the ordinance of 1787." Senator Powell said, "I understand that it starts with the idea of producing the Jeffersonian Ordinance . . . That ordinance I will read: 'There shall be neither slavery nor involuntary servitude in the said territory otherwise than in punishment of crime whereof the party shall have been duly convicted.' " [40] And on the same day Senator Sumner said the Judiciary Committee had selected what was intended for the old Jeffersonian Ordinance " . . . although they have not imitated it closely." He preferred that they use the actual words of the ordinance and not as reported by the Committee.[41]

Amendment XIV. 1. *The Legislative History of the Amendment.* On December 5, 1865, Thaddeus Stevens introduced in the House a joint resolution proposing an amendment to the Constitution of the United States. It read: "Article XIII. All national and state laws shall be equally applicable to every citizen, and no discrimination shall be made on account of race and color." It was referred to the Committee on Judiciary.[42]

On December 6, John A. Bingham of Ohio also introduced a joint resolution to amend the Constitution of the United States to empower Congress to pass all necessary and proper laws to secure to all in every state equal protection in their rights, life, liberty, and property. This was also referred to the Committee on Judiciary.[43] Bingham on February 13, 1866, reported back the resolution from the Joint Committee on Reconstruction,[44] appointed on December 13 (of six members of the Senate and nine members of the House [45]).

On February 28, on motion of Conkling, the resolution was postponed till the second Tuesday in April. The New York *Herald* of March 2 suggested that the cause of this was the fear that the elections in New Hampshire and Connecticut might go against the party in power on account of the radical nature of the proposed amendment.[46]

On April 30, 1866, Stevens reported from the Joint Committee on Reconstruction an amendment to the Constitution of the United States, consisting of five sections providing for the five things mentioned as necessary to secure in the report of the Committee.[47] The first section contained no definition of citizenship. In the debate, Garfield offered an amendment providing for the exclusion of all persons who had participated in the late insurrection, from holding any office of trust or profit under the United States forever. This was defeated and the amendment passed on May 10 by a vote of 128 to 37, nineteen not voting.[48]

In the *Senate*, the article was attacked first by Reverdy Johnson of Maryland, who moved that section three, providing that all persons who had voluntarily adhered to the Southern Confederacy or given them aid and comfort, should be deprived of the right to vote for representatives in Congress and presidential electors until July 4, 1870, be stricken out. The motion was agreed to unanimously. On May 29 Senator Howard of Michigan moved to amend section one by prefixing a definition of citizenship as follows: "All persons born in the United States and subject to the jurisdiction thereof, are citizens of the United States and of the states wherein they reside."[49] He said in support of his amendment: "This is simply declaratory of what I regard as the law of the land already." It would of course not include the families of ambassadors or foreign ministers accredited to the United States government. "It settles the great question of citizenship, and removes all doubt as to what persons are or are not citizens of the United States." It was adopted. This made United States citizenship primary, and settled the vexed question as to what persons were citizens of the United States. The words "or naturalized" very important in the amendment, were suggested by Senator Fessenden of Maine, and agreed to without objection.

The clause in Section 2 reading: "But whenever in any state the elective franchise shall be denied to any portion of its male citizens," was amended by Senator Williams of Oregon to read as in the Constitution.[50] Senator Howard moved an amendment as a substitute for section three, which had been stricken from the resolution on motion of Reverdy Johnson. This was adopted and stands as section three in the Constitution. An amendment was moved by Senator Clark as a substitute for sections four and five of the amendment as it passed the House. This was accepted and stands as section four in the Constitution. No change was made by the Senate in section five. The resolution as amended was then passed by the Senate on June 8, 1866, by a vote of 33 to 11 with five senators absent.[51]

The amendment was again brought before the House on June 9, and Boutwell gave notice that the resolution, as amended by the Senate, would be called up on June 13. Time was doubtless required for the majority to consult and decide on the course to be pursued regarding the amendment.[52] When called up on June 13, Stevens stated that the amendments proposed by the Senate had been examined by the Union portion of the Reconstruction Committee, and that the committee reported unanimously that the House ought to agree to them, and that one hour would be given the minority to use as they pleased before moving the previous question at three or three-thirty. The House passed the amendment without change by a vote of 120 to 32, thirty-two being absent.[53] This time the Republicans voted solidly for the amendment, which was a Republican measure.

2. *The Purpose of the Fourteenth Amendment.* The purpose was:

(1) *To place the Civil Rights Bill beyond the possibility of repeal, and its constitutionality beyond question.* The Civil Rights Bill had been enacted on April 9, 1866. Its purpose was, Senator Trumbull declared, to abolish and prevent discrimination against the negro by the laws of the Southern states, and to enforce the thirteenth amendment. But the constitutionality of the Civil Rights Act was questioned. Both Democrats and Republicans, and the ablest constitutional lawyers in Congress, declared the act unconstitutional on the ground that Congress had no power under the Constitution to regulate civil rights. The Southerners seeking seats in Congress, leading Republican newspapers, like the Cincinnati Commercial and the National Intelligencer, supposed to be the administration organ at Washington, resolutions adopted by Republicans and Democrats gathered in mass meetings, and state courts all declared the Civil Rights Act unconstitutional.[54]

The Republicans, therefore, determined to make the act a

part of the Constitution and thus place its constitutionality beyond question, and make its repeal impossible except by another amendment. This was the reason why an amendment was chosen. Stevens said: "Some answer, 'Your Civil Rights Bill secures the same things.' That is partly true, but a law is repealable by a majority. . . . This amendment once adopted cannot be annulled without two-thirds of Congress." [55] Broomall explained that if they were entirely safe with the Civil Rights Bill, it would do no harm to become the more effectually so, and prevent a mere majority from repealing the law and thus thwarting the will of the loyal people.[56] Garfield also declared the purpose was to put the Civil Rights Bill beyond the possibility of repeal by Congress.[57] By making the Civil Rights Bill an amendment to the Constitution, its constitutionality was also placed beyond question.[58]

(2) *To define citizenship and make it clear once for all who were citizens of the United States.* The Supreme Court of the United States had held that negroes could not be citizens.[59] The Republicans refused to accept this doctrine, but many in the country did accept it as good law. This question must not be left open to cavil, doubt, or dispute. Senator Wade proposed as a substitute for the phrase "citizens of the United States" the words "persons born in the United States or naturalized by the laws thereof." He offered the substitute for the purpose of removing doubt as to what persons were included in the term "citizens." He said he had no doubt himself, but he thought that all doubt should be removed, especially since the courts had thrown doubt on the question. Senator Stewart had also offered an amendment defining citizenship on May 14, 1866. Senator Howard then seized on Wade's suggestion, and on May 29 offered the amendment defining citizenship which became part of the first section.[60]

Dr. Flack does not think the main purpose of the Fourteenth Amendment was to declare who were citizens, because this part of the amendment was not added in the House, or the question of citizenship raised during the three days' debate on the amendment. The House, he thinks, took it for granted that negroes were citizens. All had acquiesced in that part of the Civil Rights Bill which made them such.[61] Professor Willoughby thinks the main purpose of the amendment was to

make them citizens.[62]   The Supreme Court of the United States
has declared that the main purpose was "to settle the question
upon which there had been a difference of opinion throughout
the country, and in this court, as to the citizenship of free
negroes." [63]

Justice Gray in the case of United States v. Wong Kim
Ark said: "Its main purpose doubtless was, as has been often
recognized by this court, to establish the citizenship of free
negroes, which had been denied in the opinion delivered by Chief
Justice Taney in Dred Scott v. Sanford, and to put it beyond
doubt that all blacks as well as whites born or naturalized
within the jurisdiction of the United States are citizens of the
United States." [64]   If the Dred Scott decision were good law,
then, nothing but a constitutional amendment could make negroes citizens, and President Johnson and many others believed
it was good law.

(3) *To make the Bill of Rights binding on the states.*   As
Bingham pointed out, the Supreme Court had held in the case
of Barron v. The Mayor and City of Baltimore that the bill
of rights (or the first ten amendments to the Constitution of
the United States) was binding on the United States but not
on the states.[65]   There was, therefore, absolutely nothing in
the Federal Constitution to prevent a state from enacting laws
denying the equal protection of the laws to her own citizens,
or depriving them of life, liberty, or property without due process of law.   Congress felt it necessary to correct this situation,
especially in view of the so-called "black codes" enacted by the
Southern legislatures to protect the Southern people but which
deprived the negroes of their civil rights.   Bingham told Congress there was a conspiracy extending through every Southern
state to do this, and the clerk read from the Norfolk Post to
prove the statement.[66]

Hence, the amendment, said Bingham, was simply a proposition "to arm the Congress of the United States by the consent of the people of the United States with the power to
enforce the bill of rights as it stands in the Constitution today."
This immortal bill of rights "rested for its execution and enforcement hitherto upon the fidelity of the states."   The
purpose of the amendment was to give "the whole people the
care in future of the unity of the government which constitutes

us one people and without which American nationality would cease to be." [67]   Stevens said the Constitution limited only the action of Congress and was not a limitation on the states. The amendment supplied that defect, "and allows Congress to correct the unjust legislation of the states, so far that the law which operates upon one man shall operate upon all."

The Supreme Court of the United States has held that while the Fourteenth Amendment is binding on the states, it does not make the bill of rights, or the first ten amendments to the Constitution of the United States, operative or binding on the states.[68]   "Undoubtedly, it gave much less effect to the Fourteenth Amendment than some of the public men active in framing it intended, and disappointed many others," said the Supreme Court in the case of Twining v. State of New Jersey. The amendment gives protection against acts of states, but does not protect against acts of individuals unless such individuals are official representatives of states.[69]

(4) *To establish political equality between the white and colored races of the South, or to secure the negroes in their civil rights.*   Davis of New York said the power to be centralized in Congress was "intended to be exercised in the establishment of perfect political equality between the colored and the white race of the South."   The amendment gave Congress full power to enact all laws essential to their protection, and was designed to "enforce political equality in races."

Stevens asserted that the amendment was intended to meet discrimination in the states against color, and to provide against their oppressive laws.   Woodbridge of Vermont alleged that the amendment was intended to give Congress power to enact laws which would give the citizen of the United States those rights, or "those privileges and immunities which are guaranteed to him under the Constitution of the United States." [70]

(5) *To carry out the recommendations of the Joint Committee on Reconstruction.*   The committee declared that Congress would not be justified in admitting the Southern states to participation in the government of the Union, till Congress had first provided such constitutional or other guarantees as would secure the civil rights of all citizens of the republic. They must guarantee a just equality of representation, pro-

tection against claims for damages founded in rebellion and crime, a restoration of the right of suffrage to those who have not participated in efforts to destroy the Union, and the exclusion from positions of public trust of all whose crimes had proven them unworthy of public confidence and enemies of the Union.[71] Congress then undertook to secure all the necessary guarantees by a Constitutional amendment covering all the points involved.

The purpose of the exception to citizenship under the Fourteenth Amendment contained in the words, "and subject to the jurisdiction thereof" in section one was threefold—to exclude (a) the children of Indians as they were unknown to the common law; (b) the children of alien enemies born while the enemy is in hostile occupation of American territory; (c) the children of ambassadors or other diplomatic representatives who are subject to the jurisdiction of their own government. Those born on public ships or war vessels are also excluded, though the children of consuls are not excepted.[72]

The *purpose* of section two was:

(1) *Political—to perpetuate the Republican party in power.* The Democratic party in Congress charged the Republicans with this, and McKee unblushingly acknowledged that he supported the measure for that very purpose. This was to be accomplished by reducing the power of the South and the Democratic party, and enfranchising the negro who would, as a matter of course, vote for the party which had made him free and given him the suffrage. This union of the Southern colored vote and the Northern Republican vote would ensure the success of the Republican party at the polls and secure for the party permanent control of the government of the country.[73]

(2) *Penal—to punish the South.* According to Senator Henderson, this was the leading motive.[74]

The *purpose* of section three was:

(1) *Penal—to punish the Southern leaders.* That is, treason was to be made odious by excluding the Southern leaders from Congress, and from holding any office, civil or military, under the United States or a state.[75] Its effect was to prevent the ablest men in the South from holding office.

(2) *Political—to prevent the South from adopting the Fourteenth Amendment till after the election of 1868.* Shank-

lin said the purpose was to disfranchise the Southerners till the Republican party should be able to control the South at will. It enabled the Republicans to control the election and the political situation by disfranchising the South.[76]

The *purpose* of section four was to prevent the repudiation of the debt of the United States incurred during the Civil War, and to repudiate the Southern debt and prevent its payment forever, or the payment of claims for slaves. The Constitution prohibits payment of the Southern debt incurred in aid of the rebellion. The Republicans feared that the Northern Democrats in Congress and the Southern members might combine to secure control of the government, and then repudiate the Union debt and validate the Confederate debt. This fear found expression in section four. The Joint Committee on Reconstruction declared this was one of the things to be provided against.

The *purpose* of section five was to give Congress power to enforce all the guarantees of the amendment, in spite of any hostile legislation on the part of the states. "Here is a direct affirmative delegation of power to Congress," said Senator Howard, "to carry out all these guarantees, a power not found in the Constitution." [77]

3. The Objections to the Fourteenth Amendment. The main objections were:

(1) *The amendment would centralize power in the federal government.* Hale and Davis urged against it that it centralized power in the federal government and destroyed the sovereignty of the states. Woodbridge of Vermont answered that it did not destroy the sovereignty of the states, but merely keeps whatever sovereignty they may have in harmony with a republican form of government and the Constitution. It tends on the contrary to keep the states within *their orbits.*[78]

(2) *It would interfere with the reserved rights of the states.* This objection was urged by several gentlemen, Bingham stated. One of these was Hale. Bingham's reply was that no state had a reserved right to deprive any citizen of his privileges under the Constitution of the United States, and he asked Hale for his authority for supposing any state had a right to deny to a citizen of any other state any of the privileges or immunities of a citizen of the United States.[79]

(3) *The amendment ought not to be passed in the absence of eleven states of the Union.* To this, the Republicans in Congress replied that they were not responsible for their absence, and because of their treasonable actions those states ought not to be given the privilege of participating in the government of the Union which they had attempted to destroy.[80] Majority rule, it was argued, was a fundamental principle of the government of the United States.

4. *The Sources of the Fourteenth Amendment.* These were: (1) *The Constitution of the United States.* On February 26, 1866, Bingham said the amendment stands in the very words of the Constitution as it came from the hands of the illustrious framers. Every word was in the Constitution "save the words conferring the express grant of power upon the Congress of the United States." The residue is the language of Article Four, section two, and a portion of the fifth amendment.[81] Higby added to these Article One, section eight, clause eighteen, and the amendment was held to be already in the Constitution but dormant. Hale replied that Higby's argument was so admirable he had never heard it paralleled, except in the case of the gentleman who undertook to justify suicide from the Scriptures by quoting two texts: "Judas went and hanged himself," and "Go thou and do likewise." [82] However, Article IV, section two, clause 1, and a portion of amendment V make up a part of the Fourteenth Amendment.

(2) *The Civil Rights Bill.* The principle of the first section of the Civil Rights Bill was incorporated in section one of the Fourteenth Amendment. Nearly everybody in both the majority and minority parties in Congress recognized this. Thayer and Eldridge both said the first section incorporated the Civil Rights Bill. Rogers declared it "an attempt to embody in the Constitution of the United States that outrageous and miserable Civil Rights Bill." [83]

(3) *The English common law.* In the case of the United States v. Wong Kim Ark, 1898, the Supreme Court said the fundamental principle of the common law with regard to English nationality was that birth within the allegiance of the King made one a citizen. The children of foreign ambassadors or of alien enemies were excluded, but all others born within the jurisdiction of the King were natural-born subjects.

This fundamental principle of the common law was laid down in Calvin's case, or the case of the Post-nati, 1608, which was heard before the Lord Chancellor and all the judges of England. "It thus clearly appears that by the law of England for the last three centuries, beginning before the settlement of this country . . . every child born in England of alien parents was a natural-born subject, unless the child of an ambassador or other diplomatic agent of a foreign state, or of an alien enemy in hostile occupation of the place where the child was born. This same rule was in force in all the English colonies upon this continent, down to the time of the Declaration of Independence, and in the United States afterwards." The Fourteenth Amendment, therefore, simply "follows the English common law principle that birth within the territorial limits of a state makes one a citizen of that state." It does not lay down any new law for America. It is merely declaratory of what has always been the law in England and America.

"The Fourteenth Amendment is declaratory of existing rights, and affirmative of existing law," and simply "affirms the ancient and fundamental rule of citizenship by birth." Even "before our Revolution all free persons born within the dominions of the King of Great Britain, whatever their color or complexion, were native-born British subjects." [84] The Fourteenth Amendment, then, merely applies this English common law rule for the purpose of determining American nationality.

(4) *The state constitutions.* These had in several cases applied the common law rule and recognized free negroes as citizens and admitted them to the franchise. This was true of the constitutions of New Hampshire, Massachusetts, New Jersey, New York, and North Carolina. It was the New York constitution of 1821, the New Jersey constitution of 1844, and the amendments to the North Carolina constitution of 1835 which deprived persons of color in those states of the right to vote. [85]

The *authorship* of the Fourteenth Amendment has been ascribed to Judge Neal, and to Robert Dale Owen of Indiana. Doctor Flack decides in favor of Owen's claims. [86]

Amendment XV. 1. *The Legislative History of the Fifteenth Amendment.* In the thirty-ninth Congress, Eliot of Massachusetts had offered a resolution providing that suffrage should not be denied or abridged on account of race or color, but this was unpopular at that time.[1] On January 20, 1866, Senator Fessenden of Maine and James G. Blaine introduced similar resolutions in Congress, the purpose of which was to guarantee suffrage to negroes. Fessenden secured it by a direct guarantee; Blaine attempted to secure it indirectly by excluding the excluded from the basis of representation in Congress, hoping thus to influence the South to grant negro suffrage for the sake of the additional representation in Congress.

The Joint Committee on Reconstruction favored the Blaine plan by a vote of eleven to three, and it was adopted by the House but rejected by the Senate.[2] The difficulty was that the granting of negro suffrage would require interference by Congress with the suffrage within the states. Congress had no right to interfere, it was believed; hence, there was considerable opposition even in the Northern states. New York, Connecticut, Ohio, Kansas, Minnesota, and Wisconsin voted against it.[3]

After all danger from opponents of negro suffrage in the elections had passed, William D. Kelly and John M. Broomall of Pennsylvania introduced joint resolutions on December 7, 1868, proposing to amend the Constitution to prevent discrimination in voting by reason of race or color. Broomall's differed in including Congress in the prohibition as well as the states. Both were read twice and referred to the Committee on Judiciary.[4]

On January 27, 1869, Messrs. Bingham, Shellabarger, and Ward offered three amendments which were voted down, and then the House on January 30 adopted the Boutwell joint resolution, reported by the Judiciary Committee as a substitute, by the necessary two-thirds vote. Thirty-one members failed to vote.[5]

In the Senate on December 7 and 10, 1868, Senators Craigin and Pomeroy introduced resolutions for amending the Constitution which were referred to the Committee on Judiciary.[6] Then, on January 10, 1869, the Judiciary Committee reported a constitutional amendment as article fifteen which read as it stands in the Constitution.[7]

Doctor Mathews points out that on the question of amending the Constitution, there were four parties in Congress.

(1) The *politicians*, who "aimed at Congressional control over Southern elections."

(2) The *nationalists*, who desired a strong central government and would, therefore, give the general government greater control over suffrage in the states.

(3) The *humanitarians*, or universal suffragists, who sought to base political rights on humanity itself, a remnant of inalienable rights.

(4) The *local autonomists*, "jealous of national interference in local affairs." No one of these parties was strong enough to control Congress.[8]

The politicians desired to give suffrage to the negro for practical political ends. Howard of Michigan was one of these, and he moved to substitute for the amendment proposed by the Judiciary Committee the following: "Citizens of the United States of African descent shall have the same right to vote and hold office as other citizens." Howard said frankly: "Give us the colored man, for that and that only is the object that is now before us." This, of course, was a suffrage amendment limited to one race. The humanitarians could not accept that; hence, the amendment was defeated.[9]

The politicians feared that if the proposition of the Judiciary Committee were adopted prohibiting discrimination on account of race, color, or previous condition of servitude only, then the Southern states might exclude the negroes by means of educational and property qualifications. The result was that the politicians united with the humanitarians and adopted the proposal of Senator Wilson of Massachusetts prohibiting discrimination "in any state on account of race, color, nativity, property, education or creed." Though the deadlock was broken by the coalition, a storm of indignation broke against the Senate from all over the country for prohibiting educational qualifications; and the House refused to concur in the Senate amendment.

To break the deadlock, conference committees were appointed by the houses. They agreed on a resolution which omitted the words "hold office." This was at once accepted by the House by a vote of 144 to 44.[10] The Senate was indignant because the words "hold office" had been stricken out, and was inclined to reject the amendment; but, moved by the *fear* of absolute failure to secure any amendment, and the *belief* that they had better take what they could get, the Senators and all who wanted a suffrage amendment of some kind were rallied; and on February 26, 1869 they adopted the amendment by a vote of 39 to 13. It was a compromise between the four parties in Congress.[11]

The attitude and intention of the House were clearly shown by a vote taken on a motion to suspend the rules for the purpose of introducing the following resolution: "Resolved, that in passing the Fifteenth Amendment . . . this House never intended that Chinese or Mongolians should become voters." This was rejected by a vote of 42 to 106.[12]

2. *The Purpose of the Fifteenth Amendment.* The purpose was: (1) *To deprive the states of all power to disfranchise negroes.* Boutwell of Massachusetts said the purpose was to deprive the states of power to deny men the privilege of voting on account of their race, color, or previous condition. Butler of Massachusetts urged that they stick to such a form as would remove from the states the power to disfranchise the blacks, which was the great disgrace of the country. Cullom said the language of the amendment should be broad enough to protect the people in future, not merely against oppressive legislation by the states on account of race, color, or previous condition, but also to protect them against capital, monopolies, or anything else.[13]

(2) *To enfranchise the negroes.* Cullom said it was an amendment guaranteeing a republican form of government "by securing the elective franchise to citizens deprived of it by reason of race, color, or previous condition." The animus of this amendment, said Dixon, "is a desire to protect and enfranchise the colored citizens of the country." "The manifest object," said Senator Williams, "is to extend to persons of African descent in the United States the right to vote and hold office." Senator Willy of Connecticut said the same thing. It provides that certain classes shall not be disfranchised on account of race, color, or condition.[14]

(3) *To guarantee the permanency of negro suffrage in the South.* The reconstruction programme of Congress had forced negro suffrage on the South. When the control of Congress ended, was negro suffrage guaranteed, or would the whites on

securing control in the seceding states immediately re-amend
their state constitutions by cutting out the provisions granting
negro suffrage? Congress believed they would do this; and the
attitude of the Southern states was such as to confirm Congress in this belief. The only thing for Congress to do, therefore, was to secure an amendment to the Federal Constitution
which would give Congress permanent control over the suffrage
in the reconstructed states. Hence, the Fifteenth Amendment
was adopted securing this object.[15]

(4) *To secure equality of rights and privileges.* Senator
Wilson said its purpose was "to make every citizen equal in
rights and privileges." Senator Stewart declared its object
was to make "all men without regard to race or color, equal
before the law. . . . It is the only guarantee against peon laws
and against oppression."[16]

(5) *To enable the Republicans to control the elections in
the South by means of the negro vote.* Davis of Kentucky
charged in the Senate that this was the real purpose of the
amendment. J. M. Mathews regards this as the motive of the
politicians in Congress.[17]

(6) *To provide for the obvious break-down of the Fourteenth Amendment.* Wherever the whites secured control of
the state governments, the negro was denied the right to vote.
This was done by getting around the Fourteenth Amendment
on the ground of race, color, or previous condition of servitude. The Republicans in Congress believed this amendment
had given the right to vote, or at least, they hoped that the
Southern states would readily grant suffrage to the negro for
the sake of the increased representation in Congress. This
proved a disappointment and Congress determined to stop all
weakness of the Fourteenth Amendment by adopting the Fifteenth, taking from the states all power to discriminate against
the negro, or any citizen of the United States, on account of
race, color, or previous condition. Senators Sumner and Welsh
cited the case of Georgia which had expelled the colored senators from her legislature, as showing the need for the amendment.[18]

Section Two. Bingham said the purpose of section two
was to invest Congress with express authority to enforce the
limitation of the Fifteenth Amendment.[19]

3. The Objections to the Fifteenth Amendment. The leading objections urged against it were:

(1) *All the states are not represented in Congress; therefore, the action of Congress would be null and void.* This was also urged against the thirteenth and fourteenth amendments.[20]

(2) *The amendment encroaches on the reserved rights of the states.* The country was endangered, it was said, by a concentration of power, which might result in a concentrated tyranny which would destroy the rights of the states. The objection was urged by different senators from different angles. Senator Fowler said it transferred power to Congress which belonged to the states. Senator Howard objected to giving Congress power to prescribe qualifications for voting and holding office which the Constitution gave to the states. Butler of Massachusetts said it would take from the states the power to make any educational or other test or to enact a registration law.

In answer, it was said, "Our Constitution having been made by the people, may be amended by the same authority." Our dangers have arisen from decentralization, not from centralization. Why should there be danger from the central government? The Senate is elected by the states, and the Representativs and President by the people. "The Congress and the government are but an expression of the whole people's will." "There is no basis in its structure on which to found a tyranny."[21]

(3) *Congress had no power to propose such an amendment.* Senator Davis of Kentucky urged that Congress was not omnipotent, but a body with limited and delegated powers; and Congress had not been delegated any power to subvert the Constitution by amending it so as to regulate the whole force and power of suffrage, and of holding office in the state. Senator Fowler argued that they ought not to put into the Constitution an arbitrary and fixed rule that cannot be changed or reformed without revolution; and he thought the change ought to be made by the states themselves and not by Congress. The answer to all this was that the power to amend belonged to the sovereign people.[22]

(4) *Dixon of Connecticut objected that the amendment destroyed the sovereignty and independence of the states by taking*

the regulation of the suffrage from them. Warner replied that the question was not one of negro suffrage, but of suffrage itself. The question is whether a state shall have the right to humiliate every citizen of the republic who shall choose to dwell within her borders. Sovereign power belongs to the people, who have the right to decide who shall exercise political power. To allow the states to do this, "is to give away the most essential and vital attribute of sovereignty."[23]

(5) *It enfranchised negroes and Chinese and excluded American women.* Senator Fowler objected to giving the natives of China, Africa, and India a right to control the destinies of American women, and excluding them from the suffrage. Senator Pomeroy asked the ballot for woman "because she is a citizen of the Republic, amenable to its laws, taxed for its support, and a sharer in its destiny." Some favored woman suffrage, but as it was regarded as an impracticable dream at that time, they did not dare to do more than champion the idea.

It was clearly understood by all that "race" and "color" applied to negroes, Chinese, or Indians. The question of Chinese suffrage, however, came up quite unexpectedly; and Williams and Corbett of Oregon declared that to deprive the states on the Pacific coast of the power to exclude Chinese from the suffrage would lead to political degradation and moral pollution. The local autonomists opposed imposing the Chinese vote on those states, but the humanitarians favored the principle.[24]

Of course, Chinese, Japanese, and Hindoos have been rendered ineligible to citizenship by statute and decisions of the Supreme Court, and, therefore, cannot vote. Those born in the United States are citizens under the Fourteenth Amendment and may vote like other citizens.

4. *The Sources of the Fifteenth Amendment.* The working principle and phraseology had been in part used in the First Civil Rights Act of April 9, 1866, which declared that "citizens of every race and color, without regard to any previous condition of slavery," should have the same civil rights.[25] The principle and phraseology are also found in the constitutions of South Carolina of March 17, 1868, Texas of June 1, 1868, Florida of January 20, 1868, and in the Enabling Act for Wyoming of July, 1868.[26]

This amendment was characterized by Ward of New York as "the capstone in the great temple of American freedom." [27]

NOTES TO CHAPTER XVIII

1. 2 Dallas, 466, 473 seq. 479; McClain, Cases in Const. Law, 705.
2. 134 U. S. 2; McClain, Cases, 704.
3. Annals of Cong., III, 651.
4. Id. IV, 25, 29, 30, 31; Journal of the Senate, II, 19.
5. Annals, IV, 225, 476-7; McClain, Cases in Const. Law, 705.
6. Elliot, III, 555.
7. Id. 533.
8. Hans v. La., 134 U. S. 1; McClain, Cases on Const. Law, 705-8.
9. Elliot, I, 333-6.
10. Annals of Congress, X, 1021-1033.
11. Annals, X, 155.
12. Annals, VI, p. 1824.
13. Id., 7, 493, 494; 9, 2919; 10, 410; 941-6; 11, 509, 190, 629, 259, 1289-90, 1294, 303, 304, 1296; 12, 303, 486; 449, 493; 13, 372, 375-377, 380-381; XIII, 383, 16.
14. Annals, XIII, 16, 85, 124, 376, 377.
15. Id. 126, 92, 97, 419, 421, 428, 515.
16. Annals, XIII, 128, 129.
17. Id. 209, 210, 683, 775-6, 777.
18. See Doc. Hist. of the Const., II, 411, 451, for acts of ratification.
19. Annals, XIII, 155, 156, 537, 704, 208.
20. Id. 119-122.
21. Id. 155.
22. Id. 704, 428, Mr. Gregg. See also Letter of Gouverneur Morris, Sparks, Life of Gouverneur Morris, Vol. 3, 173, 176.
23. Anals, XIII, 123.
24. Id. 123.
25. Cong. Globe, 38 Cong. 1 Sess. pt. 1, 19.
26. Id. 19.
27. Cong. Globe, Vol. 34, pt. 1, 145, 521, 522.
28. Cong. Globe, 1 sess., 38 Cong., pt. 2, 1313.
29. Cong. Globe, Vol. 34, pt. 2, 921, 1370, 1424.
30. Cong. Globe, Vol. 34, pt. 1, 921.
31. Id. 521, 522; Id. pt. 2, 1 sess., 38 Cong., 1325.
32. Cong. Globe, 1 Sess., 39 Cong., 41, 1490.
33. Cong. Globe, pt. 2, 1 Sess. 38 Cong., 1325; pt. 4, 2939, 2943, 2995.
34. Cong. Globe, 1 Sess. 38 Cong., pt. 4, 3000, 3357, 138.
35. Id. 531.
36. Cong. Globe, pt. 2, 1 Sess. 38 Cong., 1314.
37. Id. 1314.
38. Cong. Globe, pt. 2, 1 Sess. 38 Cong., 1482, 1315, 1324, 1369, 1370, 1420-22.
39. Poore, 432 (Art. VI). See for example, Ohio, 1802, Poore, 1461; Ind. 1816, 509; Ill. 1818, 445; Mo. Enabling Act, 1820, 1104; Mich. 1835, 990; Ia., 1846, 538; Kan. 1855, 581; Oregon 1857, 1506.
40. Cong. Globe, pt. 2, 1 Sess. 38 Cong., 1488-9.
41. Cong. Globe, pt. 2, 1 Sess. 38 Cong., 1482, 1483.
42. Id. 1 Sess., 39 Cong., 10.
43. Id. 39 Cong., 14.

44. Id. 44, 45.
45. Id. 813.
46. Flack, Adoption of the Fourteenth Amendment, 59.
47. Cong. Globe, 1 Sess. 39 Cong. 2286. For history of the amendment in the Reconst. Com. see Journal 7 seq. Flack, 60 seq.
48. Cong. Globe, pt. 3, 1 sess. 39 Cong., 2545.
49. Id. 2869.
50. Cong. Globe, 1 sess. 39 Cong., pt. 4, 2890, 2897, 3040, 3029, 3039.
51. Id. 2869, 3040-3042.
52. Flack, Fourteenth Amendment, 93.
53. Cong. Globe, 1 Sess, 39 Cong., pt. 4, 3148-9.
54. Flack, Fourteenth Amendment, 21, 40, 41, 44, 47 seq.
55. Cong. Globe, 1 Sess. 39 Cong., 1088.
56. Id. 2498.
57. Id. 2462.
58. 2498; 19 Howard, 393.
59. Dred Scott decision, 19 Howard 393.
60. Flack, Adoption of the Fourteenth Amendment, 88-9; Cong. Globe, 1 sess. 39 Cong., 2768, 2869.
61. Flack, Adoption of the Fourteenth Amendment, 83.
62. The Am. Const. System, 245.
63. 112 U. S. 94, 101.
64. 169 U. S. 676.
65. Cong. Globe, 1 sess. 39 Cong., 1089-90; 7 Peters, 243, 551; McClain, Cases, 15.
66. Cong. Globe, 1 sess. 39 Cong., 1089-92; 7 Peters, 551.
67. Cong. Globe, 1 sess. 39 Cong. 1088, 1034. See also Mr. Higby of Cal., 1054; and others, 2542-3, 2498, 2765-6.
68. Id. 2459; 176 U. S. 581; 211 U. S. 78; 16 Wallace 36.
69. Evans, Cases, 116; 211 U. S. 78; 92 U. S. 542.
70. Cong. Globe, 1 sess. 39 Cong., 1085, 1087, 2549, 1088.
71. Report of the Joint Committee on Reconstruction, XVI-XVIII.
72. U. S. v. Wong Kim Ark, 169 U. S. 649, 657.
73. Cong. Globe, 1 sess. 39 Cong., 2461, 2535; Flack, Adoption of the Fourteenth Amendment, 97-127.
74. Id. 105; Cong. Globe, Id. 115-122, app.
75. Id. 133, 252.
76. Flack, Adoption of the Fourteenth Amendment, 127-133; Cong. Globe, 1 sess. 39 Cong., 2500.
77. Id. 2765, 2766, 2768, 2940, 3147.
78. Cong. Globe, 1 sess. 39 Cong. 1063, 1064, 1087-1089.
79. Id. 1088, 1089.
80. Id. 1088; Id. Vol. 35, 181; Journal of the Reconstruction Committee, 5.
81. Cong. Globe, 1 sess. 39 Cong., 1034.
82. Id. 1062, 1063.
83. Flack, Adoption of the Fourteenth Amendment, 54, 81; Cong. Globe, 1 sess. 39 Cong. 2465, 2506, 2538.
84. 169 U. S. 649, 657, 659; 3 Pet. 99; 19 How. 573; McClain, Cases, 966, 967, 970; Willoughby, Am. Const. System, 248.
85. 19 How. 573; Poore, 1411, 1416, 1285, 1299, 1311, 1315, 1344, 1343, 962, 973, 979; 4 Devereaux, 25, 26; 44 Maine 507; House Docs., 59 Cong. 2 sess. 326; Yale Law Journal, XV, 263.
86. Adoption, 69-71.

NOTES TO AMENDMENT XV

1. Cong. Globe, 1 sess, 39 Cong. 406.
2. Cong. Globe, 1 sess. 39 Cong., 1032; Mathews, Legis. and Judg. Hist. of Fifteenth Amendment, 1, 13; Journal of Recon. Com. 9, 10.
3. Cong. Globe, 1 sess. 39 Cong. 1289.
4. Id. 3 sess. 40 Cong., 9.
5. Id. 286, 638, 639, 745.
6. Id. 6, 38.
7. Cong. Globe, 3 sess. 40 Cong., 379, 542, 668, 1300.
8. Legislative and Judicial History of Fifteenth Amendment, 22, 23.
9. Cong. Globe, 3 sess. 40 Cong., 828, 985; Sen. Journal, 3 sess., 222; Mathews, Legis. and Jud. History, 33.
10. Senate Journal, 3 sess. 40 Cong., 227, 293, 449; Thorpe, Const. Hist. III, 434-436.
11. Cong. Globe, 3 sess. 40 Cong. 1626-9; Sen. Journal, 3 sess. 40 Cong. 361.
12. Mathews, Fifteenth Amendment, 35-36, 40-43.
13. Cong. Globe, 3 sess. 40 Cong., 652.
14. Cong. Globe, 3 sess. 40 Cong., 862, 900, 911, 652; Thorpe, Const. History, 427.
15. J. M. Mathews, Fifteenth Amendment, 20, 21.
16. Cong. Globe, 3 sess. 40 Cong., 668, 672.
17. Id. 288 app. Fifteenth Amendment, 22, 23.
18. Cong. Globe, 3 sess. 40 Cong., 1298, 1300; Thorpe, Const. Hist. 404-5; 92 U. S. 214, 555.
19. Cong. Globe, 3 sess. 40 Cong., 727.
20. Id. 981.
21. Cong. Globe, 3 sess. 40 Cong., 1301, 725, 980-1, 670.
22. Id. 285, 287, 670.
23. Cong. Globe, 3 sess. 40 Cong., 861, 862.
24. Id. 670, 710, 862; Mathews, Fifteenth Amendment, 41.
25. U. S. Stats. at L. 14:27. MacDonald, Sel. Stats., 142.
26. Poore, Charters and Constitutions, 1658, 1814, 358; U. S. Stats. at L. 15:180.
27. Cong. Globe, 3 sess. 40 Cong., 724.

CHAPTER XIX

Amendments Sixteen and Seventeen

1. *The Congressional History of the Sixteenth Amendment.*
On April 27, 1909, Senator Brown of Nebraska proposed a
joint resolution in the Senate to amend the Constitution relative to incomes and inheritances. Next day, it was referred to
the Committee on Judiciary.[1] On June 17, Senator Brown
introduced a joint resolution (S.J.R. 39) to amend the Constitution relative to incomes which was read twice and at his
request referred to the Committee on Finance.[2] Senator Ald-
rich then reported from the Committee on Finance on June 28,
an amendment which read as the amendment stands in the Constitution. This was ordered to be printed and to lie on the
table.[3] On July 3, Senator Brown asked unanimous consent
to lay the joint resolution before the Senate for an immediate
vote in order that it might be passed and sent to the House
before the tariff bill reached that body. Objections were offered, but it was agreed on suggestion of Senator Carter of
Montana that the vote should be taken at one o'clock on Monday, July 5. Several amendments were offered and rejected
and the vote taken as agreed. It stood 77 yeas, no nays, and
15 not voting. As two-thirds had voted for the resolution, it
had passed. The vote shows that the resolution for the amendment was both a Republican and Democratic measure.[3a] Senator
Brown said: "You cannot find a man on this floor not in favor
of the tax."[4]

The resolution was sent to the House, and on July 9 was
referred to the Committee on Ways and Means which reported
favorably on July 13 (H.Rept. No. 15). The vote was taken
in the House on the Senate resolution on July 16, 1909, and
stood, yeas 318, nays 14, not voting 55, answered present 1.
As two-thirds had voted for it, the joint resolution had passed.
On July 16, 1909, it was signed by the Speaker of the House
and the Vice-President, and on July 21 deposited with the

Secretary of State by the chairman of the Senate committee on enrolled bills. It is not necessary for the President to sign an amendment.[5]

1. *The Arguments in Favor of the Amendment.* It was argued in favor:

(1) *It was the fairest, most equitable and proper tax Congress could levy.* Messrs. Bartlett, Henry, Sulzer, Sharp, Hobson, James and others argued that it took the burden of taxation from the backs of the masses, and laid it on those who do not bear a just proportion of the expenses of government. The amendment taxed according to ability to pay. It taxes wealth and not want, and places the burden of taxation on those most able to bear it. Sulzer argued that the tariff system of taxation was unjust to the poor man, because it taxed him on the necessaries of life. "It is a damnable system which taxes want and exempts wealth," said Dies of Texas. A hod carrier should not pay as much to support the government as John D. Rockefeller. Twenty-three farmers of Illinois with $115,000 between them should not pay as much as the directors of the New York City Bank with financial power of $11,000,000,000, or one tenth of the wealth of the United States, said James.[6]

(2) *It was necessary to secure revenue.* The internal revenue laws and customs duties had failed to furnish sufficient revenue to run the government. There was a shortage here of $150,000,000 annually. There was a deficit in the Treasury, and, therefore, the amendment was necessary to secure greater revenue.[7]

(3) *It will make the proposed corporation tax unnecessary.* The corporation tax without the individual income tax, Harrison of New York argued, is the most unfair tax ever levied by motion of either Chamber of Congress. It is unfair, because it allows the man with an income of $100,000 to go free and taxes the man with an income of $10,000 because his business is incorporated. This violates the fundamental principle of taxation, namely, that its burdens should be equally distributed. It allows the man conducting a grocery business on one corner to go scot free, while the man on the next corner must pay a tax because his business is incorporated.[8]

(4) *It is necessary to enable the nation to use all its resources in time of war, or other emergency.* The question of

war is now the question of which nation has the longest pocket-book, and the power may be needed some time to save the nation, said Dickema of Michigan.[9]

(5) *Hobson of Alabama argued that direct taxation enabled a people to know how much they were taxed, and it is only with such knowledge that they could prevent abuse of the taxing power.* Today, the people are taxed ten, twenty, and thirty per cent and do not know it, he declared.[10]

(6) *Payne said he supported the amendment, because an income tax was unconstitutional under our present constitution.* The Supreme Court will not reverse itself. The decision of the Supreme Court in the Pollock case was denounced by nearly everybody.[11]

3. *The Objections to the Amendment.* These were:

(1) *It promotes falsehood and deception.* It tends, as Gladstone, said, to make a nation of liars, declared Payne and others. It is the most easily concealed of any tax that can be levied, the most difficult of enforcement, and the hardest to collect. In a word, it is a tax upon the income of the honest man, and an exemption, to a greater or less extent, of the income of rascals.[12]

(2) *It destroys the democratic principle in the Constitution.* McCall of Massachusetts argued that it abolished the rule of apportionment, and abrogated one of the fundamental principles of the Constitution. Some safeguard should be provided. The House should have the sole power to amend income tax bills, and the Senate, like the British House of Lords, should have no power to amend them.[13]

(3) *McCall also objected to giving Congress the power in time of peace and wanted it limited to time of war.*[14]

(4) *It is inquisitorial in character.* This was also urged by McCall. He said it calls for the baring of the innermost business secrets of men by means of affidavits and inspection of books and papers. "You are creating here an ideal condition for corruption, and for the political Jack Cade of the future to levy blackmail."[15] This was answered by saying that ascertaining the basis of any system of taxation was necessarily inquisitorial. Clark of Missouri declared it was monstrous to say that the accumulated wealth of this country shall not bear its just proportion of the public burdens.[16]

(5) *It is a tax on industry or wealth, said McCall of Massachusetts.* Miller of Kansas replied: "If there is any tax in this country that is not a tax upon industry or wealth, I would like to know what it is." [17]

(6) *Bartholdt of Missouri objected that it was undemocratic and un-American unless all incomes were required to pay.* Have the man with an income of $100 pay one cent, and $1,000 ten cents to the government. Let one tenth of one per cent be levied on all incomes.[18] The answer was wealth and not poverty should pay.

(7) *Another objection was urged against submitting the amendment to the legislatures instead of to conventions, by Henry DeArmond and others.* It was feared the legislatures would reject the amendment. The reply was "Why change the plan or method of amending used for one hundred years?" [19]

(8) *It is a matter of importance and should be considered with greater deliberation.* It should not be dealt with in the hurry of an extra session. Pickett replied that the question of an income tax had been considered by the leaders of the nation and people for years, and the people had already decided in its favor.[20]

(9) *It would undermine and destroy the protective system.* This was urged by the Republicans. Mr. James replied that this was equivalent to saying that in order to give a few monopolists and manufacturers a chance to reach into the pockets of all the people, you have kept the tax-gatherers from reaching into the pockets of the fortunate few. No tax was more unjust than a tax on consumption, for all must eat food and wear clothes. "I would scorn, Mr. Speaker, a government whose taxing power provides that Lazarus must divide his crumbs with the tax-gatherer, but that Dives shall not give his riches." [21]

(10) *It was also urged, by McLaurin, that the amendment did not meet the requirements of the case, so as to put the meaning and constitutionality of the income tax beyond all question before the Supreme Court of the United States.* Senator Brown replied there was no other apportionment known to the Constitution except that according to the census or enumeration.[22]

4. *The Purpose of the Amendment.* This was:

(1) *To override the decision of the Supreme Court in the case of Pollock v. Farmers' Loan and Trust Co.* The belief was general in Congress that the Supreme Court decision in this case was wrong.[23]   Senator Brown declared that even though they passed a law for an income tax amendment, and the President should veto it, they could veto the President's veto. If, however, they passed a law and the Supreme Court vetoed it, "that overrides us—it is final." We have no reason to suppose the Court has changed its opinion, and even supposing we passed a law on the subject and the Court sustained it, we have no assurance that would be permanent. Our courts have demonstrated a faculty to change their minds. This is the reason, Mr. Senators, "I present to you the imperative and commanding necessity for an amendment to the Constitution, which will give the Court a Constitution that cannot be interpreted in two ways." "My purpose is to confine it to income taxes alone and forever settle the dispute by referring the subject to the several States." The purpose, said Pickett, was to amend the Constitution so that the right of the federal government to impose an income tax will be clear and unquestioned. The purpose, it was also said, was to amend the "judicial amendment to the Constitution." [24]

(2) *To give Congress power to levy an income tax in a national emergency.* Senator Rayner appealed to those opposed to the income tax amendment to give the nation power to collect taxes from incomes in an emergency; and he quoted Justice Harlan's dissenting opinion in the Pollock case that "it strikes at the very foundations of national authority" by denying "to the General Government a power, which is or may become vital to the very existence and preservation of the Union in a National emergency." The United States, he said, was the only government on earth without power to tax incomes.[25]

The Democrats charged over and over again that the *purpose* of the Republican leaders was to defeat the income tax amendment by proposing the corporation tax amendment. Both these propositions, it was said, were put through the Senate simply as a means of defeating the income tax amendment, when it was found that all the Democrats in the Senate and a sufficient number of Republicans would vote for the income tax. Sulzer charged that the ulterior purpose of the

Republicans was to defeat the income tax in the Republican state legislatures.[26] Another purpose, was, of course, *to secure revenue.*

5. *The Sources of the Amendment.* Stone of Missouri read the declaration of the Democratic national platform promulgated at Denver, in 1908, favoring the giving of power to Congress "to levy and collect a tax upon individual and corporate incomes." He said: "The President has taken his stand on the Denver platform, and a Republican Senator has culled one of its declarations, and formulated it into the legislative proposition now before the Senate." I hope when the Senator goes before the people and the legislature of his State to urge ratification, he will not fail to inform them that he got his idea from a Democratic platform, "and from the utterances of Mr. Bryan, the leading Democrat, and most distinguished citizen of his State." Senator Brown, who was from Nebraska, did not attempt to deny Stone's statement, though he asked if he meant that the Democratic source was anything against it, thereby acknowledging its authorship.[27] The Democrats constantly charged that the Republicans had appropriated the income tax amendment from Democratic platforms—"the tariff bill of 1894," the "platform of 1896," "the war-tariff bill of 1898," and the Denver platform.[28] The Republicans did not deny the charge though repelling it in other ways.

It was said in Congress that the language used in the amendment was taken from the language of other sections of the Constitution.[29] This refers to Art. I, Sec. 8, cl. 1. "The Congress shall have power to lay and collect taxes," which reappears in Article XVI; and to Art. I, Sec. 9, cl. 4, "census or enumeration," which also reappears in Article XVI; Art. I, Sec. 2, cl. 3, also contains the phrase "apportioned among the several States."

The British income tax which runs back to the Saladin Tithe of 1188, was praised, and it was said over and over again, that the United States was the only country in the world which could not levy an income tax. An income tax was first levied in the Colony of Massachusetts Bay, 1634, and 1646.[30] For the history of the Income Tax in the United States see Roger Foster's Income Tax, p. 17, seq. and references in footnotes.

Amendment XVII. 1. *The Congressional History of the Seventeenth Amendment.* A resolution providing for the election of Senators by direct vote of the people was introduced in Congress by Storrs of New York as early as 1826. From that date to 1908 over a dozen such resolutions were introduced and killed in the Senate. In that year, the Republican and Democratic National Conventions placed themselves on record as favoring the amendment.[1] In 1909, resolutions were introduced for the purpose of amending the Constitution, but objection was made to their consideration owing to a misspelled word or printer's error. Again, in April, 1911, Messrs. Cooper of Wisconsin, Sulzer of New York, Adair of Indiana, Taylor of Colorado, Rucker of Missouri, Tribble of Georgia, and Hawley of Oregon introduced joint resolutions providing for the election of Senators by direct vote of the people, which were referred to the committee on election of President, Vice-President, and Representatives in Congress. Chairman Rucker reported without amendment on April 12. The subject was debated, and the vote taken April 13. The result was:

Yeas	296
Nays	16
Not Voting	77 [2]

The required two-thirds having voted for it, the amendment had been passed by the House. Speaker Clark directed the clerk to call his name, and the Speaker voted in the affirmative.[3]

The battle royal over the amendment occurred in the Senate. Senators Owen and Bristow stated that thirty-seven states had declared in favor of the amendment and they accused the Senate of deliberately blocking the measure. This charge appears to have been well founded. A resolution introduced by Senator Bristow of Kansas on December 13, 1909, proposing the election of Senators by the electors for six years, was reported on January 11, 1911, but the report struck Article I, Section 4. clause 1 from the Constitution. This gives the Federal Government control over elections, and as a result the joint resolution was defeated on February 28.[4] This took place after a bitter debate in which appeal was made to race prejudice, sectional feeling between North and South, and the states rights doctrine for the purpose of defeating the amendment.

A new Congress was convened on April 4, 1911. Senator Bristow made careful inquiry and found that ten senators who had voted against the amendment, and at least six of the new senators favored the change. This led him to introduce his joint resolution on April 6, 1911, in the same form in which it had been voted on in the Senate. It was referred to the Committee on Judiciary.[5]

In the meantime, the House resolution was sent to the Senate, and on April 17 was read twice by its title, and referred to the Committee on Privileges and Elections. But on April 20, it was, on motion of Senator Culberson of Texas, referred to the Committee on Judiciary. Senator Borah said the reasons for this change were: (1) It would fare better before the Judiciary Committee. The committee on Privileges and Elections had had similar resolutions before it for twenty years, but none had ever reached the Senate. It had been a slaughter house for such resolutions. (2) The Judiciary Committee had jurisdiction to consider the legal questions involved, and it would go there anyway sooner or later.[6]

On May 1, 1911, Senator Borah from the Committee on Judiciary reported the joint resolution (H. J. Res. 39) favorably without amendment and it was placed on the Calendar. On May 15, the Senate on motion of Senator Borah proceeded to consider the joint resolution, when Senator Bristow of Kansas offered an amendment in the form of his original resolution. The difference between it and the joint resolution was that it omitted the clause: "The times, places and manner of holding elections for senators shall be as prescribed in each State by the legislature thereof," contained in the joint resolution.[7] Another heated debate followed. Senator Reyner opposed the Bristow amendment on the ground that thirty-six States were required to ratify the joint resolution, and with the Bristow amendment, "You take a chance with nearly every Southern Commonwealth in this Union." "You imperil the joint resolution in every Southern State." The opposition was led by Senator Bacon of Georgia who declared that Senator Bristow's amendment gave the Federal Government power to send troops and marshals into the states to control the elections and intimidate the voters. Senator Bristow says, he must have known better, as troops and marshals were never sent into the South under Article I, Section 4, but under the Fourteenth Amendment.[8] After an amendment offered by Senator Bacon to amend the Bristow amendment had been withdrawn, the Bristow amendment was agreed to and the joint resolution, as amended, adopted in the Senate Committee of the Whole and reported to the Senate.[9] After Senator Bacon's amendment had been again offered and rejected, the vote was taken on the joint resolution and resulted in 64 yeas and 24 nays. As two-thirds had voted for it, the joint resolution had passed.[10] Senator Bristow said the resolution as adopted was identically the same as that voted on February 28, and had it not been in that form, it would have lacked two or three votes necessary to its adoption. The Southern Senators presented editorials from leading Southern newspapers like the Montgomery Advertiser, the Mobile Register, and others, declaring that the Bristow amendment gave the Federal government supreme control over the elections. These were printed in the Congressional Record.[11]

The House bill had provided for a change in Article I, Section 4, clause 1. The Senate had rejected this. On June 21, 1911, the Speaker laid the resolution (H. J. Res. 39), as amended by the Senate, before the House. The Bristow amendment was attacked and defended vigorously. Olmsted of Pennsylvania moved that the House concur in the Senate amendment.[12] The burden of all the speeches was that the Bristow amendment enlarged the power of the Federal government, while the House provision narrowed that power. The Republicans favored the Bristow amendment because it left Congress with power to control the election of Senators. The Democrats opposed it, because it did.[13] The Southern Democrats, especially, opposed interference in elections on the part of Congress. Witherspoon of Mississippi even charged wildly that the purpose of the Bristow amendment was to overthrow white supremacy in the South, and reinstate negro domination, and thus destroy Southern civilization.[14] On the other hand, Mann of Illinois charged the Southern Democrats with a purpose to secure power to deprive the blacks of the right to vote and to depress them, and of trying to deprive the national government of its power to compel honest and fair elections in the South.[15] "The power of the general government," he said, "to perpetuate itself by regulating, if necessary, the election of members of Congress, both members of the House, and of the Senate, is fundamental and necessary to the perpetuation of the Union." [16] Cullop charged that the purpose of the Bristow amendment was to prevent election by direct vote of the people and defeat the measure. On Olmstead's motion to concur on the Senate amendment, the House refused by a vote of 171 nays to 111 yeas. The failure to concur was regarded as equivalent to a motion to disagree.[17]

On July 5, 1911, the Speaker laid joint resolution No. 39 before the House "and announces that the Senate asks for a conference." Rucker of Missouri moved that the House insist on its disagreement, and agree to the conference. The House agreed, and the clerk announced Messrs. Rucker, Conry, and Olmsted as the House conferees. It was some time before the conferees could get together, as difficulty arose over the question as to whether the Senate conferees ought to notify the House conferees or vice versa. On April 17, 1912, Senator Clark of Wyoming announced in the Senate that the conference committee had been unable to reach any agreement, and he gave notice that formal report of the disagreement would be made to the Senate the following Tuesday.[18] On April 23, Senator Clark announced that the conference committee had held sixteen joint meetings, but could not reach any agreement. He explained that the cause of this was that the House resolution sought not only to provide for the election of Senators by popular vote, but *also to deprive Congress of any authority to supervise in any manner or degree the election of Senators.* The Senate amendment, on the other hand, provided simply and solely for the election of the Senators by the people, leaving the supervisory authority of Congress over the election, both of Senators and Representatives in exactly the same condition as it is now in the Constitution. "In other words, the House provides for two amendments to the Constitution—the Senate provides for one only." This means that the House amended Article I, Section 3, clause 1, and Section 4, clause 1, while the Senate simply amended Article I, Section 3, clause 1. He moved that the Senate insist upon its amendment to the joint resolution, the yeas and nays on this question stood 42 to 36.[19]

On April 26, 1912, Rucker of Missouri announced in the House that the Senate committee would not give way, and that he wished to give notice that he would move to recede from the disagreement of the House to the Senate amendment, and to concur therein.[20]   On May 13, 1912, Bartlett of Georgia offered a motion to concur in the Senate amendment: Provided Congress shall not have power to provide qualifications of electors of United States Senators, nor to authorize appointment of supervisors of elections, judges of election, returning boards, nor to authorize the use of United States marshals, military forces or troops at the polls.   This was rejected by a decisive vote of 189 nays to 89 yeas, and Rucker's motion to concur was agreed to by 238 yeas to 39 nays, and 110 not voting.   As two-thirds had voted yea, the House receded from its disagreement and concurred in the Senate amendment.[21] The Speaker signed the resolution on May 14; the Vice-President signed it on May 16; and the amendment became operative May 31, 1913.[22]

2. *The Purpose of the Seventeenth Amendment.*   The purpose was:

(1) *To meet a widespread demand on the part of the people of the United States, because Senators, being elected by the state legislatures, were not responsive to the public will.*[23]   Senator Owen said thirty-seven states had declared themselves in favor of direct election of Senators—only nine states had failed to act, namely, the New England States, New York, Delaware, and West Virginia.   Twenty-seven state legislatures had demanded the reform.   Rucker said in the House on April 13, 1911, all the resolutions had a common purpose, namely, to conform to a nation-wide demand to reform "the method of electing Senators which has sullied the fair name of States, and traduced the character of gentlemen, who have sought and won high political honors.   The people demand that Senators of the United States . . . shall be elected by a direct vote, and shall respond to the will of the people." [24]

(2) *To destroy the influence of the corporations on the government.*   The corporate interests of the United States "have tenaciously sought to control the election of Senators

friendly to their interests." They have frequently spent enormous sums in corrupting legislatures to elect Senators of their own choice. Through the influence of these "Corporation Senators," "legislation to control the trusts and monopolies has been smothered in committees and defeated in the Senate." By controlling the election of Senators they have also been able to secure the appointment of Federal judges more devoted to the corporate interests than to the welfare of the people of th United States.[25]

(3) *To enable the sovereign people to control their own government.* Senator Beveridge declared on June 14, 1910, that the purpose was to enable the people to conduct the government which belongs to them.[26] (See also arguments in favor of the amendment.)

3. *The Arguments in Favor of the Amendment.* It was argued:

(1) *The people demand the amendment.* In the House, Messrs. Rucker and Morgan argued that it was a reform demanded by the people of the whole United States.[27] Senator Owen of Oklahoma argued that twenty-seven state legislatures had demanded it. This list included Pennsylvania, nearly all the states of the middle west and West, and several Southern states. Twenty of these had sent Republican Senators to Congress. A majority of Senators representing the party in power have been instructed by their states in the matter.[28]

(2) *It would make the people supreme in the Senate of the United States.* Adair argued that the method of choosing Senators by state legislatures had made the Senate the home of men of great wealth, whose hearts did not beat in sympathy with the people.[29] Wealth, plutocracy, and subserviency to the interests would no longer be the qualifications necessary for a Senator, but rugged honesty, recognized ability, and admitted capacity, which will preserve sovereignty in the hands of the people. Robinson of Arkansas offered similar arguments.[30]

(3) *It will make the Senate more responsive to the will of the people.* Robinson argued that it would make the legislative branch of the government fairly responsive to the will of the people of the states.[31] Adair said it would make the Senators directly responsible to the individual citizen, give the people direct control over the legislative department of the

government, and make the Senators responsible to the will of the people. Corporations had come to control the legislatures so that the Senate was no longer the balance wheel, or represented the interests of the people.[32]

(4) *It will increase the confidence of the people in the Senate of the United States.* Senator Owen declared it would popularize the government, and tend to increase the confidence of the people of the United States in the Senate. This confidence had been to some extent impaired in recent years.[33]

(5) *It would promote the political education of the people.* Hobson declared this would be the result through the recurring exercise of political power.[34]

(6) *It will result in the election of better men to the Senate.* Morgan said that on the average better men would be elected to the Senate—not dark horses, but men of ability and integrity. Senator Owen said it will compel candidates for the Senate to be subjected to the severe scrutiny of a campaign before the people, and compel the selection of the best fitted men.[35]

(7) *It will result in the enactment of better laws.* Morgan argued that this would follow because the people will elect better men to the Senate.[36]

(8) *It will promote the efficiency of state legislatures.* Hobson alleged that there had been an ever increasing demoralization of state legislatures, but this change would give the people greater control over their legislatures, and raise the standard of efficiency. Senator McCumber argued that it would give relief to legislators because they would not be chosen to elect Senators, but to enact legislation.[37] Senator Owen said it would prevent the disturbance of state legislation over the Senatorship.[37a]

(9) *There will be no more legislative deadlocks.* Adair said that during the past twenty years there has scarcely been a time when one or more states were not tied up on a deadlock over the election of a Senator, and therefore, were deprived of fair and equal representation. This is an injustice to the state, and unfair to the whole country. This could not happen under the new system. Deadlocks so frequent in the past, cannot happen, Robinson of Arkansas declared. Senators Owen and McCumber also urged that deadlocks would be prevented.[38]

(10) *It will prevent corruption and scandal in state legis-*

latures. Under the present method, much corruption and fraud creep into the legislatures, Adair said, because those who covet senatorships make it their business to elect proper persons, but the new plan will remove such evils from the legislatures. Hobson declared the present method invited corruption from men of wealth seeking office, and from the great moneyed interests seeking to secure or hold unmolested power to tax the American people by controlling the Senate of the United States.[39] Robinson said it would destroy bribery and corruption in state legislatures. The only remedy for all this bribery, fraud and corruption is for the people to elect the Senators. Great financial interests which have corruptly controlled the election of Senators in state legislatures cannot longer do so.

(11) *The amendment will lessen the temptation to gerrymander the legislative districts for partisan purposes.* This is self-explanatory. Adair claimed that this would be one result.[40]

4. *The Objections to the Amendment.* These were:

(1) *It is revolutionary and socialistic.* To this, Ferris answered that it was common sense, and common justice. "It is but the doing of exact justice to the people, who have long been denied the right to select their members of Congress in both branches." [41]

(2) *If popular election is adopted, none but rich men can afford to run for the Senate.* Ferris replied that Senators are elected for six years, three times the length of time for which members of the House are chosen, and there is, therefore, no occasion for such a statement.

(3) *The present method of electing Senators grew out of the carefully balanced wisdom of the fathers, has lasted for a hundred years, and ought not therefore to be disturbed.*[43] Senator Beveridge in reply said four plans of electing Senators were proposed in the Constitutional Convention: (a) Appointment by the executive from a number nominated by the state legislatures. (b) Election by the House from a number nominated by state legislatures. (c) Election by the legislatures. (d) Election by direct vote of the people, which was "advanced by the ablest man in the Constitutional Convention —at least the man whom I believe is now recognized as the ablest lawyer" —James Wilson of Pennsylvania.[44]

The third prevailed because the states wanted equality.

Objection to election of Senators by the people was based on reasons which have since disappeared. Sherman of Connecticut gave as his reason that "the people are lacking in information, and they are easily misled." Postal service was poor, telegraphs undreamed of, and newspapers local, so there may have been some reason to think the people were not informed at that time. But these conditions no longer exist to-day. The telegraph, railroads, postal service, and rural delivery are making the people more and more capable and enlightened. The average citizen is as well informed as the average member of either House. Every farmer in the Republic reads the news as to legislation in the evening. So that the reason for legislative election of Senators no longer exists. Dickinson wanted rank and wealth to count in the Senate, and have it resemble the British House of Lords as much as possible. Dickinson represented the ruling class which existed in America at that time. The small states threw their weight on this side and it prevailed. But will any Senator dare to advance against popular election today, the same reasons advanced by Sherman and Dickinson? [45]

(4) *Senator Root objected that it was inexpedient and unnecessary to change the Constitution in regard to election of Senators.* It would result in a deterioration of the personnel of the Senate, and he held that the evils could be cured by statute without amending the Constitution.[46]

(5) *The primary system in many of the states has accomplished this same purpose.* Senator Beveridge's answer was that everybody knows the people will not turn out to vote at the primary because they vote at the later election. If you get them out at the primary, they neglect the main election; their energies are exhausted; they cannot be voting all the time. It also doubles the number of elections, of which there are already too many.[47]

(6) *Tribble of Georgia objected that the amendment would give the Federal government control over the election of Senators, thus taking from the states their constitutional rights and centralizing power in the Federal government.* This would destroy the rights of the states and carry us back to the days of reconstruction in the South.[48]

The issue here was between the House amendment, which

amended Article I, Section 4, clause 1, as well as Article I, Section 3, clause 1, by changing the words, "chosen by the legislature thereof," to "elected by the people thereof." Very stubborn and vehement objection was offered to amending Section 4. Cannon said if a State seceded, the United States would be powerless to authorize an election, and the government of the United States would exist at the mercy of the states. Utter said it would change the Constitution in such a way as to rob Congress of the right to protect itself. It transfers power of control over the election of Senators from the national government to the state legislatures. This would entirely change the relations between the national government and the several states, "and would leave the nation dependent upon the several states, and without authority of its own in respect of an essential part of the machinery necessary to its continued existence," [49] said Sutherland. He declared the Senate and House constitute one of the departments of government. "To say one branch of this department shall be in the absolutely uncontrolled power of the various state governments is to deny the supremacy of the Federal government, and to that extent make it subordinate to the government of the several States." It was necessary to regulate elections by a national statute in 1842, 1866, and 1872, and it cannot be shown that it may not be necessary in the future. The people of the United States have not sought an amendment depriving the United States of its authority over ultimate control of the election of Senators.[50]

5. *The Sources of the Amendment.* (1) *The first proposal for the election of United States' Senators by the people was made in the Federal Convention on May 13, 1787, by James Wilson of Pennsylvania.*[51] On June 7, he said he wished the Senate to be elected by the people, and moved to postpone Dickinson's motion that they be elected by the state legislatures, to take up one proposing to elect Senators by the people. Gouverneur Morris supported Wilson by seconding his motion, but it was voted down ten states to one (Pennsylvania).[52]

The *reasons* given by James Wilson for advocating the election of Senators by the people, instead of by the state legislatures, or lower branch of Congress were: (1) The Senate of the United States ought to be independent of both the state legislatures and the House of Representatives. (2) Because it was wrong to increase the weight of the state legislatures by making them the electors of the national legislature. All interference between the general and local governments ought to be obviated as much as possible. (3) If they were to establish a national government, it ought to flow from the people at large. (4) Election by the people would [53] be most likely to obtain men of intelligence and uprightness. Wilson, in advocating direct election of Senators was just a century and a quarter ahead of his age.

(2) *James Wilson had state and colonial experience behind him on which he built.* He suggested that the plan in the Constitution of New York for the election of Senators by the freemen in districts was a good model to follow.[54] Madison menitoned that Senators were elected by the people in Virginia, while the upper house was also elected in other states.[55]

In some of the colonies, as Connecticut and Rhode Island, the people elected the assistants or upper house.[56] The Pennsylvania Frame of Government of 1682, as well as the Frames of 1683, and 1696, provided for the election of the Council or upper house by the freemen.[57] At the first general court held in Boston on October 19, 1630, it was decided that *the freemen should choose the assistants,* and the assistants the Governor.[58] Of course, at the time the amendment was proposed for adoption, *the states had had long experience* in electing their Senators. The amendment simply proposed to do for the United States what had been done by the states from the beginning of national existence. The amendment became operative on May 31, 1913.

NOTES TO CHAPTER XIX

1. Cong. Record, 61 Cong. 1 Sess. 1548, 1570.
2. Id. 3377.
3. Id. 3900.
3ª. Cong. Record, 61 Cong. 1 sess. 4108, 4120, 4121, 3900, 4067-4068.
4. Id. 4114.
5. Cong. Record, 61 Cong. 1 sess. 4364, 4390, 4440-1, 4493, 4495, 3 Dallas 378.
6. Cong. Record, 61 Cong. 1 sess. 4425, 4436, 4410, 4412, 4414, 4417, 4428, 4430, 4433, 4436, 4426, 4398.
7. Cong. Record, 61 Cong. 1 sess. 4412, 4421.
8. Cong. Record, 61 Cong. 1 sess. 4399.
9. Cong. Record, 61 Cong. 1 sess. 4431, 4390.

10. Cong. Record, 61 Cong. 1 sess. 4431, 4390.
11. Id. 4402-3.
12. Cong. Record, 61 Cong. 1 sess. 4402, 4403, 4390.
13. Cong. Record, 61 Cong. 1 sess. 4391.
14. Cong. Record, 61 Cong. 1 sess. 4391.
15. Cong. Record, 61 Cong. 1 sess. 4391.
16. Id. 4437, 4391.
17. Id. 4406.
18. Id. 4419.
19. Cong. Rec. 61 Cong. 1 sess. 4411, 4419.
20. Id. 4391, 4393, 4394.
21. Cong. Rec. 61 Cong. 1 sess. 4398.
22. Id. 4109.
23. Id. 1548, 4402, 4403.
24. Cong. Rec. 61 Cong. 1 sess. 1548, 3377, 4394, 4410.
25. Cong. Rec. 61 Cong. 1 sess. 1569-70.
26. Cong. Rec. 61 Cong. 1 sess. 4409, 4410, 4418.
27. Cong. Rec. 61 Cong. 1 sess. 4106.
28. Cong. Rec. 61 Cong. 1 sess. 4404, 4405, 4412, app. 126, 131, 4392, 4397, 4398.
29. Id. 4109.
30. Cong. Record, 61 Cong. 1 sess. 4116; Plymouth Colony Laws, 74; Col. Records of Mass. Bay, II, 173, 213; III, 88; Charters and Gen. Laws of Mass. Bay (Ed. 1814) p. 70.

NOTES TO AMENDMENT XVII

1. Sen. Docs. Vol. 38, 62 Cong. 2 sess. No. 666, 3, 4; Cong. Rec. 60, 1 sess. 24, 186, 224, 364, 444, 602, 2014, 5567.
2. Cong. Rec. 61 Cong. 1 sess. 2 sess. 1920, 7111, 7495, 25, 28, 85, 183, 241, 243.
3. Cong. Rec. 61 Cong. 1 sess. 242, 243.
4. Cong. Rec. 61 Cong. 2 sess. 7113, 7120; Sen. Doc. (61 Cong. 2 sess.) No. 866, 5, 105; 3 sess. 3639.
5. Cong. Rec. 62 Cong. 1 sess. 106; Sen. Docs.; 62 Cong. 2 sess. 1911-12, Vol. 38, No. 866, 8.
6. Cong. Rec. 62 Cong. 1 sess. 306, 319, 440.
7. Cong. Rec. 62 Cong. 1 sess. 787, 788, 1205.
8. Cong. Rec. 62 Cong. 1 sess. 1736. Sen. Docs. 62 Cong. 2 sess. 1911-12, no. 866, p. 9
9. Cong. Rec. 61 Cong. 1 sess. 1884.
10. Id. 1923-25.
11. Sen. Docs. 62 Cong. 2 sess. 1911-12, Vol. 38, no. 866, p. 9; Cong. Rec. 62 Cong. 1 sess. 2122, 2381, 2453, 2695.
12. Cong. Rec. 62 Cong. 2 sess. 2404.
13. Cong. Rec. 62 Cong. 2 sess. 2412, 2416, 2417, 2426, 2419, 2425.
14. Cong. Rec. 62 Cong. 2 sess. 2415.
15. Id. 2430.
16. Cong. Rec. 62 Cong. 1 sess. 2430.
17. Id. 2408, 2433, 2438.
18. Cong. Rec. 62 Cong. 2 sess. 2649-50, 2940, 2950, 4905.
19. Cong. Rec. 62 Cong. 2 sess. 5169, 5172.
20. Cong. Rec. 62 Cong. 2 sess. 5433.

21. Cong. Record, 62 Cong. 2 sess. 6366, 6369.
22. Cong. Rec. 62 Cong. 2 sess. 6407, 6475, 6503.
23. Id. 61 Cong. 2 sess. 7110.
24. Cong. Rec. 61 Cong. 2 sess. 7110. Id. 61 Cong. 1 sess. 6803-4. Id.
62 Cong. 1 sess. 206.
25. Sen. Docs. Vol. 38, 62 Cong. 2 sess. 1911-12, no. 866, p. 4, 5.
26. Cong. Rec. 61 Cong. 2 sess. 8040.
27. Id. 61 Cong. 1 sess. 206, 228.
28. Cong. Rec. 61 Cong. 1 sess. 6803-4.
29. Id. 209.
30. Cong. Rec. 61 Cong. 1 sess. 208, 209; Id. 62 Cong. 1 sess. 220.
31. Id. 220; Id. 61 Cong. 1 sess. 6803-4.
32. Cong. Rec. 62 Cong. 1 sess. 209.
33. Cong. Rec. 61 Cong. 1 sess 7109.
34. Id. 62 Cong. 1 sess. 211.
35. Cong. Rec. 61 Cong. 1 sess. 6803-4.
36. Id. 62 Cong. 1 sess. 228.
37. Id. 211; Id. 61 Cong. 1 sess. 1880.
37ᵃ. Cong. Rec. 61 Cong. 1 sess. 6803-4.
38. Id. 62 Cong. 1 sess. 209, 213; Id. 220, 231; Id. 61 Cong. 1 sess.
7109, 1880.
39. Cong. Rec. 62 Cong. 1 sess. 209, 219, 228, 231, 211.
40. Cong. Rec. 62 Cong. 1 sess. 220, 231, 213, 209; Id. 61 Cong. 1 sess.
6803-4.
41. Cong. Rec. 62 Cong. 1 sess. 221.
42. Id.
43. Id. 61 Cong. 2 sess. 80387.
44. Cong. Rec. 61 Cong. 2 sess. 8037.
45. Cong. Rec. 61 Cong. 2 sess. 8037, 8038.
46. Cong. Rec. 61 Cong. 2 sess. 1485.
47. Id. 8039.
48. Cong. Rec. 62 Cong. 1 sess. 214-15.
49. Cong. Rec. 62 Cong. 1 sess. 213, 234, 1428.
50. Cong. Rec. 62 Cong. 1 sess. 1429.
51. Elliot, V, 139.
52. Elliot, V, 167, 168, 169, 170.
53. Elliot, V, 138, 136, 169.
54. Elliot, V, 138; Poore, 1364.
55. Elliot, V, 138; Poore, 279, 1311, 1411, 1910, 961, 1284.
56. Laws of Conn. and R. I. passim.
57. Poore, 1520, 1527.
58. Elliot, New Eng. Hist. 179; Palfrey, Hist. of New Eng. Vol. II,
9, 10.

CHAPTER XX

The Eighteenth and Nineteenth Amendments

1. *The Eighteenth Amendment: A Preliminary Historical Statement.* The Congressional Record says that the first proposition for an amendment to the Constitution prohibiting the manufacture and sale of ardent spirits was submitted by a committee of the Senate of the United States.[1] Representative Blair of New Hampshire introduced a prohibition resolution in the House on December 27, 1876, for the same purpose. Then on December 4, 1911, Richmond P. Hobson of Alabama offered a joint resolution in the House to amend the Constitution for the purpose of prohibiting the sale, and importation for sale of beverages containing alcohol. It was referred to the Committee on the Judiciary.[2]

Hobson again offered his resolution on April 7, August 5, October 29, November 13, and December 1, 8, and 10, 1913. In each case the amendment was referred to the Committee on the Judiciary.[3] The resolution was, therefore, introduced by the member from Alabama over a year before the Great War broke out and when there was no thought of war.

In the Senate, Senator Works on June 21, 1913, introduced a joint resolution to amend the Constitution by prohibiting the sale, manufacture, and importation of distilled liquor containing alcohol, except for mechanical, scientific, and medicinal purposes, on and after a period of three years. It was read the first time by *title* and the second time in *full.* Congress was given power to enforce the article by appropriate legislation, and on Senator Works' motion it was referred to the Committee on the Judiciary. The reason for three years' delay was, he said, to prevent throwing too many men out of employment, and the confiscating or destroying the value of too much property. The idea of adopting such an amendment, he declared, had originated with Mr. S. Benson of Oregon, an employer of many men. He had seen the devastating effect of alcohol in destroying the lives and efficiency of laboring men.[4] On April

373

4, 1917, Senator Sheppard introduced a joint resolution in the Senate proposing the amendment. It was referred to the Committee on the Judiciary and reported with amendments.[5] The amendment was subjected to a long and acrid debate in each house. The previous question was moved and ordered in the House on December 22, 1914. The vote resulted in 197 yeas, 190 nays; 40 not voting, and one answering present. As two-thirds of the members had not voted for the resolution, it was rejected by the first vote of the House.[6]

2. *The Arguments or Objections Against the Amendment.* The arguments both for and against the amendment were many and long, rational, and irrational, and contained much wearisome repetition. In spite of this, however, the speeches on both sides were remarkable for the array of facts presented, and the debates were generally of a very high order. It was argued:

(1) *The amendment would deprive men of their property without just compensation and throw thousands out of employment.* It would destroy $800,000,000 or a thousand million dollars' worth of property without just compensation. This would increase the taxes and bankrupt the nation. Is this fair play? In 1909, $771,516,000 was invested in the liquor industry in the United States; 77,799 persons were employed in it, and their annual wages amounted to $70,907,000. It would take the bread from the mouths of hundreds of thousands of working men, not only from those employed in distilleries and breweries, but also those employed as coopers, blacksmiths, glassblowers, wagon builders, bricklayers, and carpenters. To these would be added banks, business men, railroads, and farmers who grew barley. It would result in an economic panic unparalleled in our history. Organized labor would suffer and agriculturists would be denied opportunity to market their crops except at great sacrifice. Garret of Texas replied that the thirteenth amendment took $4,000,000,000 worth of personal property from the South, and now when the South was willing to join hands with the North in destroying the liquor traffic, the North cried out about the preservation of property. "A man has no property right in an unlawful business."[7]

(2) *The amendment would deprive the government of a*

large part of its revenue. It will cause an annual deficit in the national treasury of $280,000,000. In 1914, said Representative Underwood, the government figures show that the United States derived $245,000,000, and the states $79,000,000 from the liquor traffic. The adoption of the amendment would destroy this revenue and the evils of intemperance would still exist. Representative Bartholdt said this deficit would have to be covered by direct taxes. A new corporation tax, a new income tax, and a war revenue tax had just been imposed. "Do you propose to pile an additional quarter of a billion on top of these? No political party would ever survive the attempt." In reply it was said *that* revenue was simply blood money. For every dollar it pays the government, it costs the people three, four, or ten times as much to maintain courts, jails, hospitals, and poor houses, to say nothing of the poverty, vice, disease, and wrecked lives directly due to the traffic. The sobering of the nation will more than balance the loss of revenue. Representative Webb quoted the Supreme Court of the United States in the License Cases to the effect that if loss of revenue did result to the United States, "she will be the gainer a thousand fold in the health, wealth and happiness of the people." [8]

(3) *It abandons our policy of making temperance men and women by education, undermines manliness and respect for law, and makes men liars, sneaks, and hypocrites.* Representative Brown of Wisconsin argued that it substituted legislation and coercion for education. A citizenship should be reared that is strong enough to remain honest and sober in spite of opportunities to steal and drink. The law will be evaded in a thousand ways and the result will be a nation of lawbreakers, a condition inevitably leading to lawlessness and anarchy. [9] Representative Kahn of California said that in November, 1914, the state held an election on state-wide prohibition. A druggist in Pasadena which had voted itself dry under local option, displayed a large sign in his window, "Vote the state dry." That very afternoon he was arrested for running a "blind pig." That is a sample of the hypocrisy that follows prohibition legislation.

(4) *It attempts to make men sober by law, and will make every house a distillery or barroom.* Man cannot be made

sober by law any more than he can be made honest by law, declared Bartholdt of Missouri. You cannot change human nature by statute. The spirit of temperance which is not born of conviction will never result in voluntary abstention. It cannot be legislated into the human mind and heart by congressional enactments. It attempts to legislate the appetite and desire for intoxicating liquor out of millions of people at once by a single act of legislation that no king or monarch, except the Czar of Russia who believes in the divine right of Kings, would dare to attempt. Human laws are powerless against the laws of nature. Abolish the law of gravity by enactment and jump out of a ten story window and you will be picked up in a shovel. Our opponents say we should remove temptation. We cannot do this, but we can and should by discipline and training strengthen our power of resistance against it.

Bartholdt also argued that a man could manufacture all he pleased for his own use, and that every house in the country could or would become a distillery or a barroom. The proposition should, therefore, be styled: "A bill to promote home drunkenness." Pou of North Carolina suggested that the amendment might appropriately be entitled: "An act to legalize the illicit still in the United States"; while Mann of Illinois objected that it made manufacture easy, and liquor free, and the government would have no control over it as it was untaxed.[10] Representative Tillman of Arkansas replied that though law could not make men entirely sober, yet it worked wonders and made men do many things they do not want to do. It is a great civilizer and a great persuader. "The Ten Commandments are often violated, and yet God never did a greater kindness for humanity than when he gave us these commandments and ordered their observance. Who would wipe these from the record though they are broken by thousands every hour of the day?"

(5) *It is an invasion of personal liberty and individual rights.* This is due to the fact that it prohibits what is not wrong in itself. The majority cannot deprive us of our inalienable right to eat and drink what we please without robbing us of our liberty. We must protect ourselves against what John Stuart Mill called "the tyranny of the majority," if the nation is to remain free. "No despot in history," said Bar-

tholdt, "has ever dared to prohibit what is morally right." Kelley of Pennsylvania replied that this so-called liberty was impossible in a civilized nation, for whatever law existed there were limitations on personal liberty. There are laws limiting the highwayman, the embezzler, and the killing of game out of season. Every forward step in civilization has been taken by placing new limitations on personal liberty. The argument steps backward into savagery and anarchy. Stephens of Mississippi said there were laws against profanity, vagrancy, gambling, and prohibiting persons from being drunk in public places. Why infringe upon personal liberty? "The interest of society, morals, and good government require protection from the criminal, the vicious and immoral." [11]

(6) *It would destroy the vineyards of California.* Hayes of California said the owners had their all invested in these vineyards and on the yearly crop the owners and their families depended for their living. If the owners were to be compensated, it would be different. That is the only civilized and equitable thing to do. The people of California rejected this identical amendment by about 175,000 last year (1914). He regarded the fact that his district had rejected the amendment by over 12,000 as plain instruction to him, no matter what his personal opinion on the question at issue might be. There are 160,000 acres of wine grapes in California and the adoption of the amendment would mean a loss of $30,000,000 to the grape growers of the state. When Switzerland adopted prohibition the cantons compensated the owners. [12]

(7) *National prohibition by a constitutional amendment is unworthy of a great people.* A constitution, said Bartholdt, should be a bill of rights to protect life, liberty, and property, and especially to protect the minority. By incorporating police regulations in the national constitution, it will be perverted, defaced, and desecrated. [13]

(8) *Prohibition does not prohibit, and is a failure in the states that have tried it.* This was a favorite argument and was presented by Underwood, Bartholdt, and others. The latter said a greater percentage of drunkenness was recorded and from five to nine times as many arrests were made in those states than in liberal states like Wisconsin. Webb of North Carolina replied: "Larceny laws do not prevent stealing, and

therefore you should abolish them. Homicide laws do not prevent the killing of men, and therefore, you should have no murder laws, and so on down through the catalogue." Representative Connelly of Kansas declared emphatically: "There is no evidence anywhere that prohibition has become a failure in the state of Kansas." The records show "that the amount of intoxicating liquor shipped into the state last year (1913) averaged less than one dollar and a half for each adult male citizen of the state, while other states have an average of thirty dollars per capita." Kansas has twice as many people as Colorado, yet a smaller number of prisoners in her state penitentiary. In Kansas there are eighteen counties without a poorhouse, and twenty-nine counties without an inmate in a poorhouse. When it is desired to point out a place where prohibition has been a failure, Kansas must be left out of the calculation.[14] Senator Thompson of Kansas read one hundred letters from judges, sheriffs, chiefs of police, mayors, and other officials of the counties testifying to the great success of prohibition in Kansas. Representative Tillman of Arkansas pointed out that in the prohibition state of Maine forty-nine per cent of the heads of families owned their own houses, which was nearly twice as many as in any other state of the union. The savings banks of Maine contained a larger per capita of interest bearing accounts than any other country in the world.

(9) *It could never be enforced.* This was a common objection. Suppose twelve states, it was urged, like Massachusetts, New York, New Jersey, Pennsylvania, Ohio, Indiana, Illinois, Michigan, Wisconsin, Minnesota, Missouri, and California, having a population of 50,000,000, a majority of the people of the United States, should oppose it, could such a law throwing hundreds of thousands out of work and destroying millions of dollars' worth of property, be enforced. It will be impossible to enforce it in any community where it is not supported by public sentiment.[15]

(10) *A minority of the people may impose the law on the majority.* Senator Pomerene showed by the census of 1910 that Nevada, Wyoming, Delaware, Arizona, Idaho, New Mexico, Vermont, Utah, Montana, New Hampshire, North Dakota and Oregon had 4,657,052 people, while Ohio alone had 4,767,121, or 110,069 more than the twelve states mentioned;

and that these states with the addition of Maine, Rhode Island, Florida, South Dakota, Colorado, and Connecticut had only 8,608,432 people while New York had 9,113,614, or 505,182 more than the eighteen states mentioned.[16] Why should 90,000 people in Nevada have the same weight as 9,000,000 in New York? There are nineteen states in the Union whose combined population is less than that of New York. The will of three-fourths of the states or a minority of the people can impose the law on all the states. This is possible because the thirty-six states having the smallest number of people have a total population of 40,865,581. The other twelve states have a population of 51,106,685.

In reply it was said by Representative Morgan of Oklahoma, that the argument, if valid, would apply to all proposed amendments and would prevent the people from ever amending the constitution. Six states could defeat this resolution, as two-thirds of the members must vote for it in each house. New York with forty-three votes, Pennsylvania with thirty-two, Illinois with twenty-five, Ohio with twenty-one, and Missouri and Texas with sixteen votes each have a total of one hundred and fifty-three votes, or more than one-third of the entire membership of the House, and could defeat this or any other resolution. The interests of the states with large populations, where in the main the liquor interests are concentrated, are, therefore, amply protected against any unfair or unjust action by the representatives of the people from the smaller states.[17]

(11) *It interferes with or violates state sovereignty or state rights.* It will interfere with the police power of the states. It is entirely a question for the states. That was President Wilson's view. It is a matter wholly within the police power of the state. The fathers of the republic wisely reserved police power to the several states, and the power to pass sumptuary laws was conferred · exclusively on the states. The amendment would tear this sacred doctrine to shreds by conferring police power on the national government. "Let no Democrat mistake the issue," said Mr. Henry. "The ghost of Hamilton is abroad in the American Congress and in the country. For my part, I say, 'Get thee hence. Avaunt and quit my sight.' Democracy needs no new creed." The reply to all this was that Congress had no power to *adopt* the amend-

ment. The only thing Congress could do was to submit it for acceptance or rejection by three-fourths of the states. There is no question here of any invasion of state rights. The question is, "Shall the states enlarge the powers of the Federal government by giving it the right to control the liquor traffic?" Representative Bell of California quoted Rev. Sam. Small as follows: "Our proposition cannot win without the separate consents of thirty-six of the states—the man who would arbitrarily deny to them that right is not the friend but the enemy of state rights." The amendment, it was pointed out, simply referred the question to the states as to whether or not they wanted to change their policy on the liquor traffic. This was obedience to the doctrine of state rights and not a violation.

The formation of the government, declared Saunders of Virginia, was an invasion and curtailment of the rights of the states. "The constitution contains a body of provisions which inhibit the states from doing certain things. What are these but an invasion of state rights?"

"I do not believe it is an infringement on the rights of any state," said Quinn of Mississippi in a fiery speech, "to prevent New York or any other state from emptying its sewage, its corruption, its poison, this liquor that it makes, down into my state." "None will contend," said Stephens, "that the states are unable to delegate further powers to the general government." Senator Shepherd pointed out that if it was wrong for one state to say what another state should do, then it was wrong to have adopted the income tax amendment and to have imposed it on Connecticut and Rhode Island without their consent.[18]

(12) *Beer is healthy.* Senator Sherman of Illinois replied, some kinds may be but not the kind we are making from corn and cheap rice in this country. We have seen the legend on billboards all over the country. "The beer that made Milwaukee famous." Away down in Yucatan I saw a parody on that. It said, "We brew the beer that made Milwaukee jealous." "I went in and tried some of it. No white man could habitually drink it and live. It may be good for the men who dwell in the tropics because they are short lived and some of them think it a blessing to die anyhow—a relief from the sore

vexations of the flesh—I repeat, Mr. President, that the brew of beer out of corn and rice and cheaper processes employed, is literally a corrosive, rotting, burning slop. It has rotted more kidneys, and perforated more stomachs, and destroyed more livers by cirrhosis and abscesses than all the natural diseases to which human flesh ever fell heir. I never saw a man drink it in my life, steadily, that was not a good candidate for Bright's disease, or indigestion, or paralysis, if he kept it up long enough." [19]

3. *The Arguments in Favor of the Amendment.* The leading arguments were:

(1) *Science has demonstrated that alcohol is a protoplasmic, toxic poison.* It is an oxide derivative of the hydrocarbons; its formula is C_2H_5 (OH), and it consists of two atoms of carbon, six of hydrogen and one of oxygen. Other members of the group are carbolic acid, chloral hydrate—popularly called chloral—morphine, and strychnine. Alcohol is a toxin, and a poison to all forms of life, whether plants, animals, or men. Science declares that alcohol is a protoplasmic poison. "Any organic substance placed in alcohol is preserved indefinitely," because no living thing can penetrate the alcohol to destroy it.

The death rate in America per year is 1000 in every 61,000, but for total abstainers it is only 560 per 61,000. Alcohol not only kills but also blights the drinker's children. If both parents are alcoholics, it has been found that one child out of every seven will be born deformed and incurable; of those who survive, one in five will become insane, and one in three epileptic, or hysterical, thus "blighting the very purposes of the Almighty for the future development of the race." If you want to be blessed obey nature; but if you want to be damned, defy nature. A report of 800 German scientists says: "We should not discuss moderation with a man. The thing has long since been settled by science. The use of narcotic poisons is simply indecent and criminal." The arguments under this head may be summarized as follows: (a) Alcohol is a toxic poison to all life. (b) It is a habit-forming drug. (c) It attacks the brain and destroys will-power. (d) It shortens life. (e) It blights the offspring.[20]

(2) *The amendment is necessary for the purpose of remov-*

ing temptation. The reply to this was that it was impossible to remove everything that tempts man. "The creator himself," said Bartholdt, "put temptation into the garden of Eden. But I suppose that was a mistake." The impossible task of removing temptation should not be attempted, he declared, but the thing to do was to strengthen man's powers of resistance to enable him to defy temptation. Whatever the merit of the argument, this was, so far as it went, certainly good New Testament ethical philosophy.

(3) *The liquor traffic lowers the standard of our citizenship—physically, mentally, and morally.* The chief national asset is the character of our citizenship. The main pillars of our national strength are not our national wealth and our great national resources. For the extension of the power, influence, and principles of the American republic, for leadership among the nations of the world, and for superiority over other nations, "We must rely upon the character of our citizenship." Whatever causes our citizenship to deteriorate, weakens the government and endangers the very existence of the republic. By destroying the body, blinding the reason, and weakening and paralyzing the will of our citizens, the liquor traffic destroys the very foundations of the American republic.[21]

(4) *Why not refer the question to the will of the American people to say whether or not they wish to have national prohibition?* It requires two-thirds of each house and three-fourths of the states to add an amendment to the Constitution. If two-thirds desire to have this amendment, then one-third should not complain. Representative Webb of North Carolina declared that the amendment was backed by a public sentiment of such strength and character as not only to justify but to require Congress to submit it to the states. The moral and commercial forces of the nation have given it careful thought and approval. Congress has been overwhelmed by letters and petitions asking and pleading with Congress to submit the question to the states. Over 16,000,000 people have petitioned Congress for its submission. This is a greater number than ever petitioned Congress before on any subject. In 1907, only three states, Maine, North Dakota, and Kansas had prohibition laws. From 1907 to September 1st, 1914, only six additional states had been added, but to-day there are

twenty-seven prohibition states containing a population of 61,000,000 in the union. There are only three hundred and fifty-five wet counties in the United States out of a total 2,543 counties. Over half the world is dry today. "The time has come when Congress cannot fail to recognize the overwhelming demands that are being made from every section of this Nation, and from all classes of her people to submit this proposition to the states for their ratification," or rejection.

In the debates, there was general acknowledgment of the fact by opponents that the amendment conformed to the constitutional requirements as to the manner and method in which the Constitution may be amended, though Hardwick of Georgia claimed that the amendment violated the spirit of the Constitution.[22]

4. *The Text of the Amendment.* In the House, debate on the amendment as passed by the Senate began on December 17, 1917. It read:

"Article— Section I. The manufacture, sale, or transportation of intoxicating liquors within, the importation thereof, or the exportation thereof from, the United States, and all territory subject to the jurisdiction thereof for beverage purposes is hereby prohibited. Section II. This article shall be inoperative unless it shall have been ratified as an amendment to the constitution by the legislatures of the several states, as provided in the constitution, within six years of the date of the submission hereof to the states by the congress. Section III. The congress shall have power to enforce this article by appropriate legislation."

Several important changes were made by the House. "*After one year from the ratification of this article,*" was added to section one. The purpose of this was to give the brewers, distillers, and barrooms of the country a fair and just opportunity to wind up their business.

Sections two and three were transposed, and the judiciary committee of the House amended the third resolution by making it number two and adding, "and the several states," after congress for the purpose of reserving to the states their power to enforce their prohibition laws. If this amendment were not adopted, it was said, there might be a fight in Congress every two years over the question as to whether or not the states should be given the right to aid in the enforcement of the amendment. Every state under the police power has the right to prohibit within its boundaries the manufacture and sale of intoxicating liquors. We do not want the expense of ten thousand Federal officers going over the country to enforce the law, when the states, if willing, could do it with their own officers. Therefore, "we thought it wise to give both the congress and the several states concurrent power to enforce this article." There would not be any clashing of jurisdiction because the one getting jurisdiction first would deal with the case. For this reason they did not think it would result in double jeopardy. The principle laid down by the Supreme Court of the United States in U. S. v. Lanza and Hebert v. Louisiana (260 U. S. 367, 47 Sup. Ct. 103) that a violation of the law would be an offense against two different sovereignties, and, therefore, two distinct offenses, one against the state and one against the United States, which might be prosecuted in the courts of each without violating the rule of the Constitution against double jeopardy, does not seem to have been recognized by the members of Congress in debate.

As to the *time limitation* of seven years in article three, one objection urged against the amendment was that it would remain open for adoption by the states for an indefinite time as a raw, bleeding sore on the body politic of every state in the union. Senator Warren G. Harding had, therefore, proposed an amendment placing a time limit on its ratification for the purpose of eliminating "this unending prohibition contest in the Halls of Congress," by referring it to the people who must make the ultimate decision, and *forcing* a final settlement of this great public question within six years. The constitutional objection was urged by Senator Borah and others that the Constitution placed no limit on the time within which a state might ratify an amendment, but Senator Harding replied that article V of the Constitution gave an example when it provided that no amendment affecting the importation of slaves could become operative before 1808. Senator Borah offered an amendment proposing ten years instead of six, but the Senate rejected ten years and concurred in Senator Harding's amendment. Later, however, seven years was agreed to as a fair compromise between six and ten years. In Dillon v.

Glass the Supreme Court of the United States settled the question of constitutionality by holding that Congress may fix a definite period within which an amendment must be ratified or it will be inoperative.[23]

5. *The Vote on the Amendment.* The vote in the Senate was taken August 1, 1917, and stood, yeas 65, nays 20, not voting 11. An analysis of the vote shows that only *two* states voted 'nay' in the Senate—New York and Massachusetts—and that *twenty-one* states voted 'yea.' *Fourteen* states voted *one yea and one nay*, while *nine* states voted one yea with nine senators not voting. *Two* other states, Connecticut and Maryland, failed to vote for the amendment as one senator from each state voted nay, and one did not vote. Therefore only four states failed to cast a vote in favor of the amendment.

The census of 1910 gave the United States 91,972,266 people. If the total population of the twenty-one states whose senators both voted for the amendment, and one half the population of the states from which only one senator voted for the amendment, are added, this would give a total of over 51,000,-000 in favor of the amendment, and, about 40,000,000 people against the proposition. That is, the vote in the Senate for and against would represent approximately that number of people. The party vote in the Senate stood as follows:

	Yea	Nay	Not Voting	Total
Democrats	37	11	5	53
Republicans	28	7	6	41
Totals	65	18	11	94

Wisconsin had but one senator at the time. The vote on the resolution was taken in the House on December 17, 1917, and resulted in 282 yeas, 128 nays, and 23 not voting.[24] The vote by the major parties stood as indicated by the following diagram:

	Yea	Nay	Not Voting
Republicans	138	61	14
Democrats	136	64	9

It will be seen that the Republican and Democratic parties were badly split over the measure, and that the number of votes cast in favor of the measure by each party was about the same.

Doctor George R. Lunn of Schenectady, later Lieutenant Governor of New York, had the unique distinction of casting the only Democratic vote in the House from New York State in favor of the amendment. A few scattering 'yeas' were cast by the Independents, Progressives, Prohibitionists, and non-partisans. A further analysis of the vote shows that in twenty-eight states of the union representing over 26,000,000 people, not a single vote was cast against the amendment. Even New York gave thirteen votes for the resolution, and Massachusetts gave six votes for, and six against it. Pennsylvania's vote was split in two—eighteen in favor and eighteen against. Illinois gave seventeen votes in favor of the amendment and only six against it. The vote of Alabama and Texas was also split evenly while other states with large populations such as Michigan and Minnesota supported the amendment—Michigan by a vote of ten to two and Minnesota by eight to two. Whatever the sentiment of the people towards the amendment may be today, the vote in the House which adopted the amendment on December 17, 1917, represented an overwhelming majority of the American people. If the population of the remaining states is divided in proportion to the number of votes cast by the members of the House from each state for and against the amendment, it will be found that the votes in favor of the amendment from those states represented about 39,000,000 of people. This added to the 26,000,000 from the twenty-eight states which did not cast a single vote against the amendment gives about 65,000,000. That is, the vote in Congress which adopted the Eighteenth amendment would represent about 65,000,000 of the American people. Was 26,000,000 too large a minority to ignore in the adoption of the Eighteenth amendment? If this question is answered in the affirmative, then the Constitution ought to be amended to prevent it happening again, or a return should be made to the principle of unanimity of the Articles of Confederation—the principle which did more than anything else after the Revolution to carry the American union to the brink of destruction. The adoption of the present method of amending the Constitution saved the union in 1787 and nothing better has yet been proposed.

6. *Precedents for Constitutional Prohibition.* A number of
the states had either adopted articles establishing constitutional
prohibition or had attempted to adopt such a provision. *Kansas*, as early as November, 1880, had adopted a constitutional
amendment providing that "the manufacture and sale of intoxicating liquors shall be forever prohibited in this state, except for medical, scientific and mechanical purposes." [25] This,
in general, is the form used by the states.

The twenty-sixth amendment to the constitution of *Maine*,
approved February 21, 1883, and taking effect on the first
Wednesday of January, 1885, provided for a similar restriction in that state, except, however, that the sale for medicinal
and mechanical purposes and the arts is to be permitted under
such regulations as the legislature may provide.[26] In 1889,
North Dakota adopted article 20 of the constitution prohibiting the manufacture, sale, or gift of intoxicating liquors within
the state as a beverage. *Oklahoma* adopted a prohibition amendment in 1907; *Arizona* in 1912; *Colorado* in 1914 and South
Dakota and *Michigan* in 1916 and *Nebraska* in 1917. Article
VIII, section 11 of the constitution of *South Carolina* authorized the General Assembly to prohibit the manufacture and sale
of alcoholic liquors or beverages within the state. The state
of *Washington* submitted a prohibition article to a vote of
the people, but it was rejected at the polls. The form of the
amendment or constitutional provision was, in all these cases,
similar. The manufacture, sale, or gift of intoxicating liquors
was prohibited except for medicinal, scientific, or sacramental
purposes. Colorado also prohibited importation.[27] In addition
to these states, Iowa had adopted a prohibition amendment
which was declared unconstitutional for a technical irregularity
in entering the resolutions on the Journals though the people
had ratified the amendment by a majority of 30,000.[28] Perhaps, the most interesting of all the state prohibition amendments was that of Rhode Island adopted in 1886. It became
Article V of the state constitution and read: "The manufacture and sale of intoxicating liquors to be used as a beverage
shall be prohibited. The general Assembly shall provide by law
for carrying this article into effect." This, it will be seen, is
quite similar to the Federal Amendment in principle and operation. The interesting thing about it is the fact that three

years later, the people annulled this one by adopting another amendment which became Article VIII of the Rhode Island constitution. It read: "Article V of the amendments to the Constitution of this state is hereby annulled." This is, of course, a *precedent* for amending a prohibition amendment out of the constitution. It is significant as showing what might be done in the case of the eighteenth amendment to the Constitution of the United States. It is extremely doubtful, however, whether the eighteenth amendment could be, or would be annulled by the states. To get thirty-six states to ratify such an annulling amendment would, at present, be a practical impossibility. The state constitutions, therefore, supplied Congress with many precedents for constitutional prohibition. In 1917, thirty-three states had either legislative or constitutional prohibition. Texas, which has a very excellent constitution, did not adopt a prohibition article, but instead, adopted one providing: "The legislature may establish an inebriate asylum for the cure of drunkenness and reform of inebriates." [29]   Apparently, the Texans regarded this as the better way of dealing with the liquor problem.

Amendment XIX. On May 15, 1911, Mr. Mondell introduced a joint resolution in the House extending the right of suffrage to women. It was referred to the Committee on Judiciary. From time to time, similar resolutions were introduced during the years 1911-13. On February 29, 1912, Senator Works proposed an amendment providing that "the right of citizens of the United States to vote shall not be denied or abridged by the United States or by any State on account of sex," which was also referred to the Committee on Judiciary. Senator Ashurst reported the resolution favorably from the committee on June 13, 1913, with the recommendation that it pass. The text of the amendment was almost identical with the article as it stands in the Constitution.[1] On March 5, 1918, Senator Vardaman of Mississippi proposed to *amend* the resolution by inserting a comma after the word 'sex' and the words: "But in all other respects the right of citizens to vote shall be controlled by the State wherein they reside." Senator Williams of Mississippi proposed to amend on March 19, 1914, by inserting the word 'white' before 'citizens' so as to make the resolution read: "The right of white citizens of the United States to vote shall not be denied or abridged." The object was to exclude negroes, Chinese, and Japanese. These proposals were, however, decisively defeated.² The amendment of Senator Williams was offered again on June 27, 1918, and laid on the table. Senator Harrison also proposed it on June 3, 1919, when it was finally rejected.³ Representative Gard of Ohio offered an amendment providing, as in the case of the eighteenth amendment, for a time limit of seven years within which it must be ratified or it should be inoperative. Every amendment, he declared, should have a time limit. There was one amendment which had been wandering around the country for over one hundred years. It was idle and unwise to send it out before the people in that way. The proposal was rejected.⁴ The motion of Senator Fletcher of Florida to amend by striking out the words "or by any state" was also defeated by laying the resolution on the table.⁵ Resolutions proposing to ratify the amendment by conventions or by popular vote instead of by the state legislatures were also rejected.⁶ A vote was taken on the joint resolution in the Senate on March 19, 1914, and stood 35 yeas, 34 nays with 26 not voting. It was, therefore, rejected as the constitutional two-thirds had not voted for it. After this rejection by the Senate, Senator Thomas on April 7, 1914, reported back the joint resolution from the Committee on Woman Suffrage, and asked that it be placed on the Calendar which was done. This proposition had been referred to that committee on April 7, 1913.⁷

The debate in Congress on the merits and demerits of the amendment was bitter, brilliant, senseless, or sensible by turns.

1. *The Arguments in Favor of the Amendment.* The leading arguments were:

(1) *Women are citizens and to deny them the suffrage is to deny them the equal protection of the law.* Men can vote for or against the lawmaker, the representative, judge, or sheriff, but women are denied this right and are, therefore, assuredly denied equal justice and equal protection of the law.⁸

(2) *Woman suffrage has worked successfully and satisfactorily wherever tried.* It was said that not a single objection urged against woman suffrage had ever materialized in actual practice, and not a single state which had adopted it would

go back to the old way. The experiments in nearly half the territory of the United States have proven: (a) That women vote in about the same proportion to their numbers as men. (b) Their vote has wrought no mysterious, unfeminizing influence upon them, as the world feared, nor caused neglect of children, home, or husbands. (c) It has not overturned political parties, nor the social order, nor in any way proved an abnormal or discordant influence. (d) It has strengthened the demand for good laws governing home conditions and care of children. Wyoming has had suffrage for half a century, said Mr. Ferris, and "I deny that the women are debased or mannish in Wyoming, or that the men are mollycoddles." [8a]

(3) *Women are the mothers of all the children in the United States and educate them, a service which far outweighs any labor which men perform.* No one attempted to deny this. As women furnish the men to fight the battles, they ought to have something to say as to what conditions justify battles, it was declared.[9]

(4) *Women pay half the taxes, possess half the property, and do more than half the work in the United States, and ought, therefore, to be given the right to protect themselves.* If "taxation without representation" justified our fathers in waging war, shall our mothers endure this injustice? The American people, said Senator McKellar, are a peculiar people. They threw off the British yoke in 1776, and one of their reasons for rebelling against George III was "for imposing taxes without our consent." They succeeded in winning their freedom in great part on this slogan, and yet ever since, they have taxed the women half of their population without giving them any representation in the government. Suffrage is necessary to protect property. Shall women be denied the power to protect their own property by refusing to give them a voice in the election of the representatives who make and execute the laws which control their property.[10]

(5) *It is simply a matter of justice to women.* Women demand nothing but justice, it was said, and "the responsibility cannot be shifted to our political party or to the revival of state rights." The members of this Congress, said Mr. Hersey of Maine in the House, have the responsibility and the power. We, too, can say to the women of this country as Pilate said

of old, "Knowest thou not that I have power to crucify thee and power to release thee?" "I do not see how we can consistently talk democracy while disfranchising the better half of our citizenship," said Senator Jones of Washington. Mr. Cantrill of Kentucky read a statement written by President Wilson in which he frankly and earnestly advised the members to vote for the amendment "as an act of right and justice to the women of the country and of the world." "What answer can we give to the nations of the earth," he asked, "when we send millions of our men, the very flower of our manhood, to fight for democracy, and then at home, deny the very fundamentals of democracy to our own women? What answer can we give when we spend billions of our wealth that the world may be free, and then at home tax millions of our own women without giving them the right to vote on questions of taxation? What answer can we give when we give our all for the freedom of foreign countries and keep in political slavery our own women? No, Mr. Speaker, *right and justice* will not permit us to do these things." Until women have the right of franchise, they cannot secure justice for themselves.[11] Mr. McKellar of Tennessee said men who were idiots and lunatics, and in many states, criminals, and men who could neither read nor write, nor speak the English language, Malays, Turks, and negroes were allowed to vote. "Women alone are the objects of our undying enmity so far as the privilege of voting is concerned."

Senator Ransdell of Louisiana said, to deny the suffrage to women because of their sex was legislative unfairness which no one can justify. Women who are college presidents, lawyers, doctors, bankers, ministers, and college graduates are denied the suffrage in thirty-five states, while most of the states give the right to illiterate men who cannot read the ballots or speak the English language. Surely this is not giving women "the square deal" of which Americans boast so proudly. "For men to determine that women ought not to vote is to destroy the equal justice to which the sexes are entitled."[12]

(6) *The Constitution gives the suffrage to negroes and denies it to women.* The answer to this was that the Constitution did not give negroes the right to vote. The fifteenth amendment was a restriction on the sovereign power of the state in the selection of its electors. The nineteenth amendment will

be the same. Mr. Bryan added: "The United States have no voters. The voters are the voters of the States." [13]

(7) *It would have a cleansing effect on politics.* To this, Dies of Texas replied: "I have no doubt that if women handled the cleaver at the beef stall, we would get cleaner steaks; but what man wants to court the butcher? (Laughter). No doubt women would make excellent peace officers; but what man wants to marry a policeman? (Laughter). It may be that the entrance of pure women into dirty politics would have a cleansing effect on the politics, but I cannot believe that it would have that effect upon the women. And in a case of that kind, we had better have soiled linen than soiled laundresses." [14]

(8) *The boys at the front have voted for it two to one.* Miss Rankin of Montana declared the boys at the front voted two to one for woman suffrage. "The New York soldiers voted to give their mothers the ballot." [15]

2. *The Arguments Against the Amendment.* These were very numerous and were chiefly:

(1) *It would bring women into politics.* The reply to this was that there was just as much right for denying men the suffrage on this ground as there was for denying women the privilege.[16]

(2) *Many women would not vote.* This was no reason for denying to *all* women the power to discharge the duties of citizenship properly, Senator Jones declared. It is wholly without justification to punish those who want to do their duty because others neglect theirs. Many men do not vote but that is no good reason for denying the privilege to women. Where women vote, the percentage voting is the same as that of men.[17]

(3) *Women have great influence now and vote through their husbands, fathers, brothers, and sons.* Give her the vote, was the reply, and she will still have the influence she now has, and in addition power to remedy conditions and solve great social problems. To exclude women from voting on this ground would be just as reasonable as to exclude all red-headed men from voting on the ground that they would have some relative who was not red-headed who could do their voting for them. The objection overlooked the fact that eight million women had no husbands.[18]

(4) *Women should not have the right to vote because they*

cannot bear arms or discharge all the public duties imposed upon men. The answer was that ability to bear arms was not a requisite of male suffrage. All male voters are not held to the same duties and responsibilities. Some are excused from serving on juries. Some pay poll-taxes while others are exempt. "You might as well deny man the right of suffrage because he is no good as a wet-nurse as to deny woman because she cannot bear arms," said Huling of Pennsylvania in the House.[19]

(5) *To give women the vote will break up the home.* The reply was that this was absolutely without foundation and contrary to experience. It strengthened home ties and made more of a community interest between mother and son, brother and sister, and husband and wife. Mr. Bryan declared that in all the equal suffrage states, the percentage of divorces was in excess of the average in the United States. Others said woman suffrage would cause dissensions and quarrels about politics between husband and wife and increase the number of divorces. Senator Shafroth had written a letter to each of the district judges of Colorado and he read the replies in the Senate from sixteen judges, all of whom said such a thing had never originated any quarrel or divorce. One judge said, he had granted over five hundred decrees of divorce, and no case involving separation or divorce had come to his knowledge in which the cause of action was in anywise induced by differences concerning politics, parties, or candidates.[20]

(6) *It is a reserved right of the state to determine who its electors shall be, and the amendment would take away the power of the states to regulate or restrict the suffrage within their borders.* The Republican platform recognized the right of each state to settle the question for itself. The Democratic caucus of Congress voted for the following resolution: "Resolved, that it is the sense of this caucus that the question of suffrage is a State and not a Federal question."

The Democratic platform of 1916 declared: "We recommend the extension of the franchise to the women of the country *by the states* upon the same terms as to men." [21] The amendment, it was argued, would deprive the states of their sovereign power. In reply, Mr. Mondell of Wyoming said: "The Nation has seen fit to prohibit discrimination on account of race, color, or previous condition of servitude. The Nation may with equal

or greater propriety prohibit discrimination on account of sex."
On August 5, 1918, Senator Sheppard of Texas replied: "To
the states, as coequal units of an inseparable whole, acting
through a three-fourths majority, belong alone the right to say
whether the Federal suffrage amendment shall become a part of
the Constitution. The Senator who denies them that prerogative is a usurper of their functions and a despoiler of their
rights." [22]

(7) *The right to vote would destroy woman's charm, de-
tract from her nobility of character, and unsex her.* The supporters of woman suffrage replied that there would have to be
a new creation to transform the feminine into the masculine,
to make the mother forget her child and turn a deaf ear to the
helpless. The same things were said one hundred years ago
when women demanded an equal opportunity for education. The
charge that women would be corrupted by politics, said Senator Vardaman, has been shown to be utterly fallacious. "Suffrage has not in any respect," declared Senator Poindexter,
"changed the nature of women." This has been proven in the
West.[23]

(8) *It would give the right to vote to bad, colored, and
alien women.* If we give the privilege to all kinds and conditions of men, I cannot see the justice of denying it to all sorts
and conditions of women, said Senator Sutherland.

Senator Borah wanted to know if it would give colored
women of the South the right to vote. "I do not believe," he
declared, "in putting into the Constitution another hypocritical
clause to be disobeyed. . . . The negro is to-day a disfranchised man under the American flag" by one portion of the
country and connived at and consented to by another portion.
Is that wise? "We have one blunder—the Fifteenth amendment. It ought to be repealed," said Senator Williams. To
give colored women the right to vote in the Southern states
where the colored population outnumbered the whites would be
to produce a condition that would be absolutely intolerable, it
was argued. Senator Smith of South Carolina said: "Those
of us from the South, where the preponderance of the negro vote
jeopardized our civilization, have maintained that the fifteenth
amendment was a crime against our civilization. . . . Here is
exactly the identical same amendment applied to the other half

of the negro race." Past history strongly supported these arguments. It was also urged in opposition to the amendment that it would allow thousands of alien women who marry Americans, to vote while alien men had to wait five years and become naturalized. New York overcame this objection by providing by law that such women must have been inhabitants of the United States for five years before voting.[24]

(9) *The word of God inveighs against woman suffrage.* This was, perhaps, the most fantastic of the many fantastic arguments used in the debate on the amendment. Mr. Clark of Florida urged against woman suffrage that woman was to be the 'helpmeet' of man, and man the head of the family, and any attempt to change this order was an attempt to overthrow the decrees of the Almighty. From Paul's First Epistle to the Corinthians, he proved to his own satisfaction that women were forbidden to speak in the public service of the Master. Then "what is it in the sight of God," he asked, "for her to stand upon a goods box on the corner and appeal to the gaping crowd for votes? To give her the ballot is to unsex her and replace the tender, loving, sweet-featured mother of the past with the cold, calculating, harsh-faced, street-corner scold of politics." He further proved from Paul's Epistle to the Ephesians that wives were to be in subjection to their husbands. "If they believe this, how can they insist on what they are pleased to call 'equal rights' for man and woman?" Representative Huling of Pennsylvania replied: "You say Paul said 'Wives obey your husbands,' but Paul did not know anything at all about American politics." The argument utterly fails to show that woman should be politically subject to other women's husbands.[25]

(10) *One state ought not to say what another state may do, and the small states have power to force the amendment on the large states.* Senator Sheppard answered this was not the proposition involved in the Federal suffrage amendment. The proposal was that *three-fourths or more of the states* may say what *all the states* shall do in the matter of the amendment.

Senator Pomerene said Ohio had rejected woman suffrage three times. Nevada with 81,875 people has the same voice as Ohio with 4,761,121 people, and the thirteen states of Nevada, Wyoming, Delaware, Arizona, Idaho, New Mexico, Utah, Montana, New Hampshire, Rhode Island, North Dakota, South Dakota and Oregon, according to the census of 1910 with a population of 23,415 less than the state of Ohio, shall have thirteen times the voice of Ohio in determining the question.

In the twelve smallest states of the Union, it was said, there are less than 4,000,000 people, and they have twelve times the voice of New York with a population of 9,000,000. In the twelve largest states are over 50,000,000 people—more than half the population of the United States—yet the twelve small states have an equal voice with the twelve large states in adopting the amendment. This was, however, recognized as the constitutional method of amending the organic law.[26]

3. *The Purpose and Interpretation of the Amendment.* The purpose was said to be to prevent any state from denying the right to vote to a citizen solely upon the ground that the particular citizen was a female. The amendment does not grant women the right to vote but it does grant the right to be exempt from discrimination on the ground of sex. "The right to vote," said Senator Ashurst of Arizona, "is not granted by the Federal Constitution, but the right to be exempt from certain discriminations is granted. This amendment secures to females the right to exemption from being discriminated against because they are females. A state could not deny to a citizen the right to vote because a female." This agrees with the decision of the Supreme Court of the United States as to the meaning of the fifteenth amendment, which uses the same language as the nineteenth except that the words "race, color, or previous condition of servitude" are used instead of the word "sex." [27]

4. *The Vote on the Amendment.* The final vote on the joint resolution was taken in the House on May 21, 1919, and stood yeas 304, nays 90, not voting 33, and present 1. As the required two-thirds had voted for it, the amendment had been adopted.

In the Senate, the final vote was taken on June 4, 1919, and stood 56 yeas, 25 nays, and 15 not voting. As two-thirds of the Senators *present and voting* had voted for it the joint resolution was passed. The Supreme Court of the United States has held that the constitutional two-thirds vote of the House and Senate required to adopt an amendment is two-thirds of those present, or two-thirds of a quorum, and not two-thirds of all the members elected to each house. The Speaker signed the resolution on June 4, 1919, and the Vice-President signed it on the same date. A resolution providing for an amendment does not require the signature of the President.[28] The Southern states, Alabama, Florida, Mississippi, North and South Carolina, voted solidly against the amendment in the Senate. In the House these states voted against it except that the majority of the Florida representatives voted in favor of the amendment. Virginia, Georgia, and Louisiana voted against it. The cause of Southern opposition was the fact that the amendment would enable colored women to vote. All the states west of the Mississippi except South Dakota, Nebraska, Idaho, Arkansas, and Louisiana voted for it in the Senate. In New York, while neither Senator voted for it, thirty-two members of the House—thirteen Democrats and nineteen Republicans—voted in favor of it. Over two hundred Republican members voted for it in the House, and about one hundred Democratic members. Most of the states west of the Mississippi voted for it in the House.

5. *The Sources of the Amendment.* Constitutional woman suffrage was not new in the United States in 1919. The first constitution of New Jersey, 1776, permitted women to vote and for thirty-one years after 1776, they voted.[29] When the nineteenth amendment was adopted, Arizona, California, Colorado, Idaho, Kansas, Montana, Nevada, New York, Oregon, Utah, Washington, and Wyoming had adopted a constitutional provision on the subject. The constitutions of Wyoming, Utah, and Kansas contained the following clause: "The rights of citizens of the state of ———— to vote and hold office shall not be denied or abridged on account of sex." The oldest of these three constitutions was that of Wyoming, ratified November 5, 1889. The language is that of the nineteenth amendment. A comparison of Article VI, section 1, of the constitution of Wyoming with the fifteenth and nineteenth amendments shows that the Wyoming provision was simply the fifteenth amendment with some slight changes in the phraseology and especially the substitution of the word "sex" for "race, color, or previous condition of servitude," while the nineteenth amendment adopted the phraseology of the fifteenth and added the Wyoming substitution [30] of the word 'sex.'

NOTES TO CHAPTER XX

1. Cong. Rec. Vol. 52, pt. 1, 339; Id. 63 Cong. 3 sess. 563.
2. Id.
3. Cong. Rec. Vol. 50, pt. 1, 92; Pt. 4, 3128, 5816, 5919, 32, 504, 659.
4. Cong. Rec. Vol. 50, pt. 3, 2119-22.
5. Cong. Rec. Vol. 55, pt. 465 cong. 1 sess. pp. 197-8, 3438.
6. Id. Vol. 52, pt. 1, 63 cong. 3 sess. p. 616.
For adoption and vote, see later history, this article.
7. Cong. Rec. Vol. 52, pt. 163 cong. 3 sess. 498, 500, 521, 526, 549, 584, 569.
8. Cong. Rec. Vol. 52, pt. 1, 63 cong. 3 sess. 519, 530, 549, 550; Id. 50, pt. 3, 2119-22.
9. Cong. Rec. Vol. 52, pt. 1, 63 cong. 3 sess. 531, 549-50, 533.
10. Cong. Rec. Vol. 51, pt. 1, 744, 745; Id. Vol. 52, pt. 1, 506, 531, 533, 549, 550; Vol. 56, pt. 1, 450. This was incorrect as seen in U. S. v. one Ford coupé automobile. Even liquor illicitly made is subject to taxation. 47 Sup. Ct. 154 seq.
11. Cong. Rec. Vol. 52, pt. 1, 63 cong. 3 sess. 506, 547, 549-50, 584, 593.
12. Id. 63 Cong. 3 sess. 547; Vol. 56, pt. 1, 65 cong.
13. Cong. Rec. Vol. 52, pt. 1, 63 cong. 3 sess. 549-50.
14. Cong. Rec. Vol. 52, pt. 1, 63 cong. 3 sess. 515, 530, 549-50; Vol. 55, pt, 6, 65 cong. 1 sess. 5600-5618; vol. 56, pt. 1, 65 cong. 2 sess. 450.
15. Cong. Rec. Vol. 52, pt. 1, 63 cong. 3 sess. 531, 543.
16. Id. Vol. 55, pt. 6, 65 cong. 1 sess. 5641.
17. Cong. Rec. Vol. 52, pt. 1, 63 cong. 3 sess. 508; Id. Vol. 51, pt. 1, 517, 531, 552; Vol. 52, 572; Vol. 55, pt. 6, 65 cong. 1 sess. 5644.
18. Cong. Rec. Vol. 52, pt. 1, 63 cong. 3 sess. 336, 512, 519, 529, 539, 548, 549-50, 563-4, 593-4, Vol. 55, pt. 6, 65 cong. 1 sess. 5553.
19. Cong. Rec. Vol. 55, pt. 6, 65 cong. 1 sess. 5625-6.
20. Cong. Rec. Vol. 51, pt. 1, 737-8, 513; Vol. 52, pt. 1, 63 cong. 3 sess. 604, 605
21. Cong. Rec. Vol. 51, Pt. 1, 63 Cong. 3 sess. 517.
22. Cong. Rec. Vol. 51, pt. 1, 63 cong. 3 sess. 518; Id. Vol. 56, pt. 1, 65 cong. 2 sess. 427, 437; Id. Vol. 55, pt. 6, 65 cong. 1 sess. 5586.
23. Cong. Rec. Vol. 52, pt. 1, 63 cong. 3 sess. 552; Id. Vol. 55, pt. 6, 65 cong. 1 sess. 5665; Id. Vol. 56, pt. 1, 65 cong. 2 sess. 423, 424-5, 444, 469, 427; Adv. Ops. U. S. Sup. Ct., June 15, 1921, p. 611.
24. Cong. Rec. Vol. 55, pt. 6, 65 cong. 1 sess. 5666.
25. Thorpe, Charters and Constitutions, 1284, Art. 15, Sec. 2.
26. Id. Vol. 3, 1666.
27. Thorpe, Charten and Constitutions, Vol. 5, 2889, 2892; 1 Ok. Cr. 254. Comp. Ok. State. Vol. 1, 276; Kettleborough. The State Constitutions, 55, 263. 1285, 706. 1241, 1471.
28. 60 Ia. 543, 61 Ia. 504.
29. Const. Art. XVI, sec. 42.

NOTES TO THE NINETEENTH AMENDMENT

1. Cong. Rec. Vol. 47, pt. 1, 62 Cong. 1 sess. 1023, 1122; Id. Vol. 48, 634, 686, 1004; Id. pt. 3, 2 sess. 2596; Id. Vol. 50, pt. 1, 63 Cong. 1 sess. 57, 91, 92, 307; Id. pt. 2, 1988-9.
2. Cong. Rec. Vol. 51, pt. 5, 63 Cong. 2 sess. 4339, 5106.

3. Id. Vol. 56, pt. 8, 62 Cong. 2 sess. 8346; Id. 65 Cong. 2 sess. pt. 11, 10984; Id. Vol. 58, pt. 1, 66 Cong. 1 sess. 557-8.

4. Cong. Rec. Vol. 56, pt. 1, 65 Cong. 2 sess. 809-10.

5. Id. pt. 11, 10987.

6. Id. pt. 1, 62 Cong. 2 sess. 807; Id. Vol. 58, pt. 1, 66 Cong. 2 sess. 93.

7. Cong. Rec. Vol. 51, pt. 5, 63 Cong. 2 sess. 5162; Id. pt. 7, 6317; Id. Vol. 50, pt. 1, 63 Cong. 1 sess. 57.

8. Cong. Rec. Vol. 51, pt. 5, 63 Cong. 2 sess. 4273.

8a. Cong. Rec. Vol. 51, pt. 5, 63 Cong. 2 sess. 4271. Id. Vol. 56, pt. 1, 62 Cong. 2 sess. 772, 780.

9. Id. Vol. 51, pt. 5, 63 Cong. 2 sess. 4274; Id. Vol. 52, pt. 2, 63 Cong. 3 sess. 1408.

10. Cong. Rec. Vol. 51, pt. 5, 63 Cong. 2 sess. 4274; Id. Vol. 56, pt. 11, 65 Cong. 2 sess. 10782; Id. Vol. 51, pt. 2, 2 sess. 5094.

11. Cong. Rec. Vol. 52, pt. 2, 63 Cong. 3 sess. 1409; Id. Vol. 56, pt. 1, 62 cong. 2 sess. 778; Id. 65 cong. 2 sess. 764, 765.

12. Cong. Rec. vol. 56, pt. 1, 65 cong. 2 sess. 765.

13. Id. 766; Id. Vol. 51, pt. 5, 63 Cong. 2 sess. 4198.

14. Cong. Rec. Vol. 52, pt. 2, 63 Cong. 3 sess. 1431.

15. Id. Vol. 56, pt. 1, 65 Cong. 2 sess. 772, 799.

16. Id. Vol. 50, pt. 5, 63 Cong. 1 sess. 5121.

17. Cong. Rec. Vol. 50, pt. 5, 63 Cong. 1 sess. 5121.

18. Cong. Rec. Vol. 50, pt. 5, 63 Cong. 1 sess. 5121; Id. Vol. 56, pt. 11, 65 Cong. 2 sess. 10786; Id. pt. 1, 62 Cong. 2 sess. 807.

19. Cong. Rec. Vol. 50, pt. 5, 63 Cong. 1 sess. 5121.

20. Cong. Rec. Vol. 50, pt. 5, 63 Cong. 1 sess. 5121; Id. Vol. 51, pt. 4, 63 Cong. 2 sess. 4140-2; Id. pt. 5, 63 Cong. 2 sess. 4209.

21. Cong. Rec. Vol. 50, pt. 5, 63 Cong. 1 sess. 5122; Id. Vol. 56, pt. 11, 65 Cong. 2 sess. 10777-8; Id. Vol. 52, pt. 2, 63 Cong. 3 sess. 1441, 1464

22. Cong. Rec. Vol. 56, pt. 1, 65 Cong. 2 sess. 765; Id. Vol. 52, pt. 2, 63 cong. 3 sess. 1430; Id. Vol. 56, pt. 11, 62 Cong. 9206.

23. Cong. Rec. Vol. 51, pt. 2, 63 Cong. 2 sess. 2027; Id. pt. 5, 63 Cong. 2 sess. 4274; Id. Vol. 56, pt. 8, 65 Cong. 2 sess. 8040.

24 Cong. Rec. Vol. 51, pt. 4; 63 Cong. 2 sess. 3600; Id. pt. 5, 4195, 4214; Id. Vol. 52, pt. 2; 63 Cong. 3 sess. 766; Id. Vol. 56, pt. 11, 65 Cong. 2 sess. 10776, 10781; Id. Vol. 58, pt. 1, 66 Cong. 1 sess. 618, Const. N. Y. Art. II, sec. 1.

25. Cong. Rec. Vol. 52, pt. 2, 63 Cong. 3 sess. 1414-15.

26. Cong. Rec. Vol. 56, pt. 11, 62 Cong. 2 sess. 9207; Id. 65 Cong. 2 sess, 10789; Id. Vol. 51, pt. 5, 63 Cong. 2 sess. 4336.

27. Cong. Rec. Vol. 51, pt. 4, 63 Cong. 2 sess. 4148; U. S. v. Reese, 92 U. S. 215; Leser v. Garnett.

28. Cong. Rec. Vol. 52, pt. 2, 63 Cong. 3 sess. 1441; Id. Vol. 51, pt. 5, 63 Cong. 2 sess. 5162; Id. Vol. 56, pt. 11, 65 Cong. 2 sess. 10987-8; Id. Vol. 57, pt. 3, 65 Cong. 3 sess. 3062; Id. Vol. 58, pt. 7, 66 Cong. 1 sess. 93-4, 635, 662, 669, Prohibition cases. Adv. Ops. July 1, 1920, P. 612; Hollingsworth v. Va. 3 Dall. 378.

29. Cong. Rev. V, 50, pt. 2, 63 Cong. 1 sess. 1989; Poore, Charters, 1311; N. J. Const. art. IV.

30. Const. Kansas, Art. V, sec. 8; Id. Nev. II, 1; Id. Utah IV, 1; Id. Wyoming VI, 1.

THE END

INDEX